POVERTY FOR PROFIT

Also by Anne Kim

Abandoned: America's Lost Youth and the Crisis of Disconnection

POVERTY FOR PROFIT

How Corporations Get Rich off America's Poor

Anne Kim

NEW YORK
LONDON

Published in the United States by The New Press, New York, 2024
Distributed by Two Rivers Distribution

ISBN 978-1-62097-781-1 (hc)
ISBN 978-1-62097-865-8 (ebook)
CIP data is available

The New Press publishes books that promote and enrich public discussion and understanding of the issues vital to our democracy and to a more equitable world. These books are made possible by the enthusiasm of our readers; the support of a committed group of donors, large and small; the collaboration of our many partners in the independent media and the not-for-profit sector; booksellers, who often hand-sell New Press books; librarians; and above all by our authors.

www.thenewpress.com

Composition by Dix Digital Prepress and Design
This book was set in Fairfield Light

Printed in the United States of America

2 4 6 8 10 9 7 5 3 1

Contents

POVERTY
FOR PROFIT

Introduction

District Heights, Maryland, is a suburb of Washington, DC, nine miles southeast of the U.S. Capitol, across the Anacostia River. It's one of the most segregated communities in the United States, the result of decades of redlining and housing discrimination.[1] Nine in ten of its roughly six thousand residents are Black; less than 3 percent are white.[2] Though the city's median household income is a hair below the national median ($69,099 versus $70,784 in 2021), the community is far less prosperous than other DC-area suburbs.[3] Its poverty rate is more than double that of affluent Arlington, Virginia, and nearly five times that of its northern Maryland neighbor, Bethesda.[4] At nearby Suitland High School, part of the Prince George's County school system, two-thirds of students qualify for free or reduced-price lunch.[5]

The city's main commercial thoroughfare is Pennsylvania Avenue (you can follow it north straight to the Capitol), which culminates in Penn Station, a massive collection of strip malls at the corner of Pennsylvania and Silver Hill Road. But this is not the kind of shopping center you'd find in mostly white suburbs, with a Panera next to Starbucks and big-box stores like Target and Old Navy. Instead, you'll find an Ace Cash Express, Penn Station Liquors, dd's Discount clothing store, and Ashley Outlet, which sells rent-to-own furniture. You'll also find dialysis centers, bail bondsmen, and predatory tax preparers nearby. Within a ten-minute drive of this intersection is a microcosm of "Poverty, Inc."—the vast ecosystem of industries that owe their profits and existence to the exploitation of low-income, often minority, Americans and government programs for the poor.

Across from Penn Station and visible to traffic from all directions is a DaVita dialysis center, a low-slung, gray-white, one-story building with a blue roof. A drive-through liquor store—"Open 7 Days," as its signage announces—sits next door. The DaVita center is one of at least four dialysis centers in and around District Heights. US Renal Care runs a clinic inside Penn Station, and there is another DaVita less than ten minutes away in nearby Coral Hills. Three minutes up Silver Hill Road in Suitland, Maryland, is yet another facility, Fresenius Kidney Care.[6] Because of the wildly inequitable toll that kidney disease takes on Black and low-income Americans, dialysis is big business in places like District Heights, especially when Medicare foots the bill. The vast majority of dialysis services in America are provided by just two companies, whose centers are disproportionately located in low-income neighborhoods—such as District Heights, Maryland—hardest hit by diabetes and kidney disease.[7]

Tax prep is another popular business in District Heights, given the concentration of low-income residents, many of whom are eligible for the federal Earned Income Tax Credit (EITC) for low-wage earners. On busy Marlboro Pike, about a mile away, is an outpost of the tax-preparation franchise Liberty Tax. Known for its costume-clad sign spinners, the company earns much of its revenues from low-income taxpayers claiming the EITC. It charges hundreds of dollars in preparation fees for every return filed, plus hundreds more in fees for instant cash refund "advances." This particular office is in a faded strip mall sharing space with a boarded-up barber shop, a tattoo parlor, and the "Pretty Girl Intimate Venue." On one drizzly morning in March 2022, a sign holder dressed as a gray-green Statue of Liberty sat huddled on the curb, occasionally flicking his sign toward passing cars (though on this day no one stops).

More than twenty tax-prep firms dot the area, ranging from big franchises such as Liberty Tax, Jackson Hewitt (located inside Penn Station), and H&R Block, to smaller outfits such as Assiduous Tax and Accounting and Nubian Tax Express in nearby Capitol Heights. In 2020, Maryland taxpayers claiming the EITC lost at least $50 million to tax-preparation fees, according to the nonprofit CASH Campaign of Maryland.[8]

Businesses dependent on the combination of poverty and government intervention permeate nearly every aspect of life in District Heights. Need to visit a dentist? There's Pine Dentistry, a chain of offices heavily reliant on Medicaid patients, especially children. It was formerly known as "Kool Smiles" before federal fraud charges prompted a rebranding.[9] (More on this in chapter 4.) Its District Heights office is not far from Penn Station, in a mostly empty strip mall whose other principal tenants are a liquor store, a beauty parlor, and a storefront church.

If you need a place to live, there's the Woodland Springs Apartments, a complex of three-story red-brick buildings with about five hundred units, a three-minute drive from Pine Dentistry. Originally built in the 1940s, the complex was renovated in the 1990s through a mix of government subsidies, including the Low Income Housing Tax Credit (LIHTC).[10] Its current manager is Reliant Realty Services, which specializes in low-income properties and manages 10,000 units in six states, according to its website.[11] In the fall of 2023, the rent for a two-bedroom, one-bath unit at Woodland Springs was $1,009, well below the average rent for a two-bedroom apartment in District Heights. Many residents also receive rental assistance through the Housing Choice Voucher Program (formerly Section 8).[12] The discount rent, however, comes with other costs. In May 2022, a drive-by shooting at the complex injured two boys, one of them a four-year-old.[13] In 2017, two men were found fatally shot in one of the complex's parking lots.[14] Online reviews by current and former tenants complain of roaches, flooding, and safety issues.[15] "If your not ready to be getting shot at while walking out of your building then don't move to woodland springs," one reviewer wrote in 2021. "Horrible place! Roaches everywhere then when it rains or thunderstorms water comes from in the windows [*sic*] IM READY TO PACK UP AND LEAVE!," wrote another tenant.[16]

The federal government spends about $900 billion a year on programs that directly or disproportionately impact poor Americans. This includes about $857 billion a year on antipoverty programs such as the EITC, Medicaid, affordable housing vouchers and subsidies, homeless shelters, the Supplemental Nutrition Assistance Program (SNAP, formerly food stamps), school lunch, job training programs, and cash benefits for welfare.[17] It also includes about $12 billion for child welfare and $7.8 billion for prisons.[18] States and local governments spend tens of billions more, including $80 billion a year on jails and prisons alone.[19]

These enormous sums fuel "Poverty Inc.," the vast collection of industries that make their living off the poor. Collectively, these profiteers pose formidable structural obstacles to reducing poverty. Their business models depend on their ability to exploit low-income Americans, and their political influence ensures a thriving set of industries where everyone profits except the poor—and U.S. taxpayers foot the bill.

Many of these private interests are third-party contractors directly deputized by federal, state, and local governments to administer public programs and services. These include the myriad job-training firms that work with unemployed workers and welfare recipients, the major banks that process food stamp benefits, and private prisons. President Ronald Reagan's push to "privatize" government during the 1980s led to an explosion of both nonprofit and for-profit firms that have taken on quasi-governmental duties as social service providers. Private contractors, in fact, now deliver much of the social services poor Americans receive. Companies enjoy multi-million-dollar contracts to act as government agents, determining eligibility, denying or granting benefits, and enforcing sanctions against those who don't comply with work requirements and program rules. Other firms participate in lucrative "public–private partnerships"—such as to build public housing—that benefit them more than low-income Americans.

Other industries enmeshed in the corporate poverty complex are ancillary to public systems, such as criminal justice, and exploit the opportunities created by legislation or regulation to make markets for themselves. Bail bondsmen, for instance, offer high-interest loans to those who can't afford to make bail and collect debts even after an acquittal. Debt collectors pursue unpaid fines and fees and child support on behalf of states and cities, collecting fat commissions. Towing companies profit from impoundments. Dialysis providers rely on a steady stream of low-income, minority patients whose treatment is paid for by Medicare. The result is a coterie of cottage industries dependent on government largesse—and determined to keep their niche. These businesses profit mightily at the expense of poor Americans.

The malign impacts of these corporate interests help explain poverty's seeming intractability. Nearly sixty years after President Lyndon B. Johnson declared "unconditional war on poverty," poverty remains stubbornly persistent, to the frustration of both policymakers and the public.[20] At the end of 2022, the official national poverty rate was 11.5 percent—half of what it was in 1959 but far from LBJ's goal "not only to relieve the symptom of poverty, but to cure it and, above all, to prevent it," especially among the Americans most likely to be poor.[21]

Despite nearly $2 trillion in federal aid deployed during the coronavirus pandemic, roughly one in four households headed by single women (24.7 percent) lived in poverty in 2022.[22] The overall Black poverty rate was more than half again that of whites (17.1 percent versus 10.5 percent), while Hispanic poverty stood at 16.9 percent.[23] Children under eighteen were also half again as likely to be in poverty compared to seniors over age sixty-five (15.0 percent versus 10.2 percent). Black children were more than twice as likely to be impoverished compared to whites (21.6 percent versus 9.7 percent).[24]

What many Americans think of as the "American Dream"—the ability to rise into the middle class and beyond—is also fading. Twice as many Americans today live in neighborhoods with a poverty rate of 30 percent or more compared to a generation ago.[25] Children born in the poorest fifth of households have a less than 10 percent shot at reaching the top 20 percent, according to Harvard University researcher Raj Chetty, and only about half of sons can expect to earn more than their fathers.[26] Downward mobility is a threat. A Black child born in the top fifth of households, finds Chetty, is as likely to fall to the bottom as they are likely to remain at the top.[27]

Too many Americans face structural barriers such as low-quality schools, housing segregation, mass incarceration, and lack of access to good jobs. The nation has yet to undertake systemic reforms that recognize and rectify these historic inequities. Government antipoverty programs could also be more generous. In 2017, for instance, government benefits and tax relief lifted more than 39 million Americans out of poverty, according to one analysis, and lowered the poverty rate by 12 percentage points.[28] Bigger investments could certainly mean greater impacts.

But while federal underinvestment is one reason the war on poverty has stalled, more money isn't enough to fix what's gone wrong with U.S. social policy.

Poverty profiteers undercut the efficacy of federal antipoverty programs by diverting desperately needed dollars from poor families and subverting federal policies to their own benefit. Low-income Americans pay the price of keeping these businesses afloat, while taxpayers wonder why government programs don't "work." These entrenched for-profit interests contribute to persistent poverty in multiple ways: (1) they are often ineffective, failing to deliver services that will improve low-income Americans' lives, or they are actively harmful; (2) they are often wasteful and inefficient, diverting needed resources from the populations they are charged to assist; and (3) they are resistant to reform, blocking efforts to improve programs that could also endanger their revenue streams. Bail bondsmen have organized to oppose bail reform and the abolition of cash bail, while the dialysis industry has spent hundreds of millions to shape federal and state policy. In California, dialysis companies poured $233 million into political campaigns from 2017 to 2020 to defeat regulatory measures aimed at their industry.[29]

The failure of the war on poverty is a failure of investment. But as this book argues, it's also a failure of governance that demands reckoning if U.S. social policy is to succeed.

The chapters that follow describe the multiple industries that are infiltrating almost every aspect of the lives of the poor—health care, housing, justice, job training, and nutrition. They also explain how these businesses are aided and abetted by public policies such as the wholesale privatization of government services and the political influence these industries wield on lawmakers and regulators.

In the many years I've spent writing about social policy, I've seen that much of the political conversation around poverty is binary—focused either on individual behavior or on the adequacy of government programs. Many conservatives, for instance, favor policies to "incentivize" "personal responsibility," like work requirements for people on welfare. Many liberals, however, want to boost federal funding or create new programs, like a "universal basic income" guaranteed to all households as a monthly stipend.

This book, however, seeks to open new ground by spotlighting the often pivotal role of private industry as intermediaries between government and people in poverty. As I argue in this book, these companies are not neutral administrators of government programs; they're a silent but powerful pillar of the poverty bureaucracy, with interests often at odds with both the government and the people they purport to serve. This corporate colonization of U.S. social policy, moreover, didn't occur in a vacuum but rather in the confluence of history, politics, ideology, and opportunism. It's a context that helps explain how the business of poverty has become so entrenched and why it ultimately may prove hard to unravel without a sincere commitment to the reform of governance. But by showing how the current political and policy logjam on poverty has enabled the rise of the industries I describe, I hope that liberals, conservatives, and centrists alike can find common ground in the pursuit of better and more accountable governance, the more efficient use of taxpayer dollars, and the elimination of blatant corporate abuses. Though a breakthrough might be unlikely, given the current state of U.S. politics, consensus-driven, incremental change can still ultimately lead to larger reforms.

I do not come to this book as a dispassionate observer. As the child of Korean immigrants who struggled to establish themselves in this country, I've benefited personally from some of the programs I write about here. Medicaid helped care for my grandmother in the last few years of her life. Free school lunches kept me fed when our family's grocery budget was $30 a week. I don't doubt the support these programs provided as my parents worked to secure a place for us in the middle class. My goal with this book is to help ensure that the nation's safety-net programs are as effective as they can be.

The infrastructure of poverty is big business. And as such, it is a major component of the systemic barriers low-income Americans face. No systemic understanding of poverty can be complete without a hard look at the businesses that profit from—and perpetuate—the structural disadvantages that hold back so many Americans.

1

The Price of Paying Taxes

At the Rogers Car-Mart in Rogers, Arkansas, you can both buy a used car and get your taxes done—a combination not uncommon in many low-income neighborhoods. The "buy here pay here" dealership offers financing "regardless of your past credit history (bad credit and/or no credit), previous repossession, or bankruptcy."[1] It's one of 151 Car-Mart locations nationwide that offers on-site tax preparation through Tax Max, a Tampa-based company that works with three thousand car dealerships across the country.[2]

Preparing a federal Form 1040 at the Rogers Car-Mart costs $149, according to the salesperson I spoke with in the spring of 2022. A state return costs an additional $49. I'd also pay a $93 "bank fee" if I got a refund, plus a $27 "check printing fee" if I wanted the dealership to loan me an advance on my money instead of waiting for the IRS to cut the check. The grand total would be $318—or about 15 percent of the average federal refund in 2022 of $2,201.[3] The remainder, the salesperson told me, could go toward the down payment on a car, such as the 2017 Chevy Trax with 114,000 miles or the 2020 Kia Soul with 67,000 miles in the Car-Mart inventory that day.[4] I could get my taxes done, qualify for a refund, and walk out with every penny due to me going to the dealership instead.

That, of course, is the idea.

In addition to places like Car-Mart, Tax Max works with money services businesses (such as check cashers), collections companies, and even mobile home dealers—all with the goal of helping these companies capture a chunk of their customers' tax refunds each spring. "You can send your customer down the street to file their taxes, but that refund can take 7 days or as much as 7 WEEKS to arrive," says the company's pitch to prospective partners on LinkedIn.[5] "That's 7 to 50 days for them to continue shopping and change their mind. Tax Max allows you to capture that sale on the spot and print the customer's tax refund on-site, in YOUR printer! (sic)."

Tax Max's CEO is a gray-haired, fifty-something, Florida-based entrepreneur named Bill Neylan. According to his LinkedIn bio, Neylan founded his first tax-prep firm in 1995, two years after graduating from the University of South Florida with a degree in accounting.[6] After starting out with a "handful of dealerships" in Florida, his bio says, his firm bought Tax Max, along with another company called Tax Deals 4 Wheels. Today, he's something of an industry impresario. In 2021, he helped launch BHPH United, a new trade association for buy-here-pay-here car dealers that holds its annual summit in Las Vegas.[7] At the end of a short YouTube video promoting the organization's inaugural event, which attracted nearly four hundred attendees according to its website, Neylan yanks down the lever of a giant neon-bordered slot machine, signifying the jackpots to be had in his business.[8] "Are you in? I'm in. I'm definitely in," he says.

What companies like Tax Max and its brethren are after is a cut of the Earned Income Tax Credit (EITC), the federal government's most generous tax benefit for low-income workers. In tax year 2022, the federal government refunded about $64 billion to workers and families through the EITC, according to the Internal Revenue Service (IRS).[9]

The amount of the refund depends on the amount of earnings and the number of children in a taxpayer's household, with the largest benefits going to households earning about $25,000 a year.[10]

Benefits diminish ("phase out") as workers' earnings increase.[11] The EITC is also a "refundable" credit, which means taxpayers can receive it even if they don't otherwise have tax liabilities. While the average EITC refund was $2,043 in 2022, according to the IRS, many families qualify for much more.[12] The maximum EITC for a family with three children, for instance, was $6,935 for tax year 2023, while families with two children qualified for up to $6,164.[13] For many households, an EITC refund is the biggest chunk of money they see all year.[14] For some families, according to one federally funded analysis, it accounts for as much as a quarter of their annual income.[15]

It's sums like these that are irresistible to tax-time predators, who skim tens of millions of dollars each year from refunds intended for low-income families, blunting the benefit's impact while keeping themselves rolling in profits. In Maryland, for instance, where 492,000 taxpayers received an average EITC refund of $1,950 in 2022, at least $50 million was diverted to tax preparers, says Robin McKinney, co-founder and CEO of the nonprofit CASH Campaign of Maryland.[16] That's $50 million not going to groceries, rent, to pay down student debt, or to meet other pressing needs. It's "epic bleeding," McKinney says.

It doesn't have to be this way. The tax-prep industry's birth and growth are the direct—if unintended—result of misguided public policies. Convoluted tax laws, for instance, drive taxpayers into the arms of paid preparers who promise to ease the hassle of filing returns. The EITC is especially complex, with plentiful traps for the unwary. Though intended to ensure that only "deserving" (working) taxpayers receive the benefit, the credit's complicated provisions create abundant confusion—and a perfect business opportunity for paid preparers. Other aspects of the law specifically burden EITC claimants, such as legislation passed by Congress that delays EITC refunds—and only EITC refunds—until at least February 15 (more on this to come). While the stated purpose of this provision is to allow the IRS more time to check for errors or fraud, its impact has been to buoy the market for refund advance loans and other "fast cash" products for cash-strapped consumers eager for their refunds.

Meanwhile, the industry has battled hard to preserve the status quo. It's fought efforts to ensure minimum competency and licensing standards for tax preparers and resisted efforts to simplify the tax code or the process of filing returns. Tax-prep giants H&R Block and Intuit have spent millions to block the government's efforts to experiment with automatic, "return-free" filing. In 2016 alone, according to a 2017 ProPublica report, the companies spent as much as $5 million to advance legislation prohibiting the federal government from offering taxpayers this service.[17]

What's happened with the commercial tax-prep industry is a perfect example of how Poverty, Inc., has come to be across multiple sectors of social policy. An otherwise well-intentioned and potentially effective program gets subverted by, and then becomes subservient to, an industry it creates and to which it becomes captive. The result is an abdication of governmental responsibility toward the nation's most vulnerable citizens, whom profiteers are only too happy to exploit.

Cashing In on Complexity

More than half of U.S. taxpayers rely on paid help to file their taxes, including a majority (54 percent) of those earning less than $40,000 a year.[18] Tax prep is big business. In 2023, the industry was worth $13.9 billion, according to an estimate by market research firm IBISWorld.[19]

While on the one hand are mainstream firms like H&R Block and Intuit (the makers of Turbo Tax), the industry also includes outfits like Tax Max and other businesses that target lower-income taxpayers. One government study uncovered a wide array of low-rent enterprises touting tax-prep services at tax time, including a discount shoe store in Maryland ("free pair of shoes with tax preparation"); a pawn shop in New Hampshire ("$5 to $10 discount on buying back previously pawned item"), a rent-to-own store in

Mississippi ("willing to negotiate a discount on rental items"), and, of course, used car dealers ("free tax preparation with purchase of car").[20]

Less income should mean simpler taxes—lower-income taxpayers don't typically qualify for the mortgage interest deduction or other tax breaks that complicate the returns of middle-class filers. The EITC, however, is excessively convoluted. As a social program disguised as a tax benefit, the EITC's structure reflects the bureaucratic complexity of a government program—including Congress's exacting preferences for eligibility (i.e., who is "deserving").[21] That's why so many lower-income taxpayers seek paid help at tax time. One Urban Institute study, for instance, found that among low-income parents, 66.8 percent sought help from tax preparers, including 73.4 percent of those who didn't finish high school, 71.5 percent of Hispanics, and 73.2 percent of Blacks.[22]

The IRS's current instructions for the EITC involve a forty-four-page booklet with a twelve-step checklist and ten pages of tax tables.[23] In a 2020 special report on the EITC, the IRS's National Taxpayer Advocate noted eight different formulas for calculating the benefit, depending upon "the presence and number of qualifying children, the taxpayer's earned income, adjusted gross income (AGI), investment income and marital status."[24] As the Center on Budget and Policy Priorities points out, the IRS instructions for the EITC "are nearly three times as long as the fifteen pages of instructions for the Alternative Minimum Tax," which almost exclusively applies to wealthier taxpayers.[25]

One especially confusing provision is the definition of a "qualifying child," the most important factor determining the generosity of a refund. Here's how the Taxpayer Advocate describes what it takes to be a "qualifying child":

> First, the individual must have a specific relationship to the tax filer (son, daughter, adopted child, step child, foster child, brother, sister, half-brother, half-sister, step brother, step sister, or descendent of such a relative such as a grandchild,

> niece, or nephew). Second, the individual must share a residence with the taxpayer for more than half the year in the United States. Third, the individual must be under the age of 19 (or age 24, if a full-time student) or be permanently and totally disabled.[26]

Aside from the arbitrariness of its requirements (why six months? Why age nineteen?), these criteria differ from what's required for the child tax credit, for which many families also qualify.[27] (The child tax credit, for instance, can only be claimed for children under age seventeen—versus nineteen or twenty-four under the EITC—and the child must be a U.S. citizen or legal immigrant, which the EITC does not require.)[28] The EITC's three-part test also does not align with the shifting realities and living arrangements of modern families, leading to bizarre and irrational outcomes.[29] Because of the shared residency requirement, for instance, a mother who separates from her husband may or may not qualify for the credit depending on when during the year the separation occurred.

This kind of complexity has made millionaires of people like John Hewitt, the founder of the best-known chains in the low-income tax-prep business—Jackson Hewitt and Liberty Tax.

Now in his seventies, Hewitt grew up in Hamburg, New York, a suburb just south of Buffalo, and got his start in the tax business at age nineteen. A graduate of Hamburg High, he went to the University of Buffalo but didn't finish, according to an interview he gave the *Buffalo News* on the eve of his fortieth high school reunion in 2007.[30] Instead, he took a job with H&R Block, where he became an assistant district manager for western New York in 1971 and then district manager in 1975. In 1981, he and his father built what he said was the first tax-prep software for Apple computers, which would prove essential to growing his empire. "The philosophy was to have a decision tree software that made the first-year tax preparer as good as a 20-year tax preparer," Hewitt recalls in an episode of his podcast, *iCompete*, in which he touts the advantages of running a tax-prep franchise.[31] His goal was to democratize the tax business, which he did with extraordinary success.

In 1982, Hewitt and his father bought the Mel Jackson Tax Service, a small tax-prep franchise that at that point had only six offices, and renamed it Jackson Hewitt. ("[Jackson] had died, and his widow was running it," Hewitt told the *Buffalo News*.) Fifteen years later, the business had exploded to 1,300 offices across the country, all of them franchisees licensing his proprietary software. In 1997, the financial services firm HFS Inc. (now Cendant) bought Jackson Hewitt for $483 million.[32]

Hewitt then promptly launched Liberty Tax Service in Canada, which eventually expanded to more than 2,500 locations in the United States, went public in 2011, and is now one of Jackson Hewitt's principal competitors.[33] Today, Jackson Hewitt and Liberty Tax Service together operate more than 8,000 offices nationwide.[34] In 2018, Jackson Hewitt was acquired by the private equity firm Corsair Capital, which held $10.0 billion in assets as of June 2023.[35] In 2021, Liberty Tax was bought by Nextpoint Financial, a special-purpose acquisition company (SPAC) based in Canada.[36] In its final annual report as a U.S.-based public company, Liberty Tax reported total revenues of $132 million in fiscal 2019.[37]

Hewitt has since focused on a third tax-prep franchise, ATAX, which caters to Hispanic and non-English-speaking taxpayers.[38] He announced this effort on March 6, 2019—one day after the expiration of a non-compete agreement between Hewitt and Liberty Tax, according to a 2020 interview Hewitt gave the *Franchise Times*.[39] (ATAX is actually only one of a suite of franchise opportunities Hewitt is now offering under his current venture, Loyalty Brands. In addition to tax prep, potential franchisees can also invest in Zoomin Groomin, a "custom mobile grooming franchise" for pets, or open up a local branch of The Inspection Boys, which offers "Honest and Authentic Home Inspection."[40]) As of the fall of 2023, ATAX had sixty-three offices nationwide. But its growth, the site predicts, "is going to be exponential."[41]

As Hewitt himself tells it, the secret of his success is simple:

The tax code is complex, and taxpayers are fearful. "Thousands of people have told me they're afraid of the IRS," he says in his podcast.[42] "Guess how many people have told me they were afraid of the CIA or FBI? Very few or none. So I say, thank you, IRS. That fear of the IRS drives people to have someone prepare their return."

How a Tax Break for the "Deserving Poor" Became an Industry Cash Cow

For low-income taxpayers, the tax-time anxiety that benefits people like Hewitt isn't accidental. The forty-four pages of instructions for the EITC are the result of deliberate policy choices intended to limit access.

Like so much of modern U.S. social policy, the EITC was crafted to reward the "deserving poor," an idea with deep roots that has fundamentally shaped the politics of poverty in America (more on this in chapter 3). The credit is available only to working taxpayers with "earned income" to report, and the most generous benefits are reserved for those with children to support. It is only because of its design to "make work pay" that the EITC has enjoyed enduring bipartisan support since its enactment nearly fifty years ago. At the same time, the statutory and regulatory contortions necessary to ensure that the credit *only* goes to those "deserving" of it are responsible for the complexity that's spawned the likes of Jackson Hewitt, Tax Max, and its competitors. As the credit has grown over the years, additional legislative and administrative changes—including "fixes" that have gone awry—have only served to entrench the tax-prep industry.

The "father" of the EITC was Louisiana senator Russell B. Long, son of legendary Louisiana governor and U.S. senator Huey Long (whose life inspired the book and the movie *All the King's Men*).[43] First elected to the Senate in 1948, days shy of his thirtieth birthday, Russell Long eventually rose to the chairmanship of the powerful Senate Finance Committee, which he ruled from 1965 to 1981.[44] From that perch, he exercised such profound influence over the nation's tax laws that the *Wall Street Journal* reportedly dubbed him "the fourth branch of government."[45] That legacy would come to include the EITC, which Long framed as "tax relief" for the working poor.[46]

What Long originally proposed, in 1972, was a "work bonus" equal to 10 percent of wages for low-income workers earning less than $4,000 per year. Speaking on the floor of the Senate, Long described the idea as a "dignified way to provide help to a low-income working person, whereby the more he works the more he gets." And, he added, "this way will benefit many working poor, many of whom are not on public welfare, and many of whom we hope will not be."[47]

By then, welfare reform was already in the crosshairs of conservative policymakers, including President Richard M. Nixon. Between 1960 and 1970, the number of people on Aid to Families with Dependent Children (AFDC) nearly tripled, from 3.1 million 9.0 million.[48] If poverty was the pressing social problem of the 1960s, "welfare dependency became the social problem of the 1970s," as legal historian Dennis J. Ventry Jr. writes in his political history of the EITC.[49]

Long's "work bonus" was an alternative to Richard Nixon's welfare reform plan, which aimed to replace the federal welfare program with a "negative income tax" modeled after a 1962 proposal by economist Milton Friedman.[50] Though Nixon's "Family Assistance Plan (FAP)" included a work requirement as a condition of receiving benefits, Long and other lawmakers disliked the idea of a "guaranteed income" on the grounds it would discourage work.[51] At one Senate hearing in 1973, Long showed how a father could get more in benefits under FAP if he were unemployed than if he were working. "In other words, he can increase his family's income by . . . quitting work entirely," Long said.[52]

Despite—or perhaps because of—his image as a populist champion of the working class, Long was deeply critical of the federal welfare program, AFDC. In March 1972, Long presided over a Senate Finance Committee hearing titled "Welfare Cheating," in which he condemned AFDC as "being manipulated and abused by malingerers, cheats and outright frauds."[53] Welfare "cheats," he argued, included not just those who lied about their circumstances to qualify for benefits, but also the able-bodied who did not work. Particularly irritating to Long were the men he imagined to be living with the mothers of their children receiving AFDC, who were allowed to "sponge off the welfare check, thus depriving the dependent children, on whose behalf the check was provided in the first place, of their food and clothing." "Why should that be permitted?" he railed. "If he is there acting like the man of the house and enjoying the privileges of the man in the house, why should not he be obligated to bear the burdens of the man of the house?"[54]

Nixon's plan faltered and ultimately failed, but it wasn't until 1975 that Long's proposal passed Congress. By that point, Long's "work bonus" was renamed the Earned Income Credit and cast as a temporary offset to payroll taxes for low-income families then struggling in recession.[55]

Once ensconced in the tax code, the EITC quickly became "the Anti-Poverty Program of Choice for Many," as the *Wall Street Journal* once declared.[56] Beginning with the Revenue Act of 1978, which increased the maximum credit to $500 and made it permanent, Congress has expanded or modified the EITC more than half a dozen times.[57] In 1993, President Bill Clinton signed legislation doubling the size of the benefit, which his administration proclaimed to be "the largest EITC expansion ever."[58] By 1998, the credit was lifting 4.6 million people out of poverty, and studies showed significant gains in the share of low-income mothers joining the workforce (thereby validating proponents' claims of its work incentives).[59]

Today, the credit pulls at least 5.6 million Americans out of poverty every year, says the Center on Budget and Policy Priorities, including 3 million children.[60] Its $64 billion in annual cost is more than triple the federal spending on Temporary Assistance for Needy Families (TANF, the successor to AFDC), making it the nation's largest antipoverty program by far.[61]

The EITC's growth and impact, however, have also elevated the role and fortunes of tax-time profiteers, who essentially now serve as brokers for the EITC and exact an exorbitant toll for access to this vital benefit.

Low Standards, High Prices, and Predatory Products

Low-income taxpayers often don't get the expertise or peace of mind they want from paid preparers, whose principal goal is often diverting as many dollars as possible away from taxpayers and toward themselves. Service can be shoddy and the practices predatory. "It's an industry that's been built up just to suck money out of people," says David Langley, outreach coordinator at Prepare + Prosper, a nonprofit that offers free tax-preparation services in the Minneapolis metro area.[62]

In the DC metro area, for instance, tax-prep fees charged to EITC filers run from $400 to $1,200, according to Joseph Leitmann-Santa Cruz, who is CEO and executive director of the Washington, DC–based Capital Area Asset Builders (CAAB)—making the Arkansas Car-Mart I mentioned at the start of this chapter a relative bargain.[63] "There is so much money to be extracted from people facing poverty," he says.

National data on the average cost of tax preparation doesn't exist—in part because the industry's fee structure is "a black box," says the National Consumer Law Center (NCLC). The "near uniform refusal to provide upfront price information has long allowed tax preparers to ignore consumers' demands for pricing clarity," says a 2021 NCLC report. As a result, "abusive pricing schemes proliferate."[64] Frequently, tax preparers don't disclose the cost until after they've gathered all the taxpayer's information, arguing that the complexity of the return determines the price. By that point, taxpayers might be invested in the process and reluctant to start over again elsewhere for the sake of comparison shopping.

This is what happened to Baltimore resident Carleigh S., who relied on paid preparers before becoming a client of the free tax-prep services provided by the nonprofit CASH Campaign of Maryland.

"They said, well, you know, we can't really tell you how much it's going to cost because we don't know what your taxes look like right now," she said of the commercial tax preparers she used to use. "That was always the line that was fed to me." The bottom line, when revealed, was also always higher than she expected. "There were always hidden fees," she said.[65]

When I called the Nubian Tax Express, one of the many tax preparers that dot the low-income neighborhoods of District Heights, Maryland, the man who answered the phone also told me he could not quote a specific price for filing a 1040.[66] But he told me that if I emailed over my documentation—a photo of my W2, Social Security number, etc.—he'd be happy to come up with an estimate. (I did not take him up on his offer.)

Some firms prey on immigrant taxpayers, charging astonishingly high fees for the ministerial task of renewing an Individual Tax Identification Number (what the IRS uses for noncitizens who don't have a Social Security number). Those fees can run $150 per taxpayer, says Alejandro Valenzuela Jr., tax and financial services director at Minnesota's Prepare + Prosper. "If it's a married couple and they both need to be renewed, that's $150 each plus the returns, and now you're looking at over $500 in fees."[67]

Sometimes the price-gouging veers into outright fraud. The U.S. Department of Justice's Tax Division maintains a roster of hundreds of preparers barred from business for committing tax crimes.[68] Preparer fraud is also perennially on the IRS's annual list of "Dirty Dozen Tax Scams."[69] Many of the enforcement actions brought by prosecutors involve low-income taxpayers and the EITC, such as the one brought against the Nubian Tax Express (the same firm that wanted me to email over my personal information).

In that instance, the owner of the firm was sentenced to jail time and six months' home detention in 2011 for submitting income tax returns that "falsely claimed credits to which Nubian clients were not entitled, thereby generating fraudulent income tax refunds," according to the U.S. Attorney's office for the District of Columbia.[70] Among his victims were welfare recipients, whose returns were altered so that Nubian could claim larger refunds. "Unbeknownst to the taxpayers, [the defendant] was keeping a larger part of the money than the Nubian clients were aware he had obtained from the IRS as a result of the fraudulently filed income tax returns," prosecutors said.[71]

The nation's largest tax chains aren't above these behaviors either. In 2007, the Department of Justice (DOJ) sued five Jackson Hewitt franchisees operating more than 125 outlets in Chicago, Atlanta, Detroit, and Raleigh-Durham, North Carolina, charging them with tax fraud.[72] The DOJ alleged that these businesses "'created and fostered a business environment' at the Jackson Hewitt franchises 'in which fraudulent tax return preparation is encouraged and flourishes.'" Among other things, the DOJ accused the stores of "filing false returns claiming refunds based on phony W2 forms; using fabricated businesses and business expenses on returns to claim bogus deductions; claiming fuel tax credits in absurd amounts for customers clearly not entitled to any credits; and massive fraud related to claiming the federal earned income tax credit."[73] (The DOJ's later settlement with the franchisees included restrictions, monitoring, and, in some cases, temporarily barring some of the franchise owners from the industry.)[74]

In 2019, the DOJ announced the settlement of ten separate suits filed between 2013 and 2018 against a dozen Liberty Tax Service franchisees, also for fraud.[75] In its complaint, the DOJ alleged that these franchisees had claimed over $28 billion in federal tax refunds, including more than $12 billion from the EITC.[76] Some franchisees "recruited customers, including homeless individuals, and then prepared fraudulent federal income tax returns on their behalf . . . to claim the EITC," said the DOJ.[77] The government also alleged that Liberty Tax encouraged this behavior by recognizing six of the twelve franchisees sued by the DOJ as members of the "Elite 18" of the Liberty Tax Service system, a status "'reserved' for top franchisees" "to recognize a special category of franchisees who's [sic] performance and attitude have set the standard for the [Liberty Tax Service] organization.'"[78] (As part of its settlement,

Liberty Tax agreed to "enhanced compliance measures" and independent monitoring.)

High tax-prep fees aren't the only scam tax preparers perpetrate. Many firms further gouge their customers with "fast cash" "refund advance" products, such as "refund anticipation loans (RALs)," "refund transfers," and "refund anticipation checks (RACs)" for customers who want—or need—their refund money right away.[79]

RALs work like payday loans. Taxpayers borrow against their refund for a cash advance, which gets paid back once the IRS sends the refund. When they first hit the market in the 1990s, annualized interest rates for these loans—which sometimes lasted only a week—ranged from 67 percent to 774 percent, according to the NCLC.[80] At the height of the RAL boom, around 2000, the NCLC estimated, consumers spent $810 million in RAL fees, with much of this money coming from EITC recipients.[81]

At Jackson Hewitt, customers can start borrowing against their refunds as early as mid-December. "Need money for the holidays?" asked the Jackson Hewitt site in late 2021.[82] "Early Refund Advance is here! . . . Book your appointment now. Spaces fill up fast." The site went on to promise fast, easy money: "You could get up to $1,000 in minutes on a prepaid card." "No one offers a tax refund advance loan this big, this early." "Get started with just your paystub or proof of income." The fee for this loan, the site disclosed, was $70, or a 35.9 percent APR.

At H&R Block, customers can apply for "Emerald Advance," a "fixed rate term loan" of up to $1,300 secured by their anticipated refund.[83] Taxpayers can apply for Emerald Advance as early as November 1, according to the H&R Block site, and funds are loaded onto "an H&R Block Emerald Card" or to an account through the banking app Spruce. Customers must pay the balance down to zero by March 31, and the interest rate is 35.9 percent (along with "additional fees" that "may apply," according to the site).

Alternatively, taxpayers can opt for refund anticipation checks (RACs) or "refund transfers," which are technically not loans.

Instead, they're a mechanism for taxpayers who don't have bank accounts to receive their refunds by direct deposit from the IRS instead of waiting weeks for a paper check. Companies selling RACs and refund transfers partner with a bank to create short-term bank accounts, expressly for this purpose. (The accounts typically exist for about three weeks.) When the refund arrives, the company deducts whatever fees the taxpayer owes for tax prep (and for the RAC itself) and then issues a debit card (which carries its own fees) for the balance.[84]

While the fees charged for a RAC appear to be relatively reasonable—between $32.95 and $34.95, according to a 2019 Government Accountability Office (GAO) study—taxpayers also often face an onslaught of "junk" fees that drive up the final price tag, in addition to inflated fees for tax prep.[85] "It's a bank account so it's not a 'loan' and the APR rules don't apply," says CAAB's Leitmann-Santa Cruz. "But it just so happens that the amount of fees that get charged over three weeks ends up being pretty exactly about a 300 percent interest rate." GAO's study found that the prepaid bank cards used to disburse refunds often carried monthly fees of about $5, along with additional charges every time consumers visited the ATM, deposited more money on the card, or if they didn't use the card for a certain period of time.[86] In addition, tax preparers pile on "software fees," "technology fees," and "processing fees" to run up the bill even more.

One reason tax-prep firms can get away with these practices is that customers don't pay fees upfront. "They always said don't worry about it—we'll just take it out of your refund and you're not even going to notice," as CASH client Carleigh S. said of her former experiences with paid preparers. Another reason so many EITC recipients use these products is that they can't afford tax prep otherwise. One firm interviewed by the Urban Institute indicated that "at least 90 percent of those requesting RALs at his firm cannot pay for tax preparation fees . . . so they turn to a RAL or a RAC as a way to pay for tax preparation."[87]

Though companies argue that taxpayers of all income levels

take advantage of these services, lower-income households—many of them EITC-eligible—are much more likely to purchase RACs, RALs, and other tax-time financial products. One study by the Urban Institute, for instance, estimates that EITC recipients buy 64 percent of RALs and of RACs.[88] Households with incomes between $30,000 and $39,000 were 61 percent more likely to buy a tax-time product than households earning $60,000 or more, according to the GAO.[89] Black-headed households were also more likely to rely on these products than those headed by whites.

The result is fat profits for tax-prep firms. In 2018, according to the NCLC, Liberty Tax earned more than a quarter of its revenues from refund anticipation loans and refund anticipation checks. It sold these products to a little less than half of all of its clients, collecting $42 million in fees that year.[90] In 2014 (the most recent year for which figures are available), more than 21 million consumers bought RACs, for a combined cost of at least $648 million, according to the NCLC and the Consumer Federation of America.[91]

The banks that lend the money for RALs and set up the accounts for RACs and refund transfers profit handsomely too. For instance, H&R Block's "financial partner" MetaBank (now Pathward) reported $1.84 billion in loan originations for "tax services" in fiscal 2021 and $1.9 billion in fiscal 2022.[92] Republic Bancorp, which offers "Easy Advance" loans through the tax-prep firms it works with, reported $250 million in loan originations in fiscal 2021—a sum that the company admits is dependent on the business of EITC recipients.[93] "[A] substantial number of clients utilizing . . . [Easy Advance] and [refund transfer] products are consumers that are eligible for the EITC when filing their income tax returns," the company acknowledges among the "risk factors" disclosed in its 2021 annual report.[94] Losing these customers, the company warns, "could lead to a significant decline in usage of [the company]'s . . . tax products" and, in consequence, revenues.[95]

Federal Policy Failures Help Tax-Prep Firms Flourish

Despite the abuses rife within the tax-prep industry, policymakers have largely failed to act. If anything, some spectacularly misguided policies—in addition to the overall complexity of the tax code that created the industry in the first place—have helped paid preparers maintain their grip on the EITC and the financial fortunes of low-income taxpayers. These policies warrant a closer look.

The IRS Gave Free Underwriting for Predatory Tax-Time Products

Instead of regulating RALs and other toxic tax-time products, the federal government for years actually *encouraged* their use by offering a service that helped tax-time lenders assess the risk of making a loan. Banks typically "underwrite" a loan before they issue it—they might verify a potential borrower's income and assets and determine the risk of nonpayment. Interest rates charged to "riskier" borrowers are often higher than for other consumers, ostensibly to compensate lenders for the greater possibility of default.

In the case of RALs and other tax-time loans, the risk of nonpayment is low to begin with because the lender pays itself from borrowers' refunds. (This fact alone is an argument against the usurious fees charged for these products.) The IRS's "debt indicator" program reduced lenders' risks even further by alerting preparers if customers filing electronically had outstanding tax liabilities. If a taxpayer already owed the IRS, the lender could refuse to make a loan; conversely, no outstanding tax debts meant that preparers could collect their full fees when a refund was issued, without fear of nonpayment. The bottom-line benefit of this service was to give banks and tax-prep firms free underwriting for refund loans. "The debt indicator promotes RALs by assuring lenders that the taxpayer's refund will be issued and thus the loan will be repaid," as the National Consumer Law Center wrote in a 2005 critique. "As one IRS employee stated, the debt indicator was a 'federally supplied security blanket' and 'we were doing their credit check for them.'"[96]

The IRS had begun providing the debt indicator in the early 1990s (then called the Direct Deposit Indicator) to encourage electronic filing, then just getting off the ground. But the service was discontinued in 1994 "because it was thought to be a contributing factor to fraudulent claims for the Earned Income Tax Credit," as the IRS acknowledged in a regulatory notice about the program.[97] The relatively quick turnaround on electronic returns meant that unscrupulous preparers could overclaim refunds and grab their fees before the fraud was even detected (at which point the taxpayer would be on the hook).[98] But after its elimination "elicited 'screams of rage' by the RAL industry," as the NCLC put it, citing industry sources, the IRS reinstated the debt indicator in 1999.[99]

While the IRS justified this service as "useful to taxpayers who wish to use their anticipated individual income tax return refunds to apply for bank products, for example, refund anticipation loans," it's clear the RAL industry benefited the most.[100]

After the IRS ended the debt indicator for the first time, in 1994, RAL volume dropped from 9.5 million loans in 1994 to 6 million in 1999. But when service resumed that year, RAL volume skyrocketed, reaching 12.7 million loans by 2002, according to the NCLC.[101] Sustained outcry from consumer advocates (including the NCLC) finally led the IRS to end the debt indicator for good in 2010, at which point the RAL industry promptly collapsed. In fact, the loss of the debt indicator contributed to the 2011 bankruptcy of Jackson Hewitt, after banks supplying the funds for RALs pulled out of the business.[102] (Jackson Hewitt eventually emerged from bankruptcy before it was bought by its current owner, Corsair Capital.)[103] But by then, the damage had been done. In 2008 alone, for instance, NCLC estimated, RALs "skimmed $738 million from the refunds of 8.4 million American taxpayers," with fees running as high as 500 percent APR.[104]

As noted earlier, RALs still survive today, though they've declined in popularity compared to their upstart cousins, "refund transfers" and "refund anticipation checks." One can only imagine, however, the billions of dollars taxpayers could have saved had the IRS not facilitated the RAL industry for nearly a decade.

Congress Singles Out EITC Taxpayers for Refund Delays

Congress gave the tax time products industry yet another assist—though perhaps unwittingly—when it passed the Protecting Americans from Tax Hikes Act of 2015 (the PATH Act). This legislation includes a provision requiring the IRS to withhold refunds from any taxpayer claiming the EITC or the Additional Child Tax Credit until at least February 15.[105] (Many taxpayers due refunds file early.) Though intended to give the IRS "additional time to help prevent revenue lost due to identity theft and refund fraud," its biggest impact, advocates say, has been to give cash-strapped taxpayers yet more reason to buy RALs or RACs. "People are being incentivized to get whatever mechanism gives them money faster," says the Capital Area Asset Builders' Joseph Leitmann-Santa Cruz.[106]

Moreover, these mandated delays discourage taxpayers from opting for the free (and federally funded) tax-preparation service CAAB offers through the Volunteer Income Tax Assistance (VITA) program.[107] "There is no way to compete with the private sector," says Leitmann-Santa Cruz. "If I have a family of four with adjusted gross income below $25,000, they could be receiving as much as $9,400 from the EITC and child tax credits in one year alone . . . But when we inform them that the money will not be received by the family until potentially the middle of March, it behooves them to go to a paid preparer so they'll have access to the money faster, depending on their short-term financial needs at that point." This is how the federal government is undermining its own programs with counterproductive policies.

Tax Preparers Don't Have to Be Competent to Ply Their Trade

Unlike most professions, from barbering to cosmetology to home inspection, tax preparation is utterly unregulated.[108] While the IRS offers tax preparers the opportunity to become "enrolled agents" who pass a credentialing exam and can represent taxpayers before the IRS, this program is entirely voluntary.[109] Four states—California, New York, Maryland, and Oregon—regulate tax preparers, but standards vary widely. California and New York, for instance, require preparers to register and take a qualifying class, but do not require a qualifying exam.[110] (For some reason, New York also mandates that preparers must certify that they're not four months or more in arrears on child support.)[111] Maryland and Oregon, however, do require preparers to pass a state test.[112]

There are, however, no federal minimum competency standards for paid preparers, and most paid preparers have no credential of any kind, as a coalition of consumer advocates pointed out in a 2016 letter to the Senate Finance Committee.[113] At H&R Block, for instance, about 85 percent of tax preparers are uncredentialed ("unenrolled"), according to the NCLC.[114]

Becoming a tax-prep franchisee is, in fact, ridiculously easy, provided you have the capital to invest and access to tax-prep software. "Anyone can hold herself or himself out as a return preparer with almost no knowledge or skill by simply sitting with a taxpayer and working through the tax return preparation software's question-and-answer format," as the National Taxpayer Advocate noted in a 2021 blog post calling for the tax-prep industry to be "professionalized."[115] At Liberty Tax, which franchises more than 2,500 offices nationwide, its webpage for potential franchisees promises that, "contrary to popular belief, you don't need to be a CPA to be a franchisee with us."[116] "No prior tax experience necessary!" the site continues.[117] (What potential franchisees do need, however, is about $75,000 to invest in a storefront, including up to $60,000 in capital costs, and $15,000 in "franchise fees."[118])

Unregulated preparers submit the vast majority of returns claiming the EITC, resulting—predictably—in high error rates. As many as 1 in 4 EITC dollars—between $14.9 billion and $17.6 billion—was "issued improperly" in fiscal 2017, according to the Treasury Department.[119] About half of the EITC returns prepared by unenrolled (uncredentialed) preparers—between 49 percent and

54 percent—involved overclaims of the credit. "Unenrolled [i.e., uncredentialed] preparers submit more EITC returns than all credentialed paid preparers combined," writes tax policy expert John Wancheck of the Center on Budget and Policy Priorities. "In fact, about 400,000 preparers who prepare more than 13 million EITC claims each year *never* have to pass any test to certify that they know the tax rules or to take any training on changes in tax rules."[120]

In a 2014 investigation by the Government Accountability Office (GAO), nineteen "mystery shoppers" fanned out across a major metro area, visiting paid tax preparers to ask for help with their returns. Investigators posed as waitresses or mechanics, in both instances with imaginary dependents at home and relatively simple finances (including, for the waitress, wages low enough to qualify for the EITC).[121] Just two of the nineteen tax "professionals" scouted by GAO investigators prepared a return correctly, and errors in the refunds due ranged from "$52 less to $3,718 more than the correct amount."

But because "unenrolled" preparers are also not authorized to represent taxpayers before the IRS, they don't bear liability for these faulty returns. Instead, they're able to shift the risk of their inexperience or incompetence onto taxpayers, who face the risk of audits, enforcement, and penalties.[122] The IRS audits low-income families at five times the rate of everyone else, according to researchers at Syracuse University.[123] In fact, 54 percent of the audit letters sent by the IRS in tax year 2021 targeted taxpayers earning less than $25,000 and claiming the EITC.[124] (This is despite abundant research showing tax evasion to be much more common among high earners, who have far more to gain by cheating on their taxes.)[125]

Free and Return-Free Filing Fail

The industry's biggest wins, however, have been in blocking federal efforts to simplify the tax-filing process or to expand access to free filing options for low- and moderate-income taxpayers—both of which the industry sees as existential threats.

In its fiscal 2022 annual report, filed with the Securities Exchange Commission, H&R Block made clear what's at stake. "The adoption or expansion of any measures that significantly simplify tax return preparation, or otherwise reduce the need for third-party tax return preparation services or financial products . . . could have a material adverse effect on our business and our consolidated financial position, results of operations and cash flows," the company says in the "risk factors" it discloses to investors. "Offers of free services or products could adversely affect our revenues and profitability," the company goes on to warn.[126]

From 1998 to 2013, tax-preparation companies spent $28 million lobbying Congress, reports the Sunlight Foundation, with most of that money going toward fighting proposals for "return-free" filing.[127] In 2020, H&R Block spent $3.5 million on lobbying expenses, while Intuit spent $3.4 million, and affiliates of both companies donated generously to politicians, according to OpenSecrets.[128] Donations attributable to H&R Block totaled $870,646 in 2020, including $83,529 to President Joe Biden and $41,139 to former president Donald Trump.[129] Election-year contributions attributable to Intuit, meanwhile, totaled $1.1 million, including $146,211 to Biden and $31,852 to Senator Bernie Sanders (D-VT). (Interestingly, there were no contributions to Trump.)[130]

As described by economist and former chairman of the Council of Economic Advisers Austan Goolsbee, return-free filing would allow the IRS to "pre-fill" tax returns using data already available to it from employer withholdings and other sources. "Filing a tax return would entail nothing more than checking the numbers, signing the return, and then either sending a check or getting a refund," Goolsbee writes in a 2006 report for the Brookings Institution.[131] Such a system, Goolsbee argues, could benefit up to 40 percent of taxpayers and "save up to 225 million hours of time and more than $2 billion a year in tax preparation fees," with much of that benefit flowing toward lower-income taxpayers. According to the Tax Policy Center, thirty-six countries already offer their citizens some sort of return-free filing.[132]

In a series of exposés, the nonprofit news organization ProPublica documented just how thoroughly H&R Block and Intuit have worked to stymie any IRS or congressional efforts to pursue this idea.[133] Both companies have, for instance, advanced legislation effectively prohibiting the IRS from offering taxpayers its own free filing alternative.[134] And to further forestall IRS competition, both firms have worked industriously to promote the "Free File Alliance," an industry-led effort that purports to offer free filing options to low-and moderate-income filers.[135] Under an agreement first negotiated with the IRS in 2002, the Alliance commits to offer a free electronic tax filing option for all filers earning less than about $66,000 a year.[136] According to the Alliance's website, up to 70 percent of taxpayers could qualify for this service.

The Alliance has, however, proved to be something of a Potemkin village—far more show than substance. In a 2020 audit, the IRS's inspector general (IG) found that "only 2.5 million (2.4 percent) of the 104 million eligible taxpayers obtained a free return filing through the [Free File Alliance]" because of "complexity, confusion and lack of taxpayer awareness."[137] Moreover, the IG concluded, "more than 14 million taxpayers met the Free File Program criteria and may have paid a fee to e-file their Federal tax return." Some companies participating in the program did not clarify, for instance, that taxpayers must use the IRS.gov "Free File" web page to qualify for free filing, which meant that some taxpayers mistakenly used commercial websites to file their taxes, thus incurring a fee.[138]

Taxpayers also faced inconsistent participation requirements from each of the twelve companies in the Alliance, which sometimes meant that taxpayers didn't learn they didn't qualify for free filing until after they had typed in all their information. "At this point, the taxpayer has spent significant time to research and select a [participating Free File company] and to enter tax information into that particular . . . [company]'s software, and thus may pay the fee rather than restart the time-consuming process," says the IG's report. "This may explain why the members do not disclose all of their exclusionary criteria on the IRS.gov Free File web page."[139]

The IG also noted press reports alleging that some companies even "hid their Free File web page from Internet search engines" by tinkering with the code.[140] The IG's office independently researched this claim and concluded that five companies "had coding that prevented Internet search engines from displaying the web page in search results." In 2021, Intuit left the Free File Alliance, arguing that doing so would allow the company "to focus on further innovating in ways not allowable under the current Free File guidelines and to better serve the complete financial health of all Americans through all of our products and services, in tax preparation and beyond."[141]

In March 2022, however—barely a year after leaving the Free File Alliance—Intuit was sued by the Federal Trade Commission (FTC) for "deceiving consumers with bogus advertisements pitching 'free' tax filing that millions of consumers could not use."[142] Two months later, in May, the company agreed to a $141 million settlement of a suit brought by the attorneys general of nine states alleging the company had engaged in "deceptive" advertising by promising free tax prep and then diverting customers toward paid products.[143] "Intuit cheated millions of low-income Americans out of free tax filing services they were entitled to," said New York's attorney general, Letitia James, in a statement announcing the settlement.

In one major potential setback for the industry, Congress in 2022 gave the IRS a green light to explore return-free filing. As part of the sweeping Inflation Reduction Act of 2022, which also dramatically expanded funding for the IRS, Congress set aside $15 million for the agency to study and design a "'direct efile' tax return system."[144] It could be years, however, before such a system becomes a reality, especially if tax-prep firms—as is likely—fight tooth and nail to block its implementation. Nor is there any guarantee that an IRS free-filing alternative would end the hassles and complexity that low-income taxpayers must contend with to access the EITC.

The fact remains: The gatekeeper of the federal government's most important antipoverty program is a profit-making industry whose top priority isn't the well-being of low-income families.

What's happened with the EITC illustrates how a parasitic cottage industry can hijack a government program and subvert it to its own ends. As beneficial as it is for low-income families, the EITC is also now a subsidy for corporate interests, paid for by the fees extracted from low-income workers trying to access the benefits to which they're entitled.

It would be easy to blame this result solely on the greed of corporations or the unscrupulousness of exploitative entrepreneurs. But that is too facile an explanation. Nor will it lead to the right solutions. Banning private tax prep, for instance, won't solve the underlying problem of the tax code's complexity or address the deeper philosophical question of whether the most significant benefit now available to low-income families should be delivered by the IRS.

At bottom, the rise and growth of the tax-prep industry is a failure of governance, as well as a consequence of Americans' parsimonious insistence that government assistance be reserved for the "deserving" poor.

2

Corporate Welfare

Maximus, Inc. is among a coterie of multi-billion-dollar government contractors anchored in northern Virginia, a club that includes aerospace giant Northrop Grumman, consulting powerhouse Booz Allen Hamilton, information technology firm SAIC, and countless others just a short hop from the Pentagon, Capitol Hill, and the CIA's complex at Langley.

The company's headquarters occupy a sleek office tower in the tony suburb of Tysons Corner. Across the street is the Tysons Galleria mall, which boasts a Saks Fifth Avenue, a Neiman Marcus, upscale eateries like a Japanese donburi place with $20 rice bowls, and boutiques by Italian designers. Maximus's offices are just as luxe. The building includes "a cafe on every floor of the building and free healthy snacks, a fitness center with cardio and strength equipment, recharge rooms, [and] open-concept floor plans with abundant natural lighting," according to a press release about the space, where the company moved in 2022.[1]

But unlike its peers, Maximus doesn't supply the government with fighter planes, satellites, or cybersecurity solutions; instead, it makes much of its money running government-funded antipoverty programs. Maximus is one of a handful of firms providing turnkey assistance to states that have hired private companies to run their welfare systems or other government services like Medicaid. Maximus manages applications, determines eligibility for benefits, and enrolls recipients in the programs for which they qualify.[2] The company also runs job-training programs for beneficiaries who must meet the work requirements established by welfare reform legislation in 1996. The company provides coaching, skills assessment, and career planning services, according to its site, as well as help with job placement and training.[3]

In Texas, the company has run an "integrated" one-stop portal for the state's cash assistance (welfare) program, Supplemental Nutrition Assistance Program (SNAP, formerly known as food stamps), Medicaid, and the Children's Health Insurance Program (CHIP) for needy children since 2007.[4] In addition to eligibility and enrollment, the company handles complaints, grievances, and benefit denial appeals.[5] Though not apparent to visitors of yourtexasbenefits.com, the site through which low-income Texans apply for aid from the Department of Health and Human Services, Maximus *is* the Texas welfare agency.

These contracts are lucrative. In fiscal 2022, Maximus—whose stock is publicly traded—reported total revenues of nearly $4.6 billion, including $3.9 billion from its domestic operations (it also runs welfare systems abroad).[6] Fees from its contracts with Texas, according to the state's contracts database, will total $1.9 billion between fiscal 2014 and 2024.[7]

Though the company launched in 1975, it wasn't until 1996, with the passage of welfare reform, that its fortunes skyrocketed. The law abolished the old federal cash welfare program, Aid to Families with Dependent Children (AFDC), and created Temporary Assistance to Needy Families (TANF), federally funded but run by the states. The law's provisions also opened the floodgates to commercial interests by ending restrictions on who can administer welfare programs.[8] States overwhelmed by the law's new requirements were quick to outsource to contractors promising expert help.

In the first five years after reform, Maximus's revenues swelled more than fivefold, from $88.4 million in 1995 to $487.3 million in 2001, according to M. Bryna Sanger of the Brookings Institution.[9]

By 2011, revenues had doubled again, to $929.6 million. Nor was Maximus alone in profiting from the new welfare marketplace. Companies as big as Lockheed Martin, as well as niche players like America Works, have all had their finger in the pie. As Maximus notes on its website, "~$1 trillion is spent annually by federal, state and local governments" and "80+ federal programs support low-income households"—meaning that the market for welfare services is immense.[10]

But while companies like Maximus have benefited handsomely from welfare reform, the intended beneficiaries of safety-net programs have fared less well. TANF reaches just a sliver of households in poverty—barely 1 in 5, according to the Center on Budget and Policy Priorities.[11]

And the central promise of reform, to move recipients from welfare to work, has proved a sham. Work requirements are all too often about "checking the box"—or having an excuse to shove someone off the rolls—than about genuine investments in moving a recipient to economic self-sufficiency.

In New York City, for instance, a 2004–2005 audit found that Maximus, the city's principal welfare-to-work contractor, had placed just 8 percent of recipients into jobs—despite a contractually agreed job placement goal of 46 percent.[12] At the same time, the company had expelled 76 percent of its clients for perceived rules violations. "But in the new world of welfare reform," as Donald Cohen and Allen Mikaelian write in *The Privatization of Everything*, "this counted as a success," and the company's contract was renewed in 2006. As of November 2023, Maximus still had half a dozen multi-million-dollar contracts, worth more than $53 million, to provide "employment services" to New York City's Department of Social Services.[13]

The national record is no better. Despite the billions in TANF dollars spent on job training and education each year, fewer than half of recipients (47.1 percent) were working in pre-pandemic 2019, and 21 states reported that less than a third of their recipients were participating in work activities.[14]

What has succeeded all too well, however, is the corporate takeover of social services, facilitated by a decades-long conservative campaign to slash the size of government and privatize it out of existence. Privatization was a defining policy of President Ronald Reagan's administration—and that of President Bill Clinton as well, though under the guise of "reinventing government." In tandem with the devolution of federal power to the states—another conservative priority—privatization and welfare reform generated a surfeit of opportunities for welfare profiteers.

Many states' welfare systems are now largely in the hands of private contractors who enjoy top-to-bottom control of the government benefits many poor Americans receive. They process applications and determine who qualifies—a role once reserved for public agencies. They manage debit cards for delivering cash assistance, collecting fees from both the government and recipients with each transfer or withdrawal. They provide job training and other services to recipients compelled to meet federal work requirements as a condition of receiving aid. Though the stated purpose of welfare reform was to offer low-income families a path into self-sufficiency, its bigger achievement might be the path to riches it created for companies in the privatized welfare marketplace.

Government Business Becomes the Business of Government

The man whose work enabled the rise of companies like Maximus is Emanuel S. Savas, widely acknowledged to be the "father" of privatization. Over the course of four decades, Savas and his allies enshrined privatization as a pillar of conservative antigovernment theology and fostered its weaponization by President Ronald Reagan.

A former city bureaucrat, Savas credits a snowstorm for sparking his crusade to bring the private sector into government. On February 9, 1969, a historic blizzard struck the Northeast, burying New York City in fifteen inches of snow. The storm paralyzed the city, killing forty-two people, injuring 288 and stranding thousands, including more than 200 people who spent a night huddled in the Jamaica station of the Long Island Railroad.[15]

Forecasters would later call this event the "100-hour snowstorm of 1969," and it's still the worst recorded Nor'easter in history.[16] But it would also be dubbed the "Lindsay storm," after then-Mayor John Lindsay and his administration's catastrophic failure to clear the streets in the storm's wake.

Nearly 40 percent of the city's snow removal equipment was defective, investigations later found, and the city had only eleven bulldozers at its disposal.[17] While the city's sanitation department struggled to cope, garbage piled up as high as the snowdrifts—"at the rate of 10,000 tons a day," reported the *New York Times*.[18] Snowed-in residents emerged to boo the mayor during a tour of the city's cleanup efforts (which he had to conduct in a four-wheel-drive truck after his limo got stuck).[19] Nobel-prize-winning diplomat Ralph J. Bunche, then undersecretary general for the United Nations, even sent Lindsay a telegram decrying the "shameful performance by the great city of New York." Commuting to the UN's midtown's headquarters was impossible, Bunche wrote. "I may as well be in the Alps," his missive read.[20]

The disaster ultimately derailed Lindsay's political career (he ended up switching parties, from Republican to Democrat, then losing a bid for the Democratic presidential nomination in 1972).[21] But it proved revelatory for Savas, then a relatively junior official in Lindsay's administration.

A Public Servant Becomes Privatizer in Chief

As he writes in his 2000 book, *Privatization and Public-Private Partnerships,* Savas says he discovered the city's sanitation department to be "actually out plowing streets only about half the time; the rest was spent on warm-up breaks, fueling breaks, coffee breaks and wash-up breaks."[22] He wondered if the private sector could do better—and discovered his silver bullet: privatization.

When he compared the city's services to those of private trash companies, Savas writes, he found that the city's service "cost almost three times as much per ton of trash collected."[23] He recommended the pilot privatization of garbage services in three of the city's sixty-three sanitation districts—a suggestion that generated both interest and controversy but stalled along with Mayor Lindsay's post-storm political fortunes.

Undeterred, Savas pursued his idea in academia, where he quickly became a self-described "advocate for prudent privatization."[24] A lively and persuasive writer, he churned out papers, articles, and books proselytizing from perches at Columbia University and at Baruch College.[25] Savas would soon become one of the nation's most ardent and effective champions of privatization, touting the benefits of abdicating public services to the private sector.[26] His allies would include Stuart Butler of the Heritage Foundation, and Robert Poole Jr., an MIT-trained engineer who co-founded the Reason Foundation in 1978.[27] Another wildly prolific writer, Poole authored a policy paper in 1988 proposing the nation's first private toll road in California—the 91 Express Lanes now connecting Orange and Riverside Counties.[28] The project would inspire hundreds of other "public-private partnerships" privatizing toll roads and bridges nationwide.

Poole's organization, the Reason Foundation, would also establish itself as the nation's pre-eminent pro-privatization think tank. The organization extolled the idea's virtues in policy briefs, its namesake magazine *Reason*, and its *Annual Privatization Report*, launched in 1986 after a meeting between Poole and arch-conservative billionaire David Koch of Koch Industries, Inc., a Reason Foundation trustee.[29]

Populism and "Public Choice"—the Politics of Privatization

Savas was a hands-on advocate, using his bureaucratic expertise to implement the nuts and bolts of privatization in multiple contexts. As an assistant secretary in the Department of Housing and Urban Development (HUD) under President Reagan, he single-handedly transformed U.S. affordable housing policy through his championship of "housing choice vouchers" as an alternative to public housing (more on this in chapter 6). He also took his gospel abroad, advising the governments of Poland, Botswana, and Lesotho, among others. In 1994, he helped to privatize Ukraine's bus service after he noticed long lines for public buses during a 1993 visit.[30] His 1987 volume, *Privatization: The Key to Better Government*, was translated into twelve languages.[31]

But Savas's biggest coup was to popularize the notion that the private sector can replace much of government and improve upon it. He helped to sell the public on privatization's virtues and promoted its mainstream acceptance. He normalized the idea of privately delivered government, which is one reason it doesn't raise more eyebrows today.

Savas invented simple but powerful vocabulary to enhance privatization's political appeal. As Cohen and Mikaelian put it in *The Privatization of Everything*, Savas's "enticing but thoroughly dishonest language turned governments into 'monopolies,' while citizens became 'customers' and 'competition' emerged as the panacea."[32] Even now, they write, "advocates of privatization consistently employ Savas's language and lines of attack, including images of lazy, unionized bureaucrats; looming bureaucracies that are remarkably both inefficient and nefarious; and the utopian promise of competition."[33]

In building this framework, Savas drew heavily from the "public choice" theory of political economy then gaining favor in conservative economic circles. Its creator, James M. Buchanan, would even win the 1986 Nobel Prize in Economics for his work.[34]

Public choice theory argues that government agencies, like any other entity, are prone to seek their self-interest above other priorities. Self-interested bureaucrats, the theory goes, strive to maximize their budgets and job security, while the constituencies that benefit from federal spending likewise organize themselves into powerful interest groups committed to preserving the status quo.[35] Insulated from competition, government programs become less efficient and increasingly detached from the public interest. (The irony, of course, is that this is exactly what's happened to private contractors who've colonized federal antipoverty programs, as this book explores.)

Savas used this line of argument to "perfect . . . the art of the attack on public servants," argue Cohen and Mikaelian, characterizing even teachers and firefighters "as utterly self-interested to the point of, in the case of his hometown, 'victimizing the entire city, and holding all eight million New Yorkers hostage.'"[36] Yet Savas also waged his attacks as a champion of good governance, maintaining that "the purpose of privatization is to improve government performance and thereby improve the lives of those most dependent on [it]," as he wrote in *Privatization: The Key to Better Government.*[37]

This disingenuous messaging—to propose the shredding of government in the name of reforming it—would prove especially potent in the hands of President Ronald Reagan. In the name of "efficiency" and "better" government, Reagan would gut the safety net and lay the foundation for the current welfare marketplace.

Reagan Repudiates the Great Society

Like Savas, President Ronald Reagan sensed the populist appeal of bashing big government, and he made dismantling federal government a signature focus of his agenda. "Government is not the solution to our problem; government is the problem," Reagan famously declared in his 1981 inauguration speech. Under his administration, privatization would become official federal policy; government business would soon become the business of government.

Also, like Savas, Reagan positioned himself as a reformer, not a destroyer. "It's not my intention to do away with government. It is rather to make it work—work with us, not over us; to stand by our side, not ride on our back," he said in his first inaugural address. "It is no coincidence that our present troubles parallel and are proportionate to the intervention and intrusion in our lives that result from unnecessary and excessive growth of government."[38]

Privatization Rides the Antigovernment Wave

Reagan's tenure was exceptionally fertile ground for privatization, thanks to an antigovernment backlash fueled by a rapid expansion in federal spending; burgeoning concerns over the federal deficit; and public disappointment with the unfulfilled promises of President Lyndon Johnson's Great Society.

Between 1960 and 1981, when Reagan took office, federal spending ballooned from $92.2 billion to $678.2 billion (in nominal dollars), largely due to the expansion of Social Security and Medicare but also because of massive increases in social services spending that accompanied the War on Poverty.[39] From 1965 to 1970 alone, federal spending on social services nearly tripled, from $812 million to $2.2 billion, according to Steven Rathgeb Smith and Michael Lipsky.[40] (These sums seem trivial today but were shockingly large at the time.)

In contrast to the post-war boom that fueled the optimism of the Great Society, the U.S. economy of the 1970s was faltering, further shaking public faith in the nation's strength. The oil shock of 1973–74 triggered a global energy crisis as well as domestic "stagflation"—stagnant growth coupled with high inflation.[41] The federal budget began running larger and larger deficits during the 1970s, breaking a historic cycle of wartime deficits and peacetime surpluses.[42] It was also clear by then that the War on Poverty was falling short; from 1969 to 1970, the number of Americans in poverty *grew* by 1.2 million. The number of Americans then in poverty—25.5 million—sent the poverty rate soaring to 13 percent, a five-percentage-point increase in that single year even as the welfare rolls swelled.[43]

Public confidence in government plummeted. In a 1980 survey, nearly 4 in 5 Americans thought the government "wasted a lot of money," compared to 43 percent who thought the same in 1958.[44] In one 1981 Gallup poll, notes public management expert Don Kettl, Americans thought the federal government wasted as much as 48 cents for every dollar—the result, he writes, of cynicism born of crushed expectations.[45] "Especially in the ambitious years of the Great Society . . . we dreamed such big dreams—to train the unemployed for jobs, to provide housing for the homeless, and most of all to end poverty—that disappointment was inevitable," Kettl writes in *Government by Proxy*.[46]

Conservatives moreover capitalized on Cold War fears of communism to spread fear of the perils of "big government" and the encroachment of state control. "Over the years we have gradually but steadily transferred the responsibility for financing, supplying and managing a staggering number of services from the private sector to the state," warned Idaho Republican senator Steve Symms in a 1982 hearing by the Joint Economic Committee.[47] This "creeping collectivization," Symms argued, "hampered our economy and prevented most of our citizens from attaining higher standards of living."[48]

Big business, in contrast, enjoyed a halo of competence. In the existential fight against communism, and in the face of apparent governmental failings, titans of capitalism became the guardians of democracy and American economic dominance. The celebrity entrepreneurs of the 1980s included Lee Iacocca, whose bestselling 1984 memoir, *Iacocca: An Autobiography*, chronicled his rescue of the Chrysler Corporation from bankruptcy; Donald Trump, whose 1987 book *The Art of the Deal* planted him firmly in the American consciousness; and billionaire Ross Perot, whose sponsorship of a daring rescue of two employees from pre-revolutionary Iran was memorialized in a 1984 book by Ken Follett and a 1986 mini-series starring Burt Lancaster.[49] These men appeared to epitomize efficiency, creativity, and boldness—traits seemingly missing from government.[50]

Antigovernment ideologues swooped in to make their case: That whatever government could do, business could do better, and that an entrepreneur on their worst day could beat a bureaucrat on their best. "There is mounting evidence that government is big rather than strong; that it is fat and flabby rather than powerful; that it costs a great deal but does not achieve much," wrote corporate management guru Peter Drucker in an essay for *The Public Interest*:[51]

> Government has proven itself capable of doing only two things with great effectiveness. It can wage war. And it can inflate the currency. Other things it can promise, but only rarely accomplish. . . . The best we get from government in the welfare state is competent mediocrity. More often we do not even get that; . . . And the more we expand the welfare state, the less capable even of routine mediocrity does it seem to become.[52]

Businesses, in contrast, were inherently innovative, flexible, and incentivized to be effective, Drucker argued. "Of all social institutions, it is the only one created for the express purpose of making and managing change," he wrote.[53]

Reagan took these sentiments to heart. To make good on his intention "to curb the size and influence of the Federal establishment," Reagan used two high-profile commissions to showcase his efforts.[54] The first of these was the so-called Grace Commission, headed by J. Peter Grace, CEO of the chemical company W.R. Grace & Company. Its official name was the President's Private Sector Study on Cost Control in the Federal Government and involved the recruitment of about two thousand business executives to look for ways to root out waste in federal spending. In his autobiography, *An American Life*, Reagan says the idea for the Grace Commission came from a similar effort he launched as governor of California to streamline state government. "The idea had worked in Sacramento; why not in Washington?" he wrote.[55]

The Commission's 1984 report came back with about 2,500 recommendations—excellent fodder for Reagan's crusade to badmouth government and extol business's virtues. "These volunteers discovered things going on in government that businesses hadn't been doing for a generation," Reagan wrote.[56] For example, "It cost the Veterans Administration between $100 and $140 to process (not pay) a medical claim—versus $3 to $6 for doing the same thing at private insurance companies . . . The Army spent an average of $4.20 on administrative costs to issue a paycheck, versus an average of $1 in private business."

Reagan later claimed that he implemented nearly eight hundred of the Commission's recommendations, "which saved taxpayers tens of billions of dollars and kept the deficit from growing even larger than it did."[57] For example, he boasted, "we eliminated seventy-five federal printing offices that we didn't need (and eliminated about half the government's publications, including such best sellers as *How to Buy Eggs*)."[58]

In his second term, Reagan appointed the President's Commission on Privatization to identify the swathes of government the private sector could take over. The Commission's resulting 1988 report included sweeping plans to privatize everything from low-income housing, public schools, and air traffic control to jails and prisons and Medicare.[59]

At the same time, Reagan proposed a sustained campaign of deep reductions in federal anti-poverty spending, with the goal of shrinking the government's role in fighting poverty. During his first year in office, Congress passed a historic $35 billion in budget cuts, including $25 billion in reductions to AFDC, food stamps, housing assistance, Medicaid, and other programs for those living in poverty.[60]

Clinton "Reinvents" Government

Nevertheless, Reagan was not America's most pro-privatization president, as Reason Foundation co-founder Robert Poole would point out in his essay for the twentieth anniversary edition of the *Annual Privatization Report*, in 2006. "In fact," Poole writes, "the Clinton administration's privatization successes exceeded those of Reagan."[61] These "successes" would include the dramatic expansion of the markets for human services after welfare reform in 1996. Coupled with the "devolution" of federal programs to state and local control, Clinton's embrace of privatization would birth the current corporate marketplace of social services that controls so much of the lives of those living in poverty. If Reagan launched the privatization revolution, Bill Clinton would complete it.

Like Reagan, Clinton discovered that antigovernment rhetoric was good politics. His co-option of privatization helped resurrect the Democratic Party's electoral fortunes—even as the long-term consequences of his policy decisions would prove dire.

By the time Clinton won the presidency in 1992, Democrats had suffered three embarrassing failures in their efforts to capture the White House. Reagan had crushed President Jimmy Carter in 1980, winning the Electoral College 489 to 49, and humiliated Walter Mondale in 1984, with an Electoral College tally of 525 to 13.[62] Reagan's defeat of Mondale was in fact the fifth biggest landslide in U.S. history, outdone only by Franklin Delano Roosevelt's lopsided victory against Alf Landon in 1936; James Monroe's election in 1820 (he ran unopposed); and George Washington's two terms, won by universal acclimation.[63]

In 1988, Reagan's vice president, George H.W. Bush, continued the GOP streak, trouncing former Massachusetts governor Michael Dukakis with an Electoral College vote of 426 to 111.[64] While Dukakis's disastrous campaign might best be remembered for his infamous photo op atop an M-1 Abrams tank, Bush also successfully capitalized on antigovernment sentiment, labeling Dukakis a "Massachusetts liberal" who favored high taxes and big government.[65]

Clinton, who was serving as governor of Arkansas when he decided to run for president, refurbished the Democratic Party's image. Working with the Democratic Leadership Council, a coalition of moderate and conservative, mostly southern, Democrats, Clinton ran as a fiscally conservative "New Democrat" who pledged to balance the budget, get tough on crime, and to "end welfare as we know it."[66] His goal was to win back the centrists and "Reagan Democrats" who had defected to the GOP and to rebuild a Democratic center-left coalition that could break Republicans' electoral dominance. He co-opted Republican talking points on welfare reform and taxes while still seeking progressive goals—a "third way" strategy that Democratic consultant Dick Morris would later famously call (and critics would later deride as) "triangulation."[67]

Clinton also adopted Reagan's critique of government, in repudiation of perceived big-government apologists like Carter, Mondale, and Dukakis. "Bill Clinton and Al Gore . . . are a new generation of Democrats, and they don't think the way the old Democratic Party did," says an ad from the 1992 campaign.[68] "Clinton's balanced 12 budgets . . . and they've proposed a new plan . . . detailing $140 billion in spending cuts they'd make right now."

Clinton fulfilled his pledge of reform by launching "reinventing government," after a 1992 book of the same name by journalist David Osborne and longtime city manager Ted Gaebler. In 1993, Clinton ordered a "National Performance Review" of the federal government's effectiveness, which resulted in a massive report titled *From Red Tape to Results: Creating a Government That Works Better and Costs Less.* Its preface, signed by Clinton and Gore, was Reaganesque but optimistic:

> We can no longer afford to pay more for—and get less from—our government. The answer for every problem cannot always be another program or more money. It is time to radically change the way the government operates—to shift from top-down bureaucracy to entrepreneurial government that empowers citizens and communities to change our country from the bottom up. We must reward the people and ideas that work and get rid of those that don't.[69]

Perhaps one of the few (maybe only) public management books to crack the *New York Times* bestseller list, Osborne and Gaebler's *Reinventing Government* articulated a highly readable, inspirational vision of what government could and should be. Drawing on case studies from across the country, the authors promoted a new model of "entrepreneurial government" that is "lean, decentralized and innovative . . . flexible, adaptable, [and] quick to learn new ways when conditions change."[70] And in an echo of Drucker and Savas (who are credited in the acknowledgments), Osborne and Gaebler touted "competition, customer choice and other non-bureaucratic mechanisms to get things done as creatively and effectively as possible."[71] In Phoenix, Arizona, for instance, the public works department revamped its trash collection services after losing bids to private contractors and eventually won back the city's business.[72] The Illinois Department of Public Aid started adjusting the amount of Medicaid reimbursements nursing homes received based on publicly available quality ratings, resulting in better care for residents and more information for consumers.[73]

Osborne and Gaebler also popularized the idea of "market-oriented government"—policies that "structur[e] markets to achieve a public purpose" or use market mechanisms to nudge private actors toward publicly beneficial aims.[74] This philosophy underlay the creation of programs such as the "New Markets Tax Credit," established in 2000, which provided tax credits to developers investing in low- and moderate-income neighborhoods; and the Low Income Housing Tax Credit (LIHTC), created in 1986 but made permanent in 1993, which subsidizes the construction of affordable housing (more on this in chapter 6).[75] Programs like these are also a form of privatization, though perhaps not as direct as contracting, because they rely on the private sector to ultimately deliver a desired service. Under the LIHTC, for instance, developers build privately run affordable housing complexes (in exchange for tax credits) instead of the government building public housing.

Despite their enthusiasm for competition and "performance-based" business practices like Total Quality Management—the management system devised by W. Edwards Deming that became ubiquitous in the 1980s—Osborne and Gaebler were careful not to oversell the virtues of privatization.[76] "Privatization is one arrow in government's quiver. But just as obviously, privatization is not *the* solution," they wrote. "Those who advocate it on ideological grounds—because they believe business is also superior to government—are selling the American people snake oil."[77]

But as theory turned into practice, the battleship that is the federal government proved difficult to steer. As envisioned by Osborne and Gaebler, reinventing government requires enormous investment upfront to delineate a program's goals, pinpoint the right outcomes, and establish systems for accountability. It also requires creativity alien to bureaucratic thinking.

Perhaps inevitably, "reinventing" government defaulted to shrinking it. Clinton began his second term in 1996 declaring that "the era of big government is over."[78] By 1998, two years into Clinton's second term, the administration bragged of having cut the federal workforce by 351,000 workers—making it "the smallest since Kennedy held office and, as a percentage of the national workforce, the smallest since 1931."[79] While the vast bulk of these reductions came from cuts in defense spending—a result of the "peace dividend" accompanying the end of the Cold War—the administration also used privatization as a strategy to slim down the federal payroll.[80] "Hence, the Clinton years saw the privatization of the Naval Petroleum Reserve and the Helium Reserve, the U.S. Enrichment Corporation, the Alaska Power Marketing Administration, Sallie Mae, . . . and a serious effort to create a nonprofit corporation to take over air traffic control," as the Reason Foundation's Poole wrote in 2006.[81]

In 1998, Clinton signed the Federal Activities Inventory Reform (FAIR) Act, which accelerated privatization still further by requiring agencies to create an annual list of the functions performed that are not "inherently governmental" and that could be contracted out.[82] The result has been what some analysts call a "shadow government" of contractors, who now vastly outnumber federal employees. From 2000 to 2006, federal spending on contracts mushroomed from $203 billion to $412 billion, according to public management expert Don Kettl. By 2017, federal contractors and grantees employed a total of 5,162,800 full-time workers, according to New York University professor Paul Light, compared to 1,956,900 workers directly on the federal payroll.[83] That's 2.6 contractors for every federal employee (versus a ratio of 1:1 in 1984).[84]

This overall ratio, however, masks significant variations from agency to agency. In the Department of Agriculture, for instance, federal workers still outnumber contractors, according to Light, while defense contractors outnumber federal employees 3.5 to 1.

But the single-most outsourced agency by far is the Department of Health and Human Services (HHS), which runs the government's principal safety-net programs, such as welfare and Medicaid. There, the ratio of contractors and grant employees to federal workers is a whopping 35.9 *to 1*.[85] (Coming in at a distant second is the Department of Transportation, where contractors outnumber feds 10.4 to 1.) In 2017, Light finds, HHS employed a mere 15,500 federal employees—while supporting 556,800 full-time workers in the private sector (including those at both for-profit and not-for-profit entities).

While governments have long relied on nonprofits to deliver social services at the local level, the federal welfare reform legislation signed by Clinton in 1996 turbocharged a shift in the administration of antipoverty programs from government to the private sector.

Welfare as We Know It Becomes the Business of Poverty

The welfare reform legislation signed by Clinton in 1996 was historic in its scope and impacts. It scrapped a sixty-year-old entitlement and replaced it with a time-limited, conditional benefit that dramatically reduced the number of recipients (and pushed many back into poverty). It transformed what had been a central pillar of the safety net into a vestige of itself and radically altered the government's relationship with the poor. It also launched a gold rush among companies eager to stake out fresh territory—including those with no connection to the welfare system.

In 1996, the *New York Times* reported on a three-way bidding war that pitted a subsidiary of defense contracting giant Lockheed Martin against two other mega-firms, Andersen Consulting and Electronic Data Systems (the company founded by Ross Perot).[86] The prize was not a new weapons system for the Department of Defense but a $563 million contract to run the Texas welfare system. The winner would not only process benefits for the 255,000 Texas households then on welfare but also set up systems to determine eligibility for new recipients and monitor their compliance with the new requirements of the 1996 welfare reform legislation. (This is the same contract, incidentally, now held by Maximus.)

The Texas contract was only one of many similar contracts with other states that Lockheed and its competitors were hoping to nab. "We're approaching this marketplace the way we approach all other marketplaces," as Holli Ploog, senior vice president of business development at Lockheed Information Management Services, told the *New York Times*. By 1997, the *Orlando Sentinel* reported, Lockheed IMS had inked eleven contracts in three states, including multiple deals in Florida for welfare services and child support enforcement.[87] According to the *Sentinel*, the company collected $5.5 million from the state for collecting $46.6 million in delinquent child support from 1996 to 1997. It was also set to receive $2.8 million for providing counseling, training, and education to welfare recipients in four Florida counties surrounding Orlando.[88]

The 1996 law included several features that encouraged states to outsource their welfare programs to private companies. First was its radically divergent funding structure. Instead of paying directly for benefits, as was the case under AFDC, TANF provided "block grants" to states to spend as they saw fit, so long as they met federal requirements. States could design their own rules, programs, and delivery systems, so long as they met federal targets for work participation and other "performance" measures. This flexible funding freed states to rely more heavily on contractors if they wished (and many did).

Second, the law removed restrictions on who could administer welfare programs. Before reform, deciding who could qualify for benefits was exclusively in the domain of public employees. Federal law "essentially prohibited states from contracting out initial welfare . . . intake and eligibility determination functions," according to the Urban Institute.[89] The 1996 legislation, however, allowed states to delegate these responsibilities to private companies, including to for-profits. States could, in fact, contract out the entire system, as Texas did in soliciting Lockheed's bid.

Third, the law's new work requirements—convoluted and complex—required the creation of massive new bureaucracies to monitor recipients' compliance. "Work" could include up to six weeks of job search and could include a wide variety of activities, including paid internships, community service, job training, or vocational education, each of which had to be tracked and tallied. The number of work hours required per week per recipient also varied; single mothers were initially required to work twenty hours a week but would have to work thirty hours a week by 2000, while recipients in two-parent families had to work thirty-five hours weekly.[90]

The law also required each state to raise the share of welfare recipients "working" (as defined by the law) from 25 percent in 1997 to 50 percent by 2002. That meant tracking overall data on applications, caseloads, work participation, and spending. States that pushed a lot of families off the rolls could qualify for a "caseload reduction credit" that reduced the target percentage of recipients who had to work—but that too required monitoring and accounting.[91] States, moreover, faced a "maintenance of effort" requirement, which mandated that they match a portion of federal dollars with state funds and use at least some of it for work "supports" such as child care.[92] This was yet another detail to be tracked and reported.

In addition, the legislation included a crackdown on child support enforcement, requiring each state to operate a child support enforcement program meeting federal requirements to receive

TANF funding.[93] Among other features, these new systems had to include a "central registry of child support orders" as well as centralized collections.[94] States were also required to work with each other so that delinquent dads could be tracked across state lines.

Privatization appealed to states "because of concerns over cost and the need to meet specific federal goals very quickly," as the Urban Institute notes.[95] Companies like Lockheed and EDS promised instant expertise in setting up complex data and accounting systems. The market for TANF administration and services sprouted virtually overnight.

Whereas the primary activity of state welfare programs pre-1996 was cutting checks, the new law now required states to provide recipients with a wide array of services to facilitate their transition to work. "These mandates . . . created extraordinary pressures on the service capacity of existing public agencies to find and engage large numbers of clients," M. Bryna Sanger wrote for the Brookings Institution in 2003. "Compliance required the provision of intensive and extensive services on a large scale to serve two to three times more clients than were previously serviced."[96]

By 2001, Sanger writes, states were spending more than $1.5 billion on contracting out for TANF-funded services, and in nineteen states, more than a quarter of those funds were going to for-profits.[97] States contracted out everything: job training and employment services for welfare-to-work; child welfare services such as foster care and adoption placement and mental health treatment; child support enforcement systems, including payment processing, parent location, and paternity establishment; and TANF-related services, including case management, child care, transportation, and other supports for recipients entering the workforce.[98]

"Corruption, Favoritism, and Cronyism"

Unsurprisingly, controversies trailed the deluge of TANF dollars into states, as companies battled for lucrative contracts and state agencies adjusted to the sudden shift in their roles from service providers to contract managers. Contrary to the grandiose promises of privatization advocates, privatized welfare was neither cheap nor effective.

One of the more attention-grabbing scandals involved Wisconsin's welfare program, Wisconsin Works (W2), widely celebrated for its "success" in welfare to work. (W2 was in fact the model for the 1996 law.[99]) The brainchild of then-Governor and future Secretary of Health and Human Services Tommy Thompson, W2 was the first state program to experiment with work requirements and time limits on benefits, under waivers from federal law granted first by the George H.W. Bush administration and then President Clinton.[100] Thompson signed W2 into law in April 1996, four months before Clinton signed his historic welfare reform legislation.[101] Soon after, W2 was in the hands of five contractors, including Maximus, tasked with administering the program.[102]

In 2000, state auditors released a report questioning more than $1.6 million in expenses Maximus incurred using W2 funds, including "a $23,000 payment to a nationally known musical performer for a speech to 40 W-2 participants and Maximus employees" and $15,471 for holiday parties, hotel rooms at Lake Geneva, and other social events.[103] The company spent $22,248 on restaurant meals "for which there was no documented business purpose," $1,498 on flowers, and as much as $1.1 million on advertising, including $104,900 for "backpacks, fanny packs, and coffee mugs with imprints of the Maximus name."[104]

Other investigations alleged that Maximus was as ineffective as it was wasteful. Ten months after W2's launch, 67 percent of Maximus's clients had no work assignments, according to *New York Times* reporter Jason DeParle in a 2004 book on the aftermath of welfare reform.[105] "Many clients waited months for assignments," he wrote. "Others ignored their assignments and got paid anyway . . . In the country's most famous work program, only 8 percent of clients were working [in paid jobs]."[106]

At around the same time, Maximus was under fire in New York City, where the company had won $104 million in welfare-to-work contracts in 1999. Then-Comptroller Alan Hevesi tried to block the contracts, citing "corruption, favoritism and cronyism" in the bidding process under then-Mayor Rudy Giuliani. Hevesi accused the company of failing to disclose its ties with former senior members of the Giuliani administration, one of whom allegedly helped to prepare the company's bid.[107] The dispute embroiled the city in litigation for a year before the contracts finally took effect.[108]

Maximus wasn't the only contractor caught in controversy in the years leading up to and after reform. A *New York Times* investigation of the for-profit welfare-to-work provider America Works concluded that the company "performed poorly and cost too much," despite enthusiasm for the firm's approach from both Mayor Giuliani and then-New York Governor Mario Cuomo. Under a 1989 contract with New York State, said the *Times*, the state paid nearly $1 million to the company in job placement fees for people "who never found permanent work."[109] The *Times* also noted that Ohio had canceled a contract with the company after calculating that placement costs were totaling $24,000 per person and had a low rate of success.

Subpar contracting practices were one reason for these failures. Because of the Reagan era's attack on government, says public management expert Don Kettl, "oversight is weak, and capacity is low. It's relatively easy for contractors to get by with all kinds of things."[110]

States were learning how to manage contractor performance, on the one hand, while on the other, companies were writing provisions to benefit themselves. Lockheed Martin's 1997 bid to provide welfare services in Florida, for instance, proposed a fee of "$450 for each person it processes—regardless of whether the person finds a job," the *Orlando Sentinel* reported.[111] Moreover, the bid contained "a built-in $260,000 profit and an additional $117,000 line item for 'overhead.'"

At the time of the *New York Times* investigation, America Works received about 20 percent of its $5,500 fee per recipient "simply for enrolling clients in its program—whether or not the welfare recipients get jobs."[112] In the case of Maximus and W2, reporter Jason DeParle found, the state had budgeted for 50,000 recipients with the passage of reform, but only 23,000 enrolled. Awash in extra funds, writes DeParle, the state "had little incentive to cut costs," while Maximus "found itself with a big pot of someone else's money to spend."[113] Hence the holiday parties, concerts, and Maximus-branded fanny packs.

A 2003 report on the privatization of welfare services commissioned by the U.S. Department of Health and Human Services (HHS) warned against multiple "unintended consequences" potentially resulting from poorly worded contracts:[114]

> Contractors may work to find a job for the client quickly but not help clients find jobs that offer high wages, benefits, and the possibility of upward mobility. This may occur if performance standards focus on placement only.
>
> Contractors may choose to place fewer resources into contacting clients and enrolling them into the program if they believe that those who are harder to enroll are less likely to have positive outcomes. . . .
>
> Contractors may put less effort into conducting thorough assessments and making appropriate referrals for clients if performance measures focus only on employment outcomes.
>
> Contractors may attempt to fine tune service data in order to influence performance measures for example, by estimating hours for work participation generously.

The report also cautioned that competition—the driving rationale behind privatization—"is not automatic" and can in fact be difficult to achieve.[115] And in truth, the vaunted benefits of competition never came to pass. The biggest problem, as public management expert Don Kettl points out, is that there isn't an independent market for welfare services. "Social service programs are in existence only because the government has chosen to fund them," he says. Because they create the market, "governments are essentially dealing with a small collection of suppliers for whom there aren't ready alternatives," says Kettl.[116] And once a provider lands a contract, the advantages of incumbency kick in, reducing the odds that a new provider will take over a contract when it's up for bid again.[117] States are at the mercy of a handful of firms that even now maintain an oligopoly on welfare services.

Contractors Get Fat; TANF Shrinks

The growth of companies like Maximus hollowed out the nation's welfare system. Cash assistance, once a pillar of the safety net, now reaches just a fraction of households in poverty and is meager gruel to boot.

Caseloads plummeted in the aftermath of welfare reform, from 12.6 million recipients in 1996 to 4.3 million by 2001.[118] In 2022, TANF served just 1.9 million Americans.[119] Despite the unparalleled hardship brought on by the coronavirus pandemic—which should have swelled the rolls as unemployment surged—participation fell to historic lows in 2020, according to the Center on Budget and Policy Priorities (CBPP). The program reached just 21 percent of families living in poverty in 2020, compared to 68 percent in 1996.[120] In fourteen states, says the CBPP, TANF reached less than 10 percent of impoverished households.

In some states, like Michigan, TANF is practically nonexistent, even though the state's poverty levels are consistently higher than the national poverty rate.[121] The state's average monthly TANF caseload in 2022, for instance, was just 8,729 families (out of nearly 4 million households)—a "record low cash assistance rate," according to Peter Ruark, senior policy analyst at the Michigan League for Public Policy (MLPP).[122] This despite the fact that the state received $777 million in federal funding for TANF in fiscal 2020.[123]

Moreover, very little TANF funding now goes toward cash

assistance directly benefiting recipients. Of the $31.6 billion in total federal and state spending for TANF in 2020, only 22 percent was spent on cash benefits while 10 percent went toward "program management" and the remainder toward a smorgasbord of work "supports," such as child care or to supplement state spending on child welfare and other services.[124] In Michigan, the state used the money freed up by having a lower caseload as a slush fund for itself. MLPP's Ruark discovered that TANF money was funding college scholarships largely flowing to wealthy students attending private schools—which was perfectly legal under the "flexibility" afforded by the law. "The general purposes of TANF are so broad you can drive a truck through the loopholes," Ruark told me.

Most tragic, TANF has failed to bring recipients the promised path to self-sufficiency through jobs; in fact, many families are worse off. A review of federally funded "welfare-to-work" programs from 1996 until 2004 showed modest impacts at best, with most participants unable to find stable employment. Those who did work earned an average wage (in 2004 dollars) of only $8 an hour and had no access to employer-sponsored benefits like health insurance (albeit many continued on Medicaid).[125] Welfare recipients subject to work requirements "were more likely to live in deep poverty than to have incomes above the poverty line," according to a lengthier 2016 analysis by the Center on Budget's LaDonna Pavetti, whose data included the Great Recession.[126] Gains in earnings were minimal or offset by cuts in benefits, and many recipients were trapped in dead-end, low-wage jobs. A 2023 investigation by *The Uncertain Hour* podcast on public radio likewise found that the "welfare-to-work industrial complex" "often places poor and vulnerable Americans into jobs that do not support their families and often leave them on government assistance."[127]

Contractors, however, continue to make hay. In New York City, for instance, Maximus has expanded its turf and is running the state's Medicaid program as well. It won a thirteen-year, $2.9 billion contract that runs through 2025[128] (that's in addition to its contracts for "employment services" mentioned previously[129]). America Works also still enjoys multiple contracts in New York; CheckbookNYC lists nine contracts totaling $55.8 billion for "employment services" to be provided across the city through 2023.[130]

The ultimate irony is that for all the talk of welfare reform's stated goal to "end dependency," the statute in fact birthed a new class of dependents—the companies reliant on government funding of social programs for their existence.[131] Maximus, for instance, disclosed in its annual report for fiscal 2022 that 35 percent of its revenues for the year came from state contracts and 49 percent from contracts with the federal government (with the remainder coming from foreign government contracts and municipalities).[132] Contracts with the state and city of New York alone accounted for 9 percent of the company's total revenue in 2021, according to the firm's 2021 annual report.[133] Maximus's reliance on public money is a fact the company acknowledged in the "Risk Factors" section of its 2022 annual report: "Any significant disruption or deterioration in our relationship with federal, state, and local governments and a corresponding reduction in these contracts would significantly reduce our revenue and could substantially harm our business."[134]

Conservatives Win

Gutting the federal safety net—consequences be damned—is likely what the conservatives who initially agitated for welfare reform have wanted all along. Privatization was an instrument and accelerant of that destruction.

The old welfare system, AFDC, unquestionably needed reform. When the program was created in 1935, its purpose was to support young moms who'd lost their breadwinner husbands. "It was originally designed for white widows, a population deemed deserving of aid and one expected to stay home and raise children rather than enter the workforce," as noted by *Vox*.[135] Eligible families received benefits indefinitely, so long as they met the definitional criteria for eligibility and their incomes stayed below a certain level. Like Social Security, it was an "entitlement" program for all who qualified, which meant federal spending was unlimited.[136]

Conservatives blamed the program for discouraging work and rewarding single parenthood, because it predicated eligibility on the absence of a second parent who could help support a child. Even liberals did not like the program's disincentives for work because every dollar earned at a job meant losing a dollar of benefits—a punitively high "marginal tax" on beneficiaries. Analysts at the left-leaning Urban Institute, for instance, called AFDC the "twice-poverty trap" because "work at even two times poverty-level income, or, more precisely, two or three times minimum wage, often yields little reward."[137]

The 1996 legislation, however, was less a reform of AFDC for the better than a wholesale surrender to conservative demands for "personal responsibility" from mothers living in poverty (in fact, the official name of the law is the Personal Responsibility and Work Opportunity Reconciliation Act of 1996 [PRWORA]).[138] This capitulation, however, was born of the politics of necessity.

In repudiation of Clinton's victory in 1992, the GOP roared into Congress with the 1994 midterm elections, winning fifty-four seats in the House and eight seats in the Senate.[139] Republican House candidates also won a majority of the popular vote for the first time since 1946. Instrumental to these victories was the GOP's "Contract with America," a ten-point legislative plan that promised middle-class tax cuts, term limits for legislators, and budget reform, among other priorities.[140] Drafted by soon-to-be House speaker Newt Gingrich and future House majority leader Dick Armey, the agenda also included an exceptionally harsh proposal for welfare "reform," which would become the blueprint for the 1996 law.

As initially contemplated, the GOP's proposed "Personal Responsibility Act" denied welfare benefits to mothers under age eighteen (and gave states the option to deny benefits and housing to mothers under age twenty-one); allowed states to kick recipients off the rolls after just two years; required mothers to declare the paternity of their children as a condition for receiving benefits; and required all recipients to work at least thirty-five hours per week. Most significantly, the bill proposed to end welfare as an entitlement, instead converting the program into the fixed, lump-sum "block grants" to states that TANF is today.[141]

Clinton had already vetoed two GOP reform efforts as too punitive, but the results of the 1994 election shifted political momentum in the GOP's favor.[142] By then, Clinton's failure to pass welfare reform—despite his pledge in 1992 to "end welfare as we know it"—also threatened to become a problem for his re-election campaign.[143] Unwilling to risk the political fallout from a third veto, Clinton signed PRWORA on August 22, 1996, despite acknowledging the legislation had "serious flaws."[144] (He reportedly described the measure as "a decent welfare bill wrapped in a sack of s–t," according to *Time*.)[145]

Unfortunately, the bipartisan imprimatur Clinton bestowed on welfare reform has since calcified the politics of poverty. Unwinding major elements of the 1996 legislation—such as its block grant structure and work requirements—would take a miracle politically.

Conservatives have moreover doubled down on the idea of work requirements as a condition of receiving benefits. The Trump administration, for instance, proposed in 2019 to tighten work requirements that the 1996 welfare law also imposed on some recipients of SNAP (food stamps).[146] The U.S. Department of Agriculture estimated that those restrictions would have ended benefits for about 688,000 Americans.[147] President Donald Trump also approved efforts in thirteen states to impose work requirements on Medicaid beneficiaries.[148] (Most of these initiatives, however, were later struck down by courts and rescinded by President Joe Biden. One exception is Georgia, where a federal court in 2022 allowed the "Georgia Pathways" program to continue.)[149]

Rather than move low-income Americans out of poverty, these efforts are purely punitive and aimed at preventing "idleness" rather than creating genuine opportunities for advancement.

For much of the nation's history, however, work has separated the "deserving" from the "undeserving" poor, and policymakers remain committed to "training and education" as the path to self-improvement for impoverished Americans with limited skills. Absent a radical—and unlikely—shift in the politics of poverty, work requirements are here to stay.

3

Bridges to Nowhere

International College is a for-profit school in East Los Angeles, California, where 96 percent of residents are Hispanic, more than a quarter of children live in poverty, and only 9 percent have a bachelor's degree or higher (compared to 36 percent statewide).[1] In the fall of 2022, International College offered just five courses, including basic graphic design, small-business bookkeeping, "computer operation and applications," and an online cake decoration class for $5,100 that promised to teach students "how to properly bake and ice a cake, as well as how to cover a cake board."[2]

According to the "School Performance Fact Sheet" that all for-profit schools must file with the state of California, the school enrolled eighty-six students in its bookkeeping class in 2020, thirty-four of whom finished.[3] Just thirty-three students completed the graphic design class (out of 105 who enrolled). Cake decoration boasted a 100 percent completion rate in 2020—but only three students took the class.

Utterly unknown is whether any of the graduates of International College landed jobs because of their new credentials. Although the state requires for-profit schools to disclose job placement rates and wages, International College's report includes none of this data (tables meant to display this information showed rows of "N/A" instead).

Yet despite its spotty record, International College is one of about one thousand "eligible training providers" (and more than 5,700 programs) approved by the state of California to receive federal training dollars under the Workforce Innovation and Opportunity Act (WIOA), the federal government's largest workforce development program.[4] Under WIOA, Congress appropriates nearly $3 billion a year to fund worker training programs through a network of nearly 2,400 "American Job Centers." Unemployed and underemployed workers eligible for WIOA assistance get "Individual Training Accounts," with a set amount of funds (typically capped at about $3,500) to pay for training from approved providers on a state "eligible training provider list" (the ETPL). If you visit CalJOBS.ca.gov, you'll see International College on the list of WIOA-approved programs.

California's ETPL includes high-performing institutions, but they are hard to distinguish from lesser schools and questionable for-profits. These include the Stellar Career College in Modesto, whose students earn a not-so-stellar median annual income of $25,723, according to the Department of Education's College Scorecard, and UEI College–Gardena, where 93 percent of students take out federal loans and 22 percent are in default or delinquent.[5] Also on California's "approved" list is American River College, a community college in Sacramento with a 33 percent graduation rate, and various branches of the Milan Institute, a for-profit cosmetology school that, among other things, offers a 50-week course in "barbering" for $18,493.86.[6]

Substandard job training options are par for the course nationwide, not just in California. While federally funded job training has been a key strategy in the War on Poverty since its inception, it's also been resoundingly unsuccessful. Dislocated workers, disadvantaged young adults, and other vulnerable populations lack a clear path to the skills they need for a well-paying job, despite the billions of dollars invested in training programs. Job Corps, for instance, is the federal government's largest and longest-running program for low-income youth, but the government's own auditors consider it a failure.[7]

No training program can compensate for under-performing K–12 schools or for the absence of jobs in impoverished communities. Training can't remedy the lack of child care, transportation, health insurance, or steady housing that poses insurmountable hurdles for many low-income workers. Policymakers also haven't defined what a "good" training program is. The surest test might be whether a graduate lands a job—but what kind of job, for how long, and at what wage?

None of these challenges, however, excuse the poor performance of a privatized job training industry that profits from lax oversight, public indifference, and public policies that demand *activity* on the part of benefits recipients but are far less concerned about outcomes.

Federal training dollars support myriad for-profit schools like International College. Contractors run many of the federal "one-stop centers" that offer job placement and other services to unemployed or dislocated workers—with desultory results. An oligopoly of contractors has a tight grip on Job Corps, the program for youth that's been flailing for decades.

Propping up the training industry is the public's insistence that recipients of public aid must "earn" their benefits through "work"—though this sentiment hasn't led to the commitments necessary to ensure that low-income workers truly get the means to reach self-sufficiency. Supporting work is a central tenet of American social policy, but the abandonment of this goal to private interests has meant the promise of work is often empty.

An Alphabet Soup of Training Failures

What's happened with WIOA and its "eligible training provider lists" is only the latest in a long line of disasters for government-funded job training programs. Over the last half century, Congress has passed a slew of legislation authorizing billions of dollars for job training to benefit unemployed and low-income workers. But the federal government has consistently failed to design effective programs or to maintain adequate oversight over funding and implementation—a situation that's allowed the training industry's mediocrity to go unchallenged.

The first wave of programs began even before the War on Poverty, with the Manpower Development and Training Act of 1962 (MDTA). Its purpose was to "retrain workers whose skills had become outmoded or had been replaced by automation."[8] Two years later, with the launch of the War on Poverty, Congress passed the Economic Opportunity Act of 1964, which created the Job Corps and Neighborhood Youth Corps programs for young adults, as well as the Work Experience and Training Program for welfare recipients.[9] In 1968, Congress created the Work Incentive program (WIN), popularly known as "workfare," and in 1971, it passed the Emergency Employment Act, which authorized the creation of public jobs for the unemployed (in an echo of President Franklin D. Roosevelt's WPA).[10]

In addition to these larger programs, there were a spate of smaller efforts, including "Operation Mainstream," which targeted unemployed adults age fifty-five and older; the Job Bank Program, which aimed to aggregate listings for public jobs; the JOBS program (an on-the-job training program); the Public Service Careers Program (yet another on-the-job training program); the Opportunities Industrialization Centers program, which funded community-based employment and training centers; and the Concentrated Employment Program (also a community-based employment training program).[11]

None of these programs succeeded. In a 1972 survey of these efforts, the Government Accountability Office (GAO) identified eleven major areas needing improvement, including "program design, eligibility and screening, counseling, occupational and academic training, job development and placement, monitoring, follow-up, program planning, supportive services, management information systems, and fiscal and financial matters."[12] In other words, nothing worked.

Further audits uncovered more problems. The Neighborhood

Youth Corps, for instance, was supposed to reduce high school dropout rates, but the GAO found that dropout rates actually rose in locations where the programs operated.[13] At some on-the-job program locations, either workers received no training "beyond that normally provided to new employees" or the "training" involved "menial tasks, such as custodial and cleaning work in buildings," rather than learning new job skills.[14] The Concentrated Employment Program placed just thirty-seven people in jobs over a fourteen-month period in Central and East Harlem (out of a program goal of 1,875 placements), while enrollees in the Mississippi Delta ended up in jobs that didn't match their training.[15] "For example, a person trained as a welder was placed as a janitor . . . and an automobile mechanic as a maintenance man," said the GAO.[16] Among the many problems at both locations were training curricula that didn't meet enrollees' needs, inadequate staffing, fragmentation of responsibilities, and contracts that didn't demand accountability for results.[17]

In 1973, Congress tried to clean house with the passage of the Comprehensive Employment and Training Act (CETA). Unlike the earlier generation of training programs, under which the Department of Labor directly administered nearly ten thousand separate grants to public and private training providers (one reason for MDTA's unimpressive results), CETA granted funds to about four hundred state and local governments as "prime sponsors" to create training opportunities for the unemployed and public service jobs in sectors like public works, social services, and parks maintenance.[18] From 1974 to its expiration in 1982, the federal government spent more than $51 billion on CETA, which at its peak funded about 725,000 public service jobs a year, in addition to 1 million training slots.[19]

Legislators hoped that CETA's model of state and local governance would lead to better training opportunities attuned to local needs as well as better oversight. But scandals overshadowed its successes.[20] In Chicago and St. Louis, for instance, CETA became a source of political patronage for city officials who hired relatives or other favored individuals.[21] Some studies found that CETA jobs didn't add to total employment but instead substituted for city or state jobs that would have existed anyway.[22] When the program expired in 1982, the GAO found that fewer than half of the workers employed by CETA were employed three months later; about half of the unemployed were back on government assistance; and about a quarter of those who did have jobs were earning less than they did before their CETA participation.[23]

In 1983, Congress tried again with the Job Training Partnership Act (JTPA), which rejected the public jobs model in favor of private-sector placements for trainees. Under the JTPA, states received federal grants to fund "partnerships" with local businesses for training opportunities, subsidized jobs, and work experience. But with earlier problems of oversight still unresolved, this effort became yet another boondoggle for state and local governments, as well as for companies.

In a 1990 screed from the Cato Institute, journalist James Bovard excoriated the program for wasting money on frivolous contracts, "providing contractors with a license to steal." "JTPA has spent taxpayers' money to set up a circus museum, teach cab drivers to smile, and enable a small-town mayor to fly to Japan," he wrote.[24] Numerous audits by GAO and the Department of Labor's inspector general faulted the program's contracting practices, wrote Bovard, and then there was the occasional graft. A 1988 investigation by *The Plain Dealer*, for instance, accused then-Ohio Governor Richard Celeste of funneling $1.4 million in JTPA contracts to campaign contributors, including $100,000 for an effort "to train 32 unemployed coal miners to become engineering aides." "Only two of the trainees got jobs, which is not surprising because there was no demand for engineering aides in the area of Ohio where the training occurred," wrote Bovard.

In 1998, Congress replaced the JTPA with the Workforce Investment Act (WIA, now the Workforce Innovation and Opportunity Act, WIOA), which created the American Job Centers and training provider lists that are the current playground of the training industry and providers like International College.[25]

The "Deserving Poor" Work

Despite all of these decades of failure, Congress can't help but continue to throw money at training programs—and, by extension, the training industry—thanks to a longstanding bipartisan consensus, buttressed by public opinion, that puts work at the center of antipoverty policy.

Willingness to work has long defined who, among the poor, Americans believe is worthy of help, as earlier chapters have alluded to. "Throughout the nation's past, Americans have held the work ethic sacred, and they have defined the undeserving poor by its absence," as Michael B. Katz writes in *The Undeserving Poor.*[26]

In nineteenth-century America, "paupers" who didn't work were undeserving of public sympathy, let alone public aid. Poverty was judged a moral condition, not an economic one, "the consequence of willful error, of shameful indolence, of vicious habits," in the words of a nineteenth-century minister quoted by Katz. "Especially in America, where opportunity awaited anyone with energy and talent, poverty signaled personal failure," Katz writes.[27]

In the 1980s and 1990s, conservatives resurrected these biases to weaponize work in their attacks on welfare. Their efforts to stigmatize (and racialize) welfare helped sour public opinion on Johnson's Great Society and create the political momentum that made the 1996 welfare reform inevitable. By the mid-1990s, many Americans shared the "widespread belief that most welfare recipients would rather sit home and collect benefits than work hard to support themselves," as political scientist Martin Gilens concluded in *Why Americans Hate Welfare.*[28]

Among the loudest proponents of work requirements in welfare reform was New York University professor Lawrence Mead, who declared "nonworking poverty" a "political disaster" that "suggests the bankruptcy of the entire progressive tradition—of our image of self-reliance as central to American politics."[29] Breaking the "politics of dependency," as Mead called it, required ending "permissive" social policies that he claimed coddled the nonworking poor and engendered public resentment:[30]

> What disturbs people most is the passivity of today's entrenched poor, their curious reluctance to help themselves in many ways. To average Americans, competence connotes not just working but a more general quality of "motivation" or "initiative" about life. They fail to see in today's poor that desire to improve oneself and one's family that has marked American society. Only when poor adults show a clearer commitment to "getting ahead" will other Americans be able to identify with them and feel more generous toward them. Most Americans will accept poverty as an economic condition and will do something to help, but they will not accept defeatism. The poor, if they are to be "deserving," cannot simply give up. They must "try," and working or attempting to work is the great badge of that effort.[31]

But liberal and Democratic policymakers have also reinforced the idea that recipients of government benefits should work. In the depths of the Great Depression, when unemployment peaked at close to 25 percent, President Franklin Delano Roosevelt was reluctant to maintain the federal government's public relief efforts, which he believed to be corrosive to the national character.[32] "The Federal Government must and shall quit this business of relief," FDR told Congress in his 1935 State of the Union address. "Continued dependence upon relief induces a spiritual disintegration fundamentally destructive to the national fiber. To dole our relief in this way is to administer a narcotic, a subtle destroyer of the human spirit. It is inimical to the dictates of a sound policy. It is in violation of the traditions of America. Work must be found for able-bodied but destitute workers."[33] Roosevelt went on to create the Works Progress Administration in 1935 (later renamed the Work Projects Administration [WPA] in 1939), which would ultimately employ more than 8.5 million Americans during its existence.[34] (It would also inspire CETA.)

Even President Lyndon B. Johnson's War on Poverty was predicated on encouraging work and improving low-income Americans' employability. Like FDR, Johnson generally eschewed the idea of public relief. On the morning of his State of the Union address in 1964—the day he declared war on poverty—Johnson told his advisors that "what we're trying to do—instead of people getting something for nothing, we're going to try to fit them where they can take care of themselves. . . . That's our program. We don't want them to get something for nothing. We want to get them where they can carry their own weight."[35]

During his speech, Johnson emphasized his principal strategy: to equip poor Americans with the capacity for self-help, through training and education. "Our chief weapons . . . will be better schools, and better health, and better homes, and better training, and better job opportunities to help more Americans, especially young Americans, escape from squalor and misery and unemployment rolls where other citizens help to carry them," said Johnson.[36]

In its 1964 report, Johnson's Council of Economic Advisors proposed "the maintenance of high employment" as its main tactic for poverty reduction, including by "accelerating economic growth," "rehabilitating urban and rural communities," "improving labor markets," "expanding educational opportunities," and "enlarging job opportunities for youth."[37] Among the administration's signature initiatives was the establishment of Job Corps, a residential job training program for young adults modeled after FDR's Civilian Conservation Corps (more on this later), and the preschool program Head Start.[38] Rewarding work was also the rationale behind Democrat Russell Long's championship of the "work bonus" that later became the EITC and President Bill Clinton's pledge to "make work pay" in his embrace of welfare reform.

On the one hand, the focus on work has helped justify significant investments in social services that Americans perhaps otherwise wouldn't support. Public opinion polls find nearly universal approval for providing welfare recipients with job training, education, and child care.[39] The strength of this support enabled Clinton not only to expand the EITC, but also to increase child-care funding for low-income workers by $4 billion and to expand Medicaid coverage to working-poor families.[40] Clinton also persuaded Congress to grant $100 million in new transportation funding (to improve transit access to jobs) and to create the Welfare-to-Work tax credit for employers who hired welfare recipients.[41]

The insistence on work, however, has also fed the notion that poverty is the consequence of personal "choices" versus the outcome of structural inequities that limit people's potential, regardless of the decisions they make. The public supports investments in job training, but the *outcome* of that training is still recipients' responsibility.

Sentiments like these have allowed job training providers to avoid accountability for the quality of their services—quality is immaterial if providers can shift the blame for any failures to trainees and their deficits in "personal responsibility." The longstanding, hardwired belief that anyone can pull themselves out of poverty if they "try" is one reason substandard job training programs have managed to justify their existence—and to collect federal funding from programs like WIOA and mechanisms like the ETPL.

Woe Is WIOA

When Congress passed WIOA in 2014, hopes were high, as was the rhetoric. "We've created a workforce system that's more nimble and adaptable, better aligned with what businesses need, and more accountable," said Senator Patty Murray (D-WA), one of the bill's bipartisan co-authors, on the eve of the legislation's passage.[42]

As enacted, WIOA called for a coordinated and comprehensive workforce development system that could deliver the skilled workers employers want; provide workers with pathways to well-paid careers; and bolster state and local officials' plans for economic development and growth.[43] WIOA's network of American Job Centers (AJCs) would serve as portals for workers seeking help with resume-writing, job search, training, or other services, and act as brokers for local companies on the hunt for skilled hires. "WIOA is designed to help job seekers . . . succeed in the labor market and to match employers with the skilled workers they need to compete in the global economy," says the Department of Labor.[44]

In some instances, federally funded job centers do live up to this vision. NOVAworks in Sunnyvale, California, offers up to three workshops a day for job seekers, hosts a robust online job board with listings from employer partners, and keeps painstaking track of its clients' progress.[45] "We track every person who gets training subsidies and every program they're in, and we watch their success or failure and their wage or placement," says Kris Stadelman, who was NOVAworks' executive director for nearly thirteen years.[46]

But more typical is the Arlington Employment Center, the designated WIOA job center for Arlington, Virginia.[47] In the spring of 2023, the online "Job Board" on its bare-bones site included a lone "featured employer," New Hope Health, along with a disclaimer that "this employer does not currently have any posted jobs."[48] According to the center's annual performance report, its thirteen full-time staffers assisted just 586 "customers" in 2021.[49] It hosted 56 "core workshops" over the year, which netted 263 attendees. The center also placed only eighty-five of its clients in jobs, for a placement rate of 15 percent (against a goal of 70 percent), and more than half of those who found work (54 percent) were earning less than the commonwealth's "living wage" of $15.63.[50]

Virginia's overall WIOA numbers aren't much more impressive. Between April 2020 and March 2021, just 3,121 people enrolled in WIOA-funded training programs for adult and dislocated workers, according to information supplied by commonwealth officials in the spring of 2022. Of those who exited their programs, median quarterly earnings were $6,156 six months later (or $24,624 on an annualized basis).[51]

Nor is the situation much better nationally. With roughly

$3.2 billion in funding, WIOA reached about 2.8 million "participants" (a term the government defines loosely) from July 2020 to June 2021, about 240,000 of whom received WIOA-funded training.[52] Though two-thirds of WIOA participants were reportedly working within six months of exiting the system, their median earnings (on an annualized basis) were $26,408[53]—significantly less than the annualized median earnings of a typical worker without a high school diploma in 2021 ($32,552).[54] The number of participants and trainees has moreover been shrinking. From 2016 to 2019, recipients of WIOA-funded training dropped by 77,000 (from 330,720 to 253,428), while the number of participants plummeted by 2 million (from 5.6 million to 3.6 million).[55]

Where WIOA has succeeded, however, is in creating myriad new and continuing opportunities for the training industry to sell its services to state and local workforce boards.

If you notice some striking similarities among the websites for Virginia's Workforce Connection, California's CalJOBS, and Florida's EmployFlorida.com, that's because they've all been built by Geographic Solutions, Inc., a Florida-based company whose entire business is developing software for state and local workforce agencies.[56] ("Building Integrated Workforce Development Systems" is its tagline.)[57] More than 120 job centers in 35 states use the company's flagship product, Virtual OneStop, according to its site.[58] In October 2023, the company hosted a four-day conference in Monterey, California, that attracted more than 325 attendees, including representatives from more than 190 agencies.[59] The $994 registration fee included pre-conference training on the company's latest software.

Other contractors purport to provide help with career "exploration" and skills assessment. The Arlington Employment Center's site, for instance, includes a link to "Career Concourse," an "assessment" tool created by Chmura Economics and Analytics, a Richmond-based labor market research firm.[60] When I took the assessment to "find careers that fit your interests" in December 2022, the thirty-one-question form asked if I "like," "dislike," or am "neutral" about activities for which I had no qualifications whatsoever, such as "build kitchen cabinets," "develop a new medicine," "write books or plays," "install software across computers on a large network," "test the quality of parts before shipment," or "develop a way to better predict the weather."

The potential careers recommended to me varied from "dancer and choreographer" to "industrial production manager" to "nuclear technician." Another tool by the same company, which promised to help "explore careers consistent with your values," asked if it was "very important," "somewhat important," or "of little or no importance" that "I make use of my abilities" or that "I would never be pressured to do things that go against my sense of right and wrong."[61] This tool recommended I consider becoming an optometrist (along with a host of other unrelated professions for which I also lacked the requisite skills).

Also on Arlington's site is a link to Skill-Up, a virtual portal to "5,500+ career readiness trainings, occupational skills trainings, career pathways trainings and more" offered through a company called Metrix Learning.[62] A click on the course catalog reveals an alphabetic listing of titles ranging from "Anger Management Essentials" to "Thinking Like a CFO." Detailed course descriptions are not available, nor is there information about the credentials someone would earn if they completed, for instance, the "Personal Development Curriculum," or how that would lead to employment.

"It's all static content with no curation and no guidance," says NOVAworks' former executive director Kris Stadelman, who said her agency briefly experimented with Metrix Learning. "It's real content, but it's not in a format that's digestible by anybody but the most introverted, self-motivated linear thinkers." In fact, she said, of the handful of her clients who tried out Metrix, no one finished a training.

Nevertheless, WIOA job centers in at least ten states and the Virgin Islands are customers of Metrix Learning, according to *Learning Solutions* magazine.[63] A 2020 request for proposal (RFP) posted on the Texas government contracts portal, TXShare, indicates that the company charges $25,000 for five hundred licenses to the platform, while the package with one thousand licenses costs $40,000. The company also charges between $170 and $900 for certificates issued when (or if) a trainee completes a course.[64] The company moreover offers access to its proprietary skill and technical assessment tool for $1,000 per location. The Arlington Employment Center's annual report does not indicate how many—if any—clients used the Metrix Learning platform or completed any trainings.

The mediocrity of these products is symptomatic of a system overrun by providers bent on capturing federal dollars, coupled with wholesale disregard for the accountability WIOA was supposed to bring. In what's now a familiar refrain, workers aren't getting the services they need, while private interests prosper. Nowhere is this more evident than on states' eligible training provider lists (ETPLs).

Ironically, the concept of "eligible training providers" was originally intended to give participants more control over their training. Under the Job Training Partnership Act, WIOA's predecessor, participants didn't pick their training but were assigned to programs chosen and contracted out by local workforce development agencies—one reason that program was ripe for abuse. This approach led to the "overconsumption" of training, as one analysis put it, and many people ended up in trainings they didn't want or where opportunities weren't available (except for the training providers).[65]

WIOA's philosophy, on the other hand, is to be "customer-focused." Individual Training Accounts provide workers with funding to pursue the training of their choice, while the ETPL is meant to ensure equality. Or at least that was the intent. What this structure has spawned instead is a training market dominated by mediocre providers scouting for easy WIOA dollars, while workers hoping to find quality programs must sort through mountains of chaff. The odds are high of choosing a program that is expensive, irrelevant, and of dubious quality.

For one thing, anyone can apply to become an eligible training provider, and most states in fact actively solicit applications. In Maryland, for instance, qualifying programs must lead to an "industry-recognized certificate or certification"—or simply to "measurable skill gains toward a credential."[66] Qualifying providers can be an "institution of higher education that holds a certificate of approval from the Maryland Higher Education Commission (MHEC)"—or simply "a community based organization" (although in the latter case the organization would also need to obtain a "not regulated status" letter from MHEC).[67] The result is a preponderance of for-profits and fly-by-night operators hoping to goose their revenues with WIOA money. In California and Virginia, for example, the number of for-profit providers on the state's approved provider lists equals or exceeds the number of public institutions, such as community colleges.

Many for-profit providers exploit their ETPL status as a badge of quality (however ersatz) in their marketing. The online training provider MedCerts, which offers IT and health care certifications, boasts on its home page that it has "approved ETPL status in 30+ states."[68]

Other providers dangle WIOA money as a tactic for recruiting students. Aryan Consulting and Staffing, a formerly approved Maryland provider that offered entry-level pharmaceutical manufacturing training, promised, "If you are unemployed and receiving government benefits, you may be qualified for complementary training and placement program (*sic*)."[69] (Aryan's website was riddled with typos and included no information on tuition costs. As of November 2023, the organization's website had disappeared.) The for-profit Medical Learning Center writes on its "Payment Options" page that it "is an approved Northern Virginia Workforce Investment (NVWIB) trainer provider for Virginia Residents.[70] Funding is provided for Nurse Aide that covers the total cost (*sic*)."

The predominance of for-profits lures students toward pricier options than necessary. (Trainees pay out of pocket for costs above the training dollars provided in their individual training accounts.) A student interested in becoming an administrative assistant, for example, could enroll in a 229-hour program with the Fairfax Public Schools Adult and Community Education for $2,616 —or they could spend $6,846 for a certificate in "clerical studies" from the Virginia Highlands Community College.[71] They could also opt for the for-profit Joshua Career Institute, which offers a 600-hour certificate program for $8,000.[72] Virginia's ETPL describes all three offerings as "administrative assistant" trainings approved by the state.

The often random assortment of providers on state ETPLs also means that programs may or may not align with the skills and credentials a local economy needs. Just because a training is offered doesn't mean jobs are available. In West Virginia, for example, many approved providers are online and based out of state, so they likely lack a connection with local employers. A scan through the state's ETPL includes providers based in Kentucky, Ohio, Pennsylvania, Maryland, Michigan, and Virginia.[73]

Among the more than 1,500 approved programs in Virginia, trainees can pursue credentials in everything from an associate's degree in diesel technology to certification as a wind turbine technician, an EMT, or a truck driver.[74] They can also seek training as a bail bondsman, an ethical hacker, or a massage therapist and get certificates in such specialties as permanent cosmetic tattooing, meat cutting, or the appropriate use of pepper spray (for aspiring security guards).[75] These might be excellent programs, but there's also no information about the availability of area jobs for students interested in these fields (that is, whether there's a local shortage of butchers or cosmetic tattoo artists).

Compounding these problems is that WIOA participants can't tell which programs work and which don't. Training providers aren't handing over outcomes data, a challenge that dates to the 1998 Workforce Investment Act. In a 2003 audit, the Department of Labor's Office of the Inspector General found that many ETPL providers considered reporting requirements to be "burdensome," especially if they didn't have many WIOA-funded students.[76] Some programs also worried that disclosing personal information about students, such as Social Security numbers and wage data, would violate students' privacy rights and subject them to liability, although regulations have since resolved those concerns.[77] In a November 2020 report, the research organization Mathematica found that in many states, local officials still said training providers "could not, or would not, provide the required performance data."[78] This report covered a pre-pandemic timeframe from 2016 to 2019—no doubt the pandemic made these reporting problems even worse.

One likely reason for this lack of information is that the data aren't worth bragging about. Over the summer of 2022, I emailed ten for-profit providers on the Virginia and Maryland ETPLs, asking about the number of WIOA-funded participants they'd served in the past year and their outcomes. Eight out of ten did not respond, and two failed to follow up after an initial response. (One of these ten was Aryan Consulting, noted earlier.)

States don't have much interest in digging too deep, says John Pallasch, who was formerly executive director of Kentucky's workforce development agency and now the CEO of One Workforce Solutions, a consulting firm. No news is good news if the alternative is failing federally mandated performance targets. "I know firsthand that in Kentucky, we cleaned the data well enough to get the performance measures and then we moved on," he says. "We didn't clean it pristinely, and there's not a state out there that does, because there's no incentive to do that."[79]

Technically, these failures to report data violate federal law. Department of Labor regulations require states to collect information from approved providers, including the number of WIOA participants enrolled in a particular course, the cost of the course, and outcomes such as the percentage of enrollees who receive a credential and whether they're working.[80] This data is supposed to be available on a state's ETPL and on trainingproviderresults.gov, a project initiated by the Labor Department in 2019 that was meant to be for training programs what the College Scorecard is for colleges.

But click on provider listings on a state's ETPL or the website, and lots of information is missing. Clicking on the "Course Performance" tab for half a dozen approved courses on West Virginia's ETPL yielded straight zeros for such measures as "wages at placement," "number employed after six months," and "number receiving degree or certificate."[81] For the three "administrative assistant" programs from Virginia's ETPL cited earlier, two listed no outcomes data as of November 2023 (all values for completion rates and earnings were listed as zeros). One program, offered by the Fairfax adult education program, reported just seven students in 2021, with median earnings of $7,656.39 six months after graduation.[82] Trainingproviderresults.gov frequently shows only asterisks for employment rate, completion rate, and earnings with the note "Data Suppressed."[83] As of the fall of 2023, the site was still relatively new, and states had not finished submitting their data. But the problems are still profound, says Pallasch, who also served as assistant secretary for employment and training at the Department of Labor under President Donald Trump and under whose watch the site was launched. "The data in there is junk because that's the data that the states are giving us," he says.

But in a final ironic twist, these reporting requirements—toothless as they seem to be—are still just burdensome enough to discourage some of the nation's best training providers from joining state ETPLs. "Many small organizations that run good programs opt out [because] it's too bureaucratic," the former director of a nationally recognized training program based in Maryland says. (They declined to use their name or the name of their institution to preserve relationships with state officials.) "We started to pursue [an ETPL application] but stopped because the process . . . was lengthy, and it was clear they were going to mess with a program we felt good about. We didn't want to change it for dribs and drabs of money."[84] Approved providers must, for instance, report performance on *all* students, not just those funded by the WIOA (though this requirement was frequently waived during the pandemic).[85] Many community colleges opt out of applying for a state's ETPL because they don't have the capacity or desire to track all of their students for this purpose.

National providers—such as LinkedIn Learning or Cisco—must also apply for each state's ETPL separately, another disincentive. These requirements are one reason you won't find Google, Coursera, or other high-profile organizations that offer online courses nationwide to adult learners. Also absent from state-approved provider lists are well-regarded, cutting-edge institutions like Western Governors University, an online institution that offers skills-based credentials, and Southern New Hampshire University, the nation's largest nonprofit online college (SNHU is not even on New Hampshire's ETPL).[86]

At the end of the day, WIOA participants don't get the information they need, poor-performing programs slide under the radar, and federal training dollars end up in the pockets of training providers while trainees waste their time in programs that might not help them find jobs. Only about one in three people who enroll in WIOA training ends up in a job related to that training, according to Labor Department data.[87]

But the slow-rolling disappointment of WIOA is not the most egregious failure in federal job training. That honor is reserved for Job Corps, a War on Poverty–era program that federal audits have faulted since its inception but has still managed to survive as the government's largest training program for disadvantaged young adults. One secret to its staying power has been the small group of contractors that has managed the program through successive presidential administrations, defeating efforts at reform—but at the expense of young people who might have benefited from more effective programs.

The Tragedy of Job Corps

The coronavirus pandemic that began the spring of 2020 has exacted an incalculable and ongoing social, economic, and human toll. But among the groups hit hardest were young adults caught in the transition to independence when the world shut down.

Young adults on the front lines of the economy in sectors like retail, hospitality, and food service lost jobs in cataclysmic numbers; unemployment among eighteen- to twenty-four-year-olds soared from 10 percent in March 2020 to 28 percent by July, according to the Urban Alliance, with Black and Latinx youth suffering the highest rates of joblessness.[88] College attendance also plummeted, with enrollment down by 1.4 million students from the spring of 2020 through the spring of 2022.[89]

From 2019 to 2021, the number of young adults ages eighteen to twenty-four neither working nor in school surged by more than 1 million, according to the labor market research firm Lightcast.[90] All told, an estimated 4.7 million young adults—or one in six—were disconnected from the mainstream economy, and the damage could linger for decades. "You will see a lifetime impact on this generation," as Michael Hicks, director of the Center for Business and Economic Research at Ball State University in Muncie, Indiana, told *Newsweek*.[91]

In theory, the federal government's Job Corps program is ideally suited for tackling this crisis. Launched during the War on Poverty, its explicit aim is to connect out-of-school, out-of-work young people with education and employment through a network of more than one hundred campus-based centers throughout the country. With an annual budget of $1.7 billion, Job Corps is still the government's largest education and training program for low-income youth.[92]

But Job Corps' pandemic performance was a miserable failure—even by the standards of the generally disastrous national experiment in remote learning from 2020 to 2021. Job Corps' residential model proved too rigid for the exigencies of the pandemic; instead of redoubling its efforts to keep young people engaged, it shut down completely. In March 2020, it sent home the thirty thousand students then enrolled in its centers and then struggled for months to move instruction online.[93]

Enrollment plunged by 56 percent over the following year, and the number of trades training completions dropped to *zero* between April 2020 and April 2021, according to a November 2021 audit by the Department of Labor's inspector general (IG).[94] The program struggled to get laptops and other equipment to students, partly because it took "almost half a year to establish its student loaner device policies," the IG's office found, and "some students were still without equipment months after centers ceased in-person instruction."[95] Among the program's self-inflicted hurdles was a mandatory "usage agreement" that held families liable for a $500 penalty if laptops and hotspots were lost, stolen, or damaged—a burden that many low-income families couldn't or wouldn't take on.[96] Some instructors mailed paper packets of materials that took weeks to arrive.[97]

After reopening in 2021, Job Corps centers struggled again, this time with recruitment and enrollment. In July 2022, Job Corps centers reported just 2,197 new arrivals nationwide.[98] For the nine-month period from July 2021 through March 2022, fourteen centers reported fewer than fifty total arrivals—and two reported none at all.[99]

The bigger scandal, though, is that Jobs Corps has performed poorly for decades. Even before the pandemic, Job Corps was barely serving fifty thousand young people a year, and enrollments were declining. Between 2007 and 2018, enrollment slid from 63,448 to 46,969.[100]

Evaluations find that while the program helps some young adults, the teenagers who make up the bulk of enrollees get no long-term benefits in earnings or employment. Government audits have been harsh, documenting mismanagement, safety problems, and persistent failures to place trainees into meaningful jobs. A scathing 2018 audit by the Department of Labor's inspector general (IG) concluded that the program "could not demonstrate beneficial job training outcomes."[101] Another report, from the Government Accountability Office (GAO), noted more than 13,500 safety incidents from 2016 to 2017 at Job Corps centers, nearly half of them drug-related incidents or assaults.[102] In 2015, two students were murdered in separate campus-related crimes.[103]

Even successful graduates call the program a last resort. "If you're really desperate and ain't got anywhere else to go, then I would do Job Corps," says Earvin Rogers, who enrolled at a New Jersey Job Corps center in 2017 after dropping out of community college. Rogers landed a hotel maintenance job before the pandemic but was unemployed when we spoke in 2021.

Rather than the young people it purports to serve, the program's biggest beneficiaries may be the tight-knit coterie of for-profit government contractors who administer the program, some of whom have held on to multimillion-dollar contracts for decades. But in a testament to congressional inertia, the program lingers on, surviving threatened closures, resisting overhauls, and garnering enough political support to maintain its funding. Worst of all, vulnerable young adults are paying the price of subsidizing the Job Corps industry. While Job Corps siphons away much-needed dollars that could support better programs, young adults aren't getting the help they need to put their education and careers on track.

Grand Vision, Modest Results

Launched during President Lyndon B. Johnson's War on Poverty, Job Corps now consists of 123 centers across the country, many of them in former military facilities and often in rural areas. A typical campus is the Woodstock Job Corps Center, which sits on sixty-four acres of tranquil woodland in rural Maryland, about an hour from Washington, DC.[104] A stately, H-shaped stone building that was once the oldest Jesuit seminary in America now houses the center, which can host up to four hundred students.[105]

The purpose of this residential setting, as program founder Sargent Shriver testified to Congress in 1964, was to "take young men from crippling environments and put them in centers where they will receive a blend of useful work, job training, and basic education."[106] Young people would get "a chance to escape from the cycle of poverty and to break out of the ruthless pattern of poor housing, poor homes, and poor education," he argued.[107]

Today, Job Corps offers training and certification in more than eighty fields, including IT, construction, manufacturing, health care, and hospitality. The program's website features smiling, clean-cut young people driving forklifts, cooking in chef's whites, and fixing cars. "Job Corps is not just a career training program. You'll also receive everyday staples AND a supportive community. *All of this for* **FREE**," the site promises.[108]

To be eligible for the program, students must not only qualify as low income but also have at least one barrier to education and employment, such as low literacy or homelessness.[109] Job Corps centers provide housing and meals, along with a small allowance, a uniform, books, supplies, and dental and medical care. Facilities also offer gyms and weight rooms as well as after-hours activities. A recruitment presentation for the Treasure Island Job Corps Center in San Francisco boasts that it has "one of the best recreation programs in the nation," with trips to bowling alleys and local beaches and special events like talent shows and picnics.[110] The San Jose center touts an Olympic-sized swimming pool and a dance floor.[111] Tuition is free.[112]

Over the years, Job Corps has unquestionably had its share of successes. The professional boxer George Foreman, who attended the program in the 1960s, was reportedly so grateful that he repaid the federal government the cost of his enrollment.[113]

Today, success stories include alumni like Shimira Mills, who was twenty-eight years old when we spoke in 2021. Mills said she enrolled in the Pittsburgh Job Corps Center in 2017 on a cousin's advice after a brief stint in culinary school did not launch her dream career of being a chef. She spent seven months living at the Pittsburgh campus, learning to be an HVAC technician. She found a job almost immediately at a small local business but had just been hired at a large residential heating and air conditioning company in Philadelphia with better pay and room for promotion. "Within the last two years, I have acquired two cars and an apartment where I'm living by myself," Mills told me. The program, she said, gave her a second chance when she needed one. Without Job Corps, Mills continued, "If I'm going to be 100 percent honest, I would probably still be working dead-end jobs."

Job Corps was also a lifeline for Ricky Gass. Now in his mid-twenties, Gass was eighteen when he fell into drugs. "I paid the price because I was with the wrong people," he said. One day he woke up in the back of a police car. "I was smoking some bad stuff one time—I don't even remember what happened," he told me. "They said I was trying to fight cops and all this crazy stuff was going on. I could have been shot and killed. . . . I got lucky I was sent to lockup and not a graveyard." Gass resolved to turn his life around, especially when he learned he had a daughter on the way. But with only a high school diploma, the best job he could get was at the local Family Dollar. "My check was $200 every two weeks," he said. "It was horrible."

In 2019, Gass enrolled at New Jersey's Edison Job Corps Center and threw himself into his classes, learning everything from putting in electrical wiring to hanging drywall. When one of his advisers offered him a training opportunity at a solar power company, Gass jumped at the chance and was hired soon thereafter. When we spoke in 2021, he was installing panels for Solar Landscape, a company that specializes in building large-scale solar projects in New Jersey. He was being paid the industry's prevailing wage, then about $62 an hour, according to Solar Landscape's director of community engagement, Katelyn Gold. In November 2021, he starred in a CNBC feature headlined "This 25-year-old makes $100K a year as a solar roof installer in Linden, NJ."[114]

But while Job Corps' defenders point to students like Mills and Gass as proof of the program's value, there are also students like Julea Shannon, who spent seven months at the Joliet Job Center in Illinois and earned certificates in Microsoft Word and other office software. While she told me she enjoyed the experience of living on campus ("You get to see how it is to live without your parents. It teaches you to be a mature adult," she said over chat on LinkedIn), the program didn't help her land a job. She ultimately went back to community college and earned an associate's degree in criminal justice in 2019. As of December 2022, her LinkedIn profile listed her as a student at Kankakee Community College in Joliet.

Formal evaluations of the program are similarly mixed. Evidence shows that for older students like Mills and Gass, Job Corps can be modestly beneficial. In a rigorous series of evaluations published in 2018, the research organization Mathematica found that students between the ages of twenty and twenty-four at the time of enrollment were 4.2 percentage points more likely to be employed twenty years later than a comparable group that did not attend.[115] They were also 1.4 percentage points more likely to be filing taxes and 3.6 percentage points less likely to be on disability. For these students, the net benefit of Job Corps to society was about $30,000 over the course of a participant's lifetime (in inflation-adjusted dollars), considering the taxes they paid on earnings, as well as savings from reductions in crime and dependency on public benefits.

But Mathematica's study told a different story about the teenagers who enroll in Job Corps—and who account for most attendees. It found no long-term gains in earnings or employment for students who started the program when they were ages sixteen to nineteen. Overall, the study concluded, Job Corps was not cost-effective, with the net cost of Job Corps running about $17,800 per participant (again, in inflation-adjusted dollars).[116] Even taking into account the benefits from older students' success, the government was losing money.

In fairness, the mission of Job Corps is a difficult one to make good on. Job Corps is taking on a group of young adults who are tough to reach successfully. Of the nearly fifty thousand young people enrolled in Job Corps in 2018, 60 percent did not have a high school diploma or GED when they entered the program, 20 percent were receiving public assistance, and 5 percent were homeless, runaways, or in foster care. About 80 percent of Job Corps students were teens and younger adults, ages sixteen to twenty.[117]

"The labor market is not very hospitable to young people without high levels of post-secondary skills," says Dan Bloom, senior vice president at MDRC, a nonpartisan policy research organization focused on social and education issues. "Put together with problems in the public schools, a harsh criminal justice [system], and a bunch of other contextual factors, and it's very difficult to change those trajectories."[118]

Job Corps graduate Malcolm Little, who served as student body president at the Woodstock Job Corps Center in Maryland in 2016, said many of his classmates were victims of crime or had witnessed violence.

"I met girls who were pimped out, put on drugs, folks trying to kill them," he told me. "There were other people, both male and female, who were sex trafficked and ex–drug dealers who were trying to get themselves together." Little said one young man he met in the program didn't go home to Atlanta for Christmas break because he feared for his life. "He told me the neighborhood he lived in was so bad that if he disappeared for three weeks and came back, people would assume he had been detained by the feds and snitched to get out, and that would have put a target on his back," Little said.

The prevalence of this kind of trauma means that Job Corps must serve as far more than a training program to its students if they are to succeed. "They need mental health, they need physical health, they need medications," says Tony Staynings, who is now the director of the Potomac Job Corps Center in Washington, DC, but was a consultant to the program when we spoke. "There's a whole element to the delivery of service that the average person looking from the outside doesn't understand."[119]

The expectations placed on the Job Corps program might be unattainable. No career and education program can, on its own, salvage the fortunes of young people whose lives have been shaped by deep-rooted systemic poverty. A young person's disconnection from the economic mainstream is the result of subpar schools, a dearth of jobs, and, often, neighborhoods beset by violence.

On the other hand, Job Corps has managed to sustain itself essentially unchanged for more than half a century. Its residential model, while its signature feature, is also the element that makes the program resistant to reform—not least because of the contractors who have a vested interest in maintaining the status quo.

The Job Corps Cartel

Proponents of Job Corps' residential model argue that living on campus can provide students with a clean break from negative influences in their lives.

"The folks who come to Job Corps need to be there in order to succeed," says Grace Kilbane, who served two separate stints as the national director of Job Corps, most recently under President Barack Obama. She is also a board member of the National Job Corps Association (NJCA), the trade association for Job Corps contractors.[120] "I met students who were homeless or had aged out of foster care and had nowhere to go," Kilbane told me. "That need has not gone away—if anything, it's gotten greater."

Yet the residential model is a major driver of the program's expense as well as its persistent problems with safety and security. "Centers do what they can to create a positive culture," says Jeffrey Turgeon, who worked for nearly five years at a Job Corps center in Massachusetts and is now the executive director of the MassHire Central Region Workforce Board. "But any time you've got a bunch of young people, especially young people who are at risk and haven't been successful in the past, they're going to come with whatever baggage or drama they bring with them."[121]

Shimira Mills, the Job Corps graduate who is now an HVAC technician, said discipline was a big part of life on campus, which she described as having a "boot camp type of vibe." "We got graded on a day-to-day basis on how our rooms were and chores that we had to complete every morning and every evening," she said. "If you've ever been to boot camp, they had the same system. Or jail—whichever one." Unlike a college campus, days were strictly regimented. Students woke up at 6 a.m.; breakfast was at 7; classes began at 8.

Many of her classmates did not make it through the program, Mills said. Her roommate was expelled after getting into a fight with another student. Other students were kicked out after failing drug tests, which are part of Job Corps' "zero-tolerance" policy toward alcohol and drugs. Of the 45,173 "separations" (graduations or other departures) from Job Corps in 2018, 65 percent of students left for jobs or the military and around 7 percent went on to further education, implying that the remaining 28 percent either left without completing the program or graduated without a meaningful placement.[122]

Both Mills and Little said their rooms were searched from time to time. "Every once in a while I'd come back and all my stuff from my dresser and my closet would be on the bed," Little said.

Former student Ricky Gass (the solar panel installer) was among a minority of students who commuted to his Job Corps center every day. Unlike most centers, which are in rural or out-of-the-way areas, the Edison Job Corps center he attended in New Jersey was reachable by public transportation, and Gass had child-care obligations for his daughter. "Sometimes I felt like I wanted to be on campus, but if I was staying there, I would have possibly gotten into a lot of different situations—like females, the drama. There was a lot of testosterone," he said. "Some situations I was shielded from by not being there on campus."

Phillip-Mathew Golden, who taught at the Woodstock Center in Maryland for four years, told me he witnessed a significant amount of turnover among the staff who managed the dorms. "They handled a lot of volatile situations," he said. "They tried really hard, they really cared, but it was hard to keep people there."[123]

On occasion, that volatility has spilled over into violence. In August 2015, four students at the Homestead Job Corps Center near Miami were arrested and charged with hacking to death a seventeen-year-old fellow student with a machete and then setting his body on fire. Earlier that year, a twenty-year-old student at the St. Louis Job Corps Center was arrested for allegedly shooting and killing another student in the dorms.[124] Between 2007 and 2016, the GAO found, Job Corps centers reported 49,836 safety and security incidents, including 6,541 incidents involving drugs and 9,299 assaults.[125]

The need to maintain safety is just one reason why the program's residential model is expensive. There are also more prosaic concerns, such as meals, laundry, water and electricity bills, and building maintenance.

Job Corps operates on what is essentially a franchise model—much like McDonald's—where a central office dictates the operation of individual centers in conformity with a single standard. Just like how every McDonald's must make its fries in exactly the same way, Job Corps contractors are obligated to deliver education, training, and residential services that are standardized across the program's 123 centers. Except for roughly two dozen centers run by the U.S. Forest Service, private contractors are effectively Job Corps franchisees.

Center specifications are spelled out in a more than 1,000-page "Policy and Requirements Handbook," which governs every aspect of center operation, including recruitment and screening of prospective students, curriculum, discipline, placement services, and tracking of performance metrics. Contractors must, for instance, have written plans for "blood borne pathogens," "respiratory protection," and "hearing conservation" (to protect students' hearing). Meal service is prescribed in exacting detail.[126] "Meals shall be planned using a minimum of a 28-day cycle cafeteria menu," the handbook dictates. Students must be offered, for example, "five choices of fresh or frozen vegetables and/or fruits," and "low-fat and/or fat free milk and dairy alternatives and water."

The intent of this specificity is consistency across centers (although in truth, performance reports issued by the Department of Labor show that centers vary widely in quality). The downside is that few contractors can comply with the complexity and sheer scale of the Job Corps requirements. "In practice, five private, for-profit contractors operate the majority of centers," says a 2022 Congressional Research Service report.[127]

Job Corps' largest contractor is Utah-based for-profit Management & Training Corporation (MTC), which operates twenty-two centers as one of several lines of business. The company also runs six immigrant detention centers and twenty-three correctional facilities in addition to prison medical departments and "community release centers" (i.e., halfway houses).[128] Another major contractor, Equus Workforce Solutions (formerly ResCare Workforce Services), runs WIOA-funded job centers, child-care services, and welfare-to-work programs in addition to its work for Job Corps.[129] Other major contractors include Adams and Associates, Inc., which runs fifteen Job Corps centers (with sidelines running WIOA services at two job centers in Maryland and one emergency youth shelter in Nevada); New York–based Career Systems Development Corporation, which runs ten centers; Kentucky-based Education and Training Resources (ETR), which operates nine locations; and Mississippi-based MINACT, which runs seven centers.[130]

Job Corps contracts involve big money. MTC, for instance, won three multi-year contracts in 2022 to run the Sierra Nevada Job Corps Center in Reno; the Edison Job Corps Center in Edison, New Jersey (where student Ricky Gass attended); and the Hawaii Job Corps Center in Waimanalo—worth a total of about $264 million.[131] Between 2019 and 2021, Career Systems Development won contracts to run the Loring Job Corps Center in Limestone, Maine ($56.3 million), as well as centers in San Jose and San Diego, California ($86.2 million and $99.6 million, respectively).[132] Many of these companies have been reeling in lucrative Job Corps contracts for years, if not decades. MINACT, for example, opened shop in 1978 when its founder "successfully competed for the company's first Job Corps Center contract," according to its website.[133] Career Systems Development notes on its site that it was one of Job Corps' original contractors when the program launched in 1964.[134]

Reliance on contractors does not, of course, make a program inherently flawed. In fact, the federal government doesn't perform much better than its contractors when it operates Job Corps centers directly. While a few of the centers still run by the Forest Service are among the best performers, others have been among the worst. In 2014, the Labor Department shut down the Treasure Lake Job Corps center, located within a national wildlife refuge in Oklahoma and run by the Forest Service. The closure came after years of underperformance in which fewer than half of the enrolled students finished their training and barely half of graduates found jobs.[135] Yet a significant chunk of Job Corps' problems throughout the years have been related to contractor performance, beginning with its launch.[136]

When the federal government announced Job Corps as a pillar in its War on Poverty, it also promised to ramp up the program on a war-time footing. In its first fiscal year, the government pledged, Job Corps would enroll 100,000 trainees, relying on a slate of high-profile contractors to help fulfill this goal. These early contractors would come to include many of the then-titans of U.S. industry,[137] including the Packard Bell Electronics Corp, which won contracts to run centers in West Virginia and New Mexico; the Xerox Corporation; Thiokol Chemical Corporation (later infamous as Morton-Thiokol, the manufacturer of the rocket responsible for the *Challenger* explosion); Radio Corp of America (RCA); Philco-Ford (builder of the NASA Mission Control Center in Houston); defense contractor Litton Industries, Inc. (perhaps best remembered as the manufacturer of microwave ovens before it was acquired by Northrup Grumman); and Graflex, Inc. (makers of the eponymous Graflex camera and the original parent of Careers Systems).[138]

But the parade of prominent firms did not prevent what historian Alice O'Connor calls "the all-too-familiar consequences of overpromise." By 1965, as she writes in *Poverty Knowledge*, Job Corps was already "reeling from a barrage of highly publicized mishaps and criticisms coming from all quarters":[139]

> Corpsmen were reportedly disillusioned by the combination of administrative unpreparedness, lack of curricular materials, and unfamiliar surroundings that greeted them at several of the new centers. Media reports of high dropout rates, overpaid staff, and isolated incidents of violence, drinking or local vandalism involving trainees added scandal to the mix.[140]

Media coverage of Job Corps' early years was in fact unrelentingly negative—and often racialized—with even the *New York Times* reveling in salacious nuggets about Job Corps' missteps. "18 Michigan Youths Jailed After Battling Job Corps" was one headline from 1966, as was "Job Corps Youth Sentenced for Possessing Marijuana."[141] The same year, the *Times* reported that a women's Job Corps center in St. Petersburg, Florida, was shuttered due to "hostile elements in the community and uncooperative city government." "During its 18 months in this city, the center tried vainly to combat gossip that its girls had loose morals," the *Times* wrote.[142] In 1970, a seventeen-year-old trainee was stabbed to death at the Clearfield Job Corps Center in Utah, then run by Thiokol, "in an argument that apparently involved two Negro teen-agers and a couple of Puerto Rican corpsmen," according to the *Times*. "In the wake of a near riot in which several hundred Job Corpsmen armed themselves with clubs and knives, state, county and local patrolmen stood guard until 123 Puerto Rican youths were moved to a National Guard camp fifty miles south of Clearfield for their protection," the *Times* reported.[143]

Stories like these bear more than a whiff of NIMBYism and bias, which might lead some to argue that perceptions of Job Corps' woes outweigh the reality. Yet both the Department of Labor's inspector general and the GAO have also consistently faulted both contractors' performance and DOL's oversight, with dozens of audits over the years examining everything from student outcomes to contracting practices, center safety, reports of cheating, and inadequate financial oversight. In every year since 2006, the IG's annual report has identified Job Corps' safety and program effectiveness as among the Department of Labor's "top management and performance challenges."[144]

A 2011 IG report, for instance, determined that the program may have spent as much as $164.6 million in 2010 on training for students who were not eligible to enroll.[145] Another audit in 2011 found that Job Corps "overstated" the success of 42 percent of 17,787 job placements, with those students taking entry-level jobs unrelated to their training. Among the mismatches were "culinary students placed as pest control workers, funeral attendants, baggage porters, concierges, tour guides, telemarketers, cashiers, telephone operators . . . and file clerks."[146]

Yet another investigation, in 2019, concluded that the program wasn't doing enough to stop cheating in its high school diploma programs. In San Francisco, for example, investigators discovered at least sixteen students who received diplomas despite having reading scores below the sixth-grade level, "which raised concerns about the integrity of the center's online high school program," as the investigation put it.[147] Meanwhile, Tulsa's Job Corps Center reportedly "neglected to follow any of its online high school program's rules of academic integrity and allowed students to print exams, search for the answers online, and then immediately take the exams."[148]

The IG's 2018 analysis further found that the program couldn't demonstrate that it placed students into "meaningful jobs appropriate to their training." Out of the fifty students for whom the IG was able to track down employment histories, more than half were placed in jobs like what they were doing before Job Corps. One student, who worked as a retail cashier before Job Corps, spent 310 days in bricklaying training only to return to the exact same store where they had worked previously. Job Corps reported this as a "successful" graduation and placement. Among 231 students for whom wage records were documented, the median annual income was just $12,105 in 2016—nearly $15,000 *less* than the median income for all workers without a high school diploma.[149] Among the program's problems, the audit found, was the poor performance of contractors hired to provide "transition services" to Job Corps graduates needing help finding jobs. "Job Corps paid millions of dollars to transition services contractors, but we found insufficient evidence demonstrating they had provided the services required by their contracts," the report concluded.[150]

Auditors have also criticized the Department of Labor's contracting practices, which have perpetuated the current contractor oligopoly. As far back as 1982, GAO complained of non-permissible "sole source" contracting for Job Corps.[151] "Job Corps Should Stop Using Prohibited Contracting Practices and Recover Improper Fee Payments" was the subject of one 1982 letter to DOL from GAO.[152] Nor have these issues been resolved in the ensuing decades. In a 2019 report, the GAO found that Job Corps was running sixty-eight of ninety-seven centers in 2016 under "bridge contracts"—either noncompetitive extensions of expired contracts or short-term noncompetitive contracts. In forty-two of those cases, contracts were awarded to companies that had *already lost* their Job Corps contracts and were formally protesting the decision.[153] The result was that these companies were able to squeeze hundreds of thousands of contract dollars from the government while their protests were being resolved.

DOL has tried to reserve some contracts for small businesses or minority-owned contractors to diversify its contractor base. But these efforts may also be less successful than DOL has hoped. That's because small businesses winning Job Corps contracts often subcontract to the bigger players. One example is Alternate Perspectives Inc. (API), a "certified woman-owned small business" that won contracts to run the Job Corps center in New Orleans and the Wind River center in Riverton, Wyoming.[154] According to a 2020 MTC press release, MTC and Alternate Perspectives entered a "partnership" to run the Wyoming center, as well as two others.[155] (The release also noted that DOL had "designated the Wind River center as a small business contract with API as the small-business lead and MTC as the sub-contractor.")

Similarly, Education and Training Resources (another of the big guns) calls itself a "major collaborator and subcontractor for Gadsden Job Corps Center (Gadsden, AL) and Treasure Island Job Corps Center (San Francisco, CA)."[156] According to SAM.gov (the federal government's contracts database), the $31 million lead contract to run Gadsden was last awarded in 2015 to the New Jersey–based Education Management Corporation, a "small, woman owned disadvantaged business, certified as both an '8(a)' corporation by the U.S. Small Business Administration and a Minority Business Enterprise/Small Business Enterprise for the state of New Jersey and the city of Philadelphia," according to its website.[157] (As of December 2022, the contract for Gadsden was out for a new bid under a set-aside for "historically underutilized businesses.")[158]

Status Quo Politics

The cabal of contractors running Job Corps has maintained its grip on the program in part through the advantages of incumbency. As "experienced" operators familiar with the program's complexities, they can easily outbid upstart firms without the same track record, efficiencies of scale, and inside connections. But more important, Job Corps has formidable political support in Congress, which has helped entrench the status quo.

To some extent, this support is another collateral result of Job Corps' residential model. Every state has at least one center, and many are an important source of local employment. "In rural areas or in a smaller town, [Job Corps] is a player in town," said one former senior Labor Department official who asked not to be identified to preserve their current relationships with members of Congress. "They have jobs, and it's something people are proud of in those communities."

Members of Congress are consequently reluctant to challenge the program. For example, this former official told me of one instance where a member refused to entertain the idea of closing a poorly performing center. "We said, 'Look, we're going to have to close it. It's not good for the students, and I wouldn't send my own kid there,' but the congressperson pushed really hard not to close it," the former official said. "They really loved having it in their community."

In 2019, the Trump administration proposed closing or privatizing the twenty-five centers run by the U.S. Forest Service, which would have resulted in the layoff of more than 1,100 federal employees in eight states.[159] The plan quickly ran into bipartisan opposition and was scrapped in a matter of weeks.[160]

Also helping to keep Job Corps' perspective and priorities in front of Congress is the NJCA (the contractors' trade association mentioned earlier). Launched in 1998 with thirty-eight charter members, NJCA now has more than double that membership, according to its website.[161] Though it doesn't disclose its full membership, NJCA's 2022 Board of Directors included Brian Fox, president of Education and Training Resources; Susan Larson, president of Adams and Associates; Scott Marquart, president of MTC; and Ramon Serrato, president of the Serrato Corporation, a "Service Disabled Veteran and Hispanic owned business" holding contracts to operate thirteen centers.[162]

Among other activities, the NJCA maintains the Congressional Friends of Job Corps Caucus, whose goals include "initiating a productive dialogue about the quality of services Job Corps provides to thousands of at-risk youth each year" and the "enhancement of legislative efforts toward protecting and strengthening Job Corps."[163] It boasted eighty-seven members from across the ideological spectrum in the 117th Congress (2021–2023).[164] The NJCA also ran a small political action committee during the 2014 and 2016 election cycles that donated a total of about $60,000 to candidates (mostly to Republicans), according to OpenSecrets, and spent $260,000 on lobbying in 2021 and 2022.[165] Its website is full of testimonials and videos of Job Corps success stories. A page on the program's economic impact cites an analysis finding that the average Job Corps center supports 228 local jobs.[166]

In truth, these anecdotal successes are enough to make Congress feel good about supporting the program and to overcome whatever misgivings are raised by government auditors. Progressive advocates who know that the Job Corps system is flawed are also loath to criticize it for fear of handing conservatives an excuse to kill the program and cut funding for an already neglected area of policy. Given that low-income young adults aren't a powerful political constituency, advocates say it's unlikely that money taken from Job Corps would be redirected toward other youth-serving programs.

Nevertheless, the money now going toward Job Corps isn't going toward more promising strategies for low-income young adults.

Young Adults Pay the Price

The post-pandemic crisis young Americans are facing requires a better solution. The surge in young adult "disconnection" prompted by the pandemic should be catalyzing substantial new investment in young adults. Sargent Shriver's vision of a second chance for young people in poverty is more relevant today than it has ever been. But young Americans deserve more and better than Job Corps.

More money, for instance, could be going to expand apprenticeships, which are effective and relatively inexpensive. "There aren't a lot of substitutes for getting young people to work in real employment situations with real supervisors, real mentors, and a real occupational goal," says Robert Lerman, an economist at the Urban Institute.[167] A well-structured apprenticeship, Lerman says, could cost the federal government as little as $5,000 per participant, given that employers pick up much of the tab.

More funding could also go to programs like Year Up, which trains students for careers in IT, sales, software development, and more, and places them in paid internships with mentoring and other support. Since its founding in 2000, the organization has enrolled more than 29,000 students, and reports an average starting salary of $42,000 for its graduates.[168] Also promising is the National Guard Youth ChalleNGe Program, a boot camp–style residential program that has achieved relatively strong results among sixteen- to eighteen-year-olds—the group that Job Corps has failed to benefit. Evaluations find that graduates earned, on average, 20 percent more than non-attendees and were 86 percent more likely to go on to college.[169]

Of course, none of these programs is a panacea. In the post-pandemic economy, it's unclear how many employers will be able to afford to hire apprentices. Apprenticeships also tend to be selective programs that favor job-ready applicants, as is also the case with Year Up. Only twenty-eight states offer the National Guard ChalleNGe Program, and its military focus isn't for everyone.

But so long as Job Corps—and its contractors—monopolize the resources available, low-income young adults won't get the help they need and risk falling further behind.

4

Every Body Profits

When I was an analyst at the Progressive Policy Institute in Washington, DC, a company called Kool Smiles reached out, asking if I wanted to learn more about its efforts to provide dental care to low-income children. Kool Smiles was a nationwide chain of dentistry practices whose patients were primarily children on Medicaid, the federal government's health insurance program for low-income Americans. They suggested a tour of one of their offices and a chance to speak to their dentists.

These kinds of offers are common in DC, where companies often deploy public relations teams to engage in "outreach" to think tanks and nonprofits influential in public policy. I ended up visiting what was then the Kool Smiles office in Winchester, Virginia, about eighty miles west of Washington, in a strip mall next to a Cici's Pizza. The waiting room was large and bright, saturated in primary colors, with an indoor playground at one end. The treatment area in back was likewise spacious, equipment gleaming. But unlike many dentists' offices, which might have a chair or two, each tucked into its own cubby, half a dozen kid-sized dentists' chairs in the center of the room sat arrayed like spokes in a wheel. I visited before the office opened for the day, but I could imagine what it looked like when the chairs were full, kids' heads just a foot or two apart.[1]

Medicaid dentistry, it turns out, is volume business. At the time of my visit, Kool Smiles ran practices in seventeen states and employed as many as five hundred dentists.[2] The company had long been the nation's largest provider of dental services to Medicaid patients, serving at least 2 million children a year nationwide.[3] It was also accused by the Department of Justice (DOJ) of performing thousands of unnecessary procedures on its pediatric patients.

Not long after my tour of the Winchester office, the Kool Smiles chain and its parent company, Benevis, agreed to pay $23.9 million to settle Medicaid fraud claims brought by federal prosecutors.[4] According to whistleblowers across the country, the chain "paid substantial bonuses to dentists who met production goals that rewarded expensive, unneeded and often painful treatments," including root canals and steel crowns for children who still had baby teeth.[5] In other instances, prosecutors said, the company billed state Medicaid programs for work that was never done. The company "ignored complaints from their own dentists regarding over-utilization," instead disciplining them if they were "unproductive," according to DOJ.[6] Sometimes the patients were mere toddlers. In 2019, an Arizona family sued Kool Smiles after a clinic installed crowns in their two-year-old son, who died four days after the procedure.[7]

The company has since changed the name of its clinics, operating variously as Pine Dentistry, Pippin Dental, Cortland Dental, Jubilee Dental, and Pinova Dental, among other names.[8] The Winchester Kool Smiles is now "Pine Dentistry and Braces" (though the office still claims to be an "official partner" of Benevis and Kool Smiles on its site).[9] Parent company Benevis (known as a "dental management organization") was running 120+ "supported practices" in fourteen states as of November 2023, including the Pine Dentistry in District Heights, Maryland, mentioned in the introduction.[10] It claimed more than 1.2 million patient visits a year.[11]

There's no dispute that Medicaid—and its companion program, Medicare—are among the greatest triumphs of U.S. social policy. Medicare and Medicaid are the nation's largest health insurance providers and among the largest in the world.[12] In 2021, the programs insured 135 million low-income, elderly, or disabled Americans—or about 40 percent of the U.S. population.[13] Medicaid pays for nearly half of all births, as well as most of the long-term care services provided to seniors and Americans with disabilities.[14] (Roughly 12.2 million elderly and disabled Americans are covered by both programs—so-called dual eligibles.)[15] The share of seniors uninsured in 2021 was a scant 1.2 percent, thanks to Medicare, while just 5 percent of children were uninsured, thanks to Medicaid.[16] The Medicaid expansion included in the Affordable Care Act of 2010 ("Obamacare") saved an estimated 19,200 lives from 2014 to 2017, according to one landmark study, and reduced annual mortality rates for older adults by as much as 64 percent.[17]

The immensity of the programs also means oceans of spending—and with it vast potential for both profit and profiteering. In 2021, the states and the federal government spent a total of $728 billion on Medicaid,[18] while the federal government spent $689 billion on Medicare.[19] Together, the two programs accounted for more than 27 percent of all federal spending in fiscal 2021.[20]

As in other contexts discussed throughout this book, the behavior of companies like Kool Smiles has sabotaged the efficacy of these programs. In 2021 alone, the Department of Justice reported recovering more than $5 billion in fraud claims involving federal health care programs, including Medicare and Medicaid—likely just a fraction of the money wasted on unscrupulous providers.[21] But far more troubling is the impact of health care profiteering on the health of the nation's most vulnerable individuals, whose interests are eclipsed by the revenues to be had.

Even the most cursory analysis of the challenges facing the U.S. health care system would consume a volume (or three). The United States spends more per person on health care than any other major industrialized nation, but our outcomes badly lag our peers.[22] A 2021 study by the Commonwealth Fund, for instance, ranks America last among countries in the OECD on measures such as access to care, administrative efficiency, equity, and health care outcomes.[23] Medical debts are a leading cause of personal bankruptcies, and the quality of care a person receives depends all too often on the color of their skin, as the coronavirus pandemic all too starkly revealed.[24]

This chapter explores just three of the myriad ways in which health care profiteers enrich themselves at the expense of government programs while at the same time jeopardizing the health of the poor. In the case of Medicaid dentistry, the problem is overtreatment—the consequence of "fee-for-service" payments and other policies that encourage the kind of volume-based treatment practices attributed to companies like Kool Smiles. In the case of Medicaid "managed care," where companies receive fixed payments per patient, patients experience the opposite problem. Companies focused on maintaining their margins deny sick people needed services. A final example profiles the dialysis industry, where a powerful duopoly makes its profits from a steady stream of disproportionately low-income and minority patients—and the government dollars that accompany them. Each of these case studies, in turn, reflects a broader systemic flaw in the U.S. health care system—that profit-driven health care all too often reinforces disparities in care instead of alleviating them.

Medicaid Dentistry: From the Mouths of Babes

In January 2017, *The Pueblo Chieftain* ran an obituary for local dentist and Colorado native Eddie DeRose, who passed away at the age of eighty-two.[25] The article lauded DeRose as a "champion of the underdog," a philanthropist and avid football fan whose generosity prompted Colorado State University to name its stadium in his honor. Among his achievements, the obituary noted, was serving low-income children eligible for Medicaid through a network of clinics he built nationally. "He was the only one in town to accept Medicaid at one time and then that spread across the country with his clinics," his son Dan DeRose told *The Chieftain*.[26] "Millions of children nationwide received dental care because of Eddie."

But DeRose's legacy was perhaps not so straightforward—or heroic. The dentistry chain DeRose founded—Small Smiles—was the target of multiple state and federal investigations, ultimately leading to a $24 million settlement with the Department of Justice (though by then, DeRose had sold his interest to other parties).[27] An exposé of his clinics' practices by the Colorado Springs *Gazette* led to new state rules restricting the use of "papoose boards"—flat boards resembling straitjackets that immobilize a child's head and limbs during dental procedures.[28] The chain also became the centerpiece of a U.S. Senate hearing on the perils of "corporate dentistry."[29] And DeRose's son, Michael, also a dentist, became the subject of another $10 million settlement to resolve fraud claims against a chain of clinics he owned in North Carolina.[30] Michael DeRose's license was suspended in North Carolina, while his license in Colorado was made permanently "inactive."[31] As with Kool Smiles, both Small Smiles and the younger DeRose's North Carolina clinics were accused of performing "medically unnecessary" procedures on their young patients, including "baby root canals" and the installation of steel crowns.[32]

These persistent patterns of practice—Kool Smiles and Small Smiles are by no means alone in their alleged behavior—point to bigger problems with Medicaid and low-income children's access to dental care. Children either aren't getting the care they need, or the care they get is substandard, from Medicaid mills run by for-profit chains.

However, governmental policies are what's allowed these companies to prosper. In most states, Medicaid reimbursements are far below what private insurers pay. It's no wonder then that Medicaid dentistry is a volume business—that's the only way to profit. And because most dentists don't accept Medicaid, Medicaid-focused practices have grabbed the market for themselves.[33] As a result, chains like Kool Smiles and Small Smiles are all too often the only option for children in poverty who need dental care—if they get treatment at all.

Dental Health Disparities and Why They Matter

In 2007, a twelve-year-old Maryland boy, Deamonte Driver, died when bacteria from an abscessed tooth spread to his brain.[34] His mother had struggled to find a dentist who would accept Medicaid, and by the time Deamonte got sick, his coverage had lapsed due to problems with paperwork. At the time of his death, authorities discovered, fewer than one in three Medicaid-eligible children in Maryland was receiving dental care.[35]

Nearly fifteen years later, too many children still aren't getting adequate dental care—even though Medicaid has required states to provide kids with dental coverage since 1967. Under Medicaid's "Early and Periodic Screening, Diagnostic and Treatment" benefit, states must cover "all medically necessary dental services" for children up to age eighteen.[36] (In contrast, states are not required to provide dental care to adults, except in the case of emergencies.) Children are supposed to get not only treatment for toothaches and cavities but also regular checkups, cleanings, and orthodontia (provided it's "medically necessary" and not simply cosmetic).

Yet only about half of all children enrolled in Medicaid saw a dentist in 2019, according to the Pew Research Center, and in some states, access is even more limited.[37] One government study of patients in California, Indiana, Louisiana, and Maryland found that 78 percent of Medicaid-enrolled kids received insufficient care, and as many as 1 million kids received no services at all over a two-year period.[38]

Oral health often doesn't get the attention it deserves, but it's a key driver of health disparities among Americans, with ramifications far beyond the pain of a toothache. In 2000, the U.S. surgeon general's first-ever report on the importance of oral health decried a "silent epidemic" of dental and oral diseases that included not just dental cavities—or tooth decay—but also gum disease, oral cancers, and infection, all aggravated by sugary, ultra-processed modern diets, and the widespread use of tobacco.[39] Research found alarming links between gum disease and diabetes, while chronic oral infections signaled a greater likelihood of strokes, heart and lung conditions, and poor prenatal health. "The mouth is a mirror," the report concluded, of a person's overall well-being.[40]

A follow-up report in 2021 noted vast disparities in both oral health outcomes and access to care, depending on income and race. Children in poverty are more than twice as likely to suffer from untreated tooth decay compared to their non-impoverished peers, for instance, as are Mexican American and non-Hispanic Black children compared to white children.[41]

This disproportionate burden worsens other inequities faced by children in poverty. Among preschoolers, for instance, untreated dental problems can mean "oral pain, chewing and sleeping difficulties, changes in behavior, and poorer school performance." Kids with toothaches often don't eat, "leading to weight loss and delayed growth and development."[42] Among older children, dental issues can seriously hamper academic performance. Children with toothaches and other dental problems are less likely to finish their homework, more likely to miss school, and have lower grade point averages than children without these concerns.[43] The parents of these children were also more likely to be absent from school or work, missing an average of 2.5 days per year.[44]

Lack of access to routine dental care drives up health care costs as well. Dental emergencies are all too common, as is the reliance on expensive hospital ER departments for care. Dental problems accounted for more than 2.4 million ER visits in 2014, according to the 2021 surgeon general's report, resulting in more than $1.6 billion in charges.[45] Much of this was paid for by the government. In fact, Medicaid pays for more than two-thirds of dental ER visits by children, according to the American Dental Association.[46] And ER care is no substitute for regular dental care. About 90 percent of the time, treatment consists of just painkillers and/or antibiotics, says the surgeon general, and appropriate follow-up care is rare.[47]

How Medicaid Dentistry Became a Niche Industry

The simplest answer for why Medicaid-eligible children aren't getting care is a shortage of dentists willing to treat them. Though Medicaid requires states to offer dental coverage, dentists are not required to participate. And most dentists opt out.

Just 33 percent of dentists nationwide participated in Medicaid or CHIP in 2017, according to a July 2022 paper by the ADA's Health Policy Institute.[48] And not all these dentists actually treated a Medicaid patient, even if they signed up for the program. In Michigan, for instance, where 71 percent of dentists were nominally enrolled as Medicaid providers, 15 percent saw no Medicaid patients at all in 2017.[49]

One reason so few dentists accept Medicaid is that it doesn't pay. In 2020, according to the American Dental Association, the average Medicaid reimbursement for treating children was just 61.4 percent of the fees paid by private insurance.[50] This rate was moreover a decline from 2017, when Medicaid reimbursements averaged 61.9 percent of the rates offered under private coverage. Reimbursement ratios also vary widely by state, ranging from a low of 27.8 percent in Minnesota to 104.8 percent in Kentucky (a definite outlier). In twelve states, Medicaid paid less than half the rates paid by commercial insurance.[51] Oregon, for instance, paid just 38.6 percent of commercial rates in 2020 and even *cut* rates in 2021 (though these cuts were later partially restored).[52] One 2017 study concluded that raising Medicaid reimbursement rates could help an estimated 1.8 million low-income children gain access to dental care.[53]

Many dentists are also coping with high (and rising) burdens of educational debt from attending dental school, which could prompt some dentists to limit the care they provide for free or at Medicaid's low rates. In 2021, new dental student graduates owed an average of $301,583, according to the American Dental Education Association.[54]

Other reasons dentists don't participate in Medicaid are

non-financial. Some, for instance, might not want to locate their practices in low-income or rural areas where Medicaid patients are more likely to live. More than two-thirds of the U.S. counties suffering acute shortages of dentists are in rural America, according to the Rural Health Information Hub.[55] White dentists are also less likely to serve Medicaid patients, according to the American Dental Association's Health Policy Institute. Just 39 percent of white dentists take Medicaid, compared to 63 percent of Black dentists, 51 percent of Hispanic dentists, and 50 percent of Asian dentists.[56]

As a result, Medicaid dentistry is concentrated among a subset of providers, many of them affiliated with larger practices or with "dental service organizations" (DSOs)—which include chains in the mold of Kool Smiles, Small Smiles, and their ilk.[57] Sixty-three percent of dentists affiliated with DSOs accept Medicaid patients, according to the ADA Health Policy Institute's analysis, compared to 41 percent of dentists without such an affiliation.[58] In stark contrast to smaller practices for whom Medicaid patients are unaffordable, these larger concerns have learned to leverage their scale to make Medicaid an engine for profit.

Corporate Dentistry Cracks the Code of Scale

Despite the controversy to come, Small Smiles' Edward DeRose was among the first dental entrepreneurs in the country to build a profitable Medicaid-only practice—profitable enough, in fact, to attract the attention of private investors and become a model for other Medicaid dentistry chains nationwide.

But it was actually the state of Colorado that gave the chain its start. According to a 2006 investment memo by Arcapita, a Bahraini-based private equity firm that would eventually buy the company, DeRose was running a Medicaid-only clinic in Pueblo when the state, "criticized for not providing adequate access to dental care for children eligible for Medicaid," "requested" that DeRose open a Colorado Springs clinic in 1995.[59] In 1999 and 2001, according to Arcapita, Colorado officials provided nearly $400,000 in grants for DeRose to open yet more clinics in Denver and Aurora[60]—which prompted the company to realize the potential opportunities waiting in other states.[61] By 2006, when Arcapita was ready to buy the chain, the company was running forty-four clinics in fourteen states, with a projected annual revenue that year of $146.5 million.[62]

DeRose's clinics (then run under an umbrella company called FORBA, LLC ["For Better Access"]) were unabashedly aggressive in maximizing revenues from their Medicaid patient base. They strategically located clinics in low-income neighborhoods, thereby ensuring a steady stream of Medicaid-eligible patients nearby. "The Company . . . is an expert in efficiently determining Medicaid/SCHIP eligibility, processing claims, confirming appointments and following up with patients who break appointments," Arcapita noted admiringly.[63] The company also overbooked patients and instituted an assembly-line approach to treatment that minimized clinic downtime from no-shows and delays:

> Importantly, FORBA's unique business model mitigates the 33% broken appointment challenge in that patients are not scheduled to have appointments with specific dentists. Instead, any one of four dentists at a clinic can see a patient. Therefore, since FORBA employs a minimum of three to four dentists per clinic, FORBA can leverage its critical mass of dentists and over-schedule appointments by 25%. Since patients are assigned "chairs," not individuals, the usual bottlenecks of appointment run-overs are cleared because the next available dentist simply sees the next patient.[64]

Also unique about FORBA's clinics—and what drew the interest of investors like Arcapita—was the management structure DeRose and his sons created to expand their Small Smiles empire. DeRose was a pioneer of the "dental management company" model (now known as DSOs).

DeRose and his sons created FORBA to provide business and management services to its affiliated clinics, including billing, marketing, administrative support, equipment, and supplies.[65] In many ways, it was not unlike the corporate parent of a franchise (McDentist versus McDonald's, you could say). Because states generally prohibit corporations from owning dental practices outright, FORBA "[did] not technically provide dental care," as Arcapita's memo put it. Instead, it entered into long-term management agreements with the dentists who nominally "owned" the company's affiliated practices. But whatever was said on paper, FORBA, in practice, "effectively own[ed] and manage[d] the clinics," according to Arcapita.[66] Among other duties, the company would select clinic sites and even negotiate the leases; it would buy equipment and computer systems; and it would recruit and hire staff, including the dentists nominally "owning" the practice. In return, FORBA received a fee from each of its clinics equal to "the greater of (i) $175,000 per month, (ii) 40% of booked patient revenue and (iii) 100% of operating profit (residual collections minus dentist compensation and other clinic operating expenses)"—a payment structure that Arcapita called "highly profitable."[67]

At the time of Arcapita's interest in Small Smiles, arrangements like these were rare, representing "less than 2% of the total dental market," according to Arcapita's analysis.[68] But Arcapita predicted (correctly) that the dental management company model would grow rapidly.[69] What FORBA had invented was a way for non-expert managers and financiers to profit from dentistry without really knowing anything about how to be a dentist. Naturally, Wall Street would find this opportunity irresistible. In 2019, according to the ADA, more than 10 percent of all dentists—including 20 percent of dentists under age thirty-four—worked for practices affiliated with a DSO.[70] As of 2021, as many as twenty-seven of the nation's thirty largest DSOs were private-equity-owned, according to the Private Equity Stakeholder Project.[71] Some analysts predict that DSOs could make up as much 50 percent of the dental industry by 2030.[72]

Certainly, DSOs have their advantages. Dentists are spared the day-to-day burdens of managing a practice, such as dealing with computers, office space, and payroll. DSOs can also leverage the same IT, billing, and finance infrastructure across their practices, thereby standardizing practices and reducing costs. In a 2014 white paper, the Association of Dental Support Organizations (ADSO) argued that DSOs "provide a way for dentists to reduce the time, expense, and stress associated with the administrative aspects of their practices."[73]

DSOs have also arguably helped alleviate the shortage of rural dentists by sponsoring visas for foreign dentists willing to work in underserved areas. Few small practices could likely manage the paperwork and expense of dealing with the U.S. immigration system.

When I visited the Kool Smiles in Winchester, Virginia, the staff orthodontic specialist, an immigrant from Syria, told me the company was sponsoring his application for a green card. (He did not want his name used because the paperwork was then still in progress.)[74] Kool Smiles also connected me to another staff dentist, this one from Venezuela, for whom the company was sponsoring an O-1 visa (the so-called genius visa for individuals with "extraordinary ability").[75] "I really thank Kool Smiles for supporting me," this dentist told me. He also noted that he was one of the few available dentists in his area. "No one wants this job in a rural area," he said. "Other dentists are not interested in Medicaid patients." He estimated seeing four hundred to five hundred patients a month, some of whom traveled two hours each way to see him. "If an immigration officer denies [my] visa, 5,000 Medicaid kids will not have a provider," he said.[76] A spokesperson for Benevis (Kool Smiles' parent company at the time) told me that about fifty of the roughly five hundred dentists they employed at the time were "in active immigration status" under H1-B or O-1 visas.[77]

According to H1-B Grader, a website that aggregates H1-B application data, federal immigration authorities approved 513 H1-B visas for dentists in 2022.[78] Western Dental, a DSO owned by a subsidiary of private equity firm New Mountain Capital, was the single largest sponsor of H1-B visas in 2022, with thirty-nine visas issued.[79] Western Dental is currently one of the nation's largest DSOs, with 175 offices in California, Arizona, Nevada, and Texas.[80] Seventy percent of its California patients are covered by Denti-Cal, California's Medicaid dental benefit.[81]

As the ADSO argued in its white paper, the administrative infrastructure provided by DSOs frees dentists to serve "a wider community base, including patients who have been previously underserved."[82] Certainly, that was true for Kool Smiles dentists like the ones who spoke with me. However, this structure has encouraged the volume-based approach to dentistry that has fueled multiple investigations into the Medicaid dental industry.

Extracting Profits and Pain

Shortly after FORBA's sale to Arcapita, the Small Smiles empire began to disintegrate. In 2008, television station WJLA aired a stunning exposé of the practices inside a Small Smiles clinic in Langley Park, Maryland, just outside Washington, DC. Video showed a four-year-old patient, Miguel, crying hysterically while strapped to a "papoose board" to restrain him during treatment.[83] A dentist pinches Miguel's nose shut to force open his mouth—a practice most dentists abandoned "years ago," according to investigative reporter Roberta Baskin, who prepared the report.

The papoose board wasn't the only disturbing practice Baskin uncovered. Former staffers spoke of winning "bonuses" of up to $1,500 a month for "converting" patients from checkups to major procedures on the same day.[84] One in three patients got crowns, whether they needed them or not. "They wanted us to tell parents they needed services on teeth that were healthy," former staffer Deborah McDaniel told Baskin.[85]

Small Smiles clinics had already come under scrutiny in Colorado for using papoose boards to restrain their patients (presumably so treatments would go faster). In 2004, the Colorado Springs *Gazette* discovered that the clinics had used the boards almost seven thousand times over an eighteen-month period.[86] In 2005, the Colorado Dental Board issued new regulations restricting the use of papoose boards except under certain narrow circumstances and only with parental consent and extensive documentation.[87] According to *The Gazette*, Michael DeRose had objected to the rules, arguing, "We should be rewarded for what we do because we're doing something that nobody else wants to do, and we work very hard."[88]

The WJLA investigation sparked multiple governmental inquiries, which ultimately led to a $24 million settlement with the Department of Justice in 2010.[89] Prosecutors accused FORBA of performing procedures "that were either medically unnecessary or performed in a manner that failed to meet professionally-recognized standards of care."[90] In addition to paying a fine, FORBA agreed to a five-year "Corporate Integrity Agreement," under which independent evaluators would monitor the quality of care.[91]

In the meantime, Small Smiles co-founder Michael DeRose was embroiled in a separate set of difficulties. Though he had shed his interest in FORBA, he apparently imported its practices into a chain of seven Medicaid dentistry clinics he launched in North Carolina with another dentist. In 2008, DeRose's Medicaid Dental Center (MDC) agreed to pay $10 million to the federal government and the state of North Carolina to settle claims of Medicaid fraud "for medically unnecessary dental services."[92] Local news stations reported that MDC had drilled and capped as many as sixteen teeth in one four-year-old patient in a single visit, using a papoose board to restrain him. "When he came out he was crying, his whole shirt was soaking wet with sweat," the boy's mother told Charlotte TV station WCNC.[93] Another boy, only three years old at the time, was subjected to seventeen root canals and seventeen caps.[94] News of the North Carolina settlement led the Colorado Dental Board to deactivate DeRose's license.[95]

Forced into bankruptcy by its problems, FORBA reemerged as Church Street Health Management (later "CSHM") but still couldn't avoid further scandal. In a 2012 investigation, NBC News documented "persistent allegations of abuse, including unnecessary root canals, shoddy work and insufficient anesthesia."[96] The

U.S. Senate Finance Committee then conducted its own investigation of "corporate dentistry," spotlighting CSHM's checkered history. The committee's nearly 1,600-page findings included multiple reports from the independent reviewers charged with monitoring Small Smiles clinics, who witnessed some highly questionable practices. At the company's clinic in Oxon Hill, Maryland, for instance:

> A large mouth prop was used in a young patient (patient #034) that stretched her lips so tight the doctor was unable to use distraction to mitigate the pain associated with administering local anesthesia to maxillary anterior teeth. The patient cried during administration of local anesthesia.[97]
>
> In another instance, monitors reported, a child undergoing a "baby root canal" "screamed and fought the entire time":
>
> She vomited approximately halfway through the procedure. The dentist immediately turned the patient on her side and suctioned her mouth and throat. This child's airway was in jeopardy because the mouth prop opened her mouth so wide it restricted her ability to swallow and protect her airway. The patient was screaming and gasping, leaving her airway open and vulnerable.[98]

In 2014, the Department of Health and Human Services' inspector general banned CSHM from participating in federal health care programs, including Medicaid, which led to its final demise as a DSO powerhouse.[99]

Unfortunately, the end of Small Smiles has not meant an end to predatory dentistry. If anything, the over-treatment and over-billing practiced by Small Smiles has been normalized as the standard of care in Medicaid dentistry. The Small Smiles saga served not as a cautionary tale but as a blueprint for dental profiteers. In a December 2022 article published by the *Journal of the American Dental Association (JADA)*, researchers found that children on Medicaid were much more likely to have experienced multiple root canals compared to children with private insurance, and that these procedures were much less likely to have been performed by a specialist (an endodontist).[100]

Investigations and settlements have also become the norm. In 2011, an investigation by television station WFAA in Dallas-Fort Worth, Texas, discovered that Texas's Medicaid program paid $184 million in a single year—more than the spending of the next ten states combined—to put braces on 120,000 children.[101] Among the chief culprits was a chain of clinics called All Smiles, whose owners lived in a Dallas mansion with a private water park and traveled via clinic-owned corporate jets.[102] In 2020, a Travis County district court held former All Smiles owner Dr. Richard Malouf responsible for 1,842 instances of Medicaid fraud, including "more than 100 claims he filed while he was vacationing out of country."[103] Malouf was also required to pay $16.5 million in penalties, interest, and attorney fees.

Another WFAA investigation, in 2015, found Dallas dentists who were paying patients to come to their clinics. In one instance, the station interviewed a mother who received more than $200 to take her kids to a clinic called Sunshine Dental. That clinic, WFAA found, later billed Medicaid nearly $20,000 for procedures performed on four of this woman's children.[104] In another instance, WFAA interviewed six children who said "they were paid $10 to get into unmarked vans, taken to a southeast Dallas dental clinic called All About Dentistry, and drilled without their parents' permission."[105]

In 2017, federal prosecutors entered an $8.45 million settlement with yet another Texas-based DSO, MB2 Dental Solutions, whose nineteen affiliated clinics allegedly billed Medicaid for services that "were not rendered, were tainted by kickbacks, or falsely identified the person who performed the service."[106] The Department of Health and Human Services' inspector general's office also conducted a series of investigations in four states—Indiana, Louisiana, New York, and California—and found a distressing amount of "questionable billing" by a subset of dentists.[107] One New York dentist, for instance, provided fillings "on forty-two separate tooth surfaces for the same child during the same visit," while another performed extractions on 76 percent of his patients (compared to an average of 10 percent for all dentists in New York).[108] In California, the IG's office identified 229 dentists who were providing at least seventy-six services per day (compared to an average of twenty-four statewide). One of these dentists provided more than one thousand services per day on ninety-seven days, including a high of 1,658 services on a single day. "If this dentist spent only 5 minutes performing each service, it would have taken over 138 hours," the IG's office calculated.[109] The majority of the suspect dentists in each of these states, the IG's report also noted, were affiliated with dental chains.[110]

In 2020, *USA Today* published a year-long investigation into the North American Dental Group, which owns two hundred offices in thirteen states. Among other practices the paper uncovered, "North American Dental pits office against office and dentist against dentist by sending out monthly tables ranking dentists and hygienists by who's making the most money per appointment. Offices failing to hit their goals are colored in red—and told to step it up."[111]

And then, of course, there was the Justice Department's $23.9 million settlement in 2018 with Benevis and Kool Smiles, whom the government accused of submitting "false claims to state Medicaid programs for medically unnecessary pulpotomies (baby root canals), tooth extractions, and stainless-steel crowns, in addition to seeking payment for pulpotomies that were never performed." According to a whistleblower who worked in one of the chain's Connecticut clinics, "Kool Smiles dentists wrapped child patients in papoose-like cocoons to keep them still and kept a hair dryer to dry children's clothing when they wet themselves during treatment."[112] This whistleblower also told their lawyer that Kool Smiles dentists "were young, foreign-born, in the U.S. on visas and dependent on Kool Smiles' salaries," according to the *Hartford Courant*.[113]

Unfortunately, the problem of Medicaid dentistry brooks no easy answers. Simply raising the rates Medicaid pays, for example, may not prompt more dentists to accept Medicaid patients, thereby easing the shortage of high-quality providers. And it could even backfire, by encouraging profit-mongering. According to a 2012 *Frontline* investigation, Connecticut raised the fees it paid to Medicaid dentists in 2008, which attracted a slew of new dentistry chains to the state, including Kool Smiles. "Within months," *Frontline* reported, the state's Medicaid dental director saw "a disproportionate spike in kids getting stainless steel crowns to treat cavities." That's because the state was paying about $230 per crown, versus $100 for a filling.[114]

Likewise, in Texas, more money for Medicaid has not meant better care. As the result of a class-action lawsuit filed in 1993 on behalf of the state's indigent children, the state of Texas agreed to dramatically increase its spending on Medicaid, including on dental benefits, to improve access to care.[115] But as Dr. Christine Ellis of the University of Texas Southwestern testified to Congress in 2012, the result was an explosion in fraud, typified by the All Smiles case noted earlier. "Texas has spent a lot of money straightening basically already straight teeth and has gained a lot of fraudulent orthodontic providers," Ellis testified.[116] "We have used the mouths of children to enrich unethical providers and private equity investors."

Unless and until the profession of dentistry can solve the problem of equitable access to dental services, low-income children will remain at the mercy of unscrupulous practitioners using government dollars to deliver substandard care.

"Managed" Care, Growing Profits

In January 2015, Iowa's then-Governor Terry Branstad unilaterally announced his plan to privatize the state's Medicaid program,[117] putting more than half a million Iowans' health into the hands of "managed care." Medicaid costs had risen an "unsustainable" 73 percent since 2003, state officials said, and privatization would save the state money.[118]

Instead of traditional "fee-for-service" Medicaid, where the state pays doctors and hospitals directly, the state would pay a fixed fee per patient (i.e., a "capitation" payment) to private managed care companies, which would in turn pay providers. In theory, managed-care companies can negotiate lower prices for prescription drugs, hospital stays, doctor visits, and other services. Fixed payments also theoretically encourage insurers to prioritize preventive care and the management of chronic conditions, so patients avoid expensive emergencies. "Medicaid members will receive better coordinated care so that they get the services they need to become healthier. An overall healthier Medicaid population will drive down program costs," said then-Medicaid director Mikki Stier in a 2015 press release.[119] In the first six months alone, Brandstad's team optimistically predicted, savings could total as much as $51.3 million.[120] Annual savings could reach $232 million.[121]

But just two years later, the *Des Moines Register*'s editorial board was condemning the effort as a "slow-motion train wreck."[122] Contractors had abandoned the program (or been fired), projected savings failed to materialize, doctors and hospitals were dissatisfied, and patients weren't getting adequate care. Nor did things improve. After nearly a decade in, Iowa's Medicaid program was still a prime example of privatization falling short of its promise—an outcome that would recur in other states that fell to the same allure.

Iowa's Medicaid transition was a textbook case of privatization gone awry. Less than a year into the transition, the state canceled its contract with WellCare, one of four companies hired as the state's first Medicaid contractors. Trouble with contractors has been one reason Iowa's privatization has been rocky.

In its bid to the state, WellCare neglected to mention a "corporate integrity agreement" it entered with the federal government after four of its executives were convicted of Medicaid fraud (including the CEO).[123] In a related settlement, WellCare had also agreed to pay $137.5 million to the federal government and nine states to settle the charges against it.[124] Not only had the company "misrepresented the medical conditions of patients and the treatments they received," the U.S. Department of Justice alleged, but WellCare had also "engaged in certain marketing abuses, including the 'cherrypicking' of healthy patients in order to avoid future costs; manipulated 'grades of service' or other performance metrics regarding its call center; and operated a sham special investigations unit."[125] All of this was "highly relevant information" WellCare should have disclosed to Iowa officials, ruled an administrative law judge who reviewed the bidding process after rival companies sued to protest WellCare's winning bid.[126]

By 2019, two more companies had quit the state on their own, citing "underfunding" and unacceptably low reimbursement rates.[127] UnitedHealth, for instance, claimed it had lost $250 million on Iowa's program—despite receiving more than $2 billion in state and federal Medicaid payments a year to cover about 425,000 residents.[128] As of year-end 2021, just two companies—Amerigroup and Iowa Total Care (a subsidiary of Centene)—were running Iowa's Medicaid program.[129]

Iowa also hasn't seen the savings it thought it would from privatization—even as contractors have complained of underpayment. A 2018 report by state auditors calculated $126 million in savings that year (on a nearly $5 billion program)—or less than half the amount projected by the governor's office.[130]

Privatization, instead, has been costly for doctors and hospitals who say they've struggled with added bureaucracy to justify the treatments they provide. In a 2020 state auditor's survey of Iowa Medicaid providers, nearly two-thirds (65.8 percent) said submitting claims "was more complex and took longer," while 57.9 percent said costs for staffing and administration had increased.[131] Just 6.1 percent of doctors and hospitals felt privatization had been "beneficial to quality of care," and only 9.9 percent felt it had improved access. Four in ten (41.1 percent) said they were "dissatisfied or extremely dissatisfied" with their ability to provide services to Medicaid patients, and the overwhelming majority said new restrictions on care imposed by managed-care companies were "inappropriate."[132]

Patients have, in fact, been denied necessary care—the most troubling consequence of Iowa's Medicaid privatization. In a 2021 investigation, the state auditor's office found a massive increase in illegally denied claims after managed care's takeover of Medicaid. In a comparison of pre-privatization and post-privatization appeals for claims denied, auditors found an *891 percent* increase in the number of times that courts reversed the judgment of managed-care companies (thereby finding the initial denial to be illegal).[133] "Privatized Medicaid in Iowa is substantially less likely to follow the laws and regulations regarding providing care to members," the auditor's report concluded.[134] As disability advocate Jenn Wolff told Cedar Rapids' *The Gazette,* "Iowans were made more vulnerable by privatization."[135]

Though Iowa's experience illustrates well the potential downsides of Medicaid privatization, managed care is now "the predominant delivery system for Medicaid," according to the Congressional Budget Office (CBO).[136] As of July 2020, more than 58 million Americans—or about 72 percent of Medicaid patients nationwide—were enrolled in a "comprehensive" Medicaid managed-care plan from which they received all their care.[137] The share of total Medicaid spending going to managed care has grown dramatically (from 15 percent to 37 percent between 1999 and 2012, according to the CBO).[138] In 2020, reports the Kaiser Family Foundation, payments to Medicaid managed-care organizations accounted for 49 percent of all Medicaid spending, making it the single largest category of spending within the program.[139]

The growth of Medicaid managed care has of course also meant the growth of the Medicaid managed-care industry, dominated by the "Big Five" companies: Aetna/CVS, Anthem, Centene (the company with a subsidiary in Iowa), Molina, and UnitedHealth Group. These companies control about half of the Medicaid managed-care market nationally, according to Georgetown University's Health

Policy Institute, with total 2021 enrollment of about 39.4 million.[140] Companies collect substantial amounts acting as the middlemen between patients and providers. In Iowa, for instance, managed-care companies can receive up to 12 percent of total state Medicaid costs for their fees, according to a 2018 report by the nonprofit In the Public Interest (or $57.6 million on a $4.8 billion program).[141] (The organization also points out that the state only spent between 4 percent and 8 percent on administrative costs before privatization.)[142]

Over the last twenty years, changes in federal law have helped facilitate the shift to managed care. Fiscal pressures have also prompted states to look to managed care to control spiraling budgets. But as Iowa's privatization transition shows, the promised benefits of managed care are far from guaranteed. Research shows mixed results for patients' health. The only certainty has been the steady stream of revenue flowing to managed-care companies.

The Rise of Medicaid Managed Care

Unlike Medicare, which is an exclusively federal program, Medicaid has always been administered by the states. While federal law sets broad national standards, states control program design and administration, including eligibility, payment rates—and the freedom to adopt delivery models like managed care. The federal government's chief role is to help finance the system.[143] Under a federally defined formula, poor states get more federal help with Medicaid expenditures, while wealthier states get less.[144] In Mississippi, for instance, the federal government will pay 84 percent of Medicaid costs in 2023, compared to 56 percent in Massachusetts.[145] (A formula determines the exact percentage.)

California began experimenting with managed care as early as the 1970s, according to the Robert Wood Johnson Foundation (RWJF), though these early efforts were especially disastrous. "Inexperienced entrepreneurs created dozens of new entities, which marketed door-to-door, signing up thousands of beneficiaries," as a foundation report recounted in a history of Medicaid managed care. "Within months, there were allegations of illegal marketing, inadequate access, poor quality, and undercapitalized health plans."[146]

In 1976, Congress passed legislation to prevent these kinds of misadventures, allowing only federally qualified HMOs (health maintenance organizations) to enter state managed-care contracts. This limitation would prove short-lived, however, under President Ronald Reagan's push for privatization. Throughout the 1980s, reports RWJF, Reagan encouraged states to adopt Medicaid managed care, and Congress reversed the requirement that HMOs must be federally qualified to enter state contracts.[147]

By 1992, a little more than one in ten Medicaid enrollees was participating in managed care.[148] But it wasn't until later in the 1990s that Medicaid managed care truly began to take off, catalyzed by new federal requirements expanding Medicaid and a recession that severely strained state budgets. In 1989, Congress passed legislation mandating Medicaid benefits for low-income pregnant women and children under six who lived in households with incomes up to 133 percent of the federal poverty line. Congress also expanded benefits to low-income children under eighteen living in poverty. Together, these mandates added millions of people to state Medicaid rosters, along with billions in additional expenses. "State policy-makers began referring to Medicaid as the 'Pac-Man' of state budgets, gobbling up nearly all available revenues," according to RWJF.[149] Managed care, with its promise of better care at a lower cost, became increasingly appealing to desperate states.

Congress then passed the Balanced Budget Act of 1997, which included multiple provisions creating a glide path for Medicaid managed care. First, the legislation allowed states to *require* that Medicaid enrollees participate in a managed-care plan. Second, it allowed states to limit the choice of available plan providers to only two. Third, Congress repealed federal protections allowing Medicaid beneficiaries to disenroll from a plan for any reason on one-month's notice. (The purpose of this provision was to protect enrollees from denials of service.) Instead, it enacted a provision allowing plans to "lock in" members for twelve months and requiring enrollees to show "cause" to the state if they wanted to switch.[150] In addition, Congress repealed the "75/25 rule," which had required Medicaid contractors to enroll at least 25 percent of their members from outside Medicaid.[151] Ending this requirement paved the way for companies focused solely on Medicaid enrollees. By 2009, the Medicaid managed-care market was booming, with as many as "10 publicly traded companies in this market, four of which focused almost exclusively on managing the care of Medicaid enrollees," according to the Commonwealth Fund.[152]

Among the businesses flying high was WellCare (the company that lost its contract in Iowa), whose biggest early investor was a private-equity fund connected to billionaire George Soros. Two years after going public in 2004, WellCare's stock price had already tripled, boosting the wealth of its CEO, Todd Farha, by $77 million.[153] (Farha would later be sentenced to thirty-six months in prison as one of the company's four executives convicted of fraud.)[154] Soros's fund, meanwhile, cashed out its stake for $870 million in 2006 (compared to an initial investment of $220 million), according to the *Wall Street Journal*.[155]

Companies don't need to disclose exactly how much money they make from Medicaid—a lack of transparency that Georgetown University's Health Policy Institute calls a "public policy failure"—so it's impossible to determine the total volume of governmental dollars going to managed-care companies.[156] But revenue data for California's Medi-Cal program, obtained by *California Healthline*, gives one small window into how profitable Medicaid managed care has become. According to a spreadsheet provided to *Healthline* by the California Department of Health Care Services (DHCS), companies operating in California collected about $2.9 billion in net profits from 2014 to 2020, while overall revenues ballooned from $2.8 billion to nearly $13.6 billion over that period.[157] Companies seeing the fastest growth included Blue Shield Promise, whose revenues grew from $60.7 million in 2012 to $403.7 million in 2020, and Molina, whose revenues spiked to $1.63 billion in 2020 (from $374.4 million in 2012).[158]

Like the health care and insurance industries generally, the Medicaid managed-care industry has experienced significant consolidation over the past decade (hence its current domination by the "Big Five"). Embattled WellCare, for instance, was acquired by Centene in 2019 for $17.3 billion.[159] The combined company was expected to cover 22 million enrollees nationwide in 2019 and generate $97 billion in projected revenue, according to a company press release announcing the deal.[160] In 2021, Centene acquired Magellan Health—another Medicaid-focused company—for $2.2 billion.[161] Through this transaction, according to the company, Centene acquired an additional 5.5 million members enrolled in government-sponsored health plans (including but not limited to Medicaid), as well as 41 million enrollees of a specialty managed-care program focused on behavioral health (e.g., mental health, addiction treatment, etc.). For the fiscal year ended December 31, 2021, according to its publicly filed annual report, Centene reported total revenues of $126.0 billion.[162] It also reported 72,500 full-time employees.[163]

But while companies have been thriving, many patients have fared less well. Managed care, in fact, has aggravated existing flaws in the U.S. health care system, especially when it comes to disparities in care and outcomes for lower-income Americans. Nor has it delivered the dramatic cost reductions states want.

Illusory Savings

Like Medicaid dentistry, Medicaid managed care is a volume business; the more enrollees a company signs up, the more revenue it collects. But unlike dentistry, where providers are paid for each service and have an incentive to perform as many procedures as they can, managed-care companies are under pressure to keep costs low. Because companies receive a fixed amount per patient to cover their health care costs for the year, more services provided mean less profit for the company. (Federal law does require, however, that at least 85 percent of the amounts paid to managed-care companies be spent on beneficiary care, not on administrative expenses or kept as profit.)[164]

Industry-sponsored studies insist that managed care can deliver both lower costs and high-quality care. For instance, a 2017 study by the Association for Community Affiliated Plans (ACAP) calculated that managed care "delivered nationwide Medicaid savings of $7.1 billion in 2016" compared to fee-for-service, and that ten-year savings through 2026 would total $94.4 billion.[165]

Likewise, a 2020 analysis commissioned by America's Health Insurance Plans (AHIP)—the trade association representing the nation's largest health insurers—concluded that states using Medicaid managed care for prescription drug benefits spent 25 percent less on drug costs compared to states under traditional fee-for-service plans.[166] Another AHIP-commissioned study from 2020 claimed that managed-care organizations notched dramatic improvements in quality from 2014 to 2018, as measured by national quality standards and consumer assessments.[167]

All three studies were authored by The Menges Group, a "strategic health policy and care coordination consulting" firm that also published a 2021 review of Kentucky's shift to managed care.[168] According to the group's analysis, managed care potentially saved Kentucky as much as $310 million in fiscal 2019—or up to $1.7 billion, counting the federal government's share.[169] "Kentucky's Medicaid managed care program has significantly reduced Medicaid program expenditures," the study concluded.[170]

In truth, research has found little rigorous evidence that states have saved much money by transitioning to managed care. In one analysis of state Medicaid expenditures from 1991 to 2003, when managed-care enrollment soared from 11 percent to 58 percent of all Medicaid enrollees, researchers for the National Bureau of Economic Research (NBER) concluded that "shifting Medicaid recipients from fee-for-service into [Medicaid managed care] did not reduce Medicaid spending in the typical state."[171] In fact, some states ended up spending *more* if payment rates were initially too low to attract doctors and hospitals into networks.[172]

Cutting Costs—or Cutting Corners?

Managed care hasn't meant better quality care, despite industry claims. Certainly, successes are out there, but according to the federal government's advisory commission on Medicaid (MACPAC), research is "scarce" and the results are "mixed."[173]

For instance, notes MACPAC, a 2016 study of the Texas Medicaid program found one distinct benefit from managed care for children with Type I diabetes: they were less likely than other children to be readmitted after hospitalization, "possibly indicating greater access to services that helped them prevent readmissions."[174] Meanwhile, another analysis of Texas's program found the transition to managed care worsened the incidence of infant mortality, pre-term births, and low birth weight among Black infants, compared to Hispanic children.[175] In fact, the Black–Hispanic mortality gap rose by a shocking 42 percent, according to research cited by MACPAC.[176]

Managed care's goals for cost reduction can clash with patients' needs for care. One 2021 NBER analysis, for example, examined the quality of services provided by the lowest-spending Medicaid managed-care plans. "Rather than reducing 'wasteful' spending, lower-spending plans broadly reduce medical service provision . . . and worsen beneficiary satisfaction and health," the study concluded.[177] Not only are enrollees less likely to receive any care at all, but they're also more likely to experience "avoidable" hospitalizations resulting from the lack of needed care. These cheaper plans "are not achieving savings by keeping people healthy," the researchers continued. "They are restricting access to a broad set of services with potentially harmful health consequences."[178]

At times, this lack of access can be deadly. Another NBER study, also from 2021, found that the mandatory enrollment of seniors and persons with disabilities into California's Medicaid managed-care plans led to an increase in preventable emergency room visits—and a 12 percent increase in deaths, especially among sicker enrollees.[179]

Lack of access to care can mean that needed services aren't covered or that claims are denied. It can also mean a shortage of providers willing to accept rock-bottom payment rates. In a 2014 survey of 1,800 randomly selected Medicaid providers nationwide, the HHS inspector general's office found that "slightly more than half of providers could not offer appointments to enrollees."[180] More than a third (35 percent) "could not be found at the location listed by the plan," and 16 percent said they were either not participating or not accepting new patients. Among providers who did have availability, the IG's office found, the median wait time for an appointment was two weeks (ten days for a primary care provider and twenty days for specialists). One specialist, a neurologist, had a wait time of nine months, while another offered appointments "only if the patient had a body mass index (BMI) under 40."[181]

A "secret shopper" study commissioned in 2022 by the New Mexico legislature found even worse results; investigators calling providers could schedule appointments only about 13 percent of the time, thanks to inaccurate listings and voicemails that were never returned.[182] Nevertheless, New Mexico's Medicaid program costs the state and federal government about $8.8 billion a year.[183]

Incompetence and Failures in Performance

As with Medicaid dentistry, Medicaid managed care has had its share of outrages, scandals, and government investigations.

In Kansas, for instance, the state Department of Health and Environment fired Medicaid contractor Maximus in 2020 (yes, the same company discussed earlier in this book) after years of complaints about poor performance.[184] At one point, the average wait time for calls to the KanCare service center, run by Maximus, was twenty-seven minutes.[185] The company had also failed to process Medicaid applications on a timely basis, leading to enormous backlogs.[186] The *Kansas City Star* reported that some nursing homes turned seniors away because of application delays.[187]

In California, multiple investigations by *Kaiser Health News* and state auditors led to a wholesale reboot of the entire $124 billion Medi-Cal system in 2021.[188] Kaiser's investigation found that the twenty-five managed-care companies hired to run the state's Medi-Cal program systemically outsourced their responsibilities to independent physician networks and even to other health plans. These subcontractors in turn hired their own contractors to process claims.[189] The result was a thicket of bureaucracy leading to substandard care and unjustified denials. One subcontractor investigated by Kaiser, SynerMed, was later discovered to have "falsified documents for years to cover up improper denials of care."[190] Another company, Agilon, admitted to state regulators that its employees had been altering records to pass state audits, such as by changing dates to cover up delays.[191]

State officials, meanwhile, discovered that many low-income Californians weren't receiving basic care, despite Medi-Cal's soaring costs.[192] A 2019 report by the state auditor's office ranked California fortieth in providing preventive health services to children, largely due to lack of access to care for children on Medi-Cal.[193] As many as 2.4 million children a year weren't getting required services, such as vaccinations and regular checkups, and only 25 percent of California children had received a development screening by age three.[194]

In 2021, California regulators set about rewriting the state's managed-care contracts, vowing to tighten oversight, and in 2022, the state levied a record $55 million in fines on LA Care, the state's largest Medicaid contractor, for its failures in performance.[195] It's unclear, however, just how much things will really change. In 2022, *Kaiser Health News* reported that the state's new Medicaid prescription program, awarded to Magellan Health (now owned by Centene), was "riddled with problems," including wait times of up to eight hours on call center phone lines.[196]

When the state awarded new Medicaid contracts in 2022, the biggest winners were three companies that already had major footprints in the state: Molina, Anthem-Blue Cross Partnership Plan, and Health Net of California (also now owned by Centene).[197]

In an appeal filed by longtime contractor Blue Shield, whose bids were shut out altogether, the company "accuse[d] its rivals . . . of failing to disclose hundreds of millions of dollars in penalties against them," according to *Kaiser Health News*.[198] Blue Shield's filing further attacked the winners for "poor performance 'and even mendacity'" and submitting bids "filled . . . with 'puffery,' which the state 'bought, hook, line and sinker,' without 'an iota of independent analysis.'"[199] Blue Shield CEO Paul Markovich also posted an "Open Letter to the People of California" in October 2022, warning that the state had chosen "for-profit health plans with poor track records in improving access to quality care."[200] (The letter was taken down as of January 2023.)

Molina's CEO, meanwhile, reportedly told investors that the new Medi-Cal contracts would "have a profound impact" on his company, according to the *Los Angeles Business Journal*, boosting revenues by as much as $6 billion a year.[201]

Poor Oversight, "Revenue Maximization," and Fraud

States arguably bear a good share of the blame for the problems plaguing Medicaid managed care. Federal investigators have found lax oversight, sloppy record keeping, and—on occasion—collusion to grab federal dollars.

Some states, for instance, have learned that their own coffers benefit from overbilling Medicaid, particularly if they hire "revenue maximization consultants" to help them.[202] In a spate of investigations between 2006 and 2013, the HHS inspector general's office discovered that four states—Arizona, Missouri, New Jersey, and Wisconsin—had each overbilled Medicaid with the help of Maximus (yes, that Maximus), which was acting as a "revenue maximization consultant."[203] In Wisconsin, for example, "MAXIMUS was paid contingency fees based on the amount of reimbursements it helped Wisconsin garner, creating an incentive for MAXIMUS to encourage the state to increase its billing," according to a 2019 report by the Government Contractor Accountability Project.[204] Among the reimbursements Wisconsin asked for from the federal government was $41.4 million between 2004 and 2006 for a Medicaid-financed psychiatric services program. The IG's office concluded that 95 percent of the state's claims—or $39.4 million—were actually unallowable.[205]

In 2012, a congressional hearing on Medicaid fraud aired allegations of state schemes to game federal Medicaid reimbursements in their favor. "States systematically overpaid managed care companies to cover Medicaid beneficiaries while underpaying the same plans for coverage of individuals paid for with State-only dollars," said Iowa's Senator Chuck Grassley. "This appears to be another example of the old game of States pushing the bounds to maximize Federal dollars received while minimizing State dollars spent."[206] Minnesota, for instance, was allegedly inflating what it billed the federal government for Medicaid in order to subsidize two state-funded medical programs ineligible for federal money, according to the testimony of a whistleblower, who called the scheme "a substantial and massive fraud against the Federal Government."[207]

In most cases, however, simple inattention and lack of oversight capacity are the likeliest culprits for programmatic inefficiency and waste. States have, for instance, paid tens of millions of dollars in annual capitation payments to managed-care companies for Medicaid beneficiaries they didn't know had died. In another series of investigations, from 2018 to 2021, the HHS inspector general's office discovered that California had paid nearly $74 million to managed-care companies on behalf of deceased beneficiaries, while Ohio had paid as much as $90.5 million.[208] Ohio "did not always identify and process Medicaid beneficiaries' death information," said the IG's office, which meant those residents stayed on the rolls, and companies got their payments.

In a separate 2021 investigation, the HHS inspector general's office found that most states could not provide "complete or accurate payment data" about the claims submitted to their Medicaid managed-care plans,[209] which potentially meant significant levels of improper or improperly documented claims. In fact, the Centers for Medicare and Medicaid Services (CMS) estimates that

21 percent of Medicaid claims filed in 2021 lacked proper documentation (this does not mean, however, that 21 percent of Medicaid claims were wrongly paid).[210]

One potential reason for this apparent laxity is philosophical—a principal rationale for privatization by states is to offload the hassle of running a government program. But as public management expert Don Kettl has argued, privatization doesn't work without effective contract management—which can sometimes be more difficult than program administration yet often falls by the wayside in the rush to privatize.[211]

States have also been experiencing a "brain drain" of experienced Medicaid administrators to manage program oversight—in part because they are leaving for the private sector. In 2016, the median tenure of state Medicaid directors was only two years, down from four years prior.[212]

Managed-care executives not only get paid more than state Medicaid directors but also have easier jobs, according to a 2017 study by the Government Accountability Office (GAO). Based on a ten-state survey it conducted, the GAO found that state Medicaid directors were paid an average of $152,439 in 2015, compared to the $236,007 average salary for the top executives of private managed-care organizations (whose salaries ranged as high as $1.9 million).[213] Executives also received bonuses, stocks, and other compensation averaging $78,271. State Medicaid directors also described their jobs as "very complex and time consuming" and said that they were "held accountable for their state's Medicaid program to the federal government, their governor and legislature, the media, and the public."[214] Managed-care executives, meanwhile, said their roles were "generally less complex and time consuming" and that they didn't face the same level of accountability as their public-employee peers.[215]

In its 2014 report to Congress, MACPAC cautioned that states were not investing in the administrative capacity necessary to administer their Medicaid programs effectively, especially as their size and complexity have grown.[216] "There are few clear standards to assess efficiency, value, or performance in state and federal Medicaid program administration," MACPAC concluded.[217] Nevertheless, the Medicaid managed-care industry is certain to grow, even as patient care potentially suffers.

The Dialysis Machine

As many as 37 million Americans have chronic kidney disease, often the result of diabetes, high blood pressure, and other chronic conditions.[218]

If you're white, well educated, and middle class or better, odds are you'll get the right kind of medical care that will save your kidneys. You likely have private health insurance and get regular checkups. You likely caught your condition early and are taking medicines to slow down the disease's progression. And if you're unlucky enough to be among the roughly 130,000 Americans diagnosed each year with kidney failure, or end stage renal disease (ESRD), you probably still have the resources and wherewithal to get yourself as fast as possible on the wait list for a kidney transplant.[219]

But if you're poor, less educated, or Black, odds are that your kidney disease will run unchecked, the result of longstanding disparities in access to quality care. You will likely end up on dialysis, spending three days a week, four hours a spell, at a place like the one in a run-down strip mall on Pennsylvania Avenue, SE, in Washington, DC, in a heavily African American neighborhood across the river from the Capitol. The DaVita Washington Southeast dialysis center has room for twenty-five patients at a time and takes up a full corner of the shopping center.[220] It's right next door to a liquor store and steps away from an Ace Cash Express check-cashing outlet, a barbershop, and a carryout fast-food place.

I dropped by one sunny August day, pre-pandemic, when I first started researching the dialysis industry for *Washington Monthly* magazine. An elderly, fragile-looking Black man was slumped in a wheelchair, eyes closed, just outside the center's doors, where a big sign on the glass warned visitors that firearms were not allowed inside. A MetroAccess public bus was idling in the parking lot, waiting to take other patients home.

It was mid-afternoon, but the shopping center was buzzing with knots of people hanging out by the carryout and the barbershop two doors down. Everyone I spoke to seemed to know someone on dialysis. One man in a barber's smock out for a cigarette break told me he had a friend who died at a dialysis center. He wouldn't share his name—"bad for business," he said—but he said ambulances were a constant presence at DaVita. It's not unusual for people to die on dialysis—in fact, about one in five dialysis patients die in the first year and six in ten will be dead within five years.[221] Among patients over sixty-five, who make up more than half of those who begin dialysis, 30 percent won't survive the first year.[222]

Farther down the sidewalk, I met Sharon C., who was waiting on her daughter at the carryout. Soft-spoken and fine-boned, she wore a flowing sleeveless white dress and Jackie O sunglasses, her caramel-colored hair in a ballerina bun. She said she was sixty-two years old. She too was sitting in a wheelchair, and I noticed how her left foot and ankle were grotesquely swollen, a shocking mismatch with the rest of her slender frame. It was the result of poor circulation caused by the diabetes she was diagnosed with in 2005.

Sharon is also on dialysis but goes to another DaVita center, this one at 8th and C Streets near Capitol Hill, where she spends every Tuesday, Thursday, and Saturday. "You can't miss a treatment," she said. "You can't go anywhere." She said she'd started dialysis two months earlier, when her one functioning kidney finally failed. She wasn't on the waitlist for a transplant. "I need to find a donor," she said, echoing what patient advocates say is a common misperception among dialysis patients.[223] "I don't want to be like this."

Government statistics show that people with less than a high school diploma are more than twice as likely to be diagnosed with kidney disease than people with a bachelor's degree, while someone earning $35,000 or less is about three times as likely to be diagnosed than someone earning $100,000.[224] And of the more than

800,000 Americans living with kidney failure, a disproportionate share are low-income or Black. Black Americans are three times as likely to experience kidney failure as whites, while the risk for people in poverty is more than double that of those who aren't poor.[225] Black Americans also account for 35 percent of people on dialysis, according to government statistics.[226]

This explains the profusion of dialysis centers in neighborhoods like the one in southeast Washington, DC. In the District of Columbia, where the prevalence of diabetes (a leading cause of kidney disease) is six times as common among Black residents as it is among whites, there are twenty-two dialysis centers inside the city,[227] located mostly in northeast and southeast Washington, the heavily lower-income and African American parts of the city. Another 106 dialysis centers are within a twenty-five-mile radius of DC, again concentrated in the suburbs with the largest minority and lower-income populations.[228] Just across the river in District Heights, Maryland, for example, a DaVita clinic dominates the busy intersection of Pennsylvania Ave. and Silver Hill Road, while a U.S. Renal Care clinic sits just across the street.

Like check-cashing outlets, payday lenders, and other businesses that disproportionately serve low-income and minority communities, dialysis centers are now fixtures in the urban commercial landscape. "We used to say there's a liquor store on every corner," Howard University transplant surgeon and professor of medicine Clive Callender told me. "Now we say there's a dialysis unit on every corner."

The overwhelming majority (89 percent) of these clinics are for profit, and their ownership is dominated by just two companies, Colorado-based DaVita Inc. and the German conglomerate Fresenius Medical Group.[229] According to the federal government's Medicare Payment Advisory Commission (MedPAC), the two firms control three-fourths of the nation's roughly 7,800 dialysis facilities.[230]

The bulk of their revenues, moreover, come from the federal government, which pays for the lion's share of dialysis care in the

United States. Under the current system, Medicare guarantees payment for every dialysis session, which means that clinics bill the federal government for each treatment they provide.

In 2022, according to its annual report filed with the Securities Exchange Commission (SEC), DaVita earned 67 percent of its revenues from government-sponsored health plans, including Medicare and Medicaid.[231] Revenues for the year totaled $11.6 billion, $10.6 billion of it from its U.S. dialysis operations (the company also runs clinics overseas).[232] It administered more than 28.9 million dialysis treatments in 2022, for an average of 92,506 treatments per day.[233] Though DaVita and Fresenius are private, for-profit companies, they are, like defense contractors, basically subsidiaries of the federal government given the share of their revenues that come from federal dollars.

What the federal government spends on dialysis also amounts to a shockingly large share of the federal budget. While kidney-failure patients make up about 1 percent of Medicare beneficiaries,[234] they accounted for 7.1 percent of Medicare spending in 2019 and almost 1 percent of the total federal budget.[235] On average, each patient cost the government $82,190, much of it for dialysis, but also for medications, hospitalization, and other ancillary care.[236]

Like Medicaid dentistry, the treatment of kidney failure in America is a volume-centered business aimed at keeping dialysis centers running. "You fill up a facility with so many stations, you make sure somebody is sitting in each of those chairs around the clock," said Dennis Cotter, president of the Medical Technology and Practice Patterns Institute (MTPPI). "It's the Henry Ford production model."[237]

It's a system that also arguably creates incentives to keep kidney patients on dialysis until they die. For patients with kidney failure, that means a quality of life that can be intolerable. It can also mean being steered away from other treatments, like transplants, that could improve their lives and even save the government money in the long run. For dialysis companies, however, it means steady and growing revenues, so long as the systemic inequities in U.S. health that contribute to kidney disease and kidney failure persist.

The dialysis industry would like the public to believe that dialysis centers are safe and pleasant. For instance, here's for-profit American Renal Associates describing its facilities in its 2019 annual report, filed with the SEC (the company, which operated over two hundred clinics nationwide, has since been acquired by private equity and is no longer public):[238]

> Our clinics generally contain between 15 and 20 dialysis stations, one or more nurses' stations, a patient waiting area, examination rooms, a supply room, a water treatment space to purify water used in hemodialysis treatments, staff work areas, offices and a staff lounge. Our clinics are also typically outfitted with patient-friendly features, including heated massaging chairs, wireless internet and individual television sets.

I wasn't allowed to go inside a dialysis clinic like the DaVita clinic in southeast DC (my requests were initially denied out of privacy concerns, and then the pandemic hit), but survivors say the scene inside most centers is grim.

Clinics typically consist of one big room, lined with banks of chairs and machines. Patients say they are far from luxurious. Sharon C., for example, said that while the staff at her clinic were kind, flies were a problem. "They are everywhere," she told me. "You can't eat without the flies coming everywhere."

It's not an uncommon issue. "Dialysis facilities offer a great environment for some bugs, including roaches, flies, and gnats," reads the "Bugs and Infestations" web page on the site of the Quality Insights Mid-Atlantic Renal Coalition, one of several "ESRD Networks" established under federal law to improve the quality of kidney disease care in the United States.[239]

Kidney patient Patrick Gee, who lives near Richmond, Virginia, says he remembers the first time he set foot in a dialysis clinic, after his diagnosis in April 2013. "I literally cried," he told me. "I stood there and cried. I was looking at amputees. I was looking at people who were brought in and out by paramedics. Nobody had a smile on their face. It looked dead." Patient advocate Nieltje Gedney, who was diagnosed two decades ago, recalls something similar. "That first impression of walking into the clinic was all those machines with alarms blaring, and people moaning and comatose in their chairs," she said. "I call it my PTSD moment."[240]

Amenities can't hide the fact that dialysis (technically, "hemodialysis" for the procedure performed in centers) is a grueling process.

"Your blood is leaving your body," said Dennis Cotter of the Medical Technology and Practice Patterns Institute. "It's going through a filter and getting returned. That in itself is traumatic because the blood encounters a lot of foreign surfaces, and there's a huge problem with a large variety of infections."[241]

Patients often experience cramps, chills, fever, and crippling fatigue as their bodies try to cope with a process that tries to accomplish over four hours what a pair of healthy kidneys would do over the course of two to three days. "The treatments in center are designed pretty much to beat you up," said Gedney. "That's why people are moaning and comatose, and then it takes them twelve hours to recover. You're literally stunning the body."[242] Gee said it was all he could do to keep his eyes open on the drive home after a session. "One time I got in the garage and parked the car, and my wife found me asleep behind the wheel," he said.[243]

"Dialysis is hell," says patient advocate David White, of Washington, DC, who spent nearly six years on dialysis before finally receiving a kidney transplant. "All you want to do is sleep," White told me. "You just want to rest until you feel better. And when you feel better, guess what? It's time to go back to dialysis again. It's a pretty strange way to live."

Patients' hearts must cope with the stress of pumping their blood through a machine—usually at the rate of a pint per minute.[244]

That's a big reason why dialysis is exhausting. According to the U.S. Renal Data Service, more than 40 percent of deaths among dialysis patients are due to heart problems.[245]

"I can't remember if the ambulance came for me once or twice," said White, who said he recalled one episode when his heart wouldn't stop racing for the better part of thirty minutes. "I saw one person almost die," he said. "It was really gruesome. After he was gone, there was a pool of sweat around his chair. It was unbelievable." Whenever he saw a patient carried out, he said, "It always goes through your mind that you'll never see that person again."[246]

Federal Medicare Policy: Paved with Good Intentions

In 2019, more than 490,000 Americans were dependent on in-center dialysis, living the life that David White described. The numbers diminished to about 480,000 in 2020 during the coronavirus pandemic, when medically fragile dialysis patients were especially vulnerable.[247]

More than 70 percent of kidney-failure patients who are Black and 65 percent who are Hispanic rely on in-center hemodialysis, compared to about 52 percent of whites.[248] White patients are much more likely to have received a kidney transplant (37 percent, versus 22 percent and 26 percent for Black and Hispanic patients, respectively, in 2020). White patients are also more likely to have access to home-based options for dialysis, which are gentler on the body and offer the convenience and privacy of being at home.[249]

The irony is that access to a dialysis machine—now the default treatment for low-income patients—was once rare, expensive, and precious. The well-intended changes in federal policy that led to the ubiquity of dialysis today are simultaneously a triumph, a tragedy, and a trap for both patients and the federal government.

Until the early 1970s, a diagnosis of kidney disease was literally tantamount to a death sentence. In 1962, journalist Shana Alexander published a now-classic account in *Life* magazine on the workings of Seattle's "Life or Death Committee"—a group of five anonymous citizens convened by the King County Medical Society to decide who would have access to the Seattle Swedish Hospital's ten dialysis machines. The committee—the original "death panel" if there ever was one—looked at applicants' income and net worth, marital status and children, occupation, "past performance and future potential," and references. As Alexander wrote:

> With no moral or ethical guidelines save their own individual consciences, they must decide, in the words of the ancient Hebrew prayer, "Who shall live and who shall die; who shall attain the measure of man's days and who shall not attain it; who shall be at ease and who shall be afflicted."[250]

It's not hard to guess what kinds of patients made the cut and who didn't.

In 1972, Congress and President Richard Nixon passed legislation extending Medicare fee-for-service coverage to anyone with end stage renal disease. It is still the only disease for which its sufferers are entitled to Medicare eligibility regardless of their age. According to lore, the pivotal moment for the legislation was when kidney patient Shep Glazer hooked himself up to a dialysis machine on the floor of the House Ways and Means Committee and pleaded for the means to afford his treatment. "I am forty-three years old, married for twenty years, with two children ages fourteen and ten," Glazer told the committee. "If your kidneys failed tomorrow, wouldn't you want the opportunity to live? Wouldn't you want to see your children grow up?"[251]

Medicare eligibility transformed access to dialysis from a treatment for the lucky few to something standard, commoditized, and, ultimately, a multi-billion-dollar industry—all during slightly more than a decade. It's a stark testament to government's power in creating and shaping a new market for treatment.

With a guaranteed stream of government payment for every dialysis treatment performed, dialysis clinics began springing up nationwide. Some of these were non-profit, such as the Nashville-based Dialysis Clinic, Inc. (DCI), which was established in 1971 and still exists today.[252] Others were for-profit and quickly came to dominate the nascent sector. Fresenius Medical Care is not only one of the world's two largest providers of dialysis services, it's also the world's largest manufacturer of dialysis equipment, with total global revenues in 2022 of about €19.4 billion.[253] According to Fresenius's 2021 annual report, more than 40 percent of the hemodialysis machines worldwide are made by the company.[254] It's also the principal supplier of equipment to the world's number-two dialysis provider, DaVita.[255]

The fee that Medicare pays dialysis providers is called a "bundled" payment, and it varies slightly from year to year depending on the costs reported to CMS by providers. In 2023, that payment was $265.57 per treatment and is intended to cover all the services, equipment, supplies, and drugs involved in a single session.[256]

The intent of the "bundle" is to keep costs low for Medicare, but it has also helped enable big players like DaVita and Fresenius to push out smaller players and nonprofits (in the same way Walmarts have decimated small-town mom-and-pops). This payment structure also encourages providers to perform as many treatments as they can at the lowest possible cost if they want to maximize their revenues. The benefits are efficiencies of scale and standardization of treatment, but it also prompts clinics to err toward a one-size-fits-all approach.

In a 2017 episode of *Last Week Tonight*, HBO's John Oliver dedicated an entire show to the questionable practices of dialysis companies and ridiculed the flamboyant ex-CEO of DaVita, Kent Thiry, for riding into company meetings on horseback, dressed as a Musketeer and referring to himself as the "Man in the Iron Mask."[257] Oliver also aired a clip of Thiry comparing the management of his dialysis business to that of Taco Bell. "If I had 1,400 Taco Bells and 32,000 people who worked in them, I would be doing the same stuff," Thiry tells a group of business students at UCLA.[258]

Unfortunately, Medicare's "bundled payment" approach only encourages Thiry's approach. Dialysis centers are, in fact, like Taco

Bells. In the same way that Taco Bell employees might be taught one way to make a burrito that's uniform across the franchise, dialysis center employees might be taught one way to administer dialysis.

"The typical center—the easiest thing to do is just put them on in-center hemo-[dialysis]," said surgeon Joseph Melancon, chief of the George Washington University Transplant Institute. "That's one set of skills [for the staff]. Everybody is the same. The patients come in, they sit there for their amount of time, and they come in three days a week."[259]

Patients say their treatment can reflect this factory mentality. "They are literally herding you in like cattle," says Dallas-area patient Nichole Jefferson, who endured dialysis before her transplant. "You walk in, you weigh yourself, you wash your hands, you sit down. They get to you when they get to you to stick you."[260] David White, whose advocacy has taken him behind the scenes at dialysis centers, says the patient "census" is often the top priority for facility personnel in the staff meetings he's attended as a patient representative. "The very first topic they always discuss is 'the census,'" he said. "I can't explain how it makes me feel to think that we're just numbers. But that was always the first topic of discussion at every meeting—whether they had more or fewer patients."

Putting someone on home-based dialysis, such as peritoneal dialysis, potentially means less money for providers, which might be one reason it seems discouraged as an option. One study finds that hemodialysis (i.e., in-clinic dialysis) costs an annual average of $108,656 in 2017, versus $91,716 for patients on peritoneal dialysis.[261] Setting patients up for home dialysis also requires more staff with different skills, including the ability to train patients to perform this procedure themselves. That in turn requires a different attitude toward patients, says Nieltje Gedney, who launched the advocacy organization Home Dialyzors United, after her "PTSD moment" at the center.[262] "People say about in-center that the patients are fungible—you plug one person in, they're there, you unplug them, they go home, and you replace them," she said. "Home dialysis requires a lot more one-on-one engagement."[263]

As a result, the patients most likely to get treatment at home are the ones who have the wherewithal to demand it. Kidney patient Patrick Gee, who is Black, says he believes many minority patients must fight stereotypes to access home-based modes of treatment. "My dialysis nephrologist told me, 'You can do peritoneal because you have a PhD and you're smart enough to be in compliance,'" Gee recalls. "And I'm listening to that and hearing the micro-aggression."[264] Just 9.6 percent of kidney-failure patients used in-home dialysis or peritoneal dialysis in 2020; these patients were more likely to be white.[265]

The Wrong Kind of Innovation

To its credit, the federal government has launched some recent initiatives to reform the treatment of kidney disease and improve patients' lives. In 2019, HHS Secretary Alex Azar announced pilot modifications to Medicare's payment structure intended to encourage home-based dialysis and transplants for kidney-failure patients.[266]

"The current Medicare payment system encourages in-center hemodialysis as the default treatment for patients beginning dialysis," the Centers for Medicare and Medicaid Services (CMS) acknowledged in its press release about the effort. In early 2023, CMS announced an expansion of its "Kidney Care Choices" pilot, designed to encourage comprehensive, coordinated care for patients with advanced kidney disease so they can delay dialysis or avoid it altogether through better management of their condition or through transplant.[267] According to CMS, this effort could reach as many as 250,000 Americans with advanced kidney disease or kidney failure.[268] It may take years, however, for these models to become the standard of care, assuming the hoped-for benefits materialize.

In the meantime, the current fee-for-treatment structure gives dialysis companies little incentive to invest in innovation of their own. "They have a cash cow. And there's no need to do any innovation," as Murray Sheldon, associate director for technology and innovation at the Center for Devices and Radiological Health at the U.S. Food and Drug Administration (FDA), told *Nature*.[269]

As a result, the process of dialysis has changed little over the last forty years. In fact, modern dialysis still rests on two twentieth-century breakthroughs—the first from 1944, when Dutch physician Willem Kolff invented the first "artificial kidney" in Nazi-occupied Holland using, among other things, sausage casings, orange juice cans, and a washing machine.[270] After the war, according to a history by Richard Rettig for the Institute of Medicine, Kolff sent four of his (by then refined) machines to the United States, where they were successfully used to treat soldiers suffering from kidney failure during the Korean War.[271]

The second breakthrough came in 1960, when Belding Scribner and Wayne Quinton, working at the University of Washington in Seattle, invented the "Scribner shunt," a U-shaped Teflon tube inserted into a patient's arm that made it possible to connect a patient to a machine as often as necessary.[272] Before then, the damage done to a patient's veins with each treatment made it literally impossible to administer more than a few sessions before it was no longer safe. (Today's patients typically get a "fistula," a procedure that connects an artery to a vein to create an access point for the machine.)[273]

In 2018, the American Society of Nephrologists and HHS announced "KidneyX," a "kidney innovation accelerator" that would award prizes for technological innovations in the development of an artificial kidney. Congress appropriated $5 million for the effort in 2019, and in 2021, KidneyX announced the first six winners of its Artificial Kidney Prize—none of which were affiliated with the two big dialysis companies.[274] In its 2021 annual report, Fresenius reported spending €818 million in research and development across its portfolio of companies. The only dialysis-related innovation it mentioned was the unveiling of the "FX CorAL dialyzer," which uses new and improved materials for filtering patients' blood to "reduce the side effects of dialysis."[275]

"The industry needs us sick," argues patient advocate Gedney. "We're absolutely no benefit to them if we're healthy. There's no motivation to get a patient well, and there's no motivation in dialysis to do it better because they're making a ton of money doing it poorly. So why should they have to change?"

Where the industry has innovated, however, is in its development of new business models to maximize profits. After years of acquisitions during which bigger dialysis companies swallowed up smaller ones (essentially leaving no one left to buy), companies have been entering "joint ventures" with kidney doctors, who are offered ownership stakes in new clinics that are typically built with borrowed funds.

Although the so-called federal "Stark law" generally forbids doctors from referring patients to clinics and laboratories that they own ("self-referrals"), dialysis is largely exempt from this prohibition.[276] This means nephrologists are free to refer as many patients as possible to the clinics they own. And they have every reason to do so. "A chair that is not used in a facility is not much use," explains Mark Neumann, editor-in-chief of *Nephrology News & Issues*. "You want to keep your shifts filled and you want to keep your chairs filled. It's no different from any other business."[277]

One company that worked exclusively through this model was American Renal Associates, which went public with a $100 million IPO in 2015 before its recent acquisition by private equity.[278] According to its 2019 annual report—its last public filing—the company operated 246 dialysis centers "in partnership with approximately 400 nephrologist partners."[279] In its 2021 annual report, DaVita reported that 28 percent of its revenues came from joint ventures "with nephrologists, hospitals, management services organizations, and/or other healthcare providers."[280]

DaVita acknowledges that some of these arrangements might be stretching the limits of the law. As it disclosed in its 2022 annual report:

> Our joint venture arrangements do not satisfy all of the elements of any safe harbor under the federal Anti-Kickback Statute, however, and therefore are susceptible to government scrutiny. . . . If our joint ventures are found to violate applicable laws or regulations, we could suffer severe consequences that would have a material adverse effect on our business, results of operations, financial condition and cash flows and could materially harm our reputation.[281]

The company did not mention that it has in fact already come under "government scrutiny" for past partnerships. In 2014, the Justice Department announced that DaVita had agreed to pay $350 million to resolve allegations of illegal kickbacks "to induce the referral of patients to its dialysis clinics."[282] According to the government, DaVita identified and targeted physician practices with "significant patient populations suffering renal disease" and offered them "lucrative opportunities to partner with DaVita." "To make the transaction financially attractive to potential physician partners, DaVita would manipulate the financial models used to value the transaction," the government further alleged, and lock in physicians with non-compete agreements or as "medical directors" of the joint venture clinics.[283]

The most serious consequence of these schemes, however, is the impact on patients, whose well-being might be in the hands of a physician with a financial stake in their remaining on dialysis. Some patients may not be referred by their nephrologists for a kidney transplant, which is, beyond a doubt, the best treatment for kidney failure. "A successful transplant gives you almost a normal life expectancy, particularly if you've never been on dialysis," said GW transplant surgeon Joseph Melancon. According to the latest available data, between 82 percent and 91 percent of transplant recipients survive five years after transplant (compared to just 40 percent for patients on traditional hemodialysis).[284]

Yet Howard University surgeon Clive Callender said some of his patients—who are primarily Black—were told by their nephrologists they'd be eligible for transplant "later," after spending time on dialysis. "They were told, 'We'll dialyze you for a year or two and then after that we'll put you on a transplant list," he said. "Of course, the longer you're on dialysis, the poorer your outcome is, the more likely you are to reject your transplant and the more likely you are to die."

Anecdotally, nephrologists and surgeons potentially even compete for the "best" patients. That's because the patients most likely to last the longest on dialysis—those who are younger and healthier—are also the best transplant candidates. "I think there really is a financial incentive for a dialysis nephrologist—especially if they're an 'easy' patient, a low-maintenance patient—to keep them on dialysis as opposed to referring them to transplant," said Joanne Bargman, a nephrologist and professor of medicine at the University of Toronto.[285]

Transplant surgeon Melancon is more blunt: "I'm not saying it's typical, but I've definitely heard it said, 'Wow, you took my best patients and gave them a transplant when they were doing so well on dialysis'—which is exactly the opposite of what you want."[286] Research backs up Melancon's experience. A 2014 study found that patients of for-profit chain dialysis clinics were 13 percent less likely to be put on the waitlist for a transplant than patients at nonprofit centers (of which few now remain).[287] "For-profit ownership of dialysis chain facilities appears to be a significant impediment to access to renal transplants," the researchers concluded.

Among the patients never told about transplants when he started dialysis was Patrick Gee. Gee finally received a transplant but feels he's lost valuable time. "When I was told that my kidneys were failing, I should have been told right then and there I could have had a transplant instead of dialysis," Gee said. "I think my chances of finding a living donor would have been better if I'd known. I could have had a transplant in 2013."

Over the past two decades, the Federal Trade Commission (FTC) has sought to slow the pace of consolidation in the dialysis industry and preserve competition. Unfortunately, it's had limited success; Fresenius and DaVita together now control about 75 percent of the nation's clinics.

In 2005, for instance, the FTC filed suit against DaVita for its planned $3.1 billion purchase of Gambro Healthcare Inc., then the country's third-largest provider of dialysis services, with 565 clinics.[288] The FTC characterized the merger as anticompetitive and "likely to result in monopolies for outpatient dialysis clinic provision."[289] The merger proceeded after DaVita agreed to sell sixty-nine clinics in thirty-five states to another competitor, Renal Advantage Inc. In 2010, however, Renal Advantage was bought by Fresenius.[290]

More recently, the federal government tried a more ambitious approach to the industry's anticompetitive practices—but again fell short. In July 2021, a federal grand jury indicted DaVita and then-CEO Ken Thiry on criminal antitrust charges for allegedly conspiring with three of its competitors (all led by former DaVita executives) not to poach each other's employees.[291] In 2022, however, both DaVita and Thiry were acquitted of all charges.[292]

In the meantime, as DaVita and Fresenius have continued to gain market power, they've been accused of increasingly brazen behavior to maximize revenues and maintain their market dominance, as well as the regulatory status quo.

In 2016, Fresenius agreed to pay $250 million to settle thousands of lawsuits on behalf of patients whose deaths were potentially connected to one of the company's dialysis medications.[293] The drug in question, GranuFlo, was supposed to help maintain the right pH in a patient's blood, but excess acetate in the product allegedly led to sudden cardiac arrests. According to the *New York Times*, Fresenius purportedly knew of the drug's risks and sent a warning memo[294] to its own dialysis centers—but failed to alert other dialysis centers using the product of the potential hazard.[295] The FDA later recalled GranuFlo as unsafe.[296]

In 2022, the Service Employees International Union–United Healthcare Workers West (SEIU-UHW), the National Health Law

Program, and five dialysis patients filed a complaint with the HHS Office for Civil Rights, alleging that DaVita and Fresenius dialysis clinics discriminated against Asian and Latino patients by disproportionately subjecting them to treatments at dangerously high speeds.[297] (Presumably, faster dialysis means more turnover in a chair and more revenue for the clinic.) Patients suffered "low blood pressure, dizziness, headaches and cramping" because of high-speed dialysis, while others died, according to the complaint.[298] The SEIU's analysis of facility-level data provided to the government found that the clinics with the highest proportion of high-speed treatments were disproportionately located in areas with large Asian and Latino populations. These clinics also experienced more deaths than expected, as well as higher rates of hospitalization and ER visits.[299]

In 2015, DaVita agreed to pay the federal government $450 million in settlement of claims that the company had intentionally and unnecessarily wasted dialysis medications—and then billed Medicare for the "waste."[300] According to a whistleblower, DaVita would require employees to maximize their use of two different types of dialysis drugs with each treatment so that a clinic could bill for the excess amounts. For example, the government alleged, the company's protocols required the administration of one drug in small amounts at frequent intervals so that nurses would be forced to open numerous single-use vials. Nurses would use only a portion of the vial and throw away the rest (but the clinic would bill for the entire vial).[301]

In 2017, DaVita's pharmaceutical subsidiary, DaVita Rx, agreed to pay $63.7 million to settle claims it had billed the government for drugs that were never shipped or were shipped and returned. The government also alleged that the company had offered "financial inducements" to Medicare beneficiaries in violation of the federal antikickback laws, such as by offering discounts to patients who paid by credit card.[302] In 2018, DaVita Rx was acquired by Walgreen's.[303]

In 2020, DaVita settled a class action lawsuit brought against it by shareholders who alleged the company had illegally inflated its revenues by steering kidney-failure patients away from Medicare and Medicaid and toward high-cost commercial insurance.[304] According to the complaint, filed in 2017, the rates DaVita charged commercial plans for dialysis were up to ten times or more what it received from Medicare (as much as $4,000 per treatment, versus $300)—which is why it wanted to increase the share of private-pay patients it served.[305] Clinic staff were allegedly directed to "pressure the Company's ESRD patients to forego their Medicare and/or Medicaid benefits in favor of enrolling in commercial plans," even if they could not afford the premiums.[306]

The company also purportedly helped patients pay for their insurance through an affiliated charity, the American Kidney Fund (AKF), primarily funded by the dialysis industry.[307] This financial aid lasted only so long as a person remained on dialysis, however, which meant that "if an ESRD patient obtains a life-saving kidney transplant, the AKF's premium assistance for that patient immediately ceases."[308] (Had a patient stayed on Medicare, their transplant would have been fully covered.)[309] According to a separate suit filed by a federal whistleblower in 2019, the fund allegedly steered financial aid primarily to patients of DaVita and Fresenius while denying aid to patients of other clinics that weren't fund donors.[310]

From 2017 to 2020, the dialysis industry reportedly spent more than $233 million to defeat two union-backed initiatives in California that would have put tighter regulations on the industry.[311] According to *Kaiser Health News*, DaVita was responsible for about $143 million of this spending, while Fresenius accounted for most of the rest. Also according to Kaiser, the companies spent about $111 million in 2018 to defeat Proposition 8, a union-backed effort to cap industry profits. In 2020, the industry spent $105 million to stop Proposition 23, another SEIU-backed initiative, which would have instituted patient safety protocols such as on-site physicians at every clinic. The companies have also defeated proposed legislation to set staff ratios at dialysis clinics to prevent understaffing. The industry also tried to stop AB-290, which forbids the "steering" of patients into commercial plans (as just described) and limits commercial insurance reimbursement for dialysis to Medicare rates. Governor Gavin Newsom signed AB-290 in 2019, promptly triggering a lawsuit from the industry.[312] In 2022, patient advocates put forward Proposition 29, a ballot measure that would have instituted many of the same patient safety rules as AB-290. The proposal was defeated after the industry spent $89 million on campaigns opposing the measure, according to the *Los Angeles Times*.[313]

DaVita and Fresenius have also spent plenty to maintain a presence in Washington, DC. In 2022, according to OpenSecrets.org, DaVita ponied up $1.9 million in campaign contributions and more than $3 million on lobbying, while Fresenius spent about $1 million on campaign contributions and $5.6 million on lobbying.[314] (Both companies give to both Republicans and Democrats.) Fresenius and DaVita have spent about $130 million on lobbying since 1998 and about $13 million on campaign donations since 1990.[315] As Duke University economics professor Ryan McDevitt told *Kaiser Health News*, "It's very natural for these private chains to spend millions to make billions of profits."[316]

The steady profits enjoyed by the dialysis industry are also very likely to continue. The Centers for Disease Control (CDC) predicts that the share of Americans with chronic kidney disease will grow to 16.7 percent of all adults over thirty by 2030 (up from 13.2 percent in 2010).[317] Minority and low-income Americans will moreover bear a disproportionate share of the burden of this disease, given higher rates of diabetes and high blood pressure among these populations—the result of systemic disparities in access to quality care, nutrition, and other determinants of health.[318]

Shortcomings in federal policy have not only calcified these disparities but also facilitated a rapacious industry that counts on these systemic failures to thrive.

5

Crime Pays: The Business of Criminal "Justice"

America's most famous bail bondsman might be "Dog the Bounty Hunter"—aka Duane Chapman—the star of an eponymous reality show that aired for eight seasons on A&E.[1] Before his self-inflicted implosion over a series of controversies—including multiple public revelations of racist and homophobic remarks—Chapman cut a colorful figure as the patriarch of the family-run bail business he ran with his wife and son, Da Kine Bail Bonds in Honolulu, Hawaii.[2] With his bleached-blond mullet, heavy tattoos, and trademark leather vest, he dished out "tough love" to the defendants he tracked down on his show while also portraying himself as an untiring crusader against crime. "Beware of the Dog," warns his website, where you can also buy a bag of his signature coffee—Grounds for Arrest Bounty Brew—for $19.99.[3]

Chapman's commercial success is as outsized as his on-air persona, but he's not unusual in finding a way to profit handsomely from the criminal justice system. Every year, according to FBI statistics, law enforcement arrests more than 10 million people—essentially creating and maintaining a massive market of potential clients for criminal justice profiteers, who await at every step of the process.[4] That's because many state and local governments have outsourced huge swathes of their justice systems to private contractors—while at the same time shifting the costs of running the system onto defendants. Pretrial supervision, for instance, is often in the hands of commercial bail bondsmen or private home detention companies (who charge for ankle monitors and other "services"). Private prisons housed 96,370 inmates in 2021, according to the Sentencing Project.[5]

Contractors, moreover, perform many of the functions inside government-run jails and prisons, such as providing meals and medical care. Inmates pay exorbitant fees for phone calls, commissary accounts, and access to email, also typically provided by private contractors. Sometimes, these contractors pay "commissions" to corrections authorities for access to inmates. And the return to society is often accompanied by significant debts, including those accrued during incarceration.

Among the cruelest injustices perpetrated by the criminal justice system is that there's no release from companies' pursuit of profit.

Pretrial Profits: The Bane of Cash Bail

The notoriety of shows like *Dog the Bounty Hunter* has glamorized the bail bonds industry and popularized misconceptions about its role in the justice system. Dog himself has also used his celebrity to protect his industry's standing. In recent years, Duane Chapman ("Dog") has become an outspoken opponent of bail reform, with appearances around the country and on Fox News.[6] As a growing number of states have moved to limit cash bail or even abolish it altogether, especially for minor offenses, Chapman has argued that these reforms are coddling criminals. "We tried it your way, and people are dying," he claimed on *Fox News Primetime* in 2021.[7]

With the help of larger-than-life personalities like Chapman, the commercial bail industry has cultivated the perception of offering a public service that keeps dangerous criminals off the streets. "The commercial bail system in this country is the best form of ensuring criminal defendants are returned to court and ensuring the victims of crime their rights to justice," argues the trade association Professional Bail Agents of the United States (PBUS) on its site. "It is a system paid for by the perpetuators of crime, not by the taxpaying victim."[8]

PBUS conveniently forgets that anyone out on bail is in fact awaiting trial and therefore considered *innocent.*

In truth, the commercial bail business is a lot more like loan-sharking than law enforcement, and it's been profitable enough to attract the involvement of some of the world's largest financial services firms. Its clients are low-income Americans who cannot afford the often exorbitant cash bails imposed by courts in many jurisdictions, but who also can't risk the consequences of jail. Spending more than even one day in jail "can have devastating consequences," finds Harvard University researcher Sandra Smith. The more time someone spends in detention, the more likely they are to lose their jobs and housing, to take a plea that will permanently scar their prospects, or to become re-involved in the system.[9] The commercial bail industry preys on this vulnerability for its profits and mires low-income Americans in debt—including the innocent.[10]

One such innocent caught up in the commercial bail industry's debt machine was Baltimore resident Rafiq S., whom I met in 2016 through the Baltimore city public defender's office. Rafiq had been in the wrong place at the wrong time, walking past a row house in his neighborhood that the police were about to raid. Mistaking him for someone else, they arrested him and confiscated the keys to his mother's car, parked nearby.

At his trial in 2016, police claimed that he consented to a search of his car (he didn't). They also claimed they smelled marijuana in the vehicle (there wasn't any), and they also claimed they found a gun in the glove compartment (a discovery that stunned Rafiq, who said he'd never owned a gun in his life and didn't have the key to the glove compartment in the first place). He was charged with illegal possession of a handgun and possession of a handgun in a vehicle on a public road, punishable by up to three years in prison. But because the police had no actual evidence against him—such as fingerprints on the weapon they allegedly found—a jury acquitted him on all counts after less than half an hour of deliberation.[11]

Nevertheless, Rafiq was still on the hook to his bail bondsman for $10,000—the nonrefundable "premium" that his family agreed to pay to get him out of jail two days after his arrest. Because bail arrangements are private contracts, unrelated to court outcomes, the bondsman still collects his fee regardless of what happens in court—guilty, innocent, or even if the charges are dropped, as is often the case. The Maryland Office of the Public Defender found that over one five-year period, "more than $75 million in bail bond premiums were charged in cases that were resolved without any finding of wrongdoing." This was more than double the amount of premiums paid by defendants who were, in fact, ultimately convicted.[12] "It's crazy," as Rafiq said.

In Rafiq's case, his initial bail was set at $100,000, and his bondsman set the premium at 10 percent—$10,000. Rafiq and his family paid the bondsman about $2,000 up front, with a promise to pay $100 a week until the amount was paid in full. At the time we met, he was earning $10.15 an hour installing trailer hitches for U-Haul. "I'll be paying for a long time," he said. "Like, forever."

Low Risks, High Rewards for Bail Bondsmen

Commercial bail bonds work differently from bonds posted directly with the court. Defendants who can afford to make bail on their own will get their money back when they show up for their court date.[13] That's the stated purpose of the bond—to ensure a defendant's appearance. Commercial bondsmen, on the other hand, charge a "premium" to post a bond with the court on a defendant's behalf. The bondsman gets *his* money back from the court when the defendant appears, but the "premium" collected from the client is nonrefundable. It's essentially a loan for making bail, and the "premium" is the interest.

"Do you get the bail money back if found innocent or not guilty?" asks the FAQ for Aarow Bail Bonds in Richmond, Virginia.[14] "Say it with me here. No," writes owner Dan Barto. "The premium is never returned. Whether the defendant is innocent or guilty doesn't matter. Bail bond premium is a no."

Bail bondsmen argue that the fees they charge are "premiums" because what they provide is "insurance." "Bail is similar to homeowners or auto insurance," says Jeff Kirkpatrick, a bail bondsman in Jackson, Michigan, who was executive vice president of PBUS when we spoke, around the same time I met Rafiq. "Say you went to jail for shoplifting or larceny and the judge set your bail at $10,000," Kirkpatrick says. "In most states, you would pay 10 percent to 15 percent of that bond amount as a premium. In return, the bond agent is guaranteeing the court that should you fail to appear, and the bail agent failed to produce you, they would pay the court that $10,000."[15]

In truth, the "premiums" paid by defendants cover the fees that bail agents themselves must pay to large insurance companies to guarantee payment on a bail bond.[16] If somebody jumps bail, a bondsman can call on his insurer, rather than put up the cash himself or deed over his house. Bondsmen are essentially brokers for these bigger firms. As of this writing, the largest financial services firm underwriting U.S. bail bonds is Fairfax Financial Holdings Limited, a Canadian conglomerate with multiple subsidiaries that insures bail bonds as part of its business.[17]

The profit a bondsman makes is the difference between the premiums charged to a defendant and the premiums the bondsman pays his insurer. That gives bondsmen an incentive to ensure their clients show up in court—forfeiting a bond would have the same effect on their insurance as totaling a car.

Kirkpatrick, who's been in the bail bonds business for more than thirty years, said he started out as a night shift bondsman. "I'd cover the bonds that got written in the middle of the night," he told me, before he progressed to owning his own agency. He has been PBUS's Bail Agent of the Year, according to his bio, and was inducted into the organization's Hall of Fame in 2009. He even had his fifteen minutes of fame in 2013 as a guest on Duane Chapman's spinoff show, *Dog and Beth: On the Hunt,* when the

Chapmans came to his town in search of fugitive Ricky Wheeldon (later convicted of racketeering, drug, and firearms charges).[18]

Despite the drama portrayed on Chapman's shows, Kirkpatrick says most of his job is administrative work aimed at ensuring his clients show up in court—"making sure they know when their court date is, calling them and reminding them." He argues that this aspect of his business is a public service. "The bail agents do all the work they do at no cost to the taxpayer," he told me. "It's one of those public–private partnerships that works really well. We've done a very good job of making sure that suspects appear."

Bail bonding is, in fact, a relatively low-risk business—one reason insurance companies find it appealing. According to one analysis, insurers' gross profit margin on bail bonds is as high as 83 percent—compared to 33 percent for home and auto insurance.[19] In addition to extortionately high premium rates, bail bonds contracts can be heavily skewed in favor of the bondsman, with exceedingly onerous conditions imposed on bailees to ensure they don't skip. Bail bond insurer Lexington National Insurance Corporation, for instance, offers a helpful library of "standard" contracts on its site for its bondsmen, including state-specific forms, bond approval requests, and other agreements.[20]

"Bail Standard Form No 1"—the "bail bond application and agreement" to be signed by bailees—requires that clients provide their bondsman with access to "any and all private or public information and/or records," including "credit reports, Social Security Records [*sic*], criminal records, civil records, driving records, tax records, telephone records, medical records, school records, worker compensation records, and employment records."[21]

The agreement further provides that clients "irrevocably grant" the bondsman "the right to enter your residence, or any other property that you own or occupy, without notice, at any time, for the purpose of locating, arresting and returning you to custody." In addition, the client must agree that the bondsman "may attach a location tracking device on any vehicle owned or driven by you, at any time, without notice" and "may use location technologies to locate your wireless device at any time."[22] "YOU WILL NOT HAVE THE OPTION TO OPT-OUT OF LOCATION USE OR TRACKING DURING THE BAIL PERIOD," the contract further warns. Both this contract and the Bail Bond Premium Receipt make clear that the "the premium owing or paid is fully earned upon the defendant's release from custody, and the fact that the defendant may have been improperly arrested, re-arrested, the case dismissed, or the bail reduced shall not obligate the return or forgiveness of any portion of the premium."[23]

Bail bondsmen also limit their risks by choosing their clients. They're not obligated to write a bond for anyone who asks, and bondsmen won't do business with someone who has a reputation for missing court dates. Bail bondsman and PBUS executive Jeff Kirkpatrick again analogized this practice to insurance. "Just like an insurance company that writes policies for your car or your home, if you're a person who frequently gets arrested for drunk driving, most insurance companies are going to look at [you] as a bad risk," he said. "If you have a history that you fail to appear in court all the time, you'll have a harder time getting your bond posted." Kirkpatrick said that for him, "it depends on the crime and the personal history." But "it's more times that we bond them out than we don't," he added.[24]

This kind of discretion only adds to the leverage that bail bondsmen already have over their bailees. In a 2022 report on the civil rights issues raised by cash bail, the U.S. Commission on Civil Rights expressed its concern that "those who work for the private bail industry can refuse to write a bond based on any set of attributes, stereotypes, or belief that a defendant might miss their court appearance."[25] "It's really the only place in the criminal justice system where a liberty decision is governed by a profit-making businessman that will or will not take your business," Temple University professor John Goldkamp told the Commission for its report.[26]

Given the protections bail bondsmen provide themselves, few defendants skip out on bail, which means that few bondsmen (and their insurers) will be liable for big debts to the court. In fact, PBUS acknowledges as much on a web page discouraging aspiring "recovery agents" (industry lingo for bounty hunters), which it says "can be one of worst jobs there is (sic)." "The reason you cannot make reasonable money being a recovery agent is simple," says the site. "Most bail agents do a very good job of making sure their defendants go to court." Instead, the site counsels, "Recovery agents can make more money if they are also a bail agent, which grows their network of influence and potential clients. Best of luck in the recovery agent area!"[27]

Protecting the Market for Bail

Low risks, easy profits, and a steady supply of clientele are just a few of the reasons why the commercial bail industry has lobbied industriously over the last three decades to preserve and grow its market. Though market research firm IBISWorld predicts a decline in the industry's future revenues, due to falling crime rates and an aging population (older Americans are less inclined to commit crimes), it still estimates annual revenues for the industry—i.e., the amount collected in nonrefundable "premiums"—of about $2 billion a year.[28]

According to the nonprofit Justice Policy Institute, the number of defendants released on bail—as well as the amount of the bail required—increased dramatically in the 1990s, coincident with the 1992 launch of the American Bail Coalition, an industry trade association.[29] From 1992 to 2006, the share of felony defendants released on bail doubled from 21 percent to 42 percent, while the percentage released on "personal recognizance" (without a cash bond) dropped from 41 percent to 28 percent. At the same time, the average bail amount spiked dramatically, from $25,400 to $55,500.[30] (Bigger bail amounts mean bigger "premiums" for bail bondsmen.) Not content to sit on its laurels, the industry spent at least $3.1 million from 2002 to 2011 trying to influence state policies on bail and pretrial justice, the Justice Policy Institute further reports.[31]

The bail industry's big wins in the 1990s were helped along by the conservative American Legislative Exchange Council (ALEC), which drafted and advocated industry-friendly "model legislation" expanding the use of bail and tilting state laws in favor of commercial bondsmen. For instance, ALEC's model "Crimes with Bail Restrictions Act" called for the mandatory imposition of bail for certain offenses, including murder and sexual assault and also "theft by extortion" and "resisting arrest."[32]

Echoes of this proposal live on today in the many jurisdictions where "bail schedules" dictate the bail that judges must impose. In Los Angeles County, for instance, the superior court's "2022 Felony Bail Schedule" mandated a minimum bail of $2 million (or no bail at all) for suspects charged with murder; $50,000 for vehicular manslaughter "with gross negligence"; $100,000 for "mayhem"; and $50,000 for second-degree robbery. It also mandated minimum bails of $10,000 for bookmaking; $20,000 for "grand theft of dog if value exceeds $950"; $50,000 for "own or operate a chop shop"; $10,000 for cultivating marijuana; and $50,000 for manufacturing "concentrated cannabis using volatile solvent without a license."[33] (Though California legalized recreational marijuana in 2016, only about 10 percent to 20 percent of marijuana sales are technically fully legal.)[34]

Another old ALEC model bill, the "Bail Forfeiture Relief and Remission Act," provides a grace period for the refund of a forfeited bail if a bondsman can track down a bail jumper within a specified period.[35] Florida's bail statute gives bondsmen up to two years to track down bailees and contains language identical to the ALEC model legislation.[36] It also allows bondsmen to claim a refund even if it's the police, not they, who pick up a bail jumper—so long as the bondsman had "substantially attempted" to find the defendant.[37]

Virginia, however, might win the prize for the most industry-friendly bail law. Its statute governing bail bonds requires bondsmen to charge a *minimum* premium equal to at least 10 percent (though not more than 15 percent) of the amount of the bond.[38]

The Fight over Bail Reform

Legislators in many states have nevertheless recognized the destructive impacts of cash bail—especially on those who can't afford to pay. Overstuffed jails and the unwarranted detention of innocent people are the collateral damage from the bail industry's efforts to expand the use of cash bail.

Greater reliance on cash bail has led to a steep increase in the number of people held in jails pretrial because they don't have the money to get out. In 2021, according to the U.S. Bureau of Justice Statistics, *71 percent* of jail inmates were people still presumed to be innocent and awaiting trial.[39] The share of the jail population that was "unconvicted," the government reports, has risen ten percentage points—from 61 percent to 71 percent—over the last decade.[40]

And as noted earlier, pretrial detention has catastrophic impacts on an individual's prospects. Spending time in pretrial detention raises the risk of future rearrest (and future costs for the justice system), according to a 2022 study by Christopher Lowenkamp for Arnold Ventures.[41] People in pretrial detention also tend to get longer jail sentences than those who've been released. These destructive consequences fall disproportionately on Black and Hispanic communities. Although the government hasn't collected racial demographic data on pretrial detainees since 2002, the last available data shows that a whopping 62.6 percent of pretrial detainees were Black or Hispanic (compared to about 25 percent of the overall population), according to a 2019 analysis by the Prison Policy Initiative.[42]

In 2017, New Jersey replaced cash bail with a "risk-based" assessment system for determining whether defendants should be detained or released.[43] Under this approach, whether a defendant goes free depends on their actual risk to the community, versus their financial ability to make bail. The same year, Maryland's highest court, the Court of Appeals, approved new rules requiring judges to consider whether defendants can afford cash bail when setting pretrial conditions, essentially eliminating cash bail in most circumstances.[44] (This change unfortunately came too late for Rafiq.) In 2018, California eliminated cash bail with the passage of SB 10, also in favor of a risk-based system. New York followed suit in 2019, with legislation that ended cash bail for most misdemeanors (though leaving violent felonies "bail eligible").[45] In 2022, Illinois passed a sweeping criminal justice reform bill that abolished cash bail altogether.[46]

The bail industry, however, has fought these reforms ferociously, with the result that many of these victories have been short-lived or put into limbo. In California, for example, the bail industry successfully blocked the implementation of SB 10 by securing a public referendum on the measure in 2020.[47] Voters resoundingly defeated "Proposition 25" by a margin of 55 percent to 44 percent, effectively repealing SB 10.[48] Legislation requiring bail premiums to be refunded if charges are dismissed or never filed also failed in 2022.[49] New York, meanwhile, partially rolled back its reforms in 2020 to make more offenses "bail eligible."[50] The state also made further changes in 2022 to grant judges more discretion to set cash bail.[51] In Illinois, a coalition of prosecutors and sheriff's offices filed suit to block the end of cash bail, prompting courts to halt the implementation of reform until litigation is settled.[52]

Unsurprisingly, the American Bail Coalition has helmed the industry opposition to bail reform. Its website is littered with instances of politicians condemning bail reform as a "failure," and the organization posts plentiful research purporting to show the effectiveness and cost-effectiveness of the cash bail system.[53] In January 2023, the American Bail Coalition released its "Pre-trial Roadmap," previewing the "model policies" that the industry would like to see, such as tough new limits on judges' ability to release defendants on "personal recognizance" (i.e., without cash bail).[54]

The coalition's membership page listed seven bail bond insurers as of 2023, including BailUSA, a subsidiary of Fairfax Financial; Bankers Surety, a subsidiary of Tampa-based Bankers Financial Corporation; and A1A Surety, which calls itself the nation's "oldest and largest" bail bond insurer.[55] In a 2021 investigation, Reuters calculated that the industry had spent $17 million fighting bail reform, including $7 million to defeat California's Proposition 25.[56] That's likely to be just the first tranche of spending in coming years as the industry fights to preserve its market.

The Growing Market for Home Detention

At the same time, cash bail's fall from favor in some jurisdictions has boosted the rise of another industry: for-profit home detention. For judges no longer allowed to impose cash bail but reluctant to release a defendant outright, house arrest with electronic monitoring is an appealing alternative—especially when defendants bear the cost.

Before Maryland's courts changed the rules for bail, the streets near Baltimore's detention centers downtown teemed with storefronts for bail bondsmen. The Baltimore Central Booking and Intake Center sits on Eager Street, around the corner from the Baltimore City Correctional Center (the city jail) on Greenmount Avenue. The city jail is a squat, red brick facility, but Central Booking resembles a medieval fortress with gray stone turrets and windowless walls. The building was reportedly constructed in the 1800s, when Thomas Jefferson was president.[57] The modern addition of a multi-story fence topped with razor wire adds to its foreboding air. Across the street is a dilapidated sign for "Central Booking HQ Bail Bonds," but the windows around it are boarded up, and the building looks abandoned. Online directories say the place is still open, but bail reform has clearly been bad for business.[58]

For ASAP Home Detention of Towson, Maryland, on the other hand, business has been great. ASAP (it stands for Advantage Sentencing Alternative Programs) is one of three companies that have essentially cornered the market in Baltimore for at-home detention services, including pretrial detainees.[59] Its chief competitor is Baltimore-based Alert, Inc., while A1 Trusted Monitoring, based in Upper Marlboro, Maryland, is a relative upstart in the area.[60] "I honestly can't tell you where they came from, but they've become the powerhouses of Baltimore," says Marianne Lima, an assistant public defender for the city of Baltimore, whose clients are frequently in the custody of these companies.[61]

ASAP offers home detention monitoring through ankle bracelets and GPS units made by SCRAM Systems, a leading manufacturer of electronic monitoring equipment and remote breathalyzers.[62] SCRAM's most famous user might be actress Lindsay Lohan, who agreed to wear the company's alcohol-monitoring bracelet after her 2007 arrest for driving under the influence (DUI).[63] (In its company history, SCRAM acknowledges it "became a household name as media throughout the world began covering the use of our technology on high-profile Hollywood celebrities.")[64] Alert, on the other hand, uses the OmniLink ankle bracelet to monitor its charges, while A1 relies on the BLUtag system, manufactured by Houston-based Securus Monitoring.[65]

ASAP, Alert, and A1 work directly with defendants (or "clients," as the companies prefer to call them), who "apply" for services and are "accepted" into their monitoring programs.[66] (Among other things, ASAP's "Participant Rules and Agreement" requires defendants to share all details of their schedules with the company and to promise never to submerge the ankle bracelet in water.)[67] A common practice is for defendants to get a "pre-approval" letter from a home detention company willing to take them on. Defendants then present the letter in court to support their case for home detention before trial rather than going to jail (assuming there's no bail).

This happened multiple times at a "bail review" hearing I attended in Baltimore City District Court in the summer of 2022. Typically, within twenty-four hours of their arrest (unless it's a weekend), defendants in Baltimore appear before a judge to determine the conditions of their release while charges are pending. For each defendant, an investigator for the state's Division of Pretrial and Detention Services will offer their recommendations for detention or release, depending on the severity of the alleged offense, prior criminal history, and flight risk.[68] Investigators typically describe whether a person is employed, has a stable home address, or has family in the area. They also summarize the circumstances of the arrest and the charges filed. The judge then hears from both the prosecution and the defense. Defendants' attorneys typically argue for a reduction or elimination in bail (if bail has been imposed) or a release to home detention in lieu of incarceration in the city jail. A "pre-approval" letter, defense attorneys say, makes it more likely that a judge will approve home detention. Some judges, I was told, also prefer one company over another.

Until 2021, low-income defendants in Maryland also had to pay for home detention services, which often led to hundreds and even thousands of dollars in fees accrued while awaiting trial.[69] After Baltimore County eliminated home detention fees in January 2021, the Maryland legislature followed suit, ending fees for "indigent" defendants (though not for others).[70]

Maryland, however, is the exception, not the rule. The Fines and Fees Justice Center reported that forty-three states authorized electronic monitoring fees as of 2022, and many states leave it up to companies to decide how much to charge.[71] As a predictable consequence, the market for electronic monitoring is booming.

An Explosion in E-carceration

Criminal justice advocates and researchers have noted a sharp rise over the last decade in the use of ankle bracelets and other forms of electronic monitoring, both for pretrial defendants and for people at the other end of the process, on probation or parole. In 2015, according to the Pew Research Center, more than 131,000 accused and convicted offenders were under electronic monitoring—up from 53,000 in 2005.[72]

The coronavirus pandemic accelerated the trend, and some advocates estimate that as many as 200,000 people may be subject to electronic incarceration ("e-carceration") at any given time.[73] In Chicago's Cook County, for instance, some 3,500 pretrial defendants were on home detention with ankle monitors in December 2021, compared to 2,500 the preceding April.[74]

From a public health perspective, house arrest with electronic monitoring is arguably safer than a crowded jail, especially during a pandemic. Jails and prisons were responsible for "a majority of the largest single-site outbreaks since the beginning of the pandemic," according to the COVID Prison Project at the University of North Carolina–Chapel Hill.[75] As of February 2023, more than 643,000 inmates have suffered an infection while incarcerated; nearly 3,000 have died.[76]

But ensuring prisoner safety isn't what's motivating jurisdictions to opt for electronic monitoring. Rather, it's about saving money. In Pitt County, North Carolina, for instance, authorities touted $1.2 million in annual savings from switching to electronic monitoring of pretrial defendants, prompting a similar switch in nearby Carteret County.[77] Announcing the shift in 2009, the Carteret County sheriff's office told local news outlets that housing inmates cost the county $45 a day, versus $9 a day for electronic monitoring—which defendants would pay. "The system comes at no cost to the taxpayer," then-Sheriff Asa Buck told the *Carteret County News-Times*.[78] Home detention company Alert, Inc, which operates in Pennsylvania and West Virginia as well as Maryland, claims on its site that its services save states $25,000 per defendant per year (though it cites no evidence for this assertion).[79]

Costs for detainees, on the other hand, can be extortionately high. In a 2021 survey of dozens of jurisdictions, George Washington University law professor Kate Weisburd documented a wide range of daily, weekly, and monthly fees for electronic monitoring, from a low of $1.50 per day in Lancaster County, Nebraska, to a whopping $47 a day in Sacramento County, California (for detainees who are self-employed). Monthly fees were as high as $350.61 in Connecticut, while some jurisdictions charged one-time fees of up to $2,275 (Ramsey County, Minnesota).[80] On average, Weisburd calculated, the average cost of spending one year under monitoring in the jurisdictions she examined was $3,284.08. Among the most expensive was Fairfax County, Virginia, which charged $7,300 a year at the time of Weisburd's analysis.[81] These fees were, moreover, on top of other charges a defendant might be asked to pay, such as for drug treatment, court costs, or other expenses related to court supervision. In some jurisdictions, these add-on charges include an equipment "installation fee" of up to $250.[82]

Fees are often directly payable to the company, rather than the court. In Maryland, for instance, state law provides that defendants "shall pay directly to the private home detention monitoring agency the agency's monitoring fee" (unless they're exempt by reason of their indigence).[83] The majority of states impose no explicit limits on what companies can charge, instead allowing the imposition of "reasonable" fees—whatever that means.[84] In most states, says the Fines and Fees Justice Center, failure to pay leads straight to incarceration.[85]

No Better Than Cash Bail?

While house arrest seems intuitively less harmful to detainees than traditional incarceration at the local jail, electronic monitoring in fact raises its own set of concerns. For-profit detention companies are capricious jailers, leading to immense harms and injustices suffered by detainees. "Electronic surveillance is not an alternative to incarceration, it's an alternative *form* of incarceration," as George Washington University's Weisburd writes.[86]

For one thing, private detention companies have exceedingly broad discretion to set the conditions of house arrest—as well as the power to decide when a detainee has "violated" the terms of their detention, which could lead to their imprisonment. Justice system advocates argue that this frequently leads to arbitrary and even abusive outcomes, especially when contracts are vague about what constitutes a violation. Weisburd's study, for instance, found that some monitoring agreements prohibited contact with people of "disreputable character" or "bad reputation" or required detainees to behave in an "orderly manner."[87] Minor violations—such as leaving the house to put out the garbage—or literally technical violations—such as a malfunctioning monitor—have sometimes been enough to result in a person's re-incarceration. In Cook

County, Illinois, for instance, which runs one of the nation's largest pretrial e-detention programs, more than five hundred people were re-incarcerated for "technical rule violations" in just the first six months of 2021, according to the Chicago Appleseed Center for Fair Courts.[88]

Detainees get minimal or no access to employment and education services or other supports that might help them set their lives on a better trajectory. (Jurisdictions are aiming to spend as little as possible, after all.) People on house arrest also can't go to job interviews or to work without court and company permission, and the obvious presence of an ankle monitor is highly stigmatizing for jobseekers.[89] Even if a detainee is allowed to go to work, they could be subject to random checks at their job site or required to ask permission from the monitoring company for any changes in their work schedule.[90] (In contrast, a person out on bail at least has the freedom to go to work or to look for a job without these kinds of constraints.)

In Baltimore, says Assistant Public Defender Marianne Lima, judges often impose "24/7 lockdown" with no exceptions except to see their lawyers. "Our clients really suffer because they've had jobs for years and then they're stuck there not able to go to work or to assist with the family, like transporting the kids to school—things they would do on a normal basis," she said. "While they're no longer detained, it's a huge deprivation of liberty that impacts the community."[91]

Detainees report significant impacts on their mental health, according to a major joint study on electronic monitoring, *Cages Without Bars*, by the Shriver Center on Poverty Law, Media Justice, and the Chicago Appleseed Center for Fair Courts.[92] Numerous participants interviewed by the researchers said they felt "humiliated and debilitated" by the trauma of 24/7 electronic surveillance.[93] "I had to pay someone to get me toilet tissue because I couldn't leave the house," one participant told researchers.[94] *Cages Without Bars* also found significant racial disparities in who is subject to electronic monitoring. In Cook County, Illinois, for instance, 74 percent of detainees in electronic monitoring are Black (compared to 23 percent of the overall population).[95]

Unsurprisingly, research to date finds that electronic monitoring has no beneficial impacts on whether defendants appear in court or avoid re-arrest.[96] Instead, the only real "benefits" of electronic monitoring are accruing to state corrections budgets and to the profit margins of monitoring companies and equipment manufacturers.

As in other industries profiled throughout this book, a relatively small group of companies have a lock on the market for electronic monitoring. According to *Cages Without Bars*, the largest of these firms is BI Incorporated, a subsidiary of private prison powerhouse GEO Group (more on GEO in the next section), followed by Satellite Tracking of People (STOP), Sentinel Offender Services, and Attenti (formerly a subsidiary of Post-It maker 3M).[97] These four companies together earned an estimated $700 million in revenue in 2018.[98]

In 2023, researchers estimate, the market for electronic marketing is projected to grow to at least $1.2 billion, although the true size of the market is difficult to gauge, given the multiplicity of federal, state, and local jurisdictions entering contracts with monitoring companies and the opacity of the players in this space.[99]

Except for GEO Group, the vast majority of companies involved in electronic monitoring are privately held. Attenti, for instance, is now owned by the private equity firm Apax Partners, which acquired the company in 2017.[100] Sentinel, likewise, is owned by Bison Capital Management, LLC, a New York–based private equity firm that holds more than $1 billion in investments.[101] In 2022, Sentinel bought equipment maker OmniLink (formerly a subsidiary of the Canada-based Sierra Wireless) for $37.6 million, which means OmniLink is now in the hands of Bison Capital as well. According to the press release announcing the acquisition, OmniLink's 2021 revenues totaled approximately $13.1 million.[102] Similarly, STOP is a subsidiary of Securus Technologies (affiliate Securus Monitoring Solutions is the maker of the BLUtag system), which is itself a subsidiary of the privately held Aventiv Technologies.[103] Aventiv's other subsidiaries include JPay, the biggest company in the country providing money transfer, email, and other prison services (more on this too in the next section).[104]

George Washington University's Weisburd, who was able to obtain seventy-six contracts between electronic monitoring companies and state or local corrections agencies, documented numerous instances of multi-year, multi-million-dollar contracts. Cook County, Illinois, for instance, agreed to pay the Track Group up to $4.1 million over three years, while the State of Texas entered a two-year contract with 3M (now Attenti) for $7.4 million.[105] Many contracts, she noted in her study, required agencies to "pay as they go." "In other words, the more devices and services they use, the more they pay," she wrote, thereby creating an incentive for firms to encourage electronic monitoring as much as possible.[106]

The persistence of commercial bail and the rise of the electronic monitoring industry show just how tough it will be to disentangle private actors from the criminal justice system. Both phenomena also illustrate the limitless capacity of profiteers to exploit low-income Americans and the difficulty of reforming a broken system.

Nowhere is this more true than in Maryland. While bail reform effectively wiped out the bail bonding business, it facilitated the ascendance of for-profit home detention, which itself has had destructive impacts on pretrial defendants. Worse yet, many judges are not releasing defendants from detention at all. In Prince George's County, for instance, the share of defendants held on cash bail declined by 11 percent after reform—but the share held with no bond at all rose by 14.5 percent, according to a 2018 report by the Color of Change and Progressive Maryland.[107]

During the bail review hearing in Baltimore I attended in 2022, none of the half-dozen defendants whose cases I saw reviewed were released, either on bail or into home detention (including the defendants with "pre-approvals" from detention companies). One of these defendants was a man arrested for driving under the influence. He was denied bail even though his attorney argued that continued detention would make it impossible for him to get the substance abuse treatment he needed, let alone keep his job.

Public defender Lima said keeping defendants detained before trial has become the default position for many judges. It's a particular disappointment for Lima, for whom bail reform was among the first projects she tackled when she joined the Office of the Public Defender as a young attorney. "Yeah, what we thought was a win to overhaul the bail system kind of blew up in our faces," she said.[108]

Prison: "A Captive Market"

Prison is pricey. America spends about $84 billion a year on jails and prisons—or a little more than the entire annual economic output of the state of Delaware (in 2021 dollars).[109] It's expensive for states and localities, where corrections departments often swallow up big chunks of the budget. In 2017, local governments spent more than $25 billion on jails, according to the Pew Research Center, at an average annual cost of $34,000 per occupied cell.[110] In some states, corrections spending equals or even exceeds state spending on other priorities, like higher education. In Delaware, for example, state and local funding for higher education in fiscal 2021 totaled $307 million—compared to a budget of $355 million that year for the Department of Correction.[111] The same year, Oregon allotted $2.2 billion to "public safety," versus $2.6 billion to post-secondary education.[112]

In many states, much of that money flows straight into the coffers of private companies that run vast swathes of the nation's corrections systems. Enticed as always by the false allure of lower costs and better performance, federal, state, and local governments have allowed the wholesale for-profit takeover of almost every aspect of the corrections system, from prison to parole. The result, in many instances, is a system less concerned about the proper administration of justice than about maximizing profits from prisoners.

The Private Detention Industry: Prisons and Beyond

As with so many other industries profiled in this book, a handful of firms dominate the private detention market. The two biggest are CoreCivic (formerly the Corrections Corporation of America [CCA]) and the GEO Group (formerly Wackenhut).[113] Smaller players include the Management and Training Corporation (the same company that holds the monopoly on Job Corps, described in chapter 3) and LaSalle Corrections (whose facilities are focused in Louisiana, Texas, and Georgia).[114] From the start, the industry has moved aggressively and creatively—including through the strategic use of public policy—to grow, preserve, and diversify their business. Prisons are in fact just a single facet of the modern "corrections" market.

The idea of prison privatization isn't new. America's first private prisons opened at least a century earlier. As early as the mid-1800s, "economizing state legislatures awarded contracts to private entrepreneurs to operate and manage Louisiana's first state prison, New York's Auburn and Sing Sing penitentiaries and others," writes prison privatization expert Byron Eugene Price in his book *Merchandizing Prisoners*.[115] Scandals and abuses led to the industry's near-demise through the 1950s before "expanding prison populations, pressures from courts to quickly add prison space and increases in prison costs" sparked a revival in the 1980s, Price writes.[116] Between 1985 and 2005, the number of Americans behind bars grew to a stunning 1.6 million—in part because of rising crime rates but also because of the "war on drugs," harsher sentences, and other policies encouraging mass incarceration.[117]

While states struggled with the influx of inmates, prison entrepreneurs saw a golden opportunity to relaunch an industry. Leading the way was Nashville-based Corrections Corporation of America (CCA, now CoreCivic), founded in 1983 by Republican Party activist Thomas Beasley and financed by venture capitalist Jack Massey.[118] Massey had already made his fortune building both Kentucky Fried Chicken (he bought the chain from founder "Colonel"

Harland Sanders for $2 million in 1964) and the Hospital Corporation of America, now the largest hospital chain in America.[119] When a court ordered Tennessee to fix its overcrowded prisons by the end of 1985, CCA boldly offered to spend $250 million—including $150 million to build two new prisons—in exchange for exclusive rights to run the state's system for ninety-nine years.[120] The company lost its bid, but brazen tactics like these would characterize the prison industry's rapid rise in the 1980s and 1990s. (CCA ultimately won multiple contracts to run private prisons in Tennessee; private facilities housed more than one-third of the state's inmates in 2021.)[121]

"Speculative Prisons" and Pro-incarceration Legislation

Perhaps the most outrageously aggressive scheme private prison companies used to facilitate their rise was so-called speculative prisons—facilities that companies built without governmental participation and then tried to foist on states. "Private providers or entrepreneurs looked at a state's fiscal problems, crime rate, and overcrowding problems and determined that the state could use another prison," Price writes in *Merchandizing Prisoners*. These companies "targete[d] rural communities with high unemployment figures and convince[d] them private prisons [were] a great economic development tool to revitalize their community."[122] The ploy often worked, according to Price. Many such speculative prisons led to multi-year, sole-source contracts because they were "move-in ready" and offered a quick fix to overwhelmed state corrections departments.[123]

This strategy was particularly successful in places like Texas, where the economy at the time was struggling. Rural counties under pressure to find jobs and sources of revenue lobbied desperately to have prisons sited in their jurisdictions. "As time went on, communities became bolder and bolder, offering incentives like country club memberships for wardens and longhorn cattle [to be raised on] prison grounds," according to one account of Texas's prison privatization.[124] "There was an almost frenzied climate in these rural, impoverished areas to compete for prison beds regardless of the speculative nature of some of the prison construction." For-profit companies gladly jumped into the fray. They "increased their lobbying efforts to persuade the Texas legislature and local counties that prison privatization would allow jurisdictions to build prisons faster, build them cheaper, build them with private financing, operate them at a lower cost, and increase the level of services," write Gerald Gaes and colleagues in their book, *Measuring Prison Performance*.[125] Today, Texas still has one of the largest private prison populations in the United States, according to The Sentencing Project.[126]

As a result of this orgy of prison building, not just in Texas but nationwide, the number of private prisoners surged 83 percent between 1999 and 2015.[127] As of 2021, private prisons held 96,370 people—or about 8 percent of all inmates.[128] And even as criminal justice reforms have reduced the overall number of individuals incarcerated, the share of private prisoners is still growing. Since 2000, says The Sentencing Project, the number of people housed in private prisons has grown about 10 percent.[129]

In addition to lobbying for more prisons, the industry has also pushed for laws to increase the supply of prisoners. As with the commercial bail industry and its efforts to tilt state laws in its favor, the conservative advocacy group ALEC was a key early ally. For instance, the organization advocated "truth in sentencing" laws, which require inmates to serve at least 85 percent of their sentence without possibility of early release, and "three strikes" laws mandating harsher sentences for repeat offenders.[130] During the 1980s and 1990s, more than twenty-five states passed "truth in sentencing" laws, while "three strikes" legislation passed in at least eleven states.[131]

Diversification and Expansion

The private prison industry today is nevertheless smaller than it used to be—the result of sentencing reforms and falling crime rates but also because of the Covid pandemic, which encouraged states and localities to accelerate decarceration. But the industry is far from dead.

Even before Covid, companies were taking steps to protect their revenue. Many contracts, for instance, include "lock-up quotas" that require states to guarantee a minimum level of payment, even if beds are empty. In a 2013 study of sixty-two prison contracts obtained by the nonprofit group In the Public Interest (ITPI), nearly two-thirds included occupancy guarantees or required payments (what ITPI called a "low-crime tax").[132] One contract, to run Ohio's Lake Erie Correctional Institution, involved a twenty-year term and a 90 percent quota, while three prisons in Arizona were under 100 percent occupancy guarantees. "These provisions guarantee prison companies a consistent and regular revenue stream, insulating them from ordinary business risks," said ITPI in its analysis. "The financial risks are borne by the public, while the private corporations are guaranteed profits from taxpayer dollars."[133]

CoreCivic and the GEO Group have also diversified their businesses to include electronic monitoring, private probation, and parole (so-called community corrections). They also run halfway houses and rehab centers. CoreCivic, for example, owns and operates twenty-six "residential reentry centers" with a total capacity of five thousand, according to its 2021 annual report.[134] In 2010, GEO Group purchased Cornell Corrections, which at the time held 16 percent of for-profit reentry center contracts with the federal Bureau of Prisons (BOP).[135] Before the merger, writes researcher Anne Lee, GEO had only two such contracts with BOP; after the merger, it had eleven.[136] In fiscal 2020, "reentry services" brought in 14.4 percent of the company's revenues—about $309 million. To signal this diversification, both companies have rebranded themselves with new corporate identities and "literally scrubbed the word 'corrections' from their names," writes Jamiles Lartey of the Marshall Project.[137] CCA became CoreCivic in 2016, when the company started buying up halfway houses and other real estate, according to Lartey, while GEO Group is on its way to becoming the nation's largest electronic monitoring company. (Lartey also points out that the company has changed how it describes the people it monitors—from "offenders tracked" to "individuals under community supervision," in an effort to soften its image.)

Both companies now also have a booming business housing immigrant detainees on behalf of Immigration and Customs Enforcement (ICE)—despite an executive order by President Joe Biden in 2021 to phase out the use of private prisons in the federal government.[138] Biden's order exempted ICE detention facilities—a move that many advocates condemned as a violation of Biden's campaign promise to end the use of private prisons.[139]

The ICE exemption has in fact become a highly lucrative loophole for prison companies to exploit, especially after President Donald Trump's "zero tolerance" policies on immigration resulted in an explosion of detainees.[140] As of 2021, private prisons held nearly 80 percent of immigrant detainees—making the federal government one of the industry's biggest current customers.[141] In fiscal 2021, for instance, CoreCivic earned 56 percent of its revenues in fiscal 2021 from federal agencies, according to its annual report, including $552.2 million from its contracts with ICE.[142] The GEO Group, meanwhile, earned $662 million in revenue from ICE in 2020—or 28 percent of that year's overall revenue.[143]

Detention capacity is growing. In 2022, GEO entered an agreement with Charlton County, Georgia, to nearly quadruple the size of the ICE detention center in Folkston, from 780 beds to 3,018, making it one of the nation's largest detention facilities. "If all of those beds were filled, the number of ICE detainees held there would total more than half of Folkston's population of about 4,400," the *Atlanta Journal-Constitution* reported.[144] In a 2021 investigation, CNN reported that at least one federal prison ostensibly shuttered because of Biden's executive order—the Moshannon Valley Correctional Center in Pennsylvania—reopened six months later as an immigration detention center.

CNN's investigation calculated that the Biden administration was spending about $3 million per day on payments to private prison companies—compared to $2.2 million per day during the Obama administration and $2.9 million per day while Trump was in office. These payments also include $255 million to GEO Group subsidiary BI Incorporated in 2021 for ankle monitors.[145] In keeping with the overall rise in electronic monitoring, BI has launched a "home curfew" program for immigrant detainees.[146]

Companies are evading Biden's order in other ways as well. In some instances, state and local governments are acting as middlemen—accepting federal money to house federal inmates but then outsourcing the work to prison companies.[147] In Youngstown, Ohio, for example, the U.S. Marshals Service reportedly signed a contract with the Mahoning County Sheriff's Office to maintain a facility run by CoreCivic. "The feds pay the county, then the county pays CoreCivic," CNN reported. "Even though the jail is still run by a private company, the company never signs a contract directly with the federal government—and avoids running afoul of Biden's order."[148] CoreCivic's stock reportedly jumped 7.4 percent after the *Wall Street Journal* detailed these "intergovernmental agreements" between the federal government and localities.[149]

As a result of their aggressiveness and creativity, private prison companies are faring just fine, despite declining crime rates and continued interest in sentencing reform. In fiscal 2022, CoreCivic reported total revenue of $1.84 billion, while GEO Group earned $2.4 billion.[150] Together, the two companies controlled about 150,000 beds in roughly 150 facilities, though it's beyond the prison walls where they're likely to see the most growth.

Prison Industries: Commissary Sales, Phone Calls, and the Exploitation of Inmate Labor

The prison economy supports myriad industries. Feeding prisoners means contracts for food and meal service. Prisons need furniture, linens, and clothing for inmates. Prisons also need to provide medical care, which means in-house clinics and medical staff. Every aspect of prison operations supports its own industry. Food service giant Aramark, for instance, is one of the prison economy's largest suppliers (in addition to the restaurants, convention centers, stadiums, and other industries it serves).[151]

The price of incarceration is highest for inmates and their families, who face a gauntlet of fines, fees, and extortionate charges in a system designed to strip them of their wealth as well as their dignity. "The cash register rings right after arrest," as David Dayen wrote in a piece for *Talking Points Memo.*[152]

In Maryland's prison system, for example, just staying in touch with an incarcerated loved one can be exorbitantly expensive. Families who want to send a care package must use the state's designated provider, Access Securepak.[153] This company boasts "the most comprehensive custom package program in the correctional industry" and is a subsidiary of the Keefe Group, one of the nation's largest suppliers of prison commissaries.[154] Another Keefe subsidiary, Access Corrections, manages inmate banking and commissary accounts.[155] (This is in addition to the ConnectNetwork account for phone services that inmates must also maintain.) According to the state of Maryland's website, friends and family can send money to an inmate's account for "as low as $3.95" by phone or $2.95 by internet.[156] There's also plenty of money to be made from the prisoners themselves, either through the sale of goods and services or as a source of inexpensive labor. For many inmates, prison is as expensive as it is demoralizing.

Phone Calls and Video Visits

Until a twenty-year-long national campaign by justice reform advocates prompted regulatory and congressional action, prison phone companies made hay on predatory pricing. Although the worst abuses have ended, it's still expensive for inmates to stay in touch with their families.

According to the Prison Policy Initiative, jails in some states once charged as much as $24.82 for an in-state, fifteen-minute call.[157] That was in addition to ancillary fees for "services" such as opening, funding, and maintaining a phone account, plus fees for money transfer services if an inmate's loved ones lacked a bank account to pay the bills. Companies like Western Union and Moneygram charged $10 to $12 to transfer $25 into an inmate's phone account.[158]

In 2014, the Federal Trade Commission (FTC) passed regulations capping the cost of an interstate call to $3.15 for fifteen minutes, and in 2021, it cracked down on abusive ancillary fees. The maximum money transfer fee, for instance, is now $5.95.[159] Congress also passed the Martha Wright-Reed Just and Reasonable Communications Act in early 2023, which clarified the FTC's authority to regulate the cost of *in-state* phone calls as well as video calls, although it will be at least a year or two until new rules take effect.

Nevertheless, the average jail still charged $3 for a fifteen-minute phone call as of the end of 2022, according to the Prison Policy Initiative, while the cost of a twenty-minute video call could be as much as $8 (not including "service" fees).[160] Moreover, many facilities are banning in-person visits, thereby forcing families to rely on expensive and often low-quality video visits if they want to communicate with incarcerated loved ones.[161] Some video visitation companies even require jails to ban in-person visits as part of their contracts.[162]

The lion's share of the revenue goes to just two companies, GTL (ViaPath, the company that services Maryland's prisons) and Securus (the same company dominating the electronic monitoring industry, as discussed in the preceding section).[163] In fact, reports the Prison Policy Initiative, these two companies controlled 79 percent percent of the jail and prison phone market as of 2022. Both companies are also major players in the video visitation industry, along with companies like Florida-based JPay, which also offers money transfer and other inmate financial services; and St. Louis–based HomeWAV, a smaller firm serving 89,000 inmates across 159 facilities as of 2023, according to its site.[164] (GTL's phone services, in contrast, reached 1.8 million inmates across 2,300 facilities.)[165]

Commissary Accounts, Education, Digital Content

Inmates spend at least $1.6 billion a year on commissary purchases, according to the Prison Policy Initiative, although the organization also cautions that the real amount is likely much higher.[166] In three states the group surveyed—Illinois, Massachusetts, and Washington—prisoners spent an average of $947 a year for basic necessities like toothpaste, shampoo, toilet paper, and feminine hygiene products.[167] Inmates in Massachusetts, for instance, collectively spent more than $215,000 on soap—a product that facilities are supposed to provide for free.

Inmates also spend significant amounts of money on food—in part, the Prison Policy Initiative argues—to supplement meager and nutritionally inadequate prison meals.[168] Unfortunately, most of what's for sale in prison commissaries and through affiliated care package services is junk food, like instant ramen, chips, and other ultra-processed items. The order form for Access Securepak's care packages, for instance, offers four kinds of sugary cereal—Cap'n Crunch, Apple Jacks, Froot Loops, and Frosted Flakes—along with seven kinds of cookies and a wide array of snacks typically found at highway rest stop vending machines: a five-ounce Brushy Creek "Salami Stick with Beef and Chicken" ($2.00); birthday cake–flavored Rice Krispie treats ($0.60, limit eight); Frito's chili cheese corn chips ($2.80); Chattanooga Strawberry Double Decker Moon Pie ($0.65, limit eight).[169] The "healthiest" item is canned tuna ($2.90), and the "vegetables" category includes just one item—Idahoan instant mashed potatoes (two-ounce packet for $0.85, limit seven).

"Digital" commissaries are also a growing market, with companies selling music, games, digital books, and educational materials. ConnectNetwork, for example, offers a "library of more than 12 million songs" inmates can access—provided they rent a ConnectNetwork tablet and open a ConnectNetwork "Debit Link" account.[170] The market for in-prison entertainment is apparently big enough that one company—Prison Music Kiosk—offers aspiring musicians a chance to sell their music to the prison market via its service. (Artists must, however, buy the company's how-to guide for $300.)[171]

Commissary sales are only part of the profit-making; companies also charge significant fees for money transfers into inmates' accounts. Prisons typically award one company a monopoly on money-transfer services, according to the CFPB, "leaving incarcerated people and their families without choice and with potentially higher costs."[172] At the Louisiana State Penitentiary, for instance, a $40 online transfer costs $6.50—or 16 percent.[173] In New York City, the comptroller's office determined that friends and family transferred more than $17.5 million into city jail accounts in fiscal 2018—but at a cost of more than $2 million in transfer fees.[174] Inmates in city and state facilities together spent more than $51 million in commissary purchases that year.

The CFPB further reports that companies often pay commissions to correctional institutions that are based on the number of transfers completed (thereby encouraging commissary sales). In one contract cited by the agency, a company promised to pay the state $1 for the first 1,000 transfers, $1.50 for up to 4,999 transfers, and then $2 for each transfer thereafter. Money transfers cost $4.95 to $12.95 per transaction, which meant "the state would receive 8 to 40 percent of each money transfer fee charged by the company."[175]

Many states are in fact fully complicit in gouging their prisoners. Nevada, for instance, reportedly marked up the prices in its prison commissaries by as much as 66 percent. In 2021, the state made more than $2.8 million in profits from prison commissary sales, according to the *Nevada Independent*.[176]

Room and Board and Health Care

States also charge fees for "room and board" and health care (in addition to all the court costs discussed earlier that inmates must also pay). All but two states have so-called pay to stay laws that authorize jails and prisons to charge inmates for the cost of their incarceration. Connecticut, for example, charged prisoners $249 a day, leading many to owe thousands of dollars to the state upon their release.[177] One Florida man was billed $54,750—$50 a day for his roughly three-year stay in state prison.[178]

Many states also impose co-pays for infirmary visits, which can result in insurmountably steep medical debts. Pre-pandemic, according to the Prison Policy Initiative, prisons typically charged $2 to $5 per appointment—which is expensive enough for an indigent inmate to forego needed care.[179] While most states suspended all co-pays during the height of the pandemic, those policies have since been rolled back, and some states—like Nevada—never suspended co-pays at all, even at the height of Covid.[180] A 2022 state audit concluded that Nevada's Department of Correction overcharged its inmates for medical services, including through co-pays that were more than twice the national average ($8 a visit versus $3.47).[181] The state also charged a frivolous "man down" fee of $50 for inmates needing help to get to the infirmary.[182]

Prison Labor

Adding insult to injury, governments and companies also profit from the value of prison labor, while inmates earn wages too low to afford their incarceration.

In New York City, for instance, the comptroller's office found that most jail jobs pay less than $0.40 per hour, "making it all but impossible for incarcerated individuals to support themselves within the correctional system economy."[183] "Skilled" workers, such as cooks and electricians, made between $0.32 and $0.39 per hour in 2018, while "unskilled" housekeepers earned even less. In 2018, the city's Department of Correction paid just $5.9 million in total wages—or about $660 per person that year.[184]

Nationally, prison wages have in fact fallen over the past two decades, according to the CFPB, from $0.93 *per day* in 2001 to $0.86 in 2017.[185] (This is in nominal, not real, dollars.) At this rate, the CFPB finds, "it would have taken a woman in a Colorado prison over two weeks to earn enough money for a box of tampons sold at the facility."[186]

At the same time, governments and companies profit mightily from prison labor, either by saving costs on personnel they don't have to hire (i.e., by using prison cooks and electricians instead of outside staff) or by selling prison-made products. States and cities often garnish what little that inmates do earn, not just to settle commissary accounts but also to pay for court fees, child support, and other debts.

Among the biggest beneficiaries of prison labor is the federal government, which runs the nation's largest prison industry program, UNICOR (formerly Federal Prison Industries). First established in 1934 with the goal of "rehabilitating" inmates and teaching them job skills, UNICOR is now a highly efficient revenue machine. In 2017, according to the agency's website, UNICOR made $483.8 million in net sales, with a stunning array of products ranging from air filters to vehicle parts, beef cattle, body armor, and T-shirts.[187] Inmates are paid between $0.23 and $1.15 an hour, half of which is "contributed" toward fines and fees, court debts, and other costs through the agency's Inmate Financial Responsibility Program.[188] In 2017, the government collected more than $941,000 from inmates' wages, according to the UNICOR website.

State and local jails and prisons can benefit from their inmate labor too, thanks to legislation passed by Congress in 1979 to encourage prison industries. Under the federal government's Prison Industry Enhancement (PIE) Certification Program, state and local facilities meeting certain standards are exempt from federal restrictions on the sale of prisoner-produced goods across state lines. Certified programs can also make bulk sales to the federal government above $10,000.[189] Among the nation's largest state-run prison program is Florida's Prison Rehabilitative Industries and Diversified Enterprises, Inc. (PRIDE), which advertises more than three thousand products for sale, including furniture, clothing, stationery, and even dentures.[190] In 2021, PRIDE generated $59.5 million in sales and paid its inmate workers between $0.20 and $0.95 an hour.[191]

The Price of Privatized Injustice

The companies that benefit from mass incarceration have made it their business to maintain the status quo. They depend on a steady supply of detainees whose wealth they can extract and whose labor they can exploit. The "benefits" they return to the public are minimal, while the damage they inflict is incalculable.

No evidence conclusively shows that privatized prisons save governments money. To the extent that savings did occur, it was at the expense of prison safety and services. Studies find, for instance, that private prisons cut costs "in such areas as rehabilitative services for inmates, lower guard salaries, fewer benefits and less training."[192] Nor did prison-building bring the economic development that companies promised. In fact, some research finds that private prisons actually *impede* job growth in some communities by depressing wages and diverting resources away from education and workforce development.[193] A 2013 study by researchers at Washington State University found that private prison employees earned a median salary of just $28,790—far below the median of $38,850 earned by state employees and the median of $50,830 paid to federal correctional workers.[194]

Private prisons' low wages, high turnover, and understaffing also contribute to safety concerns and violence. In a 2016 audit of federal prisons, the Department of Justice's Office of the Inspector General concluded that private prisons "incurred more safety and security incidents per capita" than comparable prisons run by the federal Bureau of Prisons.[195] Contract prisons, for instance, reported 4.2 assaults per month, compared to 1.6 in government-run institutions.[196] The private prisons also reported more contraband, more lockdowns, more inmate grievances, and more instances of inmates' being disciplined.

Research also shows that people who experience violence while incarcerated are more likely to recidivate than prisoners who don't. This could partly explain why some studies find higher recidivism rates among inmates in private facilities versus those in prisons that are government run. One study of more than 3,500 Minnesota prisoners released between 2007 and 2009, for instance, showed that "incarcerating a person in a private prison increased the chances of the person being rearrested by 13 percent, and increased the chances of the person being reconvicted by 22 percent."[197]

The unfairest burden, however, is the debt that dogs former inmates—for commercial bail or pretrial home detention; for commissary purchases, medical co-pays, and other expenses incurred while incarcerated; for court costs, fines, and fees; and for post-release probation and parole. These obligations make it impossible for individuals to rebuild their lives once they re-enter society. Many of these debts would also likely not exist were it not for a profit-driven industry determined to exploit a broken system for its own gain.

The exploitation of this literally "captive market," as the National Consumer Law Center puts it, continues even after individuals exit the prison gates.[198] People on parole or probation are often subject to fees for electronic monitoring—potentially by the same companies that might have monitored them pretrial (see the preceding chapter). Many individuals owe court costs, while others owe for debts racked up behind bars, such as for co-pays on health care. Nevada's Department of Corrections, for instance, reportedly saddled one former inmate with $100,000 in medical debt after his release.[199] Failure to pay can lead to reincarceration, which begins the debt-exploitation cycle anew.

Among those who've experienced the weight of these invisible shackles are the men I met at Baltimore's Civic Works Center for Sustainable Careers, a nonprofit that helps residents formerly involved with the justice system to learn new job skills and rebuild their lives. The organization runs multiple training programs for high-demand "green" careers, like solar panel installation, home weatherization, and brownfields remediation.[200] One of the city's most effective organizations, the center has placed more than nine hundred graduates since 2003, 80 percent of whom have stayed on the job for at least a year.[201]

One morning, pre-pandemic, I met half a dozen trainees enrolled in the center's weatherization program. They were learning how to blow insulation, seal up drafty windows, and maneuver in cramped attics. All the trainees I met were Black men, ranging in age from early twenties through their forties. All of them were returning citizens who'd paid their debts to society—they'd finished their time and been released.

But the government still laid claim to their lives for fines and fees they still owed; the debts followed these men post-release, crippling their prospects for economic self-sufficiency. They owed court debts, restitution, and even parking tickets.

One trainee, Arnold C., was facing $3,000 in impound fees after the police confiscated his car during a traffic stop. According to the Baltimore City Department of Transportation, towing charges are $130 to $140, plus an "initial storage charge" of $50, an "administrative fee" of $40, and impound charges of $15 a day. Arnold abandoned his car at the impound lot because he couldn't afford to get it out, but the city went after him anyway. He wanted to enter a payment plan but was told the minimum initial payment was $675. "I can't pay $675 to start," he said. "It's crazy because I have other things I have to try to accomplish. I'm trying to get my own place, so I've got to save this and save that. I still have to have gas money, and there's the phone bill and whole lot of little obstacles—these major fines end up hitting you on the head."[202]

When it comes to criminal justice, state and local governments can be just as rapacious as for-profit companies in their efforts to extract wealth from vulnerable constituents, often working in concert with private enterprise to generate fees and pursue debts. Governments like to call these "public–private partnerships," but the effect is more like a conspiracy to rob low-income citizens of their wealth.

The city of Baltimore, for instance, grants "medallions" to towing companies authorized to tow on behalf of police.[203] Cars can be towed for "blocking traffic," if they are "parked in violation of posted signs," "involved in police arrest/towing," "confirmed to be abandoned," or if the owner has just three or more unpaid parking tickets (what the city calls a "scofflaw vehicle").[204] Until 2022, towing companies were even allowed to collect fees from the victims of auto thefts whose cars were later recovered. Until this policy was instituted, the city apparently collected as much as $250,000 a year from victims of auto theft.[205]

To collect its debts, the city of Baltimore formerly relied on the Pennsylvania-based debt collection company Penn Credit Corporation. Residents who needed a payment plan to settle unpaid parking tickets had to negotiate directly with Penn Credit, according to the city's website. Drivers who owe more than $500 must pay 25 percent down and the remainder within twelve months, while debtors owing less than $500 must pay half down and the balance within six months.[206] (As of late 2023, the city no longer offers the option of a payment plan for delinquent parking tickets.)[207]

The state of Maryland likewise relies on a private debt collector, the Chicago-based debt collection agency Harris & Harris.[208] According to the state's request for proposal (RFP) soliciting bids for a debt collection contractor, state agencies refer more than $98 million a year in unpaid debts to private debt collectors, who keep 6.95 percent of the sums they collect.[209]

Many states further coerce debtors by suspending their driver's licenses (although advocacy campaigns in recent years have successfully ended these practices in several states).[210] In Baltimore, for instance, many of the trainees I met had lost their driver's licenses for failure to pay, which meant that transportation was yet another barrier for the men to overcome. Access to a reliable car is especially critical in Baltimore, where public transit is notoriously unreliable.

One man who'd lost his license, George H., said he had to leave the house at 5:30 every morning with his then-five-year-old son to make it to the center on time.[211] He took two buses and the subway to drop off his son at day care before getting to class at 7:45. George had owed about $700 in unpaid traffic fines when he left prison, which was why his license had been suspended. The staff at CivicWorks helped him work out a settlement—thirty-five hours of community service to erase $600 of tickets—which he had just completed. "It was a weight on my shoulders for years," he said.

Another trainee, Jimmy G., said his car insurance lapsed while he was in prison, subjecting him to fines that accrued into thousands of dollars by the time he was released. "Every month, I'm getting tickets and fines and parking violations while I'm incarcerated," he recalled. "I'm in jail for two years, and it's getting piled and piled and piled and then my car gets impounded, then sold, and all I come home to is a big fine." Uninsured cars are subject to a penalty of $150 after the first thirty days, according to the Maryland Motor Vehicle Administration, and then $7 a day thereafter.[212]

Even if he were to get another car and have his license reinstated, Jimmy said, he would be afraid to drive. "I'm on probation right now," he said. "One ticket, and I go back to prison. It all depends on the probation officer and how much they care. Some of them won't violate you if you get a driving ticket, but most of them will violate you and you gotta go back in."

"It's crazy that they think the solution to you not paying a fine is to make you pay more," said student Dominique J., who owed $2,000 before the center helped him get a court hearing to eliminate most of what he owed. "If I don't have it, I don't have it."

Until his license was restored, Dominique said he "drove dirty" for six months because he couldn't afford the fines he owed. "I got pulled over three times, and each time they would take my car and take it to the impound," he said. "It's a snowball effect. Once you get that first one, you get in a hole you can't get out of because they keep piling stuff on. What can you do? And I'm not about to stop driving my car, because I've got to earn money."

Not long after these conversations, in 2020, the Maryland assembly passed legislation ending driver's license suspensions for unpaid parking tickets and other minor traffic violations.[213] It did not, however, end suspensions for unpaid court costs, insurance violations, back taxes, or child support, which account for the bulk of the debts faced by the organization's clients.[214]

"To be honest, I haven't really seen much change in what it looks like for our students," case manager Sarah Kennedy told me in 2022. "That legislation passed, but I haven't felt the results of it very much on the ground."[215] Kennedy says as many as half of the center's clients still come in with licenses suspended due to unpaid fines and fees, and she spends about a fourth of her time negotiating with government agencies to get these penalties reduced and licenses reinstated. Where it can, the center helps subsidize the cost of paying off these amounts, although funds are limited. Driver's licenses should not be a "leverage point for debt collection," said the center's senior director, Eli Allen. "It's just so counterproductive for people trying to take a step forward in life."

But so long as there's money to be made, the "justice" system will be unwilling to loosen its grip on citizens and allow them to move on.

6

Sheltering Profits, Feeding Industry

In 2019, pre-pandemic, the federal government spent $51 billion on rental assistance and other programs to help low-income Americans afford housing.[1] That figure rose to $90 billion in 2021, with the addition of $33 billion in emergency rental assistance, plus other aid, for people at risk of eviction during the Covid-induced recession.[2] But despite all this spending, the national shortage of affordable housing is persistent and severe, and landlords hold the leverage. Many landlords make a handsome living from the federal government's Housing Choice Voucher program (formerly "Section 8" rental assistance), while tenants scramble for scarce vouchers and even scarcer available homes. Developers enjoy generous tax credits and subsidies for economic development.

Current federal housing policy aims to incentivize the private-sector development of affordable housing (rather than the government trying to build its own). Though these subsidies result in housing that wouldn't otherwise exist, they also create complexity, inefficiency, and fat profits for investors and middlemen. The federal government's largest tax incentive program—the Low-Income Housing Tax Credit (LIHTC)—produces about 110,000 affordable units per year, but at an annual cost of more than $10 billion.[3]

Private actors must, of course, supply basic goods like food and housing. Governments can't run grocery stores or build apartments (as the failure of public housing can attest). Meanwhile, government antipoverty programs are essentially subsidizing some of the biggest companies in America. Given their own reliance on government largesse, these companies owe it to low-income Americans to deliver the best products they can, not simply maximize their own revenues.

Building Revenues

Lyon Homes is a shabby complex of red brick townhouses and garden apartments in the Baltimore suburb of Dundalk, Maryland. Built in 1941, the complex offers 242 units, ranging from one-bedroom apartments to three-bedroom townhomes. Photos posted on apartments.com show bare gray walls and hardwood floors, Formica countertops, and dark brown particleboard cabinets.[4] But the rent here is just $760 for a one-bedroom apartment and $1,100 for a three-bedroom townhouse, and the landlords accept vouchers for federal rental assistance through the Housing Choice Voucher program (what used to be called Section 8). As a result, units are in high demand. The complex had no vacancies as of spring 2023; "WE CURRENTLY HAVE A 12-MONTH WAITLIST," the listing boasted.

Baltimore spends more than $260 million a year on affordable housing, according to the Baltimore City Department of Housing and Community Development.[5] This includes $156 million on rental vouchers to subsidize tenants' rent; $25 million on the Low Income Housing Tax Credit to encourage new affordable housing development; nearly $33 million on repairs and improvements, plus a variety of smaller grants and subsidies.

Yet the city's affordable housing shortage is still severe. More than 20 percent of Baltimore households spend at least half their income on housing, the department reports, and more than three thousand people are homeless.[6] Residents might spend years on the waitlist for a rental assistance voucher, or years to land a unit like the ones at Lyon Homes.

According to the Baltimore County Housing Authority's website, the waitlist at Lyon Homes last opened in 2021, and only for households with a disabled member. In spring 2023, just three affordable housing complexes were adding potential tenants to their waitlists—but applicants had to be either sixty-two and older or have a disability. All other waitlists were closed, including the waitlist for rental assistance vouchers.[7] When that list opened for just nine days at the end of October 2014, 10,000 people applied in the first few hours, and 58,000 applied in the first few days, according to Georgetown University researcher and author Eva Rosen in her book, *The Voucher Promise*.[8]

It's the same story across the country, where soaring housing costs have pushed the demand for rental assistance far beyond what's available. In 2019, roughly 4.5 million households received federal help with their rent, including about 2.1 million households participating in the Housing Choice Voucher program.[9] Yet the same year, more than 7.7 million households were living under what the government defines as "worst case housing needs." These are households with incomes at or below 50 percent of the area median who receive *no* government housing assistance and who spend more than half of their income on rent, live in "severely inadequate conditions," or both.[10]

In 2019, according to government data, just 23.6 percent of households eligible for federal housing assistance actually received it.[11] Families wait an average of two and a half years for a rental voucher, according to the Center on Budget and Policy Priorities, and many families wait as long as eight years, experiencing homelessness, eviction, and financial hardship in the meantime.[12] Many waitlists, like the ones in Baltimore, aren't accepting new applicants at all. A 2016 survey by the National Low Income Housing Coalition found that 53 percent of voucher waitlists nationwide were closed to newcomers, and nearly two-thirds of these had been closed for more than a year.[13] In Prince George's County, Maryland, for instance, the housing authority's website indicated (as of November 2023) that the last waitlist application period for the

Housing Choice Voucher program was October 5 through October 16—in *2015*.[14]

These extreme shortages of both vouchers and housing mean a lopsided market where low-income tenants have few options for finding a home, even if they're lucky enough to get federal help. Landlords, meanwhile, hold the power—along with plentiful opportunities to profit.

The Promise of Vouchers: "Funding the People"

With an annual price tag of about $19 billion, the Housing Choice Voucher program is the nation's largest rental assistance program.[15] It began as a pilot in the early 1970s, as the Experimental Housing Allowance Program under President Richard Nixon. After early research showed promising results, Congress in 1983 added a federal voucher program to Section 8 of the Housing Act of 1937 (hence the origin of "Section 8 vouchers").[16] In 1998, Congress passed the Quality Housing and Work Responsibility Act, which created the modern Housing Choice Voucher program and made it the federal government's principal form of assistance to low-income renters.[17]

Under the current structure, the federal government allocates vouchers to local public housing authorities, which administer the program day to day. Seventy-five percent of vouchers must go to households with "extremely low incomes"—households with incomes up to the poverty line or 30 percent of the local median income, whichever is higher.[18] In 2019, according to HUD, the median income among voucher households was just $13,450.[19] Voucher holders pay 30 percent of their monthly income toward rent, while the subsidy picks up the rest (up to a limit). A senior receiving $800 a month in Social Security, for instance, would pay $240 for a one-bedroom at Baltimore's Lyon Homes, while the voucher would cover the remainder of the $760 rent.

The architect of the voucher program was Malcolm ("Mike") Peabody, who served under Nixon as deputy assistant secretary for equal opportunity in the Department of Housing and Urban

Development (HUD). Before he pitched a federal pilot to Nixon, he had already pioneered it in Massachusetts while working for his brother, then-Governor Endicott Peabody. (The Peabodys were the quintessential Boston Brahmins—their father was an Episcopal bishop, their grandfather was the founder of the exclusive Groton School, and another ancestor was Massachusetts colonial governor John Endecott.)[20]

Housing vouchers, Malcolm Peabody argued, solved the problems then plaguing traditional public housing: crime, concentrated poverty, and segregation. "The public housing projects were getting bigger and bigger and bigger, and they were becoming just nests of crime," Peabody told me in a 2016 interview.[21]

By the 1970s, infamous "projects" included California's Jordan Downs Development, epicenter of the Watts Rebellion in 1965; and Chicago's Cabrini Green, a seventy-acre development press accounts described as a "war zone."[22] In 1972, the government demolished the troubled Pruitt-Igoe projects in St. Louis, designed by Minoru Yamasaki, a Japanese American architect who would later design the World Trade Center towers.[23] A thirty-three-building complex with more than 2,800 units, Pruitt-Igoe became a symbol of urban dysfunction, governmental incompetence, and the failure of "urban renewal." Besides the rampant crime—including drug dealing, prostitution, gang activity, and murder— "heaters, toilets, garbage incinerators and electricity all malfunctioned, and at one point the faulty plumbing let loose floods of raw sewage through the hallways," *The Guardian* reported in a 2015 retrospective.[24]

Vouchers, Peabody argued, rescued families from that kind of misery. They took away the government's power to dictate where people lived and under what conditions and gave tenants that control instead. Vouchers, he told me, "put the money at the bottom with the people rather than with the bureaucrats at the top." As he would write in a 1972 article for the *Washington Monthly*, "funding the people" would fulfill "the deepest emotional need of the poor today—the need to have freedom of choice, to have the freedom to determine the course of their own lives."[25]

Moving to Opportunity?

That belief in tenant self-determination still animates the Housing Choice Voucher program and accounts for its continued support among conservatives as well as liberals. For conservatives, vouchers embody a combination of two values held dear: market incentives and personal responsibility. For liberals, vouchers represent a promising and powerful mechanism for desegregating communities, breaking up concentrated poverty, and giving more low-income Americans the benefit of positive "neighborhood effects."[26]

Perhaps the most famous studies about the program's potential benefits involve the Moving to Opportunity (MTO) project, a ten-year experiment begun in 1994 that gave 4,600 low-income families a chance to move out of high-poverty areas (where more than 30 percent of households live below the poverty line) through vouchers. Children who moved to low-poverty neighborhoods (where the poverty rate is under 10 percent) were more likely to go to college and earn more money, studies concluded, and adults reported better mental and physical health.[27]

In reality, however, vouchers have underperformed their potential, largely because tenants haven't had anywhere near the wealth of choices the program envisioned. For one thing, the shortage of affordable housing is so severe that many voucher holders can't find a unit to use their benefits. Tenants have sixty days from the receipt of their voucher to find housing or risk having it "expire." According to some studies, as many as 20 percent of voucher holders don't succeed in finding housing.[28] In a 2021 report, HUD's inspector general (IG) found that 62 percent of local public housing authorities had unused voucher capacity—amounting to a total of about 80,000 vouchers nationwide.[29] The IG's office blamed the lack of inventory as one reason for this result.[30]

When tenants do find housing, they often don't escape neighborhood poverty. While voucher recipients are indeed less likely to live in high-poverty neighborhoods, "many voucher holders have not been able to find places to rent in mixed-income neighborhoods, the kind of move shown to have long-term positive impacts on health and economic well-being," writes Georgetown's Eva Rosen. Instead, she writes, "a great many voucher holders are concentrating in poor neighborhoods."[31] According to the Center on Budget and Policy Priorities, just 14 percent of families with children participating in the voucher program live in low-poverty neighborhoods.[32] One Urban Institute study of Chicago voucher tenants found that 55 percent lived in "mid- to high-poverty neighborhoods," and 63 percent lived in neighborhoods that were more than 90 percent Black.[33]

An especially damaging consequence of this lack of mobility is lack of access to decent schools. In one troubling study by the Poverty and Race Research Action Council (PRRAC), researchers found that while voucher holders lived near better schools than people in public housing, their neighborhood schools were still typically *worse* than the majority of schools in their state, including schools that primarily serve children in poverty.[34] On average, voucher holders with children lived near elementary schools ranked in the 26th percentile statewide (or roughly the bottom quarter).

In Dundalk, Maryland, where the Lyon Homes complex is located, the nearest schools are Dundalk Elementary and Dundalk High. According to the state's "report card," Dundalk Elementary ranked in the 10th percentile for Maryland schools in 2021–2022, while Dundalk High ranked in the 11th.[35] Fewer than 5 *percent* of Dundalk High students scored "proficient" or higher on the state's standardized math test that year, while 34.7 percent were considered proficient in English.

Section 8 Landlords

As with Medicaid, where the lack of high-quality providers is a persistent challenge, one of the housing voucher program's biggest problems is on the supply side too—with landlords unwilling to accept subsidized tenants. This is why voucher tenants tend to concentrate in particular neighborhoods, in units managed by the subset of landlords who accept vouchers and, in many cases, have made it their business.

Some landlords are reluctant to deal with the bureaucracy of administering vouchers, and others don't want the hassle of inspections to qualify for the program. Others believe voucher payments are too low, compared to what they can get on the open market (this is often not true).[36] But many landlords also won't accept voucher tenants based on racist and classist stereotypes and preconceptions about their character and behavior; some engage in blatant discrimination. In one 2018 study, researchers watched how landlords interacted with prospective tenants:

> Landlords can list specific tools that they use to screen tenants such as criminal background, residential history, and credit checks, but most admit that finding the right tenant comes down to a gut feeling. . . . They based their opinion of a prospective tenant on how she dressed for the interview, whether or not she returned phone calls in a timely manner, how she parented her children, and the types of questions she asked (or did not ask) about the unit. In an extreme example, one landlord told us about his "pet" theory: "The larger the dog, the worse the credit . . . Because if you think about it, anyone who has a large dog in a small apartment is irresponsible anyway."[37]

In three of five cities where researchers called landlords to gauge their willingness to accept vouchers, the denial rate was 67 percent or higher (with the highest rates of denial among landlords in low-poverty neighborhoods). In two cities where local regulations forbade discrimination against voucher tenants, the denial rate was lower—31 percent.[38]

As of the end of 2022, sixteen states, the District of Columbia, and 106 localities had passed so-called source-of-income laws, which prohibit landlords from discriminating against tenants based on their source of income (such as vouchers).[39] Jurisdictions that have passed such laws, says the Urban Institute, have seen an increase in the share of voucher recipients living in lower-poverty, less segregated neighborhoods.[40] Opponents, however, have argued that these laws force landlords to participate in a program that's supposed to be voluntary.[41] Some states—like Texas—have even passed legislation banning antidiscrimination ordinances, causing an affordable housing crisis in some areas. As many as one in four voucher holders can't find housing in Houston, according to the *Texas Tribune*, and many others are "steered" toward low-quality housing in high-poverty neighborhoods.[42]

Many landlords' reluctance to rent to voucher holders has, of course, prompted others to smell a profitable business opportunity, including the development of rental portfolios exclusively catering to voucher tenants. As Georgetown's Rosen points out, these landlords have learned that voucher payments provide a steady source of income that their otherwise financially precarious tenants may not be able to offer.

In Baltimore, Rosen writes, landlords even compete for tenants, offering "move-in incentives like new appliances, or even cash bonuses." One landlord she interviewed "was so desperate for the reliability of voucher tenants that he waited outside the voucher office to catch new recipients on their way out the door, offering them a ride up to see his vacant property in Park Heights [a struggling neighborhood in Baltimore]."[43]

Many landlords, however, can get away with substandard properties and no perks. Although the Housing Choice Voucher program requires units to pass routine quality inspections, standards are only as high as the ability of the local public housing authority to enforce them. And given the high demand for a limited supply of affordable housing, landlords have little incentive to do more than the bare minimum.

The results can be horrific when oversight is poor. In Washington, DC, for instance, a 2023 investigation by the *Washington Post* discovered that the DC Housing Authority was overpaying landlords "by millions of dollars every year."[44] In one case cited by the

Post, the city was paying $2,467 a month on behalf of a seventy-three-year-old tenant whose unit had no electricity—and in a neighborhood where the market rent was $1,613. At the same time, the paper reported, the city's waitlist for rental vouchers was thirty thousand people long, meaning that the city's overpayments were preventing many households from getting access to housing aid.

Numerous YouTube instructional videos, real estate investment how-to guides, and get-rich-quick gurus extol the virtues of investing in voucher-subsidized housing. Profits accrue by investing as little as possible while maximizing the stream of government revenue.

One such advocate is Peter Harris, a self-styled "Commercial Real Estate Coach, Author and Investor" whose website touts an audio program he recorded with Donald Trump: "Three Master Secrets of Real Estate Success."[45] (According to Amazon, the CD was published by Trump University Press in 2006 and out of print as of 2023.)[46] A former Silicon Valley engineer, according to his "Official Site," Harris is also the author of the more legit *Commercial Real Estate Investing for Dummies*.[47] In addition to his books and tutorials, Harris accepts applications for "Protegés"—co-investors with whom he promises to "share in the deal profits together."[48]

In a 2017 blog post, Harris echoes what Rosen's interviewees had discovered—that landlords can avoid many of the disadvantages of renting to lower-income tenants by investing in "Section 8."[49] Among the perks Harris cites are "On Time and Convenient Payments" ("You will get your rents specifically from the HUD each and every month as a check or direct deposit."); "Free Access to a Large Amount of Potential Tenants" ("There is a long verified wait list of Section 8 tenants accessible online you can use to discover potential tenants in your city."); "Higher Rental Rates" ("The rent you can get from a Section 8 tenant surpasses what you could get with a regular rental that is not in the best neighborhood."); and "Short Vacancies" ("Most urban areas have a long list of Section 8 members with vouchers, who are looking for housing.")

In addition, Harris writes, Section 8 landlords get "Security

From Tenant Financial Hardships" because the government pays the rent. In his blog post, he relates the story of a tenant, Marcy, "who disappeared on me for a considerable length of time." Had she not been on Section 8, "she no doubt would have been removed because of non-installment of her rent," he writes, but because of her voucher, "I didn't need to stress."[50]

Harris finishes out his post with "Investing Tips" for fellow potential voucher tenant landlords. "Get rid of all ceiling fans, screen doors, garbage disposals, and storage areas," he advises. "Having these things won't get you higher rents, yet they will cost you in maintenance. They are not necessities, and Section 8 does not mind whether you have them or not, so I would simply eliminate them."

He also describes a point system for screening out potentially troublesome lessees and counsels landlords to "train" their voucher tenants:

> Train your tenant, don't give them a chance to train you. Section 8 tenants are somewhat similar to youngsters. You should give structure and implement the standards, or you will wind up with unpleasant encounters. Continuously be proficient and don't get candidly involved or fall into any psychological distractions. You are the parent and they are the youngsters, so you should give them rules to abide by.[51]

The LIHTC: Boon or Boondoggle?

Unless and until the federal government's housing voucher program solves the problem of supply, landlords like Harris will continue to dominate the low-income rental market.

But, if anything, the shortage of quality affordable housing is likely to worsen in the short term. Over the next decade, nearly half a million units built over the last thirty years with the help of the nation's largest subsidy for affordable housing development—the federal Low Income Housing Tax Credit (LIHTC)—will be free of restrictions requiring their "affordability." Under the terms of the credit, first enacted in 1986, developers can take advantage of subsidies so long as a designated portion of the units they build are "affordable" for at least fifteen years, and in many cases, thirty.[52] While the credit worked to bring in a rush of new affordable housing development in its early years during the late 1980s and early 1990s, the market now faces a "thirty-year problem" as these affordability restrictions end, and a flood of units potentially leave the market.

For apartments located in desirable areas, the expiration of mandates will mean landlords can command market-rate rents, pricing out prior tenants and reducing the overall stock of affordable housing. About 9 percent of these expiring units are in areas that rank "high or very high in both desirability and opportunity," according to a joint study by the National Low Income Housing Coalition (NLIHC) and the Public and Affordable Housing Research Corporation, and most are held by for-profit developers. Rents for these units are likely to rise dramatically. Another 13 percent of units are in areas that rank "high or very high in opportunity"—meaning that they're ripe for gentrification.[53] All told, the study calculates, 52,923 units in high- or very-high-desirability neighborhoods with for-profit owners will have lost their affordability restrictions by 2029.[54]

Although the LIHTC is arguably still the nation's most "effective" affordable housing development program, as well as its largest, it's been an expensive and complex thirty-year experiment that's also spawned an industry aimed at profiting from the program's inefficiency.

Complex Market "Incentives"

In the same way that tax credits for solar panels and windmills promote green energy production, the LIHTC encourages affordable housing development by making its construction more financially attractive for builders. The credit doesn't subsidize production directly but instead relies on a more complex mechanism to create the right "market incentives."

The LIHTC is not administered by HUD, but by the IRS, which allocates a set amount of tax credits to each state depending on its population. In 2022, for instance, Alabama received an LIHTC allocation of $12.8 billion, while California's was $105 billion.[55] States in turn allocate credits to developers competing to get their projects subsidized. To qualify for the credit, developers must agree to ensure that a specified portion of a project's units will be "affordable" for at least fifteen years (or thirty years for projects begun after 1990).[56]

Here's where even more complexity comes in. The LIHTC is an offset for tax liabilities, which developers typically don't have before a project is built because there aren't yet rents coming in. So developers "sell" their credits to investors in exchange for cash to build their proposed developments. Often, these investors are banks, which also get credit under the Community Reinvestment Act (CRA) for participating in LIHTC projects.[57]

Because the law does not permit the actual sale of tax credits, developers and investors enter "partnership" agreements to cement their transactions.[58] In theory, these arrangements ensure that projects go through because investors don't want to lose the value of the tax credits they've "bought" (or lose credit under the CRA) if a developer goes under or construction doesn't finish.

LIHTC's cheerleaders argue this de facto "oversight" is one reason the program is effective—and proof of how market mechanisms can help achieve important goals in social policy. And indeed, this structure has worked well enough to produce more than 3.5 million units of "affordable" housing since 1987.[59]

But it's still potentially more a boondoggle for developers than a boon for low-income tenants.

In a 2017 joint investigation, NPR and PBS *Frontline* discovered that despite a 66 percent increase in federal spending, the LIHTC was producing far fewer units than it did twenty years ago—77,000 units in 1997 versus 59,000 units in 2014.[60] (In fiscal 2022, the program cost $10.4 billion, according to the Joint Committee on Taxation.[61]) Industry officials told NPR/*Frontline* that rising construction costs were to blame for the program's rising expenditures and lower returns, but it's impossible to tell if those claims are true, given the poor quality of state oversight. In a 2018 audit, the U.S. Government Accountability Office (GAO) cited "weaknesses in data quality" that made it difficult to assess the program's cost-effectiveness.[62] For example, the GAO reported, "few agencies have requirements to help guard against misrepresentation of contractor costs (a known fraud risk)."[63]

The complexity of the LIHTC creates plenty of opportunities for a variety of players to take their cut. "Syndicators," for instance, act as middlemen between developers and investors, and charge significant fees for their services. Syndicators collected more than $300 million in fees in 2016, according to the NPR/*Frontline* investigation.[64]

The true amount could be much higher. The 2018 GAO audit found that housing agencies "did not capture the full extent" of the fees paid to syndicators, although the IRS requires this data to be collected.[65] Of the twelve agencies the GAO examined, *none* collected data on total syndication costs, even though these fees potentially amounted to between 2 percent and 8 percent of the amount invested.[66] ("For perspective," reported the GAO, the median investment in its analysis was $7.6 million, which would mean a syndication fee of $608,000 at 8 percent.)[67] Whatever the fees are, they're high enough to support a multitude of well-heeled firms. According to *Multifamily Executive*'s list of 2021's "Top 10 Syndicators," the nation's biggest LIHTC syndicator is Boston Financial Investment Management, which reported $15 billion of investments under management.[68]

Developers charge hefty fees for their work as well, which also often amount to millions of dollars per transaction. In Florida, for instance, developer fees total about 16 percent of development costs—or a median of $2.1 million per project, according to the GAO.[69] (The National Council of State Housing Agencies recommends a maximum developer fee of 15 percent, though states are free to set their own standards.)[70]

The sum total of these fees can dramatically bring down the program's efficiency. A 2014 state audit of Missouri's LIHTC program found that just 42 cents of every tax-credit dollar "actually goes toward the construction of low income housing."[71] The remainder, said state auditors, was going to investors, syndicators, or back to the federal government as taxes.[72] Moreover, the audit found, the program generated only 8 cents in state revenue for every dollar spent and created just sixty-three new full-time jobs in the fiscal year examined. Since spending on the credit totaled $144 million that year, the program cost the state "approximately $61,000 per unit of housing or $2.3 million per job."[73]

On top of it all, the credit itself is extraordinarily generous, meaning that investors don't need much prodding to participate in the LIHTC. The program offers two levels of credits—a 4 percent credit for those that use tax-exempt bonds, and a 9 percent credit for those that don't. Most projects opt for the 9 percent credit, which effectively amounts to a 70 percent subsidy.[74] Here's how that works in practice, as Chris Edwards and Vanessa Brown Calder write in a critique of the credit for the Cato Institute:

> Consider a housing project that costs $10 million to build and receives the 9 percent credit. Investors would get tax credits of $900,000 a year for 10 years, totaling $9 million. Those credits would be worth about $7 million on a present-value basis, or about 70 percent of construction costs. The government essentially covers 70 percent of the costs of the project by allowing the investors to reduce their income taxes by a present value of $7 million.[75]

Developers in particular profit handsomely, argues American University professor Brandon M. Weiss, because they're using someone else's money, not their own, to finance their projects. "Rarely does the developer contribute any significant equity during construction to cover development costs," Weiss writes in the *Harvard*

Law & Policy Review. "In some cases, it is possible for a developer to finance a LIHTC project using little to none of its own capital, hence yielding close to infinite returns."[76]

All these costs and inefficiency might be tolerable if the evidence clearly showed how the LIHTC benefits low-income tenants. But again, it's difficult to gauge just how effective the LIHTC has been because there isn't enough reliable data to judge. The decentralized administration of the credit through the states has meant very little national-level, comprehensive scrutiny. It wasn't until 1996—nearly ten years after the credit's enactment—that the government even created a national database of LIHTC projects.[77]

A 2020 HUD report on the demographics of LIHTC tenants in 2017 complained of substantial data gaps, with many states and housing authorities "unable to submit information for all active properties."[78] Among the agencies that submitted no information, for instance, was New York City's Department of Housing Preservation and Development.[79] Many states didn't report data on the race or ethnicity of LIHTC tenants, and household income information was also woefully incomplete.[80] Oregon and Tennessee, for instance, reported no income data at all.[81]

This absence of data makes it impossible to know if the LIHTC is reaching underserved minority communities—or even if LIHTC properties are in fact "affordable" as required by the law. But what spotty evidence there is shows the program is flawed.

Like the Housing Choice Voucher program, the LIHTC isn't helping to break up concentrated poverty—in fact, it might be adding to it. One 2020 study concluded that "LIHTC units have been spatially clustered in socioeconomically disadvantaged neighborhoods over time" and that LIHTC developments tend "to increase the concentration of households that have lower income than the average household income" within a particular area.[82] Likewise, an earlier study in 2011 found that LIHTC units tend to be "highly clustered" in urban areas with high levels of poverty and racial segregation.[83] Why this happens is that the LIHTC program "does not provide any incentives to developers to generate mixed-income housing," as University of Kansas professor Kirk McClure testified to the Senate Finance Committee in 2017.[84]

At the same time, paradoxically, LIHTC units aren't actually "affordable" for many low-income households, and many LIHTC tenants are still severely rent-burdened.

Unlike the housing voucher program, where the maximum rent a tenant pays is equal to 30 percent of their income, the maximum rent on an LIHTC unit is 30 percent of an *area's* median income.[85] That means in places with high median incomes, rents can be exorbitant for many low-income residents. One national sample of LIHTC households found that nearly 40 percent of tenants with incomes less than half the area median were "severely cost-burdened, devoting more than half of their income to housing costs."[86] About 70 percent of the poorest LIHTC households—those with incomes under 30 percent of the area median—relied on additional assistance, such as vouchers, to help them pay the rent. (And, incidentally, this means a second source of subsidies for landlords.)

The looming expiration of affordability requirements will only add to tenants' burdens while padding developers' profits. As American University's Brandon Weiss writes, "These backend profits essentially amount to a massive windfall for private owners."[87] It's a statement that could be true of the LIHTC as a whole.

SNAPping Up Profits

The federal government spends enormous sums to combat hunger and food insecurity. In 2022, the federal government spent $183 billion on food and nutrition assistance, including the Supplemental Nutrition Assistance Program (SNAP, formerly "food stamps"), the Special Supplemental Nutrition Program for Women, Infants and Children (WIC), as well as emergency pandemic assistance.[88] The government also spends about $14 billion annually providing free and reduced-price meals through the National School Lunch Program.[89]

These programs are a lifeline for millions of children who would otherwise go hungry. But they also prop up big-box retailers, dollar stores, and food service conglomerates as much as they help ordinary households. Food stamp sales account for about 10 percent of dollar store revenues, according to one analysis, while Walmart reportedly takes in 18 percent of all food stamp purchases, according to *Slate*.[90] These companies' profits also potentially come at the expense of consumers' nutrition and health. Dollar stores in low-income areas often fail to stock fresh produce, instead offering low-quality, low-nutrition processed foods.[91] Big food companies churn out mass-manufactured school lunches high in fat and sodium (though they may technically meet the federal government's nutritional guidelines).

During the worst of the coronavirus pandemic, in 2020 and 2021, Congress dramatically expanded the Supplemental Nutrition Assistance Program (SNAP) to help American households cope with the economic shock of lockdown.[92]

The emergency aid increased the maximum benefit by about $90 per person on average—enough to keep 4.2 million Americans above the poverty line in the last quarter of 2021, according to the Center on Budget and Policy Priorities.[93] In fiscal 2021, federal spending on SNAP totaled a historic high of $111 billion, nearly double the amount spent pre-pandemic, in fiscal 2019.[94]

These additional benefits expired in March 2023, after Covid was declared to be no longer an emergency. But with inflation still running high and food prices spiking, the impact of these benefit cuts was immediate. At the Arlington, Virginia, food bank where I volunteer, the line for distributions stretched down the block, and the first families were in line an hour before the doors opened. The *Washington Post* reported a mile-long line at one Kentucky food pantry, where some families waited nine hours for a few bags of desperately needed groceries.[95]

Households weren't the only ones to take a hit when pandemic SNAP benefits ended. The *Wall Street Journal* reported that discount supermarkets and dollar stores expected a major slide in 2023 revenues, according to industry analyses.[96] Among the chains with the "highest exposure to SNAP dollars" were discounters like Grocery Outlet, along with Walmart, Dollar General, Family Dollar, Kroger, and BJ's Wholesale Club.[97] According to a Goldman Sachs analysis the *Journal* cited, SNAP accounted for as much as 15 percent of Grocery Outlet's 2021 sales and more than 10 percent of revenue for Walmart and other "high exposure" chains. In lower-income areas, the *Journal* reported, SNAP paid for as much as 20 percent of all grocery sales.[98]

SNAP may well be among the largest hidden federal subsidies enjoyed by American companies. Though benefits nominally go to low-income families, 100 percent of those dollars pass through to grocery stores, dollar stores, convenience stores, and other retailers. Although the government doesn't release data on the specific outlets where SNAP benefits go (potentially an impossible task, given the volume of transactions), a 2012 investigation by public health attorney and author Michele Simon uncovered eye-popping instances of how much individual retailers gain. In one year, for instance, "nine Walmart Supercenters in Massachusetts together received more than $33 million in SNAP dollars—over four times the SNAP money spent at farmers markets nationwide," Simon reported.[99] In Oklahoma, Simon wrote, Walmart stores captured about half of the nearly $1 billion spent on SNAP benefits over two years.

Like federal rental assistance, SNAP is also essentially a voucher program (except the benefits are spent on food). And like the Housing Choice Voucher program, SNAP is intended to give recipients the freedom to choose where to spend their benefit. But as with housing, the choices available to low-income consumers can be severely limited and substandard. Supermarkets are scarce in many low-income neighborhoods, as is fresh produce. Though the USDA now approves farmers markets to accept SNAP benefits, the overwhelming majority still do not.[100] As a result, too many SNAP dollars are flowing to businesses that are cementing disparities in access to healthy food by low-income consumers. It's a stunning example of how even the simplest of benefits for the most basic of necessities—nutrition assistance for poor families—can be distorted by private actors seeking profit.

Given the tens of billions of dollars it spends on SNAP every year, the federal government should have enormous leverage to ensure that beneficiaries have adequate access to healthy food. And given the tens of billions in revenue that major retailers, grocery chains, and processed food makers collect from SNAP annually, the quality of the products they offer to low-income consumers deserves greater scrutiny.

To its credit, Walmart offers a wide selection of fresh produce in its grocery departments. Walmart is, in fact, the nation's largest grocer, with grocery sales of $208 billion in 2021.[101] But in many parts of America, especially in rural areas, the closest food store increasingly isn't a Walmart but a discount chain like Dollar Tree or Dollar General, which often offers no fresh food at all.

That's the case in Craigsville, Virginia, a tiny town of about nine hundred people three and a half hours southwest of Washington, DC.[102] Three miles away is the Augusta Correctional Center, a medium-security state prison that's one of the town's principal employers. In 2021, 48 percent of residents were employed, according to Census Bureau data, and the poverty rate was 30 percent.[103] The nearest Walmart is twenty-five miles away in Staunton, Virginia, but there's a Dollar General on State Road 42—Craig Street—which runs through the heart of town. Aside from a couple gas stations, it's the town's only significant retail store.

Providing that convenience and proximity is what's propelled the chain's success against big retailers like Walmart. The company describes itself as a "small-box" store that offers "most necessities, such as basic packaged and refrigerated or frozen food and dairy products, cleaning supplies, paper products, health and beauty care items, . . . basic apparel, housewares, hardware and automotive supplies, among others," according to its 2022 annual report.[104] Its goal is to offer just enough basics that a fifty-mile round trip to Walmart becomes unnecessary—a strategy that's been wildly successful. As of fall 2023, the chain operated more than nineteen thousand stores across the country, making it the nation's largest retailer by store count.[105] (Dollar General stores, in fact, significantly outnumber Walmarts, of which there were 4,616 in 2023.[106] Dollar General even outpaces McDonald's by about five thousand outlets.)[107]

Dollar General also ranked twelfth among the nation's largest grocers in fiscal 2021, ahead of well-known chains like Aldi and Trader Joe's, according to industry publication *Supermarket News*.[108] Once again, its strategy has been to fill in the gaps traditional grocers have left by colonizing what would otherwise be "food deserts" in low-income urban and rural areas. "We generally locate our stores and plan our merchandise selections to best serve the needs of our core customers, the low and fixed income households often underserved by other retailers (including grocers)," acknowledges the company's annual rseport.[109]

Nearly 24 million Americans live in low-income areas "that are further than 1 mile from a large grocery store or supermarket," according to the federal government's Healthy People 2030 project.[110] Likewise, a 2012 government study identified 1,519 "Limited Supermarket Access" areas nationwide, where residents "must travel significantly farther to reach a supermarket" compared to residents in well-served areas.[111] Predominantly Black and Hispanic neighborhoods are much less likely to have a supermarket than neighborhoods that are predominantly white;[112] conversely, Black Americans are more than twice as likely to live in limited supermarket access areas than whites.[113] Lack of access to healthy food, in turn, worsens racial and economic disparities in health outcomes, such as higher rates of obesity and diabetes, cardiovascular disease, and cancer.[114]

But Dollar General's arrival in low-income communities has hardly turned food deserts into oases. As essentially souped-up convenience stores, Dollar General and similar chains offer inventories heavily stocked with cheap, highly processed foods and scant availability of fresh produce (you could say their bread and butter are Tastykake and Parkay). It might be great for the company's bottom line, but not for consumers' health.

In Craigsville's Dollar General, for instance, an aisle labeled "Good Choices" offered only several brands of granola bars, along with Rice Krispie treats and cheese puffs. I saw no fresh fruit or vegetables during my visit in the fall of 2022, but I did see a large sign by the register, next to a display of Bic lighters: "SNAP EBT accepted." ("EBT" stands for "electronic benefits transfer.")

In 2021, just 1,300 of Dollar General's 18,000+ stores offered any fresh produce, although the company pledged to grow that number to 10,000 over the next several years as part of a partnership with the nonprofit Feeding America.[115] How extensive these fresh offerings will ultimately be, however, is an open question. The company's business model dictates "a low-cost, no frills building with limited maintenance capital, low operating costs, and a focused merchandise offering," according to its annual report, along with limited staff and limited space.[116] The company is experimenting with a new type of store called DG Market, which will sell the top twenty fresh produce items sold by traditional grocery stores, "including lettuce, tomatoes, onions, apples, strawberries, potatoes, sweet potatoes, lemons, limes, salad mixes and more," according to an industry publication about the effort.[117] The first DG Market store opened in Tennessee in 2021.[118]

That Dollar General is making these shifts at all is the result of years of advocacy by public health and consumer groups, who've criticized dollar stores for their destructive impacts on low-income neighborhoods. A 2018 report by the Institute for Local Self-Reliance called dollar stores "an invasive species in America's left-behind places."[119] Organizations like the Center for Science in Public Interest have argued that dollar stores potentially worsen access to healthy food options by driving out competition. "When dollar stores saturate a community's grocery market, full-service food stores are deterred from opening and existing grocers are pushed out," the group wrote in a 2020 factsheet.[120] In some instances, existing grocery sales drop by as much as 30 percent when a dollar store moves into the neighborhood. Advocates also charged that dollar stores deliberately targeted low-income neighborhoods and—worst of all—counted on SNAP dollars to fuel their expansion into these areas. Between 2007 and 2017, the number of outlets accepting SNAP benefits grew from 162,00 to 250,000, driven largely by the growth in dollar stores.[121]

Congress, however, has largely ignored the dollar store phenomenon—even though the federal government has been the de facto financier of the industry's growth via SNAP. Instead, conservatives in Congress over the last several years have preferred to focus on toughening work requirements and further limiting who "deserves" aid. Some members want to eliminate SNAP benefits altogether for poor adults without children, while others want to raise the work hours demanded from "able-bodied adults without dependents" ("ABAWDs") (though the law is already quite strict).[122]

These proposals of course miss the point. The SNAP beneficiaries who are in fact the least "deserving" are the companies that profit from the program without accountability for the damage they inflict. But it's still low-income Americans—and all too often, children—who bear the toll of this lack of oversight, both with their health and as political pawns.

Lunch Money

Donna Martin is the director of nutrition for Burke County, Georgia, public schools. She is everyone's dream Lunch Lady.

When we spoke on a Monday in March 2022, she was readying the day's menu: turkey tetrazzini, broccoli, carrot sticks with homemade ranch dressing, and made-from-scratch strawberry muffins. "And we have 'fruit-mallow,' which is one of my favorites," Martin said. "It's fruit cocktail, but it's got extra cherries and marshmallows, which the kids really like." The Friday before, she'd served barbecued chicken with collards sourced from a local farmer and homemade rolls made with local whole wheat flour. "Yeah, we have amazing meals," she said.

Even more remarkably, she and her staff produced these meals on the tightest of tight budgets. Her district is poor—more than two-thirds of her 3,600 students qualify for free or reduced-price school lunch—and her cafeteria's principal source of funding is the federal government's National School Lunch Program.[123] Martin starts work at the crack of dawn and scrounges for supplies all day. A pioneer of the "farm-to-school" movement, Martin is creative and endlessly inventive so that not a scrap of food is wasted. Her meals are fresh and appealing, even to the pickiest of grade-schoolers.

But she's also a unicorn among school nutrition directors—rare enough that First Lady Michelle Obama paid her a visit in 2016 and later invited her to the White House on multiple occasions for summits on child nutrition.[124]

Far more typical of school lunch programs is what gets served every day in Fairfax County, Virginia, to the district's more than 181,000 students, about a third of whom qualify for free lunch.[125] The food comes not from cafeteria cooks but from a contractor, Premier, Inc./US Foods, one of the nation's largest food-service companies.[126]

Download a monthly menu for any of the county schools (I downloaded the March 2023 menu for Justice High School), and you'll see a dozen or so items in constant, monotonous rotation.[127] Hamburgers and cheeseburgers alternate with "baked chicken on bun" and "corn dog bites." The "beef soft taco" trades off with nachos ("tortilla chips," "Taco Meat," and "Nacho Cheese Sauce"). The "Italian Line" serves both cheese and pepperoni pizza every day, while the "Asian Line" serves General Tso's or sweet and sour chicken. The mystifyingly named "Chopped Cheese Salad" is also available daily, as is a "Yogurt Biteable," Cheez-its, and a "Spicy Chicken Wrap." Fruit and vegetable selections vary between broccoli, baby carrots, applesauce, canned peaches, and mandarin oranges. My teenage sons, who are Fairfax County students, described their cafeteria food with one word: "brown."

Though it nominally meets federal nutrition standards, the cheeseburger served at Fairfax County school lunch has more fat, calories, and sodium than a regular cheeseburger from McDonald's. According to the nutrition information provided by Fairfax County, a "cheeseburger on bun" packs 350 calories with 19 grams of fat and 820 milligrams of sodium.[128] A McDonald's cheeseburger, in contrast, clocks in at 300 calories, 12 grams of fat, and 750 milligrams of sodium, which of course is still nowhere near "healthy."[129] Fairfax County's "baked chicken on bun" is comparably salty and fatty (350 calories/14 grams of fat/630 milligrams of sodium), as is the "healthier" "spicy chicken wrap" (350 calories/18 grams of fat/680 milligrams of sodium). The "Yogurt Biteable," which includes string cheese and a soft pretzel, has significantly less fat (7 grams) but makes up for it in sugar (18 grams).

Menus like these might help explain why half of U.S. children don't eat a fruit or vegetable every day, according to the Centers for Disease Control (CDC), and why childhood obesity is rising.[130] According to a 2015 study by researchers at the University of Illinois at Chicago, pizza is the second-leading source of calories among children ages twelve to nineteen.[131] As one result, more than one in five children ages twelve to nineteen are obese, reports the CDC, and the rate of Type II diabetes among teens has nearly doubled over the last twenty years.[132]

Nevertheless, the National School Lunch Program is one of the most important supports available to low-income children. Burke County's Martin says for many of her kids, the breakfasts, lunches, and even suppers she provides might be the only food they get. Pre-pandemic, the National School Lunch Program reached nearly 30 million children a day and served 4.9 billion lunches a year.[133] In 2021–2022, nearly half of public school students (48.6 percent) qualified for free or reduced-price meals.[134] Access to free meals reduces food insecurity and improves school performance.[135] Free breakfast, in particular, reduces tardiness, absenteeism, and behavior problems triggered simply because a child is hungry.[136]

Yet despite the importance of these meal programs, school lunches are increasingly more likely to be what's served in Fairfax County: mass-produced, marginally nutritious, and indifferently prepared. Current policies have made it tough for many school districts to emulate Donna Martin and her healthful, made-from-scratch meals. Contractors, meanwhile, have made it easy for districts to rely on them to feed their students. That's how Big Food is taking over school lunch.

Unlike every other aspect of public school operations, cafeterias are largely expected to be self-sustaining.[137] They typically get no money from their districts and must instead rely on federal reimbursements from the National School Lunch Program and revenue from cafeteria sales to pay for the food they serve. This financial imperative is what's helped drive many districts into the arms of Big Food.

To cover costs, school cafeterias must maximize participation in the federal school lunch program (in order to get reimbursements) and persuade the students who can afford it to buy lunch full price. That, in turn, means offering what kids will eat—pizza, burgers, and chicken nuggets—and for the lowest cost possible.

During the pandemic, Congress raised reimbursements for school meals by 40 cents per lunch and 15 cents per breakfast through June 2023, to a maximum reimbursement of $4.50 for lunch and $2.67 for breakfast for schools with the highest needs. (Wealthier schools get lower reimbursements per meal, and reduced-price lunches are also reimbursed at lower rates.)[138] But more than half of nutrition directors surveyed for a 2023 report by the School Nutrition Association said these reimbursement rates failed to cover their costs, and nearly nine in ten said "increasing costs" were their top concern.[139]

Even Burke County's Martin said making ends meet has been a struggle. Staffing got more expensive as the labor market tightened throughout 2022; inflation sent her food costs spiraling by

25 percent. "Costs are going up and up, but the money I get from the federal government is the money I get," she said. "I'm not like a restaurant that can charge more to my customers."[140]

Rising costs aren't the only difficulty many school food programs face. For instance, finding skilled and willing staff has also been tough, especially since the start of the pandemic. In the School Nutrition Association's 2023 report, 59 percent of school nutrition directors called "staff shortages" a significant challenge.[141] "Our jobs are really hard," said Martin. "When we do all this scratch cooking, you're making rolls, you're on your feet, you're lifting 50-pound bags of flour and sugar and cases of product—it's hard, hard work. If you can go to Walmart and make $15 an hour as a cashier, people would take that in a heartbeat over the hard work in my kitchens."

And even if they can find the workers, many schools have outdated kitchens that can make food preparation difficult. Fifty-five percent of school kitchens needed infrastructure upgrades as of 2014, according to the Pew Trusts, and 88 percent needed at least one piece of kitchen equipment (federal grants for kitchen equipment have likely since mitigated this problem to some extent).[142] Federal nutrition standards are also complex, and the bureaucracy of compliance intimidating. The USDA's "Transitional Standards for Milk, Whole Grains and Sodium," for instance, is thirty-nine pages long, and there's a seven-page policy memo on the appropriate formulation of smoothies.[143]

Food service management companies, however, promise to take all these hassles away—an irresistible proposition for many cash-strapped districts. Aramark is currently one of the nation's three largest school lunch food service companies (and as noted in chapter 5, it's also the nation's largest provider of prison food services as well).[144] Its website, for instance, lists multiple benefits of its services, including "Delivering meal programs that meet USDA requirements for nutritional standards" and "Delivering a financially viable food service program that minimizes use of general fund dollars to subsidize the food program or generates a surplus for reinvestment back into the district."[145]

Aramark also posts on its site a "guide" to help school leaders overcome community opposition to contracting out school lunch. Titled "Outsourcing Is Not a Dirty Word," the pamphlet proposes talking points for overcoming objections, while including a sales pitch for the company. "Explain how the outsourcing provider will work with existing employees, deliver more specialized training and development programs and may even help create more jobs within the community," the guide counsels.[146]

In 1990, *Education Week* published a prescient piece titled "Food-Service Companies Eye $5-Billion School-Lunch Market."[147] At the time, the article reported, just 4 percent of schools participating in the National School Lunch Program used food service management companies to provide their meals, but executives interviewed in the piece projected growth rates of 15 to 20 percent a year.[148]

By 2022, the three biggest players in the K–12 market—Compass Group North America (through its subsidiary, Chartwells), Sodexo, Inc., and Aramark Corp.—were posting an estimated $3.9 billion in combined sales (though this figure includes contracts with private schools too).[149] These companies offer not just the outsourcing of a school's entire dining operation but also ready-made foods and products that school staff can heat and serve, even if they lack all the amenities of a professional kitchen. (Imagine thousands of pounds of chicken nuggets, premade burgers, and frozen waffles.)

For districts unwilling to go all in with a food service management company, big food companies are still happy to help in other ways—by selling districts cheap, highly processed foods that are easy to prepare and popular with kids. In a 2015 analysis, the Physicians Committee for Responsible Medicine identified twenty companies advertising "unhealthy meat and dairy products for school meals" in the pages of the School Nutrition Association's *School Nutrition* magazine. These businesses included ConAgra food service (Chef Boyardee beef ravioli; Gilardi stuffed-crust pepperoni pizza and cheese-filled breadsticks); AdvancePierre Foods (beef and mushroom patties); Foster Farms Food Service (chicken corn dogs); and Sarah Lee Foodservice (hot dog; corn dog).[150] In 2023, Kraft Heinz reportedly started marketing modified versions of Lunchables to school cafeterias. "The fact that a processed, packaged food meets school lunch standards is part of what needs to change in the national school lunch program," Katie Wilson of the Urban School Food Alliance told the *Washington Post*.[151]

Fast food companies also cater to school lunch programs. Domino's Pizza, for example, offers "Smart Slice," which it advertises as "locally made, NSLP compliant pizza."[152] Likewise, Pizza Hut markets to schools with its "A+ Pizza Program," featuring pizza crusts made of "51% white whole wheat flour" to comply with federal standards.[153]

Companies will even make processed foods to order for schools that participate in the USDA Foods program, which provides surplus meat and dairy to schools for free.[154] Under the government's "USDA Foods further processing" program, a district can ship thousands of pounds of USDA chicken to a contractor, who'll convert them into nuggets (for a fee). In school year 2017, districts processed $1.4 billion worth of food this way.[155] The program arguably expands access to the USDA Foods program by providing a way for districts to convert raw or bulk foods they otherwise don't have the capacity to handle "into a variety of convenient, ready-to-use end products," as the USDA puts it.[156] But it also means districts are spending a lot of money to process whole foods into products that are much less healthy. One early critique by writer Lucy Komisar noted how the Michigan Department of Education was sending its contractors free raw USDA chicken worth $11.40 a case and paying $33.45 a case to get them back as nuggets.[157]

The savings promised to schools by big food companies are either often illusory or come at the price of sacrificing nutrition. By sheer dint of their size, food service companies do have the benefit of bulk purchasing power, which can advantage smaller school districts that lack the leverage to negotiate with suppliers. But the more common strategy for cost savings is by cutting corners—providing low-cost foods that are also lower in quality. "Pizza is very, very, very cheap," as Burke County's Donna Martin points out.[158] Districts save money but shortchange students' health.

And sometimes there are no savings at all. In Washington, DC, for instance, the city's auditor released a 2016 report bluntly titled "Contracting Out School Food Services Failed to Control Costs as Promised."[159] The audit followed a $19.4 million settlement with Chartwells in 2015, after allegations that the company had overcharged the District millions of dollars and delivered poor-quality food that was sometimes spoiled.[160] The complaint against the company also claimed that instead of buying food "at the lowest possible price," as its contract required, Chartwells "used a corporate affiliate to purchase foods from 'companies that manufacture highly processed foods and charge higher prices,'" the *Washington Post* reported.[161] In quantifying the extent of these overpayments, the auditor's office found that the District had spent an average of $3.90 per school meal, compared to $2.98 paid by schools in New York and $3.62 in Fairfax.[162]

Certainly, easing the financial constraints school food programs face could reduce the pressure to rely on Big Food. More-generous reimbursements and help with infrastructure upgrades could encourage more school lunch programs to follow Donna Martin's lead in Burke County.

But there are much more powerful forces at play that influence what kids want to eat, why schools might turn to outsourcing, and why big food companies control so much of the American diet. What's happened with the national school lunch program is emblematic of Poverty, Inc.—the motive to profit can distort even the most well-intentioned of programs with the noblest of aims: feeding hungry kids.

Conclusion

Who's Really Fighting the War on Poverty?

Self-serving private interests have hijacked the war on poverty. Failures in governance and public policy have enabled predatory industries to thrive at the expense of low-income Americans and of taxpayer dollars.

The complexity of the Earned Income Tax Credit (EITC), for instance, spawned tax-time profiteering. Welfare's work requirements support a multitude of for-profit training providers offering dubious credentials and few pathways to real employment. Flawed Medicaid payment policies encourage fraudsters while hindering access to high-quality health care for the poor. Health disparities, in turn, prop up the revenues of industries like dialysis. Multi-billion-dollar conglomerates control the health, the financial security, and even the physical liberty of millions of low-income Americans, thanks to the abdication of government responsibility to contractors. All too often, these for-profit interests sabotage the effectiveness of the government programs to which they owe their livelihood, and they perpetuate the poverty that is the raw material of their business.

Over the past twenty years, so-called double-bottom-line companies have become increasingly fashionable. The idea of "doing well by doing good"—pursuing both profit and social impact—has especially caught on in the consumer market, where there's strong and growing demand for ethically sourced, environmentally responsible products.[1]

Companies boast of "fair trade" coffee, "clean" cosmetics, and "green" production methods. Certified Fairtrade coffee sales, for instance, have grown from about $43 million in 2017 to about $68 million in 2020, according to Fairtrade America.[2] Simply labeling a coffee "fair trade" increases its sales by nearly 10 percent, according to one Stanford University study.[3] Assuming the truth of their labeling, many companies are changing their practices and business models to respond to consumer pressures. And companies have incentive to do so because the U.S. consumer market is robust. There are plenty of shoppers with money to spend, which means plenty of competition for those dollars.

But this is nothing like the "market" for social services, where there's a single payer "customer" (the government) and a limited number of vendors, where product quality is tough to measure, and the end "consumers" (low-income Americans) have little to no leverage over the "services" they receive. As is clear throughout these pages, contractors hold most of the power in these situations, leaving few choices for governments and often none for low-income Americans. Just a handful of companies control the market for TANF and Medicaid administration, for instance, and the same is true of private prisons, Job Corps contractors, etc. Privatization's purported goal was to harness the private sector's innovative impulse for the public good by spurring government to be more creative, effective, and efficient. What's happened is a perversion of that entrepreneurial energy. Companies have indeed been endlessly inventive, but in their strategies for exploiting government and the beneficiaries of government programs. Meanwhile, the "competition" and "choice" promised by privatization have been illusory.

Policymakers must shed the idea that "the market" can deliver social services effectively—or at least in a way that benefits low-income Americans more than it does companies' own bottom line. The pursuit of profit is an uneasy fit for social policy, and it's a motive powerful enough to override even the best of intentions.

A case in point: Salt Lake County, Utah's 2013 experiment with "social impact bonds" to finance preschool for disadvantaged children. As originally conceived, the Utah plan was brilliant, bold, and potentially revolutionary. To finance an expansion of Salt Lake County's early childhood program, Goldman Sachs and JB Pritzker agreed to lend the county and the United Way of Salt Lake $7 million over five years to reach an additional 3,500 children.[4] The county would repay the loans (i.e., the social impact bonds) only if the program met certain metrics for "success"—namely, the avoidance of special education, which cost $2,470 per child per year. If all went well, Goldman Sachs and Pritzker would get 40 percent of the aggregate savings from these reduced expenditures as "Success Fees"—or about $1,040 per child per year.[5]

The effort began with much fanfare and high hopes. "We want [this] 'pay for success' model to be not only for Salt Lake County but throughout the nation," Salt Lake County then-Mayor Ben McAdams told me in 2014. "We want to get it to the point where you have a marketable investment that could attract private-sector dollars for solving complex government programs in a more efficient way."[6] In theory, the plan was a "win-win-win"—a return on their money for investors, an infusion of funds for the government, and more access to services for low-income children. Two years into the program, Goldman Sachs announced its first results—that 109 "at-risk" kindergarteners had successfully avoided special education, entitling the bank to its first payment of $260,000.[7]

But the effort immediately came under fire for potentially overstating its results (and thus overpaying investors). In particular, experts told the *New York Times*, the program overcounted the number of children "at risk" for special education—meaning Goldman got its "success fee" for kids who may never have needed special education in the first place. Moreover, experts said, Goldman's investment in preschool—about $1,700 per child—was too small to produce the kinds of results reported. The most successful programs documented in research typically cost four to five times as much.[8] More broadly, critics argued that the avoidance of special education as a measure of "success" encouraged officials to deny children needed services, especially those with disabilities.[9] Documentarian Nadine Pequeneza, who spent three years studying a similar preschool initiative in Chicago, concluded in the *Stanford Social Innovation Review* that social impact bonds "might be doing more harm than good."[10]

The Utah experiment illustrates the private sector's limited capabilities in social policy. For one thing, as Pequeneza points out, instruments like social impact bonds promote "simplistic solutions to complex problems."[11] It's impossible to solve a multi-faceted problem like poverty with a narrow set of "market incentives" that private actors can be paid to act upon. By itself, better access to preschool won't set a child up for success in school, especially if the rest of their education is substandard and if they face a host of other challenges at home and in their communities. It's also difficult to determine what to measure, how to measure it, and how to prevent gaming of the system. For instance, if "success" in running a Medicaid program means lower costs, "success" is a simple matter of denying access to care—as some Medicaid contractors have done (see chapter 4). In addition, effective human services require investment; they can't be done on the cheap. A high-quality preschool program, for instance, requires skilled and caring teachers, curricula tailored to each child's needs, and access to supportive services for families.[12] This requires much more spending than $1,700 per child per year (what Goldman purportedly invested in Utah).

Unfortunately, the corporatization of U.S. social policy has been half a century in the making. Disentangling the private sector from the infrastructure of government—let alone undoing the damage—is a dauntingly large and expensive task. Governments have given away so much of their administrative capacity that reclaiming and rebuilding their capabilities would require a far bigger budget and far more political will than what's currently possible in our hyper-polarized, hyper-partisan environment.

Nevertheless, Congress, federal agencies, and states can take any number of practical—and politically feasible—steps to rein in the destructive impacts of privatization and demand better performance from the companies entrusted to carry out governmental functions.

Congress could, for instance, require more transparency from states about the share of federal dollars flowing to contractors for social services and to which firms. One reason the corporate poverty complex has grown so big is that states and the federal government aren't collecting and synthesizing data about the size and reach of these businesses. At present, the most reliable data is what's gleaned from companies' annual reports—provided those firms are big enough to be publicly traded and required to disclose information to the U.S. Securities and Exchange Commission. Smaller companies that aren't public—or even large companies that are privately held (e.g., owned by private equity firms)—can operate with relatively little transparency into their revenue, the number of contracts they hold, or the amount of governmental dollars they receive. Given that so many of the companies described in this book earn the lion's share of their revenue from government, it seems only fair that they be considered "publicly" funded—and therefore publicly accountable for their activities. More and better data could also lead to new strategies for increasing competition, breaking up provider monopolies (for example, in Job Corps), or improving procurement practices (such as limiting the number of markets nationally in which a single company can serve).

Governments can also tighten up their oversight of the contractors they hire and the dollars they spend. While many agencies have already embraced so-called performance-based contracting, officials too often pick the wrong measures of "success." Job training contractors, for instance, might be paid for the number of enrollees they sign up or the "placements" they make but get no reward for longer-term job retention or wage gains among their trainees. The incentive then becomes to churn through trainees without regard for their long-term success or to cherry-pick enrollees who might be the easiest to place. Likewise, Medicaid contractors might be rewarded for keeping costs low per enrollee, but without regard to the health of beneficiaries. As discussed earlier in this book, this creates incentives to deny care, especially to the sickest patients. So long as contractors are in the mix, rethinking what's rewarded could help eliminate perverse incentives and improve the quality of services.

Governments could also limit their contracting to ministerial tasks that might benefit from the efficiency of corporate infrastructure but don't require administrative discretion in the benefits people receive. States could, for instance, hire companies to process benefit checks but disallow them from deciding eligibility. (Analogously, payroll processing companies cut paychecks, but they don't determine anyone's salary.) Over time, governments could potentially claw back the power they've given away by narrowing the scope of future contracts.

In a perfect world, the goal should be to expunge the parasitic industries dragging down U.S. antipoverty efforts and to eliminate the failures in policy that have allowed this kind of corporate opportunism. Getting there will require a fundamental re-examination of who is really running the machinery of U.S. social policy, and who in fact benefits most. To accomplish this task, policymakers should keep in mind the following five takeaways.

1. Government doesn't deliver antipoverty programs; private actors do.

Much of the government's antipoverty apparatus is not, in fact, in government hands. Often, the relationship between government and third parties involves the direct contracting out of services, such as running prisons, administering Medicaid, or managing a Job Corps center. In many other instances, however, third parties insert themselves between government and the beneficiaries of antipoverty programs. Tax preparers essentially broker the EITC for low-income Americans. Section 8 landlords, Medicare dentists, and dollar stores are the intermediaries through which low-income households receive such basic benefits as housing, health care, and food.

But when politicians and pundits talk about the efficacy of antipoverty programs, they are almost always focused on the performance of government or the behavior of the poor. What's missing from the conversation is the performance and behavior of private interests acting on behalf of the government or as middlemen to deliver services and benefits.[13] The profit seeking of these third-party players significantly diminishes the effectiveness of government programs, either by diverting resources from the intended beneficiaries (in the case of tax preparers skimming the EITC) or by providing poor-quality products that undercut a program's purpose (e.g., an unnecessary and painful "baby root canal" performed by an unscrupulous Medicaid dentist).

To be fair, commercial tax-prep firms and insurance companies aren't in business to fight poverty—their goal is to make money or to fulfill the narrow terms of a government contract. Moreover, the large public companies that dominate sectors like benefits administration are beholden first to their shareholders, not to the broader aims of U.S. social policy.

Nevertheless, policymakers should fully consider the impacts of these third-party actors when they evaluate antipoverty programs. And they should recalibrate U.S. social policy to reduce the "drag" created by unintended private-sector intermediaries. Simplifying the tax code, for instance, would allow fewer low-income Americans to rely on commercial tax preparers to access the EITC. "Source of income" laws could help break the monopoly of Section 8 landlords and induce real competition. Reforms like these could be an important step toward making federal antipoverty programs more effective.

The starting point, however, should be a "census" to quantify the universe of contractors and their impact on policies and programs. This book covers the programs forming the core of federal antipoverty policy but it's far from an exhaustive review of for-profit involvement in social services. For-profit companies own 70 percent of the nation's nursing homes, for instance, while Medicaid pays the bills for nearly two-thirds of nursing home residents.[14] Many states have also begun to privatize their foster care systems, leading to horrific consequences for at-risk children.[15] For instance, a 2015 *BuzzFeed* investigation into the nation's largest for-profit foster care placement agency, National Mentor Holdings, uncovered a host of negligent practices that resulted in abuse and even deaths at the hands of foster parents.[16] (Long-term care and child welfare reform could easily fill their own volumes, which is one reason I could not give these topics justice here.)

The devolution of social services across multiple layers of government (federal, state, and local) has allowed the for-profit social services industry to operate in the shadows relatively unmolested and in disparate, fragmented service sectors. A big-picture assessment of the collective impact—and damage—these players have wrought would help achieve the accountability that should have been demanded all along.

2. Poverty persists, in part, because it benefits the industries that profit.

For industries that depend on antipoverty programs and low-income Americans to fuel their business, the end of poverty is an existential threat. Dollar stores benefit because hungry Americans rely on SNAP. Section 8 landlords profit because households need assistance to afford their rent. Private prisons feed off a criminal justice system that disproportionately targets the poor. Industries like these have embedded themselves into the daily lives of low-income Americans. They're entrenched in the infrastructure of poverty, and they have a vested interest in maintaining the status quo.

Billions of dollars are at stake, which is why these industries have acted to protect their "markets" and block policy changes that could hurt their revenues. Some companies have sued the government or each other when they lose contracts, as has happened with Job Corps and Medicaid managed care. Others have lobbied to stop reforms that could damage their business. Commercial tax-preparation companies, for instance, have successfully undermined free filing initiatives for low-income Americans and short-circuited efforts to provide the automatic filing of tax returns. Prison companies and the commercial bail industry have propped up state lawmakers' efforts to be "tough on crime," thereby guaranteeing a steady supply of inmates for their businesses. Job Corps contractors have insulated themselves with local support from the areas where their centers are located.

The aggregate impact of these efforts is to calcify the programmatic flaws and inefficiencies that helped birth these industries in the first place (e.g., tax prep) and to trap low-income Americans into systems where these industries can continue to exploit their status. Tackling the systemic sources of poverty means confronting the institutions that have made poverty their business.

One way to begin this task might be to require more disclosure from private-sector interests about their financial interests in the policy positions they support. Another option might be to encourage legislative analyses about the financial impacts of proposed legislation on government contractors and other third-party stakeholders (like the fiscal analyses that the Congressional Budget Office and other agencies now perform to show a proposal's effect on the budget). Better understanding of the connection between policies and profit-making could help counteract poverty privateers' outsized influence.

3. "Personal responsibility" is a myth when the poverty industry controls people's choices.

One of the most enduring debates about poverty's causes is the role of "personal responsibility." Americans believe in the trope of "rags to riches"—that anyone can "pull themselves up by their bootstraps" to achieve "the American Dream." Conservatives have capitalized on these cherished notions to blame the poor for their circumstances and to enshrine a harshly punitive view toward the poor in the law (see chapter 2). Welfare work requirements, for instance, reinforce the prejudice that recipients are "lazy" and promote the simplistic idea that all anyone needs to get out of poverty is a job, no matter how poorly paid.

The choices people make do matter, of course. But what also matters—and might matter more—is the universe of choices available to individuals, depending on their zip code, race, and other factors outside their control. For many low-income Americans, the "choices" available to them are limited or non-existent, and all too often are dictated by the industries that colonize low-income communities. Many people don't have access to affordable healthy food, for instance, because dollar stores and bodegas control the food choices available in low-income neighborhoods. "Willpower" can't overcome a diet where the only options available and affordable—including at the school cafeteria—are processed foods high in fat and sodium.

Another case in point is the Housing Choice Voucher Program, where Section 8 landlords have made a mockery of what this program is supposed to represent—a ticket to opportunity in a better neighborhood. As chapter 6 describes, recipients can wait years to land a voucher, only to remain in a low-income neighborhood without decent schools or other amenities that could improve a household's prospects.

Policymakers need to recognize the paucity of choices facing many low-income Americans, as well as the private sector's role in narrowing their options. With programs like housing vouchers, food stamps, and school lunch, Congress should consider how to use the federal government's considerable buying power as leverage for improving what's available to low-income households and making true choices possible. Tougher nutrition standards, for instance, could also at least result in healthier school lunches. Bigger subsidies for fresh fruits and vegetables (and smaller subsidies for highly processed foods) could mean the greater availability of produce. As tough as it is to shape the private sector's responses to public policy, policies should at least offer some reward for the companies that are doing "the right thing."

4. We need better governance—and a lot more of it.

The rise of the companies that control so much of U.S. social policy is also a reflection of the decline in governmental oversight and authority. Much of the malfeasance chronicled in these pages is the result of someone in government dozing at the wheel.

At the same time, government workers have been both outnumbered and outgunned, both by the hordes of contractors that have accumulated over decades of privatization and by the industries adjacent to the poverty economy that operate without accountability. As chapter 2 noted, the "shadow government" of contractors and subcontractors throughout government is many multiples larger than the official federal headcount, especially in the delivery of human services. Public management experts like the University of Maryland's Don Kettl and New York University's Paul Light have sounded the alarm for years on the inadequacy of governmental efforts to manage this shadow workforce, enforce accountability, and measure performance. The ways in which poverty-related industries undermine governmental antipoverty efforts should raise these alarms to a blaring crescendo.

It's time for Reinventing Government 2.0, but this time with a focus on reclaiming governmental capacity for management, audit, and enforcement to bring the shadow workforce to heel.

Liberals have generally been averse to embracing "government reform," equating it (correctly, for the most part) to budget cuts, privatization, and conservatives' sustained attack on federal authority. But progressives must disarm conservatives' antigovernment strategy if they want to restore public trust in government and rebuild its authority. That means a genuine strategy to "build back better" (so to speak), not just bigger, with accountability as the central theme.

5. More funding for federal antipoverty programs won't solve the problem of poverty, but it will feed the poverty industry.

Many progressives have long argued that the biggest problem with the federal government's antipoverty efforts has been the lack of adequate funding. Expanding federal benefits like SNAP and the EITC would lift more families out of poverty, advocates argue, while dramatically expanding the housing voucher program would help alleviate the problem of years-long waitlists for aid.[17] Unquestionably, more money would help.

But simply growing the funding for these programs would also mean more money lining the pockets of contractors and intermediaries that also depend on these programs for their profits. Yes, the benefits will trickle down to the Americans who need them, but only after a heavy "tax" is exacted by the poverty industry.

Progressives should couple proposals for increased funding with ideas for programmatic reform, including better oversight and accountability by contractors and other intermediaries. This approach would not only have the substantive benefit of improving program performance, it would also help win political support for bigger investments in fighting poverty. Taxpayers need to know that their dollars are wisely spent, and government needs to offer proof of its commitment to accountability if they want taxpayers' trust.

It's no coincidence that the governmental failings that have given rise to "Poverty, Inc." are the result of conservative attacks both on government and on the poor. Conservative antigovernment ideology fueled Reagan's push for privatization. Conservatives' punitive views on the "undeserving" poor set up the failure of "welfare to work." Conservative stinginess encouraged states to fall for the false promise of cost-cutting through privatization.

The creation of "Poverty, Inc." is a particularly destructive consequence of conservative victories in dictating U.S. social policy. For-profit industries are now mercenaries in conservatives' broader war against America's poor. Undoing the damage will require a frontal assault on the most egregious abuses. It will also mean defeating the conservative ideology that has dominated the politics and policies around poverty for at least the past forty years.

That task has never been more urgent.

Acknowledgments

I'd like to thank Paul Glastris, editor in chief of the *Washington Monthly*, for his mentorship, ideas, and eagle-eyed editing throughout the years and for teaching me how to meld policy analysis with narrative. Multiple sections of this book also started out as articles published in the *Monthly*, and I'm grateful for the time, space, and encouragement Paul gave me to pursue the threads that ultimately became *Poverty for Profit*. Special thanks, too, to Will Marshall, Ed Kilgore, and Peter Ross Range, all of whom taught me about the intersection of politics and policy.

I'm also immensely grateful to the many people who spoke to me about their personal experiences for this book and who generously connected me, a random writer, to their networks. I'd like to thank Dave White in particular, who aptly calls himself the "Kidney Warrior." A survivor and fierce advocate, he was my guide through the harrowing world of dialysis and entrusted his own experiences to me. Dave, it's an honor to tell your story.

A huge thank you, too, to Marc Favreau and Ben Woodward of The New Press, both of whom provided invaluable support, feedback, and editing throughout the process of writing *Poverty for Profit*. Thank you for your faith in me and in this project!

Finally, my love and gratitude are bottomless for my husband, Brian, and my two boys, Alex and Elliot. Thank you, guys, for your unending love and patience (and willingness to read drafts).

Notes

Introduction

1. See "Mapping Race in America," Othering & Belonging Institute, University of California, Berkeley, https://belonging.gis-cdn.net/us_segregation_map/?year=2020&bounds=38.94%2C-76.51%2C38.75%2C-77.02&geo=tract&geoid=24033801907; Edward Cheng, Bo Kim, Angela Martinez, Mimika Thapa, and Lauren Thomas, *Redlining in Prince George's County, Maryland* (College Park, MD: University of Maryland, 2019), https://drum.lib.umd.edu/handle/1903/25554; Sarah Shoenfeld, "Mapping Segregation in D.C.," D.C. Policy Center, April 23, 2019, https://www.dcpolicycenter.org/publications/mapping-segregation-fha/.

2. "QuickFacts, District Heights city, Maryland," U.S. Census Bureau, July 1, 2022, https://www.census.gov/quickfacts/fact/table/districtheightscitymaryland/PST045221.

3. U.S. Census Bureau, "QuickFacts, District Heights"; Jessica Semega and Melissa Kollar, *Income in the United States: 2021* (Washington, D.C.: U.S. Census Bureau, 2022).

4. District Heights' 2021 poverty rate was 14.1 percent, compared to 6.5 percent in Arlington and 3.8 percent in Bethesda. U.S. Census Bureau, "QuickFacts, District Heights"; "QuickFacts, Arlington CDP, Virginia," U.S. Census Bureau, July 1, 2022, https://www.census.gov/quickfacts/arlingtoncdpvirginia; "QuickFacts, Bethesda CDP," U.S. Census Bureau, July 1, 2022, https://www.census.gov/quickfacts/bethesdacdpmaryland.

5. "Overview of Suitland High School, 2022," *U.S. News and World Report*, accessed September 30, 2023, https://www.usnews.com/education

/best-high-schools/maryland/districts/prince-georges-county-public-schools /suitland-high-school-9186.

6. The four facilities are DaVita District Heights Dialysis, 5701 Silver Hill Rd., District Heights, Maryland; U.S. Renal Care Silver Hills Dialysis LLC, 5652 Silver Hill Rd., District Heights, Maryland; DaVita Coral Hills Dialysis, 4797 Marlboro Pike, Capitol Heights, Maryland; and Fresenius Kidney Care Camp Springs, 3700a St. Barnabas Rd, Suitland-Silver Hill, Maryland.

7. Anne Kim, "The Dialysis Machine," *Washington Monthly*, November/December 2017.

8. Anne Kim, "Would You Trust a Used Car Dealer with Your Tax Refund?," *Washington Monthly*, March 26, 2022.

9. Michael W. Davis, "Kool Smiles Dental Quietly Changes the Names of Its Clinics," *Dentistry Today*, May 6, 2019.

10. Ronald Roach, "Public, Private Alliances Fix Up Rundown Housing," *Washington Business Journal*, April 21, 1997. According to this article, financing for the renovation included a "$10.976 million mortgage from the AFL-CIO Housing Investment Trust; a $14.8 million equity investment assembled by the Boston Financial Group from syndication of low-income housing tax credits; a $1.95 million mortgage from the Maryland Department of Housing and Community Development; a $350,000 mortgage from Prince George's HOME loan program; and a $6.5 million grant from the U.S. Department of Housing and Urban Development."

11. "About," Reliant Realty Services, accessed November 6, 2023, https://www.reliantrs.com/about/.

12. "Woodland Springs," Apartments.com, accessed November 5, 2023, https://www.apartments.com/woodland-springs-district-heights-md/4fz4sph/; "Rental Market Trends in District Heights, Maryland," Rent.com, November 5, 2023, https://www.rent.com/maryland/district-heights-apartments/rent-trends. "All vouchers and rental assistance programs are accepted," according to the company's site; "Woodland Springs," accessed November 5, 2023, Reliant Realty Services, https://www.reliantrs.com/property/woodland-springs.

13. Megan Rivers, "District Heights Community Frustrated Someone Opened Fire with Kids Playing Outside," *WUSA9*, May 5, 2022.

14. "2 Men Found Fatally Shot Outside District Heights Apartments ID'd," *WUSA9*, July 7, 2017.

15. "Woodland Springs," accessed November 8, 2023, ApartmentRatings.com, https://www.apartmentratings.com/md/district-heights/woodland-springs_301736597020747/.

16. Jana White, review of Woodland Springs Apartments, Google, accessed

November 8, 2023, https://g.co/kgs/UYMUQb; Maria Jones, review of Woodland Springs Apartments, Google, accessed November 8, 2023, https://g.co/kgs/APFttW. This is just a small sampling of numerous negative reviews complaining of safety and maintenance issues.

17. H. Luke Shaefer, Kate Naranjo, and David Harris, *Spending on Government Anti-Poverty Efforts: Healthcare Expenditures Vastly Outstrip Income Transfers* (Ann Arbor, MI: University of Michigan, 2019).

18. Congressional Research Service, *Child Welfare: Purposes, Federal Programs and Funding* (Washington, D.C.: Congressional Research Service, 2023); Emily D. Buehler, *Justice Expenditures and Employment in the United States, 2017* (Washington, D.C.: U.S. Department of Justice, Office of Justice Programs, Bureau of Justice Statistics, 2021), 4.

19. Buehler, *Justice Expenditures and Employment*, 4.

20. Emily A. Shrider and John Creamer, *Poverty in the United States: 2022* (Washington, D.C.: U.S. Census Bureau, 2023). Under the "Supplemental Poverty Measure," which takes into account the impact of Social Security payments, tax credits, and other governmental transfers, the poverty rate in 2022 was 12.4 percent, an increase of 4.6 percent from 2021. This dramatic rise is widely attributed to the expiration of pandemic-related benefits.

21. "President Lyndon B. Johnson's 1964 State of the Union Address," Office of the Historian, U.S. House of Representatives, accessed November 8, 2023, history.house.gov/Media?mediaID=15032450456.

22. Alicia Parlapiano, Deborah B. Solomon, Madeleine Ngo, and Stacy Cowley, "Where $5 Trillion in Pandemic Stimulus Money Went," *New York Times*, March 11, 2022. Congress allocated $1.8 trillion in stimulus payments to families and individuals, including money for emergency food aid, expanded unemployment benefits, and a monthly child tax credit. These payments kept the 2020 poverty rate at 11.5 percent—relatively low compared to the 15.1 percent poverty rate in 2010 during the Great Recession. Shrider and Creamer, *Poverty in the United States: 2022*, 3.

23. Shrider and Creamer, *Poverty in the United States: 2022*, Table A-1.

24. Ibid., Table A-3.

25. August Benzow and Kenan Fikri, *The Expanded Geography of High-Poverty Neighborhoods* (Washington, D.C.: Economic Innovation Group, 2020). According to the Economic Innovation Group, 24 million Americans lived in high-poverty neighborhoods in 2018, compared to 12 million in 1980.

26. Raj Chetty, Nathaniel Hendren, Patrick Kline, Emmanuel Saez, and Nicholas Turner, "Is the United States Still a Land of Opportunity? Recent Trends in Intergenerational Mobility," NBER Working Paper No. 19844, January 2014, JEL No. H0J0, http://www.nber.org/papers/w19844, 1; Raj

Chetty, David Grusky, Maximilian Hell, Nathanial Hendren, Robert Manduca, and Jimmy Narang, "The Fading American Dream: Trends in Absolute Income Mobility Since 1940," NBER Working Paper No. 22910, December 2016, http://www.nber.org/papers/w22910, 2.

27. Raj Chetty, Nathaniel Hendren, Maggie R. Jones, and Sonya R. Porter, "Race and Economic Opportunity in the United States: An Intergenerational Perspective," NBER Working Paper 24441, March 2018, revised December 2019, JEL No. H0,J0, http://www.nber.org/papers/w24441.

28. Danilo Trisi and Matt Saenz, *Economic Security Programs Reduce Overall Poverty, Racial and Ethnic Inequities* (Washington, D.C.: Center on Budget and Policy Priorities, 2021).

29. Samantha Young, "Dialysis Industry Spends Millions, Emerges as Power Player in California Politics," *California Healthline*, December 9, 2020.

1. The Price of Paying Taxes

For the title of this chapter, I've borrowed the title of a paper I coauthored back in 2002. As a team of four young analysts from the Progressive Policy Institute and the Brookings Institution, we surveyed 124 tax-prep businesses in the metro DC area about the prices and products they offered. We found that, on average, taxpayers could expect to spend about 10 percent of their refund on tax prep and refund products. It is shocking how little has changed. Alan Berube, Anne Kim, Benjamin Forman, and Megan Burns, *The Price of Paying Taxes: How Tax Preparation and Refund Loan Fees Erode the Benefits of the EITC* (Washington, D.C.: Brookings Institution and Progressive Policy Institute, 2002).

1. "Financing Options," America's Car-Mart, accessed November 2, 2023, https://www.car-mart.com/financing-options. "Buy here, pay here" dealerships are dealerships that offer in-house financing for the cars they sell instead of working with a financing company to provide customers with loans. For a quick primer, see Ben Luthi, "How Buy Here, Pay Here Dealer Financing Works," Experian, January 14, 2019, https://www.experian.com/blogs/ask-experian/what-is-a-buy-here-pay-here-dealership/. The federal Consumer Financial Protection Bureau (CFPB) has taken enforcement action against some dealers for predatory practices. Consumer Financial Protection Bureau, "CFPB Takes First Action Against 'Buy-Here, Pay-Here' Auto Dealer," press release, November 19, 2014, https://www.consumerfinance.gov/about-us/newsroom/cfpb-takes-first-action-against-buy-here-pay-here-auto-dealer/.

2. "Find a Location," America's Car-Mart, accessed November 8, 2023,

https://www.car-mart.com/locations/; "About Us," Tax Max, accessed November 8, 2023, https://www.taxmax.com/TaxMax/about.aspx.

3. "Filing Season Statistics for Week Ending February 4, 2022," Internal Revenue Service, last modified December 20, 2022, https://www.irs.gov/newsroom/filing-season-statistics-for-week-ending-february-04-2022.

4. "Find a Car—Rogers, Arkansas," America's Car-Mart, accessed February 23, 2022, https://www.car-mart.com/cars/012/rogers-arkansas/.

5. "Tax Max," LinkedIn, accessed November 9, 2023, https://www.linkedin.com/company/trs-tax-max/about/.

6. "Bill Neylan," LinkedIn, accessed November 9, 2023, https://www.linkedin.com/in/bill-neylan-793316b/.

7. "BHPH United Formed to Provide Improved Education and Resources to Buy Here, Pay Here Dealers," Buckeye Dealership Consulting, November 10, 2021, https://www.buckeyereinsurance.com/bhph-united-formed-to-provide-improved-education-and-resources-to-buy-here-pay-here-dealers/; "BHPH United Summit '24," BHPH United, accessed November 23, 2023, https://www.bhphunited.com/summit.

8. "Bill Neylan, CEO of TaxMax, Is ALL IN, for the BHPH United Summit—Just One Month Away!" YouTube, March 2022, https://www.youtube.com/watch?v=8KJ79W3b2PI.

9. "EITC Fast Facts," Internal Revenue Service, last modified January 6, 2023, https://www.eitc.irs.gov/partner-toolkit/basic-marketing-communication-materials/eitc-fast-facts/eitc-fast-facts.

10. Internal Revenue Service, *Publication 596: Earned Income Credit (EIC)* (Washington, D.C.: Internal Revenue Service, 2022).

11. Ibid. In tax year 2022, taxpayers with three "qualifying children" had to earn less than $53,057 ($59,187 if married and filing jointly) in order to be eligible for the credit. Workers with no children qualify for the credit if their earnings are below $16,480 ($22,610 for married filing jointly).

12. Internal Revenue Service, *Earned Income Credit.*

13. "Earned Income and Earned Income Tax Credit (EITC) Tables," Internal Revenue Service, last modified March 8, 2023, https://www.irs.gov/credits-deductions/individuals/earned-income-tax-credit/earned-income-and-earned-income-tax-credit-eitc-tables.

14. Elaine Maag, William J. Congdon, and Eunice Yau, *The Earned Income Tax Credit: Program Outcomes, Payment Timing, and Next Steps for Research* (Washington, DC: U.S. Department of Health and Human Services, Office of Planning, Research, and Evaluation, Administration for Children and Families, 2002).

15. Ibid.

16. Interview with author. State-by-state EITC data can be found here: "Statistics for Tax Returns with the Earned Income Tax Credit (EITC)," Internal Revenue Service, last modified March 17, 2023, https://www.eitc.irs.gov/eitc-central/statistics-for-tax-returns-with-eitc/statistics-for-tax-returns-with-the-earned-income.

17. Jessica Huseman, "Filing Taxes Could Be Free and Simple. But H&R Block and Intuit Are Still Lobbying Against It," *ProPublica*, March 20, 2017.

18. U.S. Government Accountability Office, *Paid Tax Preparers: In a Limited Study, Preparers Made Significant Errors* (Washington, D.C.: U.S. Government Accountability Office, 2014).

19. "Tax Preparation Services in the U.S.: Market Size, Industry Analysis, Trends and Forecasts (2023–2028)," IBISWorld, October 2023, https://www.ibisworld.com/united-states/market-research-reports/tax-preparation-services-industry/.

20. U.S. Government Accountability Office to Honorable John Lewis, Subcommittee on Oversight, Committee on Ways and Means, U.S. House of Representatives, "Subject: Refund Anticipation Loans," June 5, 2008.

21. In truth, much of U.S. domestic policy is now delivered through the tax code. The most obvious examples are subsidies for the middle class, which are disguised as tax breaks. These include the home mortgage interest deduction but also tax preferences for retirement accounts, 529 accounts for college savings, and so on. Tax breaks are politically much more palatable for Congress to pass than direct subsidies or the creation of a new program. In addition, the "cost" of tax benefits—tax "expenditures"—can be framed as lost revenue versus "government spending."

22. Elaine Maag, *Paying the Price? Low-Income Parents and the Use of Paid Tax Preparers* (Washington, D.C.: Urban Institute, 2005), 3.

23. Internal Revenue Service, *Earned Income Credit*.

24. National Taxpayer Advocate, *Earned Income Tax Credit: Making the EITC Work for Taxpayers and the Government* (Washington, D.C.: National Taxpayer Advocate, 2020).

25. Robert Greenstein, John Wancheck, and Chuck Marr, *Reducing Overpayments in the Earned Income Tax Credit* (Washington, D.C.: Center on Budget and Policy Priorities, 2019), 3.

26. National Taxpayer Advocate, *Earned Income Tax Credit*, 11.

27. "Child Tax Credit," Internal Revenue Service, last modified August 24, 2023, https://www.irs.gov/credits-deductions/individuals/child-tax-credit#.

28. Ibid.

29. For instance, said the Taxpayer Advocate: "A woman separated from and stopped living with her husband in January of last year, but they are still

married. She has custody of their children. She is *likely eligible* for the EITC because she can file using the head of household status. However . . . If the couple separated in **November,** she is ***likely NOT eligible*** for the EITC because she was not living apart from her husband for the last six months of the year and therefore cannot claim the head of household filing status." Or this: "A young man lives with and supports his girlfriend and her two kids. He and the mom used to be married, got divorced, and are now back together. He is ***likely eligible*** for the EITC because the children are his stepchildren and therefore meet the relationship requirement. However . . . If he and the mom were **never married**, he is ***likely NOT eligible*** for the EITC because the children are not related to him." (Emphasis in original.) National Taxpayer Advocate, *Earned Income Tax Credit*, 8.

30. Jonathan D. Epstein, "Meet Mr. 1040: Hamburg High Grad Founded Both Jackson Hewitt and Liberty Tax Firms," *Buffalo News*, September 9, 2007.

31. John Hewitt, "Discovering ATAX Tax Services," in *iCOMPETE: Building Your Empire with John Hewitt*, produced by Loyalty Brands, podcast, audio, 28:44, 14:41, https://loyaltybrands.com/podcasts/.

32. Emily Nelson, "HFS to Pay $483 Million in Deal for Jackson Hewitt," *Wall Street Journal*, November 20, 1997.

33. "About Us," Liberty Tax, accessed November 8, 2023, https://www.libertytax.com/about-us; "Liberty Tax Parent Files for IPO," *Accounting Today*, September 6, 2011. Hewitt couldn't start Liberty Tax Service in America because of a non-compete agreement with Jackson Hewitt after its sale. "I had a noncompete in the U.S until 2000. So we immediately purchased a tax franchise in Canada," he told the *Buffalo News*. Epstein, "Meet Mr. 1040."

34. Jackson Hewitt operates nearly 6,000 storefronts and kiosks, according to its current owner, Corsair Capital. "Jackson-Hewitt," Corsair Capital, accessed November 8, 2023, https://corsair-capital.com/insight/jackson-hewitt.

35. "About Corsair," Corsair Capital, accessed November 8, 2023, https://corsair-capital.com/firm.

36. Liberty Tax, "About Us."

37. Liberty Tax, Inc., *Annual Report on Form 10-K for the Fiscal Year Ended April 30, 2019* (Virginia, Beach, VA: Liberty Tax, Inc., 2019), 33.

38. "Our Story," ATAX, accessed November 8, 2023, https://ataxfranchise.com/our-story/. According to the company timeline on its site, ATAX began in 2007 as "the first Latino owned tax preparation, bookkeeping and payroll franchise in the United States" and became "partners" with Hewitt in 2019.

39. Beth Ewen, "Forced Out of Liberty Tax Service, Founder John Hewitt

Will Try Again," *Franchise Times,* January 24, 2019, updated October 12, 2020. Hewitt was ousted as CEO from Liberty Tax in 2018 in an especially lurid chapter in the company's history. An internal review found that Hewitt "had sex in his office and hired relatives of female employees with whom he'd had romantic relationships," according to *Fortune*. "Liberty Tax Founder John Hewitt Faces Ouster Amid Sex Scandal Allegations," *Fortune.com,* December 13, 2007. A 2018 class action suit against both Liberty Tax and Hewitt by company investors alleged that Hewitt "treated the Company as his 'playground,'" and that Liberty Tax had been "knowingly condoning and footing the bill for [Hewitt's] reckless escapades that included dating countless employees; routinely having sex with employees in his office; using Company resources to further his romantic relationships by, among other things, directing the Company to hire countless of his girlfriends' friends and relatives to 'made up' positions for which they were nevertheless unqualified, causing the Company to often exceed its annual 'new hire' budget by at least $1 million . . ." Consolidated Amended Class Action Complaint, In re Liberty Tax, Inc. Securities Litigation, No. 2: 17-CV-07327-NGG-RML (E.D.N.Y. June 12, 2018). The case was later dismissed when the court ruled that investors had no cause of action against the company for its failure to disclose the full circumstances of Hewitt's departure. IBEW Local 98 Pension Fund v. Liberty Tax, Inc. (In re Liberty Tax, Inc. Securities Litigation), No. 20-652 (2d Cir. Sep. 30, 2020). See also Michael Cohn, "Liberty Tax Ousts John Hewitt as CEO," *Accounting Today,* September 6, 2017.

40. "About Zoomin Groomin," Loyalty Brands, accessed November 8, 2023, https://loyaltybrands.com/zoomin-groomin/; "The Inspection Boys," Loyalty Brands, accessed November 8, 2023, https://loyaltybrands.com/the-inspection-boys/.

41. ATAX, "Our Story."

42. Hewitt, "Discovering ATAX Tax Services," podcast,12:31.

43. "Huey Long," directed by Ken Burns, aired December 17, 2007, https://www.pbs.org/kenburns/huey-long/.

44. John H. Cushman Jr., "Russell B. Long, 84, Senator Who Influenced Tax Laws," *New York Times,* May 11, 2003. Martin Weil and Clarence Williams, "Sen. Russell Long, 84, Dies," *Washington Post,* May 11, 2003.

45. Cushman, "Russell B. Long."

46. 118 Cong. Rec. 33011 (statement of Senator Russell Long).

47. Ibid., 33010.

48. Dennis J. Ventry, "The Collision of Tax and Welfare Politics: The Political History of the Earned Income Tax Credit, 1969–1999," *National Tax*

Journal, 53, no. 4, part 2 (December 2000): 983-1026, http://www.jstor.org/stable/41789508.

49. Ibid., 985.

50. Milton Friedman, *Capitalism and Freedom* (Chicago and London: University of Chicago Press, 1962).

51. For an excellent contemporaneous account of the debate around Nixon's proposal, see Robert J. Lampman, *Nixon's Family Assistance Plan* (Madison, WI: Institute for Research on Poverty, University of Wisconsin–Madison, 1969).

52. Ventry, "The Collision of Tax and Welfare Politics," 990.

53. Russell B. Long, *Welfare Cheating: Address of Hon. Russell B. Long, Chairman, Committee on Finance, and Supporting Material*, prepared for the use of the Committee on Finance, U.S. Senate, 92nd Congress, 2d Session, 1972, Committee Print 75-077, 1.

54. Ibid., 4.

55. Ventry, "The Collision of Tax and Welfare Politics," 995. The Senate Finance Committee's Report on the Tax Reduction Act of 1975 stated: "This new refundable credit will provide relief to families who currently pay little or no income tax. These people have been hurt the most by rising food and energy costs. Also, in almost all cases, they are subject to the social security payroll tax on their earnings. Because it will increase their after-tax earnings, the new credit, in effect, provides an added bonus or incentive for low-income people to work, and therefore, should be of importance in inducing individuals with families receiving Federal assistance to support themselves. Moreover, the refundable credit is expected to be effective in stimulating the economy because the low-income people are expected to spend a large fraction of their disposable incomes." Quoted in Congressional Research Service, *The Earned Income Tax Credit (EITC): Legislative History* (Washington, D.C.: Congressional Research Service, 2022), 4.

56. Ibid., 5.

57. Ibid., 4.

58. The White House, Office of the Press Secretary, "President Clinton Proposes to Expand the Earned Income Tax Credit in Order to Increase the Reward for Work and Family," press release, January 12, 2000, https://clintonwhitehouse4.archives.gov/WH/New/html/20000112_2.html.

59. Robert Greenstein and Isaac Shapiro, *New Research Findings on the Effects of the Earned Income Tax Credit* (Washington, D.C.: Center on Budget and Policy Priorities, 1998).

60. Center on Budget and Policy Priorities, *Policy Basics: The Earned*

Income Tax Credit (Washington, D.C.: Center on Budget and Policy Priorities, 2023).

61. Annual federal spending on TANF has been frozen at $16.5 billion since 1996. "Temporary Assistance for Needy Families," U.S. Department of Health and Human Services, Administration for Children and Families, Office of Family Assistance, last modified June 29, 2022, https://www.acf.hhs.gov/ofa/programs/temporary-assistance-needy-families-tanf.

62. Interview with author.

63. Interview with author.

64. Michael Best, Chi Chi Wu, and Lauren Saunders, *Report: 2021 Tax Season—Higher Costs for Vulnerable Taxpayers During the COVID Economic Crisis* (Washington, D.C.: National Consumer Law Center, 2021).

65. Interview with author.

66. This conversation took place in the spring of 2022.

67. Interview with author.

68. "Program to Shut Down Schemes and Scams," U.S. Department of Justice, last modified October 12, 2023, https://www.justice.gov/tax/program-shut-down-schemes-and-scams.

69. U.S. Department of Justice, "Justice Department Continues Efforts to Stop Fraudulent Tax Preparers," press release, April 6, 2022, https://www.justice.gov/opa/pr/justice-department-continues-efforts-stop-fraudulent-tax-preparers.

70. United States Attorney for the District of Columbia, "District Man Sentenced to Jail and Ordered to Pay $161,000 in Restitution in Tax Fraud Conspiracy," press release, August 16, 2011, https://www.justice.gov/archive/usao/dc/news/2011/aug/11-361.pdf.

71. Ibid.

72. U.S. Department of Justice, "U.S. Government Sues Jackson Hewitt Tax Preparation Franchises in Four States, Alleging Pervasive Fraud," press release, April 3, 2007, https://www.justice.gov/archive/opa/pr/2007/April/07_tax_215.html.

73. Ibid.

74. U.S. Department of Justice, "Corporations That Owned Jackson Hewitt Franchises in Three States Agree to be Barred from Tax Return Preparation," press release, September 28, 2007, https://www.justice.gov/archive/tax/txdv07779.htm.

75. U.S. Department of Justice, "Justice Department Announces Settlement with Liberty Tax Service," press release, December 3, 2019, https://www.justice.gov/opa/pr/justice-department-announces-settlement-liberty-tax-service.

76. Complaint, United States of America v. Franchise Group Intermediate

L 1, LLC, d/b/a Liberty Tax Service, No. 19-cv-653, 10 (E.D. Va, Dec. 3, 2019), https://www.justice.gov/opa/press-release/file/1223246/download.

77. Ibid., 14.

78. Ibid., 19.

79. For useful background, see "The High Cost of Refund Anticipation Loans and Checks," Michigan Legal Help, accessed November 6, 2023, https://michiganlegalhelp.org/self-help-tools/income-tax/high-cost-of-refund-anticipation-loans-and-checks#refund-anticipation-checks—pre-paid-cards.

80. Chi Chi Wu, Jean Ann Fox and Elizabeth Renuart, *Tax Preparers Peddle High Priced Tax Refund Loans: Millions Skimmed from the Working Poor and the U.S. Treasury* (Washington, D.C.: National Consumer Law Center and Consumer Federation of America, 2002).

81. Ibid.

82. "Tax Refund Advance Loans," Jackson Hewitt, accessed December 15, 2021, https://www.jacksonhewitt.com/refund-advance/.

83. "H&R Emerald Advance," H&R Block, accessed November 6, 2023, https://www.hrblock.com/financial-services/emerald-advanced-lending-credit/.

84. Chi Chi Wu, *Report: Tax-Time Products 2018—A New Generation of Tax-Time Loans Surges in Popularity* (Washington, D.C.: National Consumer Law Center, 2008).

85. U.S. Government Accountability Office, *Tax Refund Products: Product Mix Has Evolved and IRS Should Improve Data Quality* (Washington, D.C.: U.S. Government Accountability Office, 2019), 17.

86. Ibid., 18.

87. Brett Theodos, Rachel Brash, Jessica F. Compton, Nancy M. Pindus, and C. Eugene Steuerle, *Who Needs Credit at Tax Time and Why: A Look at Refund Anticipation Loans and Refund Anticipation Checks* (Washington, D.C.: Urban Institute, 2010), 33.

88. Ibid., 15.

89. U.S. Government Accountability Office, *Tax Refund Products*, 24.

90. Chi Chi Wu and Mandi Matlock, *Report: 2019 Tax Season—The Return of the Interest-Bearing Refund Anticipation Loan and Other Perils Faced by Consumers* (Washington, D.C.: National Consumer Law Center, 2019).

91. Chi Chi Wu, Chantal Hernandez, and Michael Best, *Minefield of Risks: Taxpayers Face Perils from Unregulated Preparers, Lack of Fee Disclosure, and Tax-Time Financial Products* (Washington, D.C.: National Consumer Law Center and Consumer Federation of America, 2016).

92. "MetaBank Announces Name Change to Pathward," *Businesswire*,

March 29, 2022; Meta Financial Group Inc., *Annual Report on Form 10-K for the Fiscal Year Ended September 30, 2021* (Sioux Falls, SD: Meta Financial Group Inc., 2021), 10; Pathward Financial Inc., *2022 Annual Report* (Sioux Falls, SD: Pathward Financial Inc., 2022), 9.

93. "Tax Refund Solutions—Easy Advance," Republic Bank, accessed November 7, 2023, https://www.republicrefund.com/Products/EASYAdvance.aspx; Republic Bancorp, Inc., *Annual Report on Form 10-K for the Fiscal Year Ended December 31, 2021* (Louisville, KY: Republic Bancorp, Inc., 2021), 52.

94. Republic Bancorp, *2021 Annual Report*, 26.

95. Ibid.

96. Chi Chi Wu, *Corporate Welfare for the RAL Industry: The Debt Indicator, IRS Subsidy and Tax Fraud* (Washington, D.C.: National Consumer Law Center, 2005).

97. Internal Revenue Service, "Announcement of Opportunity to Obtain a Debt Indicator in a Pilot Program for the Tax Year 1999 Form 1040 IRS e-file and On-Line Returns," *Federal Register* 64, no. 231 (December 2, 1999): 67621.

98. *Fraud in Income Tax Preparation, Hearing Before Subcommittee on Oversight, Committee on Ways and Means, U.S. House of Representatives*, 109th Cong. 403 (2005), 66 (Statement of Chi Chi Wu, National Consumer Law Center).

99. Wu, *Corporate Welfare for the RAL Industry*, 2.

100. Internal Revenue Service, "Announcement of Opportunity to Obtain a Debt Indicator."

101. Wu, *Corporate Welfare for the RAL Industry*, 3.

102. David Rothstein, "Jackson Hewitt Goes Bankrupt; or, That's Your Business Model?!?," New America Foundation, May 26, 2011, https://www.newamerica.org/asset-building/the-ladder/jackson-hewitt-goes-bankrupt-or-thats-your-business-model/.

103. Jackson Hewitt Tax Services, "Jackson Hewitt Tax Services Announces Strategic Partnership with Corsair Capital," press release, May 31, 2018, https://www.jacksonhewitt.com/about-jackson-hewitt/news-and-events/jackson-hewitt-tax-service-announces-strategic-partnership-with-corsair-capital/.

104. Consumer Federation of America, "Consumer Advocates Applaud End of IRS-Provided Service to Refund Anticipation Lenders," press release, August 5, 2010, https://consumerfed.org/press_release/consumer-advocates-applaud-end-of-irs-provided-service-to-refund-anticipation-lenders.

105. In 2023, the IRS told taxpayers to expect their refunds by February 28. "When to Expect Your Refund If You Claimed the Earned Income Tax Credit or Additional Child Tax Credit," Internal Revenue Service, last

modified January 25, 2023, https://www.irs.gov/credits-deductions/individuals/earned-income-tax-credit/when-to-expect-your-refund-if-you-claimed-the-earned-income-tax-credit-or-additional-child-tax-credit.

106. Interview with author.

107. The Volunteer Income Tax Assistance (VITA) program provides free tax-prep help to low-income taxpayers through grants to qualified local tax help organizations. Though Congress appropriated $30 million to the program in 2021—a big win for advocates—it's not enough. "We had 60,000 calls to fill 5,600 appointments," says Maryland CASH's McKinney, whose organization runs multiple VITA sites as part of its services. In 2019, according to the nonprofit Prosperity Now, VITA volunteers helped 1.5 million households file their returns—a tiny fraction of the taxpayers eligible for VITA help. And unlike paid preparers, VITA volunteers must undergo extensive training and pass a test. For more background on VITA, see Joanna Ain and Rebecca Thompson, "In a Year Full of Loss, a Big Win for Our VITA Field," Prosperity Now, January 12, 2021, https://prosperitynow.org/blog/year-full-loss-big-win-our-vita-field.

108. "The National Occupational Licensing Database," National Conference of State Legislatures, last modified August 12, 2022, https://www.ncsl.org/research/labor-and-employment/occupational-licensing-statute-database.aspx.

109. "Enrolled Agents—Frequently Asked Questions," Internal Revenue Service, March 1, 2023, https://www.irs.gov/tax-professionals/enrolled-agents/enrolled-agents-frequently-asked-questions.

110. "Registered Tax Preparers, California Tax Education Council," State of California Franchise Tax Board, last modified September 23, 2021, https://www.ftb.ca.gov/tax-pros/california-tax-education-council.html.

111. New York State Department of Taxation and Finance, *"Publication 58, Information for Income Tax Return Preparers* (Albany, NY: New York State Department of Taxation and Finance, 2015), https://www.tax.ny.gov/pdf/publications/income/pub58.pdf.

112. "Register via Maryland Examination—Individual Tax Preparers," Maryland Department of Labor, accessed November 8, 2023, https://www.dllr.state.md.us/license/taxprep/taxprepregexam.shtml; "Exam Requirements," Oregon Board of Tax Practitioners, accessed November 8, 2023, https://www.oregon.gov/obtp/pages/examrequirements.aspx.

113. "NTA Blog: Minimum Competency Standards for Return Preparers Are Crucial Taxpayer Protections," National Taxpayer Advocate, updated February 6, 2023, https://www.taxpayeradvocate.irs.gov/news/nta-blog-minimum-competency-standards-for-return-preparers-are-crucial-taxpayer

-protections/; Alaska Public Interest Research Group et al. to U.S. Senate Committee on Finance, letter, April 15, 2016, https://web.archive.org/web/20190522193706/https://www.nclc.org/images/pdf/taxes/letter_Tax_Preparer_Reg_senate_Finance.pdf.

114. Wu and Matlock, *Report: 2019 Tax Season*, 11.

115. National Taxpayer Advocate, "NTA Blog." Although the IRS tried to mandate standards during the Obama administration, a federal appeals court (in a decision written by now Supreme Court Justice Brett Kavanaugh) struck down the effort, ruling that the IRS had no authority to regulate paid preparers. "It might be that allowing the IRS to regulate tax-return preparers more stringently would be wise as a policy matter. But that is a decision for Congress and the President to make if they wish by enacting new legislation," Kavanaugh wrote for the majority on the U.S. Court of Appeals for the D.C. Circuit. Loving v. Internal Revenue Service, 742 F.3d 1013, 1022 (D.C. Cir. 2014).

116. "About," Liberty Tax, https://www.libertytax.com/about-us; "Franchising with Us—Low Start-Up Costs," Liberty Tax, accessed November 6, 2023, https://www.libertytaxfranchise.com/investment-information.

117. Liberty Tax, "Franchising with Us."

118. Ibid. Liberty Tax will also claim 14 percent of revenues in "royalty fees," plus an "advertising fee" of 5 percent, according to its site as of November 2023.

119. Congressional Research Service, *The Earned Income Tax Credit (EITC): Administrative and Compliance Challenges* (Washington, D.C.: Congressional Research Service, 2018).

120. John Wancheck, *IRS Needs Authority to Regulate Tax Return Preparers*, Center on Budget and Policy Priorities, May 5, 2021, https://www.cbppb.org/blog/irs-needs-authority-to-regulate-tax-return-preparers.

121. U.S. Government Accountability Office, *Paid Tax Preparers*, 10.

122. As the National Taxpayer Advocate writes: "Many believe that their preparer is responsible for a mistake, but they may be in for a rude awakening. It is the taxpayer who has to pay the IRS any additional amounts due, including penalties and interest. Taxpayers cannot simply point a finger at their tax return preparer to avoid liability for an inaccurately prepared return." National Taxpayer Advocate, *NTA Blog*.

123. "IRS Audits Poorest Families at Five Times the Rate for Everyone Else," TRAC IRS, March 8, 2022, https://trac.syr.edu/tracirs/latest/679/.

124. Ibid. These audit letters are so-called correspondence audits, where the IRS asks for documentation to justify a specific line item on a return.

125. One study by the National Bureau of Economic Research estimated

that "36% of federal income taxes unpaid are owed by the top 1% and that collecting all unpaid federal income tax from this group would increase federal revenues by about $175 billion annually." John Guyton, Patrick Langetieg, Daniel Reck, Max Risch, and Gabriel Zucman, "Tax Evasion at the Top of the Income Distribution: Theory and Evidence," NBER Working Paper 28542, March 2021, JEL No. D31,H26, https://www.nber.org/papers/w28542.

126. H&R Block, Inc., *Annual Report on Form 10-K for the Fiscal Year Ended June 30, 2022* (Kansas City, MO: H&R Block, Inc., 2022), 8–9.

127. Louis Serino, "Tax Preparers Lobby Heavily Against Simple Filing," Sunlight Foundation, April 15, 2013, https://sunlightfoundation.com/2013/04/15/tax-preparers-lobby-heavily-against-simple-filing/.

128. "H&R Block—Summary," OpenSecrets, https://www.opensecrets.org/orgs/hr-block/summary?id=D000022016; "Intuit Inc.—Summary," OpenSecrets, https://www.opensecrets.org/orgs/intuit-inc/summary?id=D000026667.

129. OpenSecrets, "H&R Block."

130. OpenSecrets, "Intuit Inc." OpenSecrets notes that organizations themselves cannot contribute to candidates and party committees and that the donations attributable to these companies are by "affiliates"—namely employees making individual contributions or through political action committees.

131. Austan Goolsbee, *The Simple Return: Reducing America's Tax Burden Through Return-Free Filing* (Washington, D.C.: Brookings Institution, 2006).

132. "How Could We Improve the Federal Tax System?," Tax Policy Center, Tax Policy Center Briefing Book, May 2020, https://www.taxpolicycenter.org/briefing-book/what-other-countries-use-return-free-filing.

133. Liz Day, "How the Maker of TurboTax Fought Free, Simple Tax Filing," *ProPublica*, March 26, 2013.

134. Jessica Huseman, "Filing Taxes Could Be Free and Simple. But H&R Block and Intuit Are Still Lobbying Against It," *ProPublica*, March 20, 2017.

135. "Free File Alliance," accessed November 9, 2023, https://freefilealliance.org.

136. "Free File: About the Free File Alliance," Internal Revenue Service, last modified January 23, 2023, https://www.irs.gov/e-file-providers/about-the-free-file-alliance.

137. U.S. Treasury Inspector General for Tax Administration, *Complexity and Insufficient Oversight of the Free File Program Result in Low Taxpayer Participation* (Washington, D.C.: U.S. Treasury Inspector General for Tax Administration, 2020).

138. Ibid., 6. Once on the members' commercial websites, *the taxpayers*

are not guaranteed a free return filing. "Eligible taxpayers with the same tax situations have different experiences filing their returns and may be charged a fee based solely on whether they access a member's website through IRS.gov or through an Internet search."

139. Ibid., 7.

140. Ibid., 9.

141. Carmen Reinicke, "Intuit Will No Longer Be a Part of an IRS Program That Helps Millions of Americans File Taxes for Free," *CNBC*, July 16, 2021.

142. Federal Trade Commission, "FTC Sues Intuit for Its Deceptive TurboTax 'Free' Filing Campaign," press release, March 29, 2022, https://www.ftc.gov/news-events/news/press-releases/2022/03/ftc-sues-intuit-its-deceptive-turbotax-free-filing-campaign.

143. Jacob Bogage, "Intuit Agrees to $141 Million Settlement over 'Deceptive' TurboTax Ads," *Washington Post*, May 4, 2022.

144. Justin Elliott and Paul Kiel, "Inflation Reduction Act Will Require the IRS to Study Free Tax Filing Options," *ProPublica*, August 16, 2022.

2. Corporate Welfare

1. Maximus, "Maximus Moves Corporate Headquarters to New Location in Tysons, Virginia," press release, May 3, 2022, https://maximus.com/news/maximus-moves-corporate-headquarters-new-location-tysons-virginia.

2. "Eligibility and Enrollment Solutions Made Simple," Maximus, accessed November 1, 2023, https://maximus.com/eligibility-and-enrollment.

3. "SNAP/TANF Employment and Training," Maximus, accessed November 1, 2023, https://maximus.com/solutions/snap-tanf-employment-training.

4. "Case Study: Texas Eligibility Support Services," Maximus, February 11, 2019, https://maximus.com/case-study/texas-eligibility-support-services.

5. Ibid.

6. Maximus, Inc., *Annual Report on Form 10-K for the Fiscal Year Ended September 30, 2022* (McLean, VA: Maximus, Inc., 2022), 28.

7. "LBB Contracts Database," Legislative Budget Board, State of Texas, https://www.lbb.texas.gov/Contract_Reporting.aspx. This figure includes a $419 million contract awarded January 1, 2023, for eligibility determination services.

8. Personal Responsibility and Work Opportunity Reconciliation Act of 1996, Pub. L. No. 104-19, 110 Stat. 2105 (1996).

9. M. Bryna Sanger, *The Welfare Marketplace: Privatization and Welfare Reform* (Washington, D.C.: Brookings Institution Press, 2003), 79.

10. "Supports and Safety Net," Maximus, accessed November 1, 2023, https://maximus.com/supports-and-safety-net.

11. Aditi Shrivastava and Gina Azito Thompson, *TANF Cash Assistance Should Reach Millions More Families to Lessen Hardship* (Washington, D.C.: Center on Budget and Policy Priorities, 2022).

12. Donald Cohen and Allen Mikaelian, *The Privatization of Everything: How the Plunder of Public Goods Transformed America and How We Can Fight Back* (New York: The New Press, 2021), 30.

13. "Maximus Human Services, Inc.: Top Ten Agencies by Active Expense Contracts," Checkbook NYC, accessed October 15, 2023, https://www.checkbooknyc.com.

14. Center on Budget and Policy Priorities, *Policy Basics, Temporary Assistance for Needy Families* (Washington, D.C.: Center on Budget and Policy Priorities, 2022); "Combined TANF and SSP-MOE Work Participation Rates, Fiscal Year 2019," U.S. Department of Health and Human Services, July 30, 2020, https://www.acf.hhs.gov/sites/default/files/documents/ofa/wpr2019table01a.pdf, Table 1-A.

15. Sewell Chan, "Remembering a Snowstorm That Paralyzed the City," *New York Times*, February 10, 2009; Sylvan Fox, "A Paralyzed City Digs Out of Snow," *New York Times*, February 11, 1969.

16. Mike Squires, "The 100-Hour Snowstorm of February 1969," Climate.gov, February 22, 2016, https://www.climate.gov/news-features/blogs/beyond-data/100-hour-snowstorm-february-1969

17. Chan, "Remembering a Snowstorm"; Richard Phalon, "Political Foes and Voters Score Lindsay on Cleanup," *New York Times*, February 12, 1969.

18. Sylvan Fox, "Areas of Queens Still Snowbound; Most of City Open," *New York Times*, February 13, 1969.

19. Fox, "Areas of Queens Still Snowbound"; Chan, "Remembering a Snowstorm."

20. Chan, "Remembering a Snowstorm."

21. Ibid.

22. Emanuel S. Savas, *Privatization and Public-Private Partnerships* (New York: Seven Bridges Press, LLC, 2000), xiii.

23. Ibid.

24. Ibid.

25. "E.S. Savas," Sage Publishing, accessed November 1, 2023, https://us.sagepub.com/en-us/nam/author/emanuel-s-savas.

26. Savas "pioneered the concept of privatization," the libertarian, pro-privatization Reason Foundation says in its description of an award it created in his honor. "He was the first to advocate private competition to improve public services." Today, the foundation's ongoing Savas Award for Privatization honors individuals "advancing innovative ways to improve the provision

and quality of public services by engaging the private sector." Winners have included former Indiana governor and Purdue University president Mitch Daniels; former Democratic New York City Council member and charter school founder Eva Moskowitz; former Federal Communications Commission chairman Ajit Pai (an Obama appointee); and former Indianapolis mayor Stephen Goldsmith. "Savas Award for Privatization," Reason Foundation, accessed November 3, 2023, https://reason.org/savas-award-for-privatization/.

27. Stuart M. Butler, ed., *The Privatization Option: A Strategy to Shrink the Size of Government* (Washington, D.C.: The Heritage Foundation, 1985); "Robert Poole," Reason Foundation, accessed November 1, 2023, https://reason.org/author/robert-poole/.

28. Reason Foundation, "Robert Poole."

29. Reason Foundation, *Transforming Government Through Privatization* (Washington, D.C.: Reason Foundation, 2006). The report's twentieth anniversary edition, in 2006, would credit Koch's "vision and support" for creating "the nation's foremost publication on privatization, outsourcing, and government reform." In recent years, having achieved the lion's share of its goals, the report has focused more narrowly on the privatization of infrastructure, including airports, air traffic control, and airport security. Marc Scribner, *Annual Privatization Report 2022: Aviation* (Washington, D.C.: Reason Foundation, 2022).

30. John Tierney, "Bringing His Gospel Home; City Hall Lends Ear to Captain of Privatization," *New York Times*, May 25, 1995.

31. E.S. Savas, *Privatization: The Key to Better Government* (London: Chatham House Publishers, 1988); Tierney, "Bringing His Gospel Home."

32. Cohen and Mikaelian, *The Privatization of Everything*, 24.

33. Ibid.

34. "James M. Buchanan Jr.," The Nobel Prize, accessed November 8, 2023 https://www.nobelprize.org/prizes/economic-sciences/1986/buchanan/facts/.

35. Donald F. Kettl, *Government by Proxy: (Mis)Managing Federal Programs* (Washington, D.C.: CQ Press, 1987), 10.

36. Cohen and Mikaelian, *The Privatization of Everything*, 24.

37. Savas, *Privatization*, 14.

38. Ronald Reagan, "Inaugural Address 1981," National Archives, Ronald Reagan Presidential Library & Museum, January 20, 1981, https://www.reaganlibrary.gov/archives/speech/inaugural-address-1981.

39. "Historical Tables," WhiteHouse.gov, https://www.whitehouse.gov/omb/budget/historical-tables/, Table 3.1. In constant (2012) dollars, federal outlays grew from $694.7 billion in 1960 to $1.65 trillion in 1981. As a share of

GDP, however, federal spending was less dramatic, swelling from 17.3 percent to 1960 to 21.6 percent in 1981.

40. Steven Rathgeb Smith and Michael Lipsky, *Nonprofits for Hire: The Welfare State in the Age of Contracting* (Cambridge, MA: Harvard University Press, 1993), 54.

41. B. Alex Beasley, "The Oil Shocks of the 1970s," Yale University, 2023, https://energyhistory.yale.edu/the-oil-shocks-of-the-1970s/. Members of the oil-producing cartel OPEC cut production to protest U.S. policies in the Middle East, including America's support of Israel during the Yom Kippur War.

42. Daniel L. Thornton, "The U.S. Deficit/Debt Problem: A Longer Run Perspective," Federal Reserve Bank of St. Louis, *Review* 4, no. 6 (November/December 2012): 441–55.

43. U.S. Census Bureau, *Poverty Increases by 1.2 Million in 1970 (Advance data from March 1971 Current Population Survey)* (Washington, D.C.: U.S. Census Bureau, 1971).

44. Kettl, *Government by Proxy*, 2.

45. Ibid.

46. Ibid.

47. *Privatization of the Federal Government, Hearings before the Subcommittee on Monetary and Fiscal Policy of the Joint Economic Committee*, 98th Cong. 1254 (1984) (statement of Senator Steven D. Symms). Symms, incidentally, was a Tea Party Republican before such a thing existed. A former apple farmer who first ran for Congress in 1972, his purported campaign slogan was "Take a bite out of big government!" His tenure included multiple controversies, including an accusation that Kitty Dukakis, wife of Democratic presidential nominee Michael Dukakis, had once burned the American flag. Personal scandals involving infidelity and a son facing criminal charges led him to decline a bid for re-election in 1992; "Symms Weighs Senate Retirement as Personal Troubles Mount," *Deseret News*, July 7, 1991, https://www.deseret.com/1991/7/7/18929577/symms-weighs-senate-retirement-as-his-personal-troubles-mount.

48. *Privatization of the Federal Government* (statement of Senator Steven D. Symms).

49. Lee Iacocca and William Novak, *Iacocca: An Autobiography* (New Providence, NJ: Bantam, 1986); Donald J. Trump and Tony Schwartz, *Trump: The Art of the Deal* (New York: Random House Publishing Group, Reprint edition, October 6, 2015); Ken Follett, *On Wings of Eagles: The Inspiring True Story of One Man's Patriotic Spirit—and His Heroic Mission to Save His Countrymen* (New York: Penguin Books, 1984); *On Wings of Eagles* (Goodland Productions, 2016), https://www.imdb.com/title/tt0090491/.

50. Of course, time has revealed that none of these emperors has clothes. Iacocca could not save Chrysler from globalization and retired in 1992 as the company's fortunes declined. It eventually declared bankruptcy in 2009 and is now a part of FCA US, owned by Fiat Chrysler Automobiles. Robert D. McFadden, "Lee Iacocca, Visionary Automaker Who Led Both Ford and Chrysler, Is Dead at 94," *New York Times*, July 2, 2019; Chris Isidore, "Chrysler Files for Bankruptcy," CNNMoney.com, May 1, 2009; "Chrysler's Complicated Parentage: Who Owns It Now?," *Motortrend*, June 12, 2020. Historians have ranked Trump the worst president in U.S. history with misdeeds too numerous to elucidate here; Tim Naftali, "The Worst President in History," *The Atlantic*, January 19, 2021. Perot, who mounted one of the most successful third-party bids for the presidency in 1992, saw his star fade when he ran again in 1996. "By then the epigrams had paled, and voters suspected that his business strengths, the risk-taking and stubborn autocratic personality, might not serve a president constrained by Congress and public opinion. And by then more was known of Mr. Perot, who could be thin-skinned and meanspirited, who had subjected employees to moral codes and lie detector tests, who was drawn to conspiracy theories and had hired private detectives to chase his suspicions," wrote the *New York Times* in his obituary in 2019; Robert D. McFadden, "Ross Perot, Brash Texas Billionaire Who Ran for President, Dies at 89," *New York Times*, July 9, 2019.

51. Peter F. Drucker, "The Sickness of Government," *Public Interest*, Winter 1969, 3.

52. Ibid., 7.

53. Ibid., 20.

54. Reagan, "1981 Inaugural Address."

55. "President's Private Sector Survey on Cost Control (Grace Commission)," National Archives, Ronald Reagan Presidential Library & Museum, https://www.reaganlibrary.gov/archives/topic-guide/presidents-private-sector-survey-cost-control-grace-commission; Ronald Reagan, *An American Life* (New York: Simon and Schuster, 2011), loc. 4907 of 12869, Kindle.

56. Reagan, *An American Life*, loc. 4915.

57. Ibid.

58. Ibid.

59. President's Commission on Privatization, *Privatization: Toward More Effective Government* (Washington, D.C.: President's Commission on Privatization, 1988).

60. Robert Benenson, "Social Welfare Under Reagan," *CQ Researcher*, March 9, 1984; Sheldon Danziger and Robert Haveman, "The Reagan Administration Budget Cuts: Their Impact on the Poor," University of

Wisconsin–Madison, Institute for Research on Poverty, *Focus* 1, no. 2 (Winter 1981–82): 13–16.

61. Reason Foundation, *Transforming Government Through Privatization*, 22.

62. "1980 Electoral College Results," National Archives, last reviewed December 10, 2019, https://www.archives.gov/electoral-college/1980; "1984 Electoral College Results," National Archives, last reviewed December 10, 2019, https://www.archives.gov/electoral college/1984.

63. Kevin Kaduk, "The 10 Biggest Landslides in Presidential Election History," *ListWire*, August 17, 2021.

64. "1988 Electoral College Results," National Archives, last reviewed December 10, 2019, https://www.archives.gov/electoral-college/1988.

65. Bob Drogin, "How Presidential Race Was Won and Lost: Michael Dukakis," *Los Angeles Times*, November 10, 1988; Mark Leibovich, "Massachusetts, The Stigma State," *Washington Post*, February 1, 2004. Bush also used racist dog whistles in his campaign—i.e., the infamous attack ad featuring convicted criminal Willie Horton, who committed additional crimes while on furlough from prison when Dukakis was governor. Erin Blakemore, "How the Willie Horton Ad Played on Racism and Fear," History.com, November 2, 2019, https://www.history.com/news/george-bush-willie-horton-racist-ad.

66. Mitchell Locin, "Clinton Says He's a 'New Democrat,'" *Chicago Tribune*, October 22, 1922; "Bill Clinton in 1992 ad: 'A Plan to End Welfare as We Know It,'" *Washington Post*, August 30, 2016.

67. In a 2000 interview with *Frontline*, Morris invoked the Hegelian dialectic to describe triangulation: "What you should do is really take the best from each party's agenda, and come to a solution somewhere above the positions of each party. So from the left, take the idea that we need day care and food supplements for people on welfare. From the right, take the idea that they have to work for a living, and that there are time limits. But discard the nonsense of the left, which is that there shouldn't be work requirements; and the nonsense of the right, which is you should punish single mothers. Get rid of the garbage of each position, that the people didn't believe in; take the best from each position; and move up to a third way. And that became a triangle, which was triangulation. For those of your viewers who are into philosophy, it really is Hegelian in concept: the idea of a thesis, an antithesis, and a synthesis. And when we originally discussed it, we did so in terms of Hegel, which we had studied at Oxford. But in American politics, we spoke of triangulation." Dick Morris, interview by Chris Bury, *Frontline*, June 2000, https://www.pbs.org/wgbh/pages/frontline/shows/clinton/interviews/morris2.html.

68. "1992 Clinton Campaign Ads," YouTube, https://www.youtube.com/watch?v=XoBFL6iwid4 at 1:39.

69. National Performance Review, *From Red Tape to Results: Creating a Government That Works Better & Costs Less, Report of the National Performance Review* (Washington, D.C.: National Performance Review, 1993).

70. David Osborne and Ted Gaebler, *Reinventing Government: How the Entrepreneurial Spirit Is Transforming the Public Sector* (New York: Plume, 1993), 2.

71. Ibid.

72. Ibid., 77.

73. Ibid., 139.

74. Ibid., 282.

75. "President Clinton's New Markets Initiative: Revitalizing America's Underserved Communities," The White House, December 14, 2000, https://clintonwhitehouse4.archives.gov/textonly/WH/new/html/Mon_Dec_18_154959_2000.html; "Briefing Book: Key Elements of the U.S. Tax System: What Is the Low-Income Housing Tax Credit and How Does It Work?," Tax Policy Center, https://www.taxpolicycenter.org/briefing-book/what-low-income-housing-tax-credit-and-how-does-it-work.

76. "Total Quality Management," *Inc.*, accessed November 8, 2023, https://www.inc.com/encyclopedia/total-quality-management-tqm.html.

77. Osborne and Gaebler, *Reinventing Government*, 45.

78. William Jefferson Clinton, "State of the Union Address, January 23, 1996," The White House, January 23, 1996, https://clintonwhitehouse4.archives.gov/WH/New/other/sotu.html.

79. John Kamensky, "National Partnership for Reinventing Government (formerly the National Performance Review): A Brief History," National Partnership for Reinventing Government, January 1999, https://govinfo.library.unt.edu/npr/whoweare/history2.html (archive).

80. Paul Light, *The Government-Industrial Complex: The True Size of the Federal Government, 1984–2018* (New York: Oxford University Press, 2019), 45.

81. Reason Foundation, *Annual Privatization Report*, 23.

82. Federal Activities Inventory Reform Act of 1998, Pub. L. 105-270, 112 Stat. 2382 (1998).

83. Light, *Government-Industrial Complex*, 23.

84. Ibid.

85. Ibid.

86. Nina Bernstein, "Giant Companies Entering Race to Run State Welfare Programs," *New York Times*, September 15, 1996.

87. Jeff Kunerth, "Lockheed Takes on Welfare," *Orlando Sentinel*, September 7, 1997.

88. Ibid.

89. Demetra Smith Nightingale and Nancy M. Pindus, *Privatization of Public Social Services: A Background Paper* (Washington, D.C.: Urban Institute, 1997).

90. "The Personal Responsibility and Work Opportunity Reconciliation Act of 1996," U.S. Department of Health and Human Services, Office of the Assistant Secretary for Planning and Evaluation, August 31, 1996, https://aspe.hhs.gov/reports/personal-responsibility-work-opportunity-reconciliation-act-1996.

91. "TANF-ACF-PI-2020-05 (Renewed Form ACF-202, Caseload Reduction Report)," U.S. Department of Health and Human Services, Office of Family Assistance, Policy and Guidance, December 30, 2020, https://www.acf.hhs.gov/ofa/policy-guidance/tanf-acf-pi-2020-05.

92. Ibid.

93. U.S. Department of Health and Human Services, "The Personal Responsibility and Work Opportunity Reconciliation Act of 1996."

94. Ibid.

95. Smith and Pindus, *Privatization of Public Social Services*, 4.

96. M. Bryna Sanger, *The Welfare Marketplace: Privatization and Welfare Reform* (Washington, D.C.: Brookings Institution Press, 2003), 35.

97. Sanger, *Welfare Marketplace*, 27.

98. Pamela Winston, Andrew Burwick, Sheena McConnell, and Richard Roper, *Privatization of Welfare Services: A Review of the Literature* (Princeton, NJ: Mathematica, Inc., 2002).

99. Demetra Smith Nightingale and Kelly S. Mickelson, *An Overview of Research Related to Wisconsin Works (W-2)* (Washington, D.C.: Urban Institute, 2000).

100. Michael Wiseman, "State Strategies for Welfare Reform: The Wisconsin Story," Institute for Research on Poverty, Discussion Paper No 1066-95, December 1995, https://www.irp.wisc.edu/publications/dps/pdfs/dp106695.pdf; Thomas Corbett, "Understanding Wisconsin Works (W-2)," Institute for Research on Poverty, https://www.irp.wisc.edu/publications/focus/pdfs/foc181-3.pdf.

101. "Governor Signs Welfare Reform Bill in Wisconsin," *Associated Press*, April 26, 1996.

102. Jason DeParle, "Dream Deferred," *Washington Monthly*, September 2004.

103. "Wisconsin Legislative Audit Bureau, Letter of Transmittal," July 28, 2000, https://legis.wisconsin.gov/lab/reports/ltrmaximus.htm; "Administration of the Wisconsin Works Program by Maximus, Inc.," Wisconsin Legislative Audit Bureau, https://legis.wisconsin.gov/lab/reports/maximus.pdf, 11.

104. Wisconsin Legislative Audit Bureau, "Administration of the Wisconsin Works Program," 12, 13.

105. Jason DeParle, *American Dream: Three Women, Ten Kids, and a Nation's Drive to End Welfare* (New York: Viking, 2004).

106. Ibid. As noted, "work" can include job training, school, job search, and a host of other activities that don't include paid work.

107. Thomas J. Lueck, "Hevesi Rejects Largest Pacts for Welfare," *New York Times*, March 23, 2000.

108. Michael Cooper, "Disputed Pacts for Welfare Will Just Die," *New York Times*, October 4, 2002.

109. Esther B. Fein, "For Job-Finding Concern, a Troubled Past," *New York Times*, March 1, 1994.

110. Interview with author.

111. Kunerth, "Lockheed Takes on Welfare."

112. Fein, "For Job-Finding Concern, a Troubled Past."

113. DeParle, *American Dream*.

114. Sheena McConnell, Andrew Burwick, Irma Perez-Johnson, and Pamela Winston, *Privatization in Practice: Case Studies of Contracting for TANF Case Management* (Princeton, NJ: Mathematica, Inc., 2003), 42.

115. Ibid., 70.

116. Interview with author.

117. McConnell et al., *Privatization in Practice*, 30.

118. "Trends in the AFDC Caseload since 1962," U.S. Department of Health and Human Services, accessed November 8, 2023, https://aspe.hhs.gov/sites/default/files/private/pdf/167036/2caseload.pdf; "TANF Caseload, 1996," U.S. Department of Health and Human Services, https://www.acf.hhs.gov/sites/default/files/documents/ofa/1996_15months.pdf; "SSP-MOE: Total Number of Families, Fiscal and Calendar Year 2001," U.S. Department of Health and Human Services, https://www.acf.hhs.gov/sites/default/files/documents/ofa/2001_15months_ssp.pdf.

119. "Temporary Assistance for Needy Families (TANF) Caseload Data, Fiscal Year (FY) 2022," U.S. Department of Health and Human Services, March 31, 2023, https://www.acf.hhs.gov/sites/default/files/documents/ofa/fy2022_tanf_caseload.pdf.

120. Center on Budget and Policy Priorities, *Policy Basics: Temporary Assistance for Needy Families* (Washington, D.C.: Center on Budget and Policy Priorities, 2022).

121. Michigan's 2021 poverty rate was 13.1 percent, compared to 12.8 percent nationwide. "QuickFacts, Michigan," U.S. Census Bureau, July 1, 2022, https://www.census.gov/quickfacts/fact/table/MI/AGE295221.

122. "Temporary Assistance for Needy Families (TANF) Caseload Data, Fiscal Year (FY) 2021," U.S. Department of Health and Human Services, March 10, 2022, https://www.acf.hhs.gov/sites/default/files/documents/ofa/fy2021_tanf_caseload.pdf.

123. "TANF and MOE Spending and Transfers by Activity, FY 2020: Michigan," U.S. Department of Health and Human Services, https://www.acf.hhs.gov/sites/default/files/documents/ofa/fy2020_tanf_moe_state_piechart_michigan.pdf.

124. "TANF and MOE Spending and Transfers by Activity, FY 2020: United States," U.S. Department of Health and Human Services, September 22, 2021, https://www.acf.hhs.gov/sites/default/files/documents/ofa/fy2020_tanf_moe_national_data_pie_chart.pdf.

125. Thomas M. Fraker, Dan M. Levy, Irma Perez-Johnson, Alan M. Hershey, Demetra S. Nightingale, Robert B. Olsen, and Rita A. Stapulonis, *National Evaluation of the Welfare-to-Work Grants Program: Final Report* (Princeton, NJ: Mathematica Policy Research, Inc., 2004).

126. LaDonna Pavetti, *Work Requirements Don't Cut Poverty, Evidence Shows* (Washington, D.C.: Center on Budget and Policy Priorities, 2016).

127. "Season 6: The Welfare to Work Industrial Complex," *The Uncertain Hour*, Marketplace, Minnesota Public Radio, March 15, 2023, https://www.marketplace.org/shows/the-uncertain-hour/season-6-the-welfare-to-work-industrial-complex/.

128. "Contracts for Maximus Inc.," New York State Office of the State Comptroller, Open Book New York, accessed November 8, 2023, https://wwe2.osc.state.ny.us/transparency/contracts/contractresults.cfm?ID=22213.

129. Database search of Checkbook NYC, Maximus Human Services, Inc., https://www.checkbooknyc.com, March 14, 2023.

130. Database search of Checkbook NYC, America Works, https://www.checkbooknyc.com, March 14, 2023.

131. One of the stated purposes of PRWORA, the statute that created TANF, is to "end the dependence of needy parents on government benefits by promoting job preparation, work, and marriage"; Personal Responsibility and Work Opportunity Reconciliation Act of 1996, Pub. L. No. 104-19, 110 Stat. 2105 (1996).

132. Maximus, *2022 Annual Report*, 7, 8.

133. Maximus, Inc., *Annual Report on Form 10-K for the Fiscal Year Ended September 30, 2021* (McLean, VA: Maximus, Inc., 2021), 23.

134. Maximus, *2022 Annual Report*, 18.

135. Dylan Matthews, "'If the Goal Was to Get Rid of Poverty, We Failed': The Legacy of the 1996 Welfare Reform," *Vox*, June 20, 2016.

136. "Aid to Families with Dependent Children (AFDC) and Temporary Assistance for Needy Families (TANF)—Overview," U.S. Department of Health and Human Services, Office of the Assistant Secretary for Planning and Evaluation, https://aspe.hhs.gov/aid-families-dependent-children-afdc-temporary-assistance-needy-families-tanf-overview.

137. Linda Giannarelli and C. Eugene Steuerle, *The Twice-Poverty Trap: Tax Rates Faced by AFDC Recipients* (Washington, D.C.: Urban Institute, 1995), 1.

138. "The Personal Responsibility and Work Opportunity Reconciliation Act of 1996," U.S. Department of Health and Human Services, Office of the Assistant Secretary for Planning and Evaluation, August 31, 1996, https://aspe.hhs.gov/reports/personal-responsibility-work-opportunity-reconciliation-act-1996.

139. Federal Elections Commission, *Federal Elections 94: Election Results for the U.S. Senate and the U.S. House of Representatives* (Washington, D.C.: Federal Elections Commission, 1995).

140. "Republican Contract with America," https://web.archive.org/web/19990427174200/http://www.house.gov/house/Contract/CONTRACT.html (archive).

141. "The Personal Responsibility Act (Welfare Reform)," https://web.archive.org/web/20001012113736/http://www.house.gov/house/Contract/persrespd.txt (archive).

142. "Clinton Vetoes GOP Welfare Reform Bill," *Baltimore Sun*, January 10, 1996.

143. For an excellent summary of the political landscape in 1996, see Ron Haskins, "Interview: Welfare Reform, 10 Years Later," Brookings Institution, August 24, 2006, https://www.brookings.edu/on-the-record/interview-welfare-reform-10-years-later/. Haskins, a senior fellow at the Brookings Institution, was a key staffer on the House Ways and Means Committee with a front-row seat at the bill's passage.

144. John F. Harris and John E. Yang, "Clinton to Sign Bill Overhauling Welfare," *Washington Post*, August 1, 1996.

145. Lily Rothman, "Why Bill Clinton Signed the Welfare Reform Bill, as Explained in 1996," *Time*, August 19, 2016.

146. Laura Reiley, "Trump Administration Tightens Work Requirements for SNAP, Which Could Cut Hundreds of Thousands from Food Stamps," *Washington Post*, December 4, 2019.

147. Ibid.

148. Madeline Guth and MaryBeth Musumeci, "An Overview of Medicaid Work Requirements: What Happened Under the Trump and Biden Administrations?," Kaiser Family Foundation, May 3, 2022, https://www.kff

.org/medicaid/issue-brief/an-overview-of-medicaid-work-requirements-what-happened-under-the-trump-and-biden-administrations/.

149. Madeline Guth, "Medicaid Work Requirements Are Back on the Agenda," Kaiser Family Foundation, April 3, 2023, https://www.kff.org/policy-watch/medicaid-work-requirements-are-back-on-agenda/.

3. Bridges to Nowhere

1. "East Los Angeles, CDP, California," U.S. Census Bureau, accessed November 8, 2023, https://data.census.gov/cedsci/profile/East_Los_Angeles_CDP,_California?g=1600000US0620802.

2. "School Catalog, January 3, 2022–December 23, 2022," International College, accessed November 6, 2023, https://drive.google.com/file/d/1qlhVgK5UpWU-Th1XVo6sMfN5T8-dARUm/view.

3. "School Performance Fact Sheet, Calendar Years 2019 & 2020, Cake Decoration (2) – 160 Hours," International College, accessed November 6, 2023, https://drive.google.com/file/d/1CiUxHTpA7awyth0u3BTMEZ522dQNZR04/view.

4. As of November 2023, CalJOBs listed about 900 "eligible training providers," including about 340 for-profit institutions. Database search of CalJOBS, November 9, 2023, https://www.caljobs.ca.gov/vosnet/Default.aspx

5. "Stellar Career College," U.S. Department of Education, College Scorecard, accessed November 8, 2023, https://collegescorecard.ed.gov/school/?444529-Stellar-Career-College; "College Scorecard, UEI College–Gardena," U.S. Department of Education, College Scorecard, accessed November 8, 2023, https://collegescorecard.ed.gov/school/?393649-UEI-College-Gardena.

6. "American River College," U.S. Department of Education, College Scorecard, accessed November 8, 2023, https://collegescorecard.ed.gov/school/?109208-American-River-College; "Provider Information: Milan Institute," CalJOBS, accessed November 9, 2023, https://www.caljobs.ca.gov.

7. U.S. Department of Labor, Office of Inspector General, *Jobs Corps Could Not Demonstrate Beneficial Job Training Outcomes* (Washington, D.C.: U.S. Department of Labor, Office of Inspector General, 2018).

8. U.S. General Accounting Office, *Implementation of the Phaseout of CETA Public Service Jobs* (Washington, D.C.: U.S. General Accounting Office, 1982). (GAO was known as the Comptroller General of the United States, then as the General Accounting Office before it became the Government Accountability Office in 2004. "100 Years of GAO," U.S. Government Accountability Office, https://www.gao.gov/about/what-gao-does/hundred-years-of-gao.)

9. U.S. General Accounting Office, *Implementation of the Phaseout of CETA Public Service Jobs*, 5.

10. Ibid., 8.

11. Ibid., 11–18.

12. Ibid., 21.

13. Ibid., 22.

14. Ibid., 29.

15. Comptroller General of the United States, *Concentrated Employment Program in New York City Has Not Met Its Employment Objectives* (Washington, D.C.: Comptroller General of the United States, 1972).

16. Comptroller General of the United States, *Problems in Making the Concentrated Employment Program Work in Rural Mississippi* (Washington, D.C.: Comptroller General of the United States, 1972), 2.

17. Comptroller General, *Concentrated Employment Program in New York City*, 23–24.

18. Comptroller General of the United States, *Progress and Problems in Allocating Funds Under Titles I and II—Comprehensive Employment and Training Act* (Washington, D.C.: Comptroller General of the United States, 1976), 1. According to a 1978 report by the comptroller general of the United States (now the Government Accountability Office), the U.S. Department of Labor reported that out of 84,000 CETA jobs it analyzed in 1977, 18 percent were in public works, 17 percent were in "environmental quality," and 25 percent were in social services and education. Comptroller General of the United States, *Information on the Buildup in Public Service Jobs* (Washington, D.C.: Comptroller General of the United States, 1978).

19. Comptroller General of the United States, *Progress and Problems in Allocating Funds Under Titles I and II—Comprehensive Employment and Training Act*, 1; Spencer Rich, "CETA: Still Going Strong Despite Doubts," *Washington Post*, July 3, 1978.

20. One area in which CETA did have some success was its promotion of local art and artists. Andrea Kirsh, "Recording the Unrecorded Art History of CETA, the Comprehensive Employment and Training Act," *Artblog*, June 23, 2022, https://www.theartblog.org/2022/06/recording-the-unrecorded-art-history-of-ceta-the-comprehensive-employment-and-training-act/.

21. Rich, "CETA: Still Going Strong."

22. Ibid.

23. U.S. General Accounting Office, *Implementation of the Phaseout of CETA Public Service Jobs*.

24. James Bovard, *JTPA: Another Federal Training Fraud* (Washington, D.C.: CATO Institute, 1990).

25. "Workforce Innovation and Opportunity Act," U.S. Department of Labor, Employment and Training Administration, https://www.dol.gov/agencies/eta/wioa.

26. Michael B. Katz, *The Undeserving Poor: America's Enduring Confrontation with Poverty*, 2d ed. (New York: Oxford University Press, 2013), 185.

27. Katz, *The Undeserving Poor*, 6–7.

28. Martin Gilens, *Why Americans Hate Welfare: Race, Media, and the Politics of Antipoverty Policy* (Chicago: University of Chicago Press, 1999).

29. Lawrence M. Mead, *The New Politics of Poverty: The Nonworking Poor in America* (New York: Basic Books, 1992), 3, 16.

30. Katz, *The Undeserving Poor*, 181.

31. Mead, *New Politics of Poverty*, 61.

32. "Great Depression Facts," Franklin D. Roosevelt Presidential Library and Museum, https://www.fdrlibrary.org/great-depression-facts.

33. Franklin D. Roosevelt, "Annual Message to Congress, January 4, 1935," The American Presidency Project, University of California, Santa Barbara, https://www.presidency.ucsb.edu/documents/annual-message-congress-3.

34. "Executive Order 7034—Establishing the Division of Applications and Information, the Advisory Committee on Allotments, the Works Progress Administration, and for Other Purposes," The American Presidency Project, https://www.presidency.ucsb.edu/documents/executive-order-7034-creating-machinery-for-the-works-progress-administration; "Works Progress Administration (WPA)," History.com, last modified September 21, 2022, https://www.history.com/topics/great-depression/works-progress-administration.

35. Guian A. McKee, "Lyndon B. Johnson and the War on Poverty," Presidential Recordings, Miller Center, University of Virginia, 2014, https://prde.upress.virginia.edu/content/WarOnPoverty2.

36. Lyndon B. Johnson, "Annual Message to the Congress on the State of the Union, January 8, 1964," The American Presidency Project, https://www.presidency.ucsb.edu/documents/annual-message-the-congress-the-state-the-union-25.

37. Council of Economic Advisors, *Annual Report of the Council of Economic Advisors* (Washington, D.C.: Council of Economic Advisors, 1964), 74, 75.

38. "Head Start History," U.S. Department of Health and Human Services, Office of Head Start, updated June 30, 2023, https://www.acf.hhs.gov/ohs/about/history-head-start.

39. Gilens, *Why Americans Hate Welfare*, 185.

40. "Clinton-Gore Accomplishments: Reforming Welfare by Promoting Work and Responsibility," The White House, December 15, 2000, https://clintonwhitehouse4.archives.gov/WH/Accomplishments/welfare.html.

41. Ibid.

42. Office of Sen. Patty Murray, "Senate Passes Murray's Historic Bipartisan, Bicameral Deal to Improve American Workforce Development System with 95–3 Vote," press release, June 25, 2014, https://www.murray.senate.gov/senate-passes-murrays-historic-bipartisan-bicameral-deal-to-improve-american-workforce-development-system-with-95-3-vote/.

43. Congressional Research Service, *The Workforce Innovation and Opportunity Act and the One-Stop Delivery System* (Washington, D.C.: Congressional Research Service, 2022).

44. "Workforce Innovation and Opportunity Act," U.S. Department of Labor, Employment and Training Administration, https://www.dol.gov/agencies/eta/wioa.

45. "NOVAworks Public Calendar," NOVAworks, https://www.novaworkss.org/calendar/nova; "Job Search," NOVAworks, https://jobboard.novaworks.org.

46. Interview with author.

47. "Arlington Employment Center," Arlington, VA, accessed March 14, 2023, https://www.arlingtonva.us/Government/Programs/AEC.

48. Accessed March 14, 2023.

49. "FY 2021 Performance Plan," Arlington Employment Center, https://www.arlingtonva.us/files/sharedassets/public/departments/documents/dhs/marcus-alert/pmps/fy2021/eid-arlington-employment-center-pmp-fy-2021-final.pdf.

50. Ibid., 11, 13.

51. Email to author from Yolanda Crewe, WIOA Programs Director, April 20, 2022.

52. Congressional Research Service, *The Workforce Innovation and Opportunity Act*; "WIOA Performance Results At-a-Glance," U.S. Department of Labor, Employment and Training Administration, https://www.dol.gov/agencies/eta/performance/wioa-performance. The DOL reports that 2,842,543 people "participated" in WIOA programs in 2021, which is defined fairly loosely. See "Definitions of Terms Related to the Performance Accountability System," U.S. Department of Labor, https://www.dol.gov/sites/dolgov/files/ETA/advisories/TEGL/2022/TEGL%2010-16%20Change%202/Attachment%20I.pdf.

53. U.S. Department of Labor, "WIOA Performance Results At-a-Glance."

54. "Employment Projections, Earnings and Unemployment Rates by

Educational Attainment, 2021," U.S. Department of Labor, U.S. Bureau of Labor Statistics, last modified September 6, 2023, https://www.bls.gov/emp/chart-unemployment-earnings-education.htm. According to the Bureau of Labor Statistics, the median weekly wage of someone without a high school diploma in 2021 was $626. Assuming full-time, full-year work, this translates into $32,552. Workers with a high school diploma earned a medium weekly wage of $809—$42,068 on an annualized basis. Median weekly earnings for all workers in 2021 was $990 ($51,580 on an annualized basis). "Median Weekly Earnings by Age and Sex, Second Quarter 2021," U.S. Department of Labor, U.S. Bureau of Labor Statistics, July 26, 2021, https://www.bls.gov/opub/ted/2021/median-weekly-earnings-by-age-and-sex-second-quarter-2021.htm.

55. 2020 saw an even more precipitous pandemic year decline to just 237,836 trainees. "WIOA by the Numbers, Interactive Data Analysis Tool," U.S. Department of Labor, Employment and Training Administration, https://www.dol.gov/agencies/eta/performance/results/interactive-data-analysis.

56. "Virginia Workforce Connection," Virginia Career Works, https://vawc.virginia.gov/vosnet/Default.aspx; CalJOBS, CalJOBS.ca.gov.

57. "Geographic Solutions," https://www.geographicsolutions.com.

58. "Virtual OneStop (VOS) Sapphire," Geographic Solutions, https://www.geographicsolutions.com/VOS; "About Us," Geographic Solutions, https://www.geographicsolutions.com/Company/About-Us.

59. "Workforce Technology Conference," Geographic Solutions, accessed November 8, 2023. https://www.geographicsolutions.com/2023-Conference/WTC2023.

60. "Career Concourse," Virginia Career Works, accessed November 7, 2023, https://alexandriaarlington.careerconcourse.com; Chmura, https://www.chmura.com.

61. "Explore Values," Career Concourse, accessed November 7, 2023, https://alexandriaarlington.careerconcourse.com/assessment/values.

62. "Skill-Up City of Alexandria and Arlington County," City of Arlington, Virginia, accessed November 7, 2023, https://www.arlingtonva.us/Government/Programs/AEC/Skill-Up-City-of-Alexandria-and-Arlington-County.

63. "U.S. Wired for Education: Skills Training for America's Unemployed," *Learning Guild*, March 9, 2011, https://learningsolutionsmag.com/articles/642/us-wired-for-education-skills-training-for-americas-unemployed.

64. "Request or Proposals for Career Pathways Platform (Web-Based Education)," TXSHARE, https://txshare.org/getmedia/8010a85a-c910-4884-83a5-88185595f2de/NCTCOG-RFP-2020-079-Career-Pathways-Platform.pdf, 29.

65. Carl E. Van Horn and Aaron Fichtner, "Eligible Training Provider Lists and Consumer Report Cards," in *The Workforce Investment Act: Implementation Experiences and Evaluation Findings*, eds. Douglas J. Besharov and Phoebe H. Cottingham (Kalamazoo, MI: W.E. Upjohn Institute for Employment Research, 2011), 153–73.

66. "Maryland Eligible Training Provider List—Workforce Innovation and Opportunity Act (WIOA)," Maryland Department of Labor, https://www.dllr.state.md.us/employment/train/.

67. Ibid.

68. MedCerts, https://medcerts.com.

69. Aryan Consulting & Staffing, https://aryanstaffing.com/training-program (site discontinued).

70. "Tuition for Medication Aide Program," Medical Learning Center, accessed November 8, 2023, http://www.medicallearningcenterva.com/medication-aide-tuition/.

71. Virginia Career Works, "Virginia Workforce Connection."

72. Ibid., accessed December 2022.

73. Database search of Workforce West Virginia, November 9, 2023, https://public.workforcewv.org/JobSeeker/JobSeekerHome.asp?SessionUID={08CB37A0-9BDB-47E4-A048-0BD3B9975811}. When I first started researching this topic in 2022, West Virginia's ETPL even included a provider in California, the Ding King Training Institute, which offered a certificate in "paintless dent repair" for vehicles for $13,000. Database search of Workforce West Virginia, April 14, 2022; "Paintless Dent Repair Training—#1 Trusted PDR School in America," Ding King, https://thedingking.com.

74. Virginia Career Works, "Virginia Workforce Connection"; According to Virginia's ETPL, workers can obtain certification as a wind turbine technician from Centura College for $29,452; As of November 2023, Virginia's ETPL included eighteen EMT programs, varying in price from $24,691 for an associate's degree in emergency medical services from the for-profit ECPI University to $400 for EMT certification from the Richmond Adult Technical Center. Commercial driver certifications are fairly consistent in price, ranging from $2,199 to $5,400 (as of November 2023). "Virginia Workforce Connection," Virginia CareerWorks.

75. WIOA-approved ethical hacker certification was available as of late 2023 from multiple providers, including Security University ($2,995) and the New Horizons Computer Learning Center of Richmond ($5,400). Among the roughly twenty approved programs for massage therapy is a certificate program from the for-profit Centura College for $16,782. According to the College Scorecard, Centura College had a 56 percent graduation rate as of

November 2023, 88 percent took out federal student loans to finance their education, and the median debt owed was $14,750 (while median earnings were $22,899). "Centura College–Chesapeake," U.S. Department of Education, College Scorecard, https://collegescorecard.ed.gov/school/?420024-Centura-College-Chesapeake. Among the approved options for permanent tattooing is a ninety-hour course for $5,050 from the Avi Career Training in Great Falls, Virginia. Virginia's ETPL includes one five-week meat-cutting course, offered online, for $925. Pepper spray certification is available for only $75 from A Security Training Academy as of November 2023, along with courses on "baton tactics" (also $75) and "bail enforcement" ($400).

76. U.S. Department of Labor, Office of Inspector General, *Implementation of the Workforce Investment Act's Training Provisions in Selected States* (Washington, D.C.: U.S. Department of Labor, Office of Inspector General, 2003).

77. "Joint Guidance on Data Matching to Facilitate WIOA Performance Reporting and Evaluation," U.S. Department of Education, updated August 2016, https://studentprivacy.ed.gov/resources/joint-guidance-data-matching-facilitate-wioa-performance-reporting-and-evaluation.

78. Melissa Mack and Kate Dunham, *Performance Accountability, Eligible Training Providers, Labor Market Information, and Evaluation Requirements Under WIOA* (Princeton, NJ: Mathematica, Inc., 2020).

79. Interview with author.

80. "Training and Employment Guidance Letter 08-19," U.S. Department of Labor, Employment and Training Administration, January 2, 2020, https://www.dol.gov/agencies/eta/advisories/training-and-employment-guidance-letter-no-08-19.

81. "Course Performance," Workforce West Virginia, accessed November 8, 2023, https://public.workforcewv.org/Jobseeker/TrainingCoursePerformanceDetail.asp?SessionUID=%7b98F2B90F-301B-4297-B0CA-AC1ED4D469EE%7d&CourseUID=%7b34E06BCF-C0F2-4C43-855C-43277A140FAB%7d.

82. Virginia Career Works, "Virginia Workforce Connection."

83. TrainingProviderResults.Gov., https://www.TrainingProviderResults.Gov.

84. Interview with author.

85. U.S. Department of Labor, Employment and Training Administration, to Larry Hogan, governor of Maryland, letter, July 7, 2021, https://www.dol.gov/sites/dolgov/files/ETA/wioa/pdfs/MD%20Signed%20ETP%20Letter%20with%20Incoming%207_7.pdf.

86. "Leadership and History," Southern New Hampshire University,

https://www.snhu.edu/about-us/leadership-and-history; "Eligible Training Provider List," nhworks, accessed September 30, 2023, https://nhworksjob match.nhes.nh.gov/vosnet/drills/program/ApprovedPrograms.aspx.

87. In fiscal 2020, for instance, the Department of Labor reported that just 37.7 percent of participants in WIOA training programs found "training-related employment." "WIOA Adult Performance Report," U.S. Department of Labor, accessed November 7, 2023, https://www.dol.gov/sites/dolgov/files /ETA/Performance/pdfs/PY%202020%20WIOA%20National%20Perfor mance%20Summary.pdf.

88. Urban Alliance, *More Than Just Pocket Money* (Washington, D.C.: Urban Alliance, 2020).

89. "Undergraduate Enrollment Falls 662,000 Students in Spring 2022 and 1.4 Million During the Pandemic," National Student Clearinghouse, press release, May 26, 2022, https://www.studentclearinghouse.org/blog /undergraduate-enrollment-falls-662000-students-in-spring-2022-and-1-4 -million-during-the-pandemic/.

90. Anne Kim, "Generation COVID: Record Numbers of Youth Opt Out of College, Work," *Newsweek*, September 28, 2022.

91. Ibid.

92. Congressional Research Service, *Job Corps: A Primer* (Washington, D.C.: Congressional Research Service, 2022).

93. U.S. Department of Labor, Office of Inspector General, *COVID-19: ETA Should Continue to Closely Monitor Impact on Job Corps Program* (Washington, D.C.: U.S. Department of Labor, Office of Inspector General, 2020).

94. U.S. Department of Labor, Office of Inspector General, *COVID-19: Safety and Remote Learning Challenges Continue for Job Corps* (Washington, D.C.: U.S. Department of Labor, Office of Inspector General, 2021).

95. Ibid., 10.

96. Ibid.

97. Ibid.

98. "Outreach and Admissions Report Card (OAOMS-10), Report Period: 7/1/2022–7/31/2022," U.S. Department of Labor, https://s3-us-west-2.ama zonaws.com/jobcorps.gov/2022-09/rpos_07312022_PY.pdf.

99. "Outreach and Admissions Report Card by Rank (OAOMS-10R), Report Period: 7/1/2021–3/31/2022," U.S. Department of Labor, https://s3 -us-west-2.amazonaws.com/jobcorps.gov/2022-06/rpor_03312022_PY.pdf. By June 2023, enrollment was still below pre-pandemic levels. Job Corps reported 27,736 "arrivals" from July 1, 2022 to June 30, 2023, far short of a stated target enrollment of 55,360. "Outreach and Admissions Report Card (OAOMS-10), Report Period: 7/1/2022-6/30/2023," U.S. Department

of Labor, http://jobcorps-gov.s3.us-west-2.amazonaws.com/2023-08/rpos_06302023_PY.pdf.

100. "Student Outcomes/Who Job Corps Serves," U.S. Department of Labor, accessed April 4, 2021, https://s3-us-west-2.amazonaws.com/jobcorps.gov/2020-05/Who%20Job%20Corps%20Serves%20PY07-PY18%2003302020.xlsx (site discontinued).

101. U.S. Department of Labor, Office of Inspector General, *Job Corps Could Not Demonstrate Beneficial Training Outcomes.*

102. U.S. Government Accountability Office, *Job Corps: DOL Could Enhance Safety and Security at Centers with Consistent Monitoring and Comprehensive Planning* (Washington, D.C.: U.S. Government Accountability Office, 2018).

103. U.S. Department of Labor, Office of Inspector General, *Student Safety in the Job Corps Program: Testimony before the U.S. House of Representatives Committee on Education and the Workforce* (Washington, D.C.: U.S. Department of Labor, Office of Inspector General, 2017).

104. "Life at Woodstock Job Corps," Job Corps, https://woodstock.jobcorps.gov/campus-life.

105. "History of Woodstock Library," Georgetown University Library, https://www.library.georgetown.edu/woodstock/history.

106. U.S. Congress, Committee on Education and Labor, Subcommittee on the War on Poverty Program, *Economic Opportunity Act of 1964: Hearings on H. R. 10440, a bill to mobilize the human and financial resources of the nation to combat poverty in the United States*, report prepared for the use of the Committee on Education and Labor, 88th Cong., 2d Sess., 1964, Committee Print 31-847, 21 (statement of R. Sargent Shriver).

107. Ibid.

108. "Careers begin at Job Corps," Job Corps, https://www.jobcorps.gov.

109. U.S. Department of Labor, Office of Job Corps, *Policy and Requirements Handbook* (Washington, D.C.: U.S. Department of Labor, 2016), Exhibit 1.1.

110. Job Corps, Powerpoint presentation, "Job Corps: Success Lasts a Lifetime," https://hcoe.org/wp-content/hcoe-files/pdf/calsoap/ccx/Job%20Corps%20PowerPoint.pdf.

111. Ibid.

112. "The Path to Success Starts Here," Job Corps, https://www.jobcorps.gov/i-am-a/parent.

113. "Foreman Repaying Job Corps," *New York Times*, February 11, 1973.

114. Emma Fierberg, "This 25-Year-Old Makes $100K a Year as a Solar Roof Installer in Linden, New Jersey," CNBC.com, November 30, 2021,

https://www.cnbc.com/video/2021/11/30/this-25-year-old-makes-100k-a-year-as-a-solar-roof-installer-in-linden-new-jersey.html.

115. Peter Z. Schochet, *National Job Corps Study: 20-Year Follow-Up Study Using Tax Data* (Princeton, NJ: Mathematica, Inc., 2018).

116. Ibid. This research has one important caveat: Because it tracked the long-term fortunes of Job Corps students for up to twenty years after they left the program, its results reflect the program as it was in 1995, versus today. But little evidence indicates that Job Corps has improved dramatically since then, as this chapter discusses in detail.

117. Department of Labor, "Who Job Corps Serves."

118. Interview with author.

119. Interview with author.

120. "Board of Directors," National Job Corps Association, accessed November 8, 2023, https://njcaweb.org/leadership/.

121. Interview with author.

122. Department of Labor, "Who Job Corps Serves."

123. Interview with author.

124. Lisa Rein, "After Murders and Other Violence, Federal Job Corps Program Comes under Scrutiny," *Washington Post*, August 27, 2015.

125. U.S. Government Accountability Office, *Job Corps: Preliminary Observations on Student Safety and Security Data* (Washington, D.C.: U.S. Government Accountability Office, 2017).

126. Job Corps, *Policy and Requirements Handbook.*

127. Congressional Research Service, *Job Corps: A Primer* (Washington, D.C.: Congressional Research Service, 2022).

128. "About Us," Management & Training Corporation, https://www.mtctrains.com/about-us/.

129. "ResCare Workforce Services Is Now Equus Workforce Solutions," Equus, https://equusworks.com/rescare-workforce-services-is-now-equus-workforce-solutions/; Equus Workforce Solutions, https://equusworks.com.

130. "Shelter Management," Adams and Associates, https://adamsaai.com/services/shelters/; Career Systems Development Corporation, https://www.careersystems.com; "Our Story," Education and Training Resources, https://www.etrky.com/company-profile/; "Our Team," MINACT, http://minact.com/our-team/key-corporate-staff/.

131. "Operation of the Sierra Nevada Job Corps Center," SAM.gov, https://sam.gov/opp/c4d63db26c59485fbe065adf8c27f7c1/view; "Operation of the Edison Job Corps Center," SAM.gov, https://sam.gov/opp/45a08a7a87a84595b1b877a00c1c33b7/view; "Operation of Hawaii Job Corps Center," SAM.gov, https://sam.gov/opp/96fc2d0146f34c3083f3c05e3aad4a18/view.

132. "Operation of the Loring Job Corps Center/OA/CTS," SAM.gov, https://sam.gov/opp/84f2e4aba27845dc9b1a77ae5c730a63/view; "Operation of San Jose Corps Center," SAM.gov, https://sam.gov/opp/244ae7bc83a24d518bbc61d5889d143d/view; "Operation of the San Diego Job Corps Center," SAM.gov, https://sam.gov/opp/b35716cc17aef1f5a305bd11ee9ee911/view.

133. "About Our Founder," MINACT, https://minact.com/about/founder-story/.

134. "History," Career Systems, https://www.careersystems.com/history/.

135. David A. Fahrenthold, "Job Corps Closing Troubled Center in Oklahoma," *Washington Post*, August 28, 2014.

136. A selected list of GAO and IG reports throughout the years includes: Robert Hast to The Honorable Alexis M. Herman, "Subject: Job Corps Training Centers: Concerns About Admission Procedures and Agreements with State and Local Prison Authorities to Enroll Prisoners," letter, December 12, 2000); U.S. General Accounting Office, *Job Corps: Need for Better Enrollment Guidance and Improved Placement Measures* (Washington, D.C.: U.S. General Accounting Office, 1997); U.S. General Accounting Office, *Job Corps: Participant Selection and Performance Measurement Need to Be Improved* (Washington, D.C.: U.S. General Accounting Office, 1997); Comptroller General of the United States, *Job Corps Should Strengthen Eligibility Requirements and Fully Disclose Performance* (Washington, D.C.: Comptroller General of the United States, 1979); U.S. Department of Labor, Office of Inspector General, *Job Corps Regional Director's Authority as Contracting Officer Raises Concerns* (Washington, D.C.: U.S. Department of Labor, Office of Inspector General, 2007); U.S. General Accounting Office, *Corrective Actions Taken or in Process to Reduce Job Corps' Vulnerability to Improper Use of Contracting Authority* (Washington, D.C.: U.S. General Accounting Office, 1983).

137. Office of Economic Opportunity, *Job Corps Reports* (Washington, D.C.: Office of Economic Opportunity, 1968), 105.

138. Gregory R. Bell, "Morton-Thiokol: Getting Off Easy," *Harvard Crimson*, December 10, 1986. "Thiokol Corporation," Encylopedia.com, https://www.encyclopedia.com/social-sciences-and-law/economics-business-and-labor/businesses-and-occupations/thiokol-corp; "Northrop Grumman Announces Completion of Merger with Litton Industries Inc.," press release, Northrop Grumman, May 30, 2021, https://news.northropgrumman.com/news/releases/northrop-grumman-announces-completion-of-merger-with-litton-industries-inc; "History," Career Systems, https://www.careersystems.com/history/.

139. Alice O'Connor, *Poverty Knowledge: Social Science, Social Policy, and*

the Poor in Twentieth-Century U.S. History (Princeton, NJ: Princeton University Press, 2001), 166–67.

140. O'Connor, *Poverty Knowledge*, 176–77.

141. "18 Michigan Youths Jailed After Battling Job Corps," *New York Times*, August 1, 1966; "Job Corps Youth Sentenced for Possessing Marijuana," *New York Times*, April 16, 1966.

142. Martin Waldron, "Hostility in St. Petersburg Shuts First Women's Job Corps Unit," *New York Times*, July 29, 1966.

143. "Stabbing Death Upsets Job Corps Center in Utah," *New York Times*, August 3, 1970.

144. See, e.g., U.S. Department of Labor, Office of Inspector General, *U.S. Department of Labor's Top Management and Performance Challenges* (Washington, D.C.: U.S. Department of Labor, Office of Inspector General, 2022). Archived reports: https://www.oig.dol.gov/topchallenges.htm.

145. U.S. Department of Labor, Office of Inspector General, *Job Corps Must Strengthen Controls to Ensure Low-Income Eligibility of Applicants* (Washington, D.C.: U.S. Department of Labor, Office of Inspector General, 2011).

146. U.S. Department of Labor, Office of Inspector General, *Job Corps Needs to Improve Reliability of Performance Metrics and Results* (Washington, D.C.: U.S. Department of Labor, Office of Inspector General, 2011).

147. U.S. Department of Labor, Office of Inspector General, *Job Corps Should Do More to Prevent Cheating in High School Programs* (Washington, D.C.: U.S. Department of Labor, Office of Inspector General, 2019), 9.

148. Ibid.

149. U.S. Department of Labor, Office of Inspector General, *Job Corps Could Not Demonstrate Beneficial Job Training Outcomes*.

150. Ibid., 2.

151. U.S. General Accounting Office, *Award and Administration of Contracts for Job Corps Centers* (Washington, D.C.: U.S. General Accounting Office, 1982).

152. Morton E. Henig to The Honorable Albert Angrisani, July 2, 1982, https://www.gao.gov/assets/140/138105.pdf.

153. U.S. Government Accountability Office, *Job Corps: Actions Needed to Improve Planning for Center Operation Contracts* (Washington, D.C.: U.S. Government Accountability Office, 2019).

154. "Our Centers," Alternate Perspectives, Inc., https://www.alternateperspectives.net/our-centers.

155. "New Partnership Will Take Wind River Job Corps to the Next Level," Management & Training Corporation, press release, August 27, 2020, https://

www.mtctrains.com/uncategorized/new-partnership-will-take-wind-river-job-corps-to-the-next-level/.

156. Education and Training Resources, "Our Story."

157. "Operation of the Gadsden Job Corps Center," SAM.gov, https://sam.gov/opp/0004551f059c41c96138aa9004644642/view; Education Management Corporation, http://www.edu-mgt.com/index.htm.

158. "Gadsden Job Corps Center w/ OA CTS," SAM.gov, https://sam.gov/opp/053ab7b8f46240d097dbbfde4b3c4de9/view.

159. Lisa Rein, "Trump Administration to Pull Out of Rural Job Corps Program, Laying Off 1,100 Federal Workers," *Washington Post*, May 24, 2019.

160. Lisa Rein, "Trump Administration Backtracks on Closure of Job Corps Program After Bipartisan Opposition from Congress," *Washington Post*, June 19, 2019.

161. "Our Mission," National Job Corps Association, https://njcaweb.org/mission.

162. "Board of Directors," National Job Corps Association, https://njcaweb.org/leadership/; "About Us," Serrato Corporation, https://www.serratocorp.com/about-us/.

163. "Friends of Job Corps Congressional Caucus," National Job Corps Association, https://njcaweb.org/friends-of-job-corps-caucus.

164. Ibid.

165. "National Job Corps Assn.," OpenSecrets.org, https://www.opensecrets.org/orgs/national-job-corps-assn/summary?id=D000054280.

166. "Job Corps Works for Communities," National Job Corps Association, https://njcaweb.org/job-corps-works/communities/.

167. Interview with author.

168. David Fein and Jill Hamadyk, *Bridging the Opportunity Divide for Low-Income Youth: Implementation and Early Impacts of the Year Up Program* (Washington, D.C.: Office of Planning, Research and Evaluation, Administration for Children and Families, U.S. Department of Health and Human Services, 2018).

169. "Program," National Guard Youth ChalleNGe, https://ngchallenge.org/about-us/program/.

4. Every Body Profits

1. This was what I recall seeing during my visit in 2018; this office has since been renamed, and the treatment area's configuration may have changed since then.

2. U.S. Department of Justice, Office of Public Affairs, "Dental Management Company Benevis and Its Affiliated Kool Smiles Dental Clinics to Pay

$23.9 Million to Settle False Claims Act Allegations Relating to Medically Unnecessary Pediatric Dental Services," press release, January 10, 2018, www.justice.gov/opa/pr/dental-management-company-benevis-and-its-affili ated-kool-smiles-dental-clinics-pay-239; Interview with Dave King, Benevis, November 2, 2017.

3. David Heath and Jill Rosenbaum, "Complaints About Kids Care Follow Kool Smiles," *Frontline*, June 26, 2012.

4. Edmund H. Mahony, "Dental Chain Will Pay $24M to Settle False Billing Claims Over Unnecessary Work on Children," *Hartford Courant*, January 10, 2018.

5. Ibid.

6. U.S. Department of Justice, "Dental Management Company Benevis to Settle False Claims Act Allegations."

7. Mike Pelton, "A 2-Year-Old Boy Died After Getting a Common Dental Procedure at Kool Smiles. The Family Is Suing," *WEWS*, January 7, 2019.

8. Michael W. Davis, "Kool Smiles Dental Quietly Changes the Names of Its Clinics," *Dentistry Today*, May 6, 2019.

9. "Children's and Family Dentist in Winchester, VA," Pine Dentistry, accessed November 8, 2023, https://www.pinedentistry.com/locations/win chester-va/. The site notes that "Pine Dentistry & Braces is an official partner of Benevis and Kool Smiles."

10. "What We Do," Benevis, https://benevis.com/what-we-do/. In 2020, Benevis was bought by private equity firm New Mountain Capital, LLC. Cision PR Newswire, "Benevis Has Been Acquired by New Mountain Capital," press release, November 13, 2020.

11. "Who We Are," Benevis, accessed November 9, 2023, https://benevis .com/who-we-are/.

12. Mark Duggan, Craig Garthwaite, and Adelina Yanyue Wang, "Heterogeneity in the Impact of Privatizing Social Health Insurance: Evidence from California's Medicaid Program," National Bureau of Economic Research, Working Paper 28944, June 2021, http://www.nber.org/papers/w28944.

13. "CMS Releases Latest Enrollment Figures for Medicare, Medicaid and Children's Health Insurance Program (CHIP)," Centers for Medicare and Medicaid Services, press release, December 21, 2021, https://www.cms .gov/newsroom/news-alert/cms-releases-latest-enrollment-figures-medi care-medicaid-and-childrens-health-insurance-program-chip.

14. Daniela Franco Montoya, Puneet Kaur Chehal, and E. Kathleen Adams, "Medicaid Managed Care's Effects on Costs, Access and Quality: An Update," *Annual Review of Public Health* 41 (April 2020): 537–49.

15. "Dually Eligible Beneficiaries," MACPAC, https://www.macpac.gov/topics/dually-eligible-beneficiaries/.

16. Katherine Keisler-Starkey and Lisa N. Bunch, *Health Insurance Coverage in the United States: 2021* (Washington, D.C.: U.S. Census Bureau, 2022); Laryssa Mykyta, Katherine Keisler-Starkey, and Lisa Bunch, "More Children Were Covered by Medicaid and CHIP in 2021," U.S. Census Bureau, September 13, 2022, https://www.census.gov/library/stories/2022/09/uninsured-rate-of-children-declines.html.

17. Kaiser Family Foundation, "Status of State Medicaid Expansion Decisions: Interactive Map," February 16, 2023, https://www.kff.org/medicaid/issue-brief/status-of-state-medicaid-expansion-decisions-interactive-map/; Hannah Katch, Jesse Cross-Call, and Matt Broaddus, "Frequently Asked Questions About Medicaid," Center on Budget and Policy Priorities, November 22, 2019, https://www.cbpp.org/research/health/frequently-asked-questions-about-medicaid.

18. "Federal and State Share of Medicaid Spending," Kaiser Family Foundation, https://www.kff.org/medicaid/state-indicator/federalstate-share-of-spending.

19. Kaiser Family Foundation, "The Facts About Medicare Spending," June 2022, https://www.kff.org/interactive/medicare-spending/.

20. Congressional Budget Office, "The Federal Budget in Fiscal Year 2021: An Infographic," September 30, 2022, https://www.cbo.gov/publication/58268.

21. U.S. Department of Justice, Office of Public Affairs, "Justice Department's False Claims Act Settlements and Judgments Exceed $5.6 Billion in Fiscal Year 2021," press release, February 1, 2022, https://www.justice.gov/opa/pr/justice-department-s-false-claims-act-settlements-and-judgments-exceed-56-billion-fiscal-year.

22. "How Does the U.S. Health Care System Compare to Other Countries?," Peter G. Peterson Foundation, July 19, 2022, https://www.pgpf.org/blog/2022/07/how-does-the-us-healthcare-system-compare-to-other-countries.

23. Eric C. Schneider, Arnav Shah, Michelle M. Doty, Roosa Tikkanen, Katharine Fields, and Reginald D. Williams II, *Mirror, Mirror 2021: Reflecting Poorly; Health Care in the U.S. Compared to Other High-Income Countries* (Washington, D.C.: The Commonwealth Fund, 2021).

24. David U. Himmelstein, Deborah Thorne, Elizabeth Warren, and Steffi Woolhandler, "Medical Bankruptcy in the United States, 2007: Results of a National Study," *American Journal of Medicine* 122, no. 8 (August 2009); Scott Gottlieb, "Medical Bills Account for 40% of Bankruptcies," *BMJ* 320,

no. 7245 (May 13, 2000): 1295; Leo Lopez III, Louis H. Hart III, and Mitchell H. Katz, "Racial and Ethnic Health Disparities Related to COVID-19," *JAMA* 325, no. 8 (2021): 719–20.

25. Joe E. Cervi, "Pueblo Dentist, Philanthropist Eddie DeRose Dies at 82," *Pueblo Chieftain*, January 22, 2017.

26. Ibid.

27. U.S. Department of Justice, Office of Public Affairs, "National Dental Management Company Pays $24 Million to Resolve Fraud Allegations," press release, January 20, 2010, https://www.justice.gov/opa/pr/national-dental-management-company-pays-24-million-resolve-fraud-allegations.

28. At dental supplier Sky Dental Supply Inc., papoose boards are available for patients as young as three months old. The boards have Velcro scraps that immobilize a patient's limbs, while another strap secures a child's head to the board. The price: $849. "Papoose Board," Sky Dental Supply Inc., accessed November 7, 2023, https://www.skydentalsupply.com/papoose-board-kids.htm; Cary Leider Vogrin, "Small Smiles Involved in Child Restraint Law," *The Gazette*, January 20, 2010, https://web.archive.org/web/20160304071228/http://gazette.com/article/92725 (archive).

29. Committee on Finance, United States Senate, and Committee on the Judiciary, United States Senate, *Joint Staff Report on the Corporate Practice of Dentistry in the Medicaid Program*, report prepared for the use of the Committee on Finance, 113th Cong., 1st Sess. 2013, Committee Print 113–16.

30. U.S. Department of Justice, "North Carolina Dental Services Chain Pays $10 Million to Resolve False Claims Allegations," press release, April 9, 2008, https://www.justice.gov/archive/opa/pr/2008/April/08-civ-282.html.

31. Stipulation and Final Agency Order, In the Matter of the Disciplinary Proceeding Regarding the License to Practice Dentistry in the State of Colorado of Michael A. DeRose, DDS, License Number 5133, State Board of Dental Examiners, State of Colorado, December 12, 2005.

32. U.S. Department of Justice, "North Carolina Dental Service Chain Pays $10 Million."

33. "ADA Estimate of Dentists Serving Medicaid Patients Drops by 11%," Texas Dentists for Medicaid Reform, September 23, 2022, https://www.tdmrs.org/ada-estimate-of-dentists-serving-medicaid-patients-drops-by-11/.

34. Mary Otto, "For Want of a Dentist Pr. George's Boy Dies After Bacteria from Tooth Spread to Brain," *Washington Post*, February 28, 2007.

35. Ibid. Maryland has since expanded dental coverage to include adults, beginning in January 2023; "Advocacy Secures Adult Dental Benefit in Medicaid," Maryland Dental Action Coalition, https://www.mdac.us.

36. CMS Informational Bulletin, "Aligning Dental Payment Policies and Periodicity Schedules in the Medicaid and CHIP Programs," Center for Medicare and Medicaid Services, May 4, 2018, https://www.medicaid.gov/federal-policy-guidance/downloads/cib050418.pdf.

37. Allison Corr and Josh Wenderoff, "Inequitable Access to Oral Health Care Continues to Harm Children of Color," Pew Charitable Trusts, March 11, 2022, https://www.pewtrusts.org/en/research-and-analysis/articles/2022/03/11/inequitable-access-to-oral-health-care-continues-to-harm-children-of-color.

38. U.S. Department of Health and Human Services, Office of Inspector General, *Most Children with Medicaid in Four States Are Not Receiving Required Dental Services* (Washington, D.C.: U.S. Department of Health and Human Services, Office of Inspector General, 2016).

39. National Institutes of Health, *Oral Health in America: Advances and Challenges* (Bethesda, MD: U.S. Department of Health and Human Services, National Institutes of Health, National Institute of Dental and Craniofacial Research, 2021).

40. Ibid., 17.

41. National Institutes of Health, *Oral Health in America*, 2A-6.

42. Ibid., 2A-7.

43. Ibid., 1–23.

44. Ibid.

45. Ibid., 1–24.

46. "Emergency Department Visits for Dental Conditions: A Snapshot," American Dental Association Health Policy Institute, accessed November 7, 2023, https://www.ada.org/-/media/project/ada-organization/ada/ada-org/files/resources/research/hpi/hpigraphic_0420_1.pdf.

47. National Institutes of Health, *Oral Health in America*, 1–24.

48. American Dental Association, "Dentists Who Participate in Medicaid: Who They Are, Where They Locate, How They Practice," Presentation, American Dental Association, September 2022, https://www.ada.org/resources/research/health-policy-institute/coverage-access-outcomes/dentists-in-medicaid.

49. Marko Vujicic, Kamyar Nasser, and Chelsea Fosse, *Dentist Participation in Medicaid: How Should It Be Measured? Does It Matter?* (Washington, D.C.: American Dental Association Health Policy Institute, 2021).

50. "Reimbursement Rates for Child and Adult Dental Services in Medicaid by State," American Dental Association Health Policy Institute, 2020, https://www.ada.org/-/media/project/ada-organization/ada/ada-org/files/resources/research/hpi/hpigraphic_1021_1.pdf.

51. Ibid.

52. Ibid.; Ben Botkin, "Oregon Lawmakers Put $19 Million Toward Medicaid Dental Cuts," *The Lund Report*, December 14, 2021.

53. Natalia I. Chalmers and Robert D. Compton, "Children's Access to Dental Care Affected by Reimbursement Rates, Dentist Density, and Dentist Participation in Medicaid," *American Journal of Public Health* 107, no. 1 (October 2017): 1612–14.

54. "Educational Debt," American Dental Education Association, https://www.adea.org/godental/money_matters/educational_debt.aspx.

55. "Oral Health in Rural Communities," Rural Health Information Hub, https://www.ruralhealthinfo.org/topics/oral-health. (The Rural Health Information Hub was formerly the national clearinghouse of the HHS's Office of Rural Health Policy.)

56. American Dental Association, "Dentists Who Participate in Medicaid."

57. Ibid.

58. Ibid.

59. "Overview," Arcapita, https://www.arcapita.com/who-we-are/; Committee on Finance, *Joint Staff Report on the Corporate Practice of Dentistry*, 225.

60. Committee on Finance, *Joint Staff Report on the Corporate Practice of Dentistry*, 225.

61. Ibid., 225.

62. Ibid., 216–17.

63. Ibid., 237.

64. Ibid., 238.

65. Ibid., 227.

66. Ibid., 217. FORBA was also the entity actually purchased by Arcapita.

67. Committee on Finance, *Joint Staff Report on the Corporate Practice of Dentistry*, 227.

68. Ibid., 226.

69. Ibid., 226. Arcapita estimated a growth rate of 23 percent per year for the dental practice management model, "substantially outpacing dental industry growth."

70. Jennifer Garvin, "DSO 101: What Is a Dental Support Organization?," American Dental Association, March 30, 2022, https://www.ada.org/publications/ada-news/2022/march/main-types-of-dsos.

71. Eileen O'Grady, "Deceptive Marketing, Medicaid Fraud, and Unnecessary Root Canals on Babies: Private Equity Drills into the Dental Care Industry," Private Equity Stakeholder Project, July 2021, https://pestakeholder.org/wp-content/uploads/2021/08/PESP_DSO_July2021.pdf, 2.

72. Ibid.

73. Association of Dental Support Organizations, *Toward a Common Goal: The Role of Dental Support Organizations in an Evolving Profession* (Washington, D.C.: Association of Dental Support Organizations, 2014), 5.

74. Interview with author.

75. "O-1 Visa: Individuals with Extraordinary Ability or Achievement," U.S. Citizenship and Immigration Services, updated March 3, 2023, https://www.uscis.gov/working-in-the-united-states/temporary-workers/o-1-visa-individuals-with-extraordinary-ability-or-achievement.

76. Interview with author.

77. Interview with author.

78. "Dentist H1B Sponsorship Data," H1B Grader, https://h1bgrader.com/job-titles/dentist-1ok8mlwz2d.

79. Western Dental is part of Sonrava Health, which owns three other brands, including Trident, Vital Smiles, and Mid-Atlantic Dental Partners; "Sonrava Health," New Mountain Capital, https://www.newmountaincapital.com/portfolio/western-dental/.

80. "Western Dental," New Mountain Capital, https://web.archive.org/web/20200731205928/https://www.newmountaincapital.com/portfolio/western-dental/ (archive).

81. Elizabeth Aguilera, "California Raised Taxes to Pay Doctors for the Poor—and Is Still Waiting for Them," *CalMatters*, March 8, 2019 (updated June 23, 2020).

82. Association of Dental Support Organizations, *Toward a Common Goal*, 5.

83. iTeamatWJLA, "I-Team: Small Smiles Investigation," YouTube, https://www.youtube.com/watch?v=pIoMaw4zC9Q at 1:50.

84. Ibid at 4:05.

85. Ibid.

86. Cary Leider Vogrin, "Small Smiles Involved in Child Restraint Law Change," *The Gazette*, January 20, 2010, https://web.archive.org/web/20160304071228/http://gazette.com/article/92725 (archive).

87. 3 CCR 709-1.

88. Brian Newsome, "Dental Company Exploited Poor Children for Profit, Government Says," *The Gazette*, January 20, 2010.

89. Department of Justice, "National Dental Management Company Pays $24 Million to Resolve Fraud Allegations."

90. Ibid.

91. Ibid.

92. U.S. Department of Justice, "North Carolina Dental Services Chain Pays $10 Million to Resolve False Claims Allegations," press release, April 9, 2008, https://www.justice.gov/archive/opa/pr/2008/April/08-civ-282.html.

93. Jeffrey Wolf, "Dentist Performed 'Unnecessary' Work on Children and Billed Taxpayers," *KUSA-TV*, April 11, 2008.

94. Ibid.

95. Colorado Department of Regulatory Agencies, Colorado Dental Board. Search of provider database: https://apps.colorado.gov/dora/licensing/Lookup/LicenseLookup.aspx.

96. Talesha Reynolds, "Firm That Manages Dental Clinics for Kids Excluded from Medicaid," *NBC News*, March 12, 2014.

97. Committee on Finance, *Joint Staff Report on the Corporate Practice of Dentistry*, 386.

98. Ibid.

99. U.S. Department of Health and Human Services, Office of Inspector General, "OIG Excludes Pediatric Dental Management Chain from Participation in Federal Health Care Programs," press release, April 3, 2014, https://oig.hhs.gov/newsroom/news-releases/2014/cshm.asp.

100. Lorel E. Burns, Nihan Gencerliler, and Heather T. Gold, "A Comparative Analysis of Public and Private Dental Benefit Payer Types for the Provision and Outcomes of Root Canal Therapy on Permanent Teeth of Children and Adolescents in Massachusetts," *Journal of the American Dental Association* 154, no. 2 (February 2023): 151–58, doi: 10.1016/j.adaj.2022.10.011.

101. "Texas Taxpayers Pay Big for Straight Teeth," *WFAA*, August 22, 2011.

102. "Documents Detail Medicaid Fraud Allegations, Investigations of Dentist," *WFAA*, October 29, 2013.

103. Mark Smith, "District Court Rules Dallas-Area Dentist Is Responsible for Medicaid Fraud," *WFAA*, August 18, 2020.

104. "Parents Say Dentist Pays for Patients," *WFAA*, August 26, 2015.

105. "Sixth Medicaid Dental Victim Comes Forward, Police Investigate," *KHOU*, August 17, 2012.

106. United States Attorney's Office, Northern District of Texas, "Texas Dental Management Firm, 19 Affiliated Dental Practices, and Their Owners and Marketing Chief Agree to Pay $8.45 Million to Resolve Allegations of False Medicaid Claims for Pediatric Dental Services," press release, January 9, 2017, https://www.justice.gov/usao-ndtx/pr/texas-dental-management-firm-19-affiliated-dental-practices-and-their-owners-and.

107. U.S. Department of Health and Human Services, Office of Inspector General, *Questionable Billing for Medicaid Pediatric Dental Services in Indiana* (Washington, D.C.: U.S. Department of Health and Human Services,

Office of Inspector General, 2014); U.S. Department of Health and Human Services, Office of Inspector General, *Questionable Billing for Medicaid Pediatric Dental Services in Louisiana* (Washington, D.C.: U.S. Department of Health and Human Services, Office of Inspector General, 2014); U.S. Department of Health and Human Services, Office of Inspector General, *Questionable Billing for Medicaid Pediatric Dental Services in New York* (Washington, D.C.: U.S. Department of Health and Human Services, Office of Inspector General, 2014); U.S. Department of Health and Human Services, Office of Inspector General, *Questionable Billing for Medicaid Pediatric Dental Services in California* (Washington, D.C.: U.S. Department of Health and Human Services, Office of Inspector General, 2014).

108. U.S. Department of Health and Human Services, Office of Inspector General, *Questionable Billing in New York*, 7, 8.

109. U.S. Department of Health and Human Services, Office of Inspector General, *Questionable Billing in California*, 8.

110. Ibid., 7; U.S. Department of Health and Human Services, Office of Inspector General, *Questionable Billing in New York*, 6; U.S. Department of Health and Human Services, Office of Inspector General, *Questionable Billing in Louisiana*, executive summary; U.S. Department of Health and Human Services, Office of Inspector General, *Questionable Billing in Indiana*, 12.

111. David Heath, Mark Greenblatt, and Aysha Bagchi, "Dentists Under Pressure to Drill 'Healthy Teeth' for Profit, Former Insiders Allege," *USA Today* and *Newsy*, March 19, 2020.

112. Mahony, "Dental Chain Will Pay."

113. Ibid.

114. *Frontline*, "Complaints About Kids Follow Kool Smiles."

115. Consent Decree, Frew v. McKinney, No, 3:93CV65 (E.D. Tex. February 20, 1996), 40.

116. Christine Ellis, "Is Government Adequately Protecting Taxpayers from Medicaid Fraud?," testimony, April 25, 2012, https://oversight.house.gov/wp-content/uploads/2012/04/4-25-12-Ellis-Testimony.pdf.

117. "Medicaid Privatization Timeline," Iowa Senate Democrats, September 18, 2019, https://www.senate.iowa.gov/democrats/2019/09/medicaid-privatization-timeline-update/.

118. Erin Murphy, "Medicaid Forcing Big Changes," *The Gazette*, May 3, 2015, https://www.thegazette.com/news/medicaid-forcing-big-changes/.

119. Rod Boshart, "State Signs Medicaid Contracts with Private Managed Care Providers," *The Gazette*, October 9, 2015, https://www.thegazette.com/news/state-signs-medicaid-contracts-with-private-managed-care-providers/.

120. Ibid.

121. David Pitt, "Audit: Iowa Medicaid Savings Barely Half What Was Projected," *Associated Press*, November 26, 2018.

122. "Editorial: Privatized Medicaid Was Supposed to Save Money?," *Des Moines Register*, May 25, 2017.

123. "Official Terminates WellCare Contract," *The Gazette*, December 18, 2015, https://www.thegazette.com/life/official-terminates-wellcare-contract/; U.S. Department of Justice, Office of Public Affairs, "Former WellCare Chief Executive Sentenced for Health Care Fraud," press release, May 19, 2014, https://www.justice.gov/opa/pr/former-wellcare-chief-executive-sentenced-health-care-fraud; U.S. Department of Justice, Office of Public Affairs, "Four Former WellCare Executives Found Guilty in Florida," press release, June 10, 2013, https://www.justice.gov/opa/pr/four-former-wellcare-executives-found-guilty-florida.

124. U.S. Department of Justice, Office of Public Affairs, "Florida-Based Wellcare Health Plans Agrees to Pay $137.5 Million to Resolve False Claims Act Allegations," press release, April 3, 2012, https://www.justice.gov/opa/pr/florida-based-wellcare-health-plans-agrees-pay-1375-million-resolve-false-claims-act.

125. Ibid.

126. *The Gazette*, "Official Terminates WellCare Contract."

127. Tony Leys, "United Healthcare, Iowa Medicaid Leaders Blame Each Other for Breakdown Affecting 425,000," *Des Moines Register*, April 1, 2019; Beau Bowman, "United Healthcare Will Withdraw from Iowa's Medicaid Program," *KCCI*, March 29, 2019; Leslie Small, "AmeriHealth Caritas Exits Iowa's Managed Care Program; Maine to Vote on Medicaid Expansion," *Fierce Healthcare*, November 1, 2017.

128. Leys, "United Healthcare, Iowa Medicaid Leaders."

129. Iowa Department of Human Services, *Iowa Medicaid Managed Care Quality Assurance System* (Des Moines, IA: Iowa Department of Human Services, 2021).

130. Pitt, "Iowa Medicaid Savings Barely Half What Was Projected."

131. Office of Auditor of State, State of Iowa, "News Release," press release, July 27, 2020, https://www.auditor.iowa.gov/reports/file/62327/embed, 1, 14, 16.

132. Ibid., 2.

133. Office of Auditor of State, State of Iowa, "News Release," press release, October 20, 2021, https://www.auditor.iowa.gov/reports/file/66425/embed.

134. Ibid., 2.

135. Michaela Ramm, "Five Years of Managed Care in Iowa: State Says Medicaid Has Stabilized but Patients Disagree," *The Gazette*, May 11, 2021.

136. Congressional Budget Office, *Exploring the Growth of Medicaid Managed Care* (Washington, D.C.: Congressional Budget Office, 2018).

137. Centers for Medicare and Medicaid Services, *Medicaid Managed Care Enrollment and Program Statistics, 2020* (Washington, D.C.: Centers for Medicare and Medicaid Services, 2022).

138. Congressional Budget Office, *Exploring the Growth of Medicaid Managed Care.*

139. Elizabeth Hinton and Jada Raphael, "10 Things to Know About Medicaid Managed Care," Kaiser Family Foundation, March 1, 2023, https://www.kff.org/medicaid/issue-brief/10-things-to-know-about-medicaid-managed-care/.

140. Andy Schneider and Allie Corcoran, "Medicaid Managed Care in 2021: The Year That Was," Center for Children and Families, Georgetown University, December 21, 2021, https://ccf.georgetown.edu/2021/12/21/medicaid-managed-care-in-2021-the-year-that-was/.

141. "Privatizing the VA: Lessons from Privatized Medicaid in Kansas and Iowa," In the Public Interest, March 2018, https://www.inthepublicinterest.org/wp-content/uploads/ITPI_PrivatizingVAMedicaid_March2018.pdf, 3.

142. Ibid.

143. "Annual Statistical Supplement, 2015: Medicaid Program Description and Legislative History," Social Security Office of Retirement and Disability Policy, https://www.ssa.gov/policy/docs/statcomps/supplement/2015/medicaid.html.

144. The federal share of Medicaid costs is known as the "Federal Medical Assistance Percentage (FMAP)," determined by a formula that compares the average per capita income in a state with the national average. Statutorily, the FMAP can't be below 50 percent or higher than 83 percent. Social Security Office of Retirement and Disability Policy, "Annual Statistical Supplement, 2015."

145. "Federal Medical Assistance Percentage (FMAP) for Medicaid and Multiplier, FY 2023," Kaiser Family Foundation, https://www.kff.org/medicaid/state-indicator/federal-matching-rate-and-multiplier/?currentTimeframe=0&sortModel=%7B%22colId%22:%22FMAP%20Percentage%22,%22sort%22:%22desc%22%7D.

146. Sarah Goodell and Michael Sparer, "Medicaid Managed Care: Costs, Access, and Quality of Care," Robert Wood Johnson Foundation, The Synthesis Project, September 4, 2012, https://web.archive.org/web/20221004101034

/https://www.rwjf.org/en/library/research/2012/09/medicaid-managed-care.html (archive), 3.

147. Ibid.

148. Ibid.

149. Ibid., 4.

150. Andy Schneider, "Overview of Medicaid Provisions in the Balanced Budget Act of 1997, P.L. 105–33," Center on Budget and Policy Priorities, September 8, 1997, https://www.cbpp.org/sites/default/files/archive/908mcaid.htm.

151. Sara Rosenbaum, "Ushering in a New Era in Medicaid Managed Care," The Commonwealth Fund, July 1, 2015, https://www.commonwealthfund.org/blog/2015/ushering-new-era-medicaid-managed-care.

152. Michael J. McCue and Michael H. Bailit, *Assessing the Financial Health of Medicaid Managed Care Plans and the Quality of Patient Care They Provide* (Washington, D.C.: The Commonwealth Fund, 2011).

153. Ibid.

154. U.S. Department of Justice, "Former WellCare Chief Executive Sentenced for Health Care Fraud."

155. Barbara Martinez, "In Medicaid, Private HMOs Take a Big, and Profitable, Role," *Wall Street Journal*, November 15, 2006.

156. Andy Schneider and Allie Corcoran, "Medicaid Managed Care: 2020 Results for the 'Big Five,'" Center for Children and Families, Georgetown University, February 23, 2021, https://ccf.georgetown.edu/2021/02/23/medicaid-managed-care-2020-results-for-the-big-five/.

157. Bernard J. Wolfson, "California's Reboot of Troubled Medi-Cal Puts Pressure on Health Plans," *California Healthline*, September 20, 2021, https://californiahealthline.org/news/article/californias-reboot-of-troubled-medi-cal-puts-pressure-on-health-plans/; "Medi-Cal Commercial Plans Net Income and Revenue Figures" (via *California Healthline*), https://californiahealthline.org/wp-content/uploads/sites/3/2021/09/Medi-Cal-Commercial-plans-Net-Income-and-Revenue-figures-DHCS.pdf.

158. Ibid.

159. Centene Corporation, "Centene Completes Acquisition of WellCare," press release, January 28, 2020, https://www.centene.com/news/centene-completes-acquisition-of-wellcare.html.

160. Ibid.

161. Magellan Health, "Centene Signs Definitive Agreement to Acquire Magellan Health," press release, January 4, 2021, https://ir.magellanhealth.com/news-releases/news-release-details/centene-signs-definitive-agreement-acquire-magellan-health.

162. Centene Corporation, *Annual Report on Form 10-K for the Fiscal Year Ended December 31, 2021* (St. Louis, MO: Centene Corporation, 2021), 1.

163. Ibid., 18.

164. MACPAC, *Medicaid Loss Ratios in Medicaid Managed Care* (Washington, D.C.: MACPAC, 2022). The proportion of health care spending to revenue is the medical loss ratio. Requirements on medical loss ratios are intended to prevent excess profits and/or spending on administrative expenses and overhead.

165. The Menges Group, "Potential Savings of Medicaid Capitated Care: National and State-by-State Estimates," July 2017, http://communityplans.wpenginepowered.com/wp-content/uploads/2017/07/ACAP-Menges-MMC-Savings-Report-FINAL-071117.pdf.

166. America's Health Insurance Plans, "New Study: Medicaid Managed Care Saves Billions on Prescription Drugs for Taxpayers Every Year," press release, February 4, 2020, https://www.ahip.org/news/press-releases/new-study-medicaid-managed-care-saves-billions-on-prescription-drugs-for-taxpayers-every-year.

167. Paige Minemyer, "AHIP study: How Medicaid Managed Care Plans Have Made Gains in Quality Improvement," *Fierce Healthcare*, March 5, 2020.

168. Austin Barselau, Manisha Gupta, and Joel Menges, "Assessment of Kentucky Medicaid Managed Care Program Impacts," The Menges Group, November 2021, https://themengesgroup.com/wp-content/uploads/2022/06/the_menges_groups_assessment_of_kentuckys_medicaid_managed_care_program.pdf, 1.

169. Ibid., 2. Kentucky's Medicaid spending more than doubled between 2000 and 2019, the report found, but the rate of growth was 20 percentage points lower than that in states that hadn't embraced managed care, as Kentucky did in 2011. The analysis used the rate of Medicaid spending growth in fee-for-service states to construct a counterfactual scenario for Kentucky.

170. Ibid., 1.

171. Mark Duggan and Tamara Hayford, "Has the Shift to Managed Care Reduced Medicaid Expenditures? Evidence from State and Local-Level Mandates," NBER Working Paper 17236, July 2011, and *Journal of Policy Analysis and Management* 32, no. 3 (2013): 505–35.

172. Duggan and Hayford, "Has the Shift to Managed Care Reduced Medicaid Expenditures?," 5.

173. "Managed Care's Effect on Outcomes," MACPAC, https://www.macpac.gov/subtopic/managed-cares-effect-on-outcomes/.

174. Citing Kathleen Healy-Collier, "Medicaid Managed Care Reduces

Readmissions for Youths with Type 1 Diabetes," *American Journal of Managed Care* 22, no. 4 (April 2016): 250–56, PMID: 27143290.

175. Citing MACPAC, "Managed Care's Effect on Outcomes."

176. The study cited by MACPAC compared outcomes between Black and Hispanic births in Texas. Ilyana Kuziemko, Katherine Meckel, and Maya Rossin-Slater, "Do Insurers Risk-Select Against Each Other? Evidence from Medicaid and Implications for Health Reform," NBER Working Paper No. 19198, July 2013, http://www.nber.org/papers/w19198.

177. Michael Geruso, Timothy J. Layton, and Jacob Wallace, "What Difference Does a Health Plan Make? Evidence from Random Plan Assignment in Medicaid," NBER Working Paper No. 27762, August 2020, Revised October 2021, http://www.nber.org/papers/w2776, 1.

178. Ibid., 5.

179. Duggan, Garthwaite, and Wang, "Heterogeneity in the Impact of Privatizing Social Health."

180. U.S. Department of Health and Human Services, Office of Inspector General, *Access to Care: Provider Availability in Medicaid Managed Care* (Washington, D.C.: U.S. Department of Health and Human Services, Office of Inspector General, 2014), 1.

181. Ibid., 11, 12.

182. Morgan Lee, "Study: Medicaid Providers Mostly Can't Be Reached by Phone," *Associated Press*, December 13, 2022.

183. Ibid.

184. Katie Bernard, "Kansas Replaced Troubled Medicaid Contractor, Maximus," *Kansas City Star*, October 5, 2020.

185. Maximus, "KanCare Clearinghouse Meeting with Legislative Oversight Committee," presentation, August 4, 2016, http://kslegislature.org/li_2016/b2015_16/committees/ctte_jt_robert_g_bob_bethell_joint_committee_1/documents/testimony/20160804_11.pdf, 16.

186. Andy Marso, "KanCare Changes Leave Seniors Struggling to Get, Keep Medicaid Coverage," *Kansas City Star*, February 22, 2018.

187. Andy Marso, "Medicaid Application Delays Are Forcing Kansas Nursing Homes to Turn People Away," *Kansas City Star*, December 15, 2017.

188. Angela Hart, "Mattresses and Mold Removal: Medi-Cal to Offer Unconventional Treatments to Asthma Patients," *California Healthline*, December 14, 2021; Bernard J. Wolfson, "California's Reboot of Troubled Medi-Cal Puts Pressure on Health Plans," *California Healthline*, September 20, 2021.

189. Bernard J. Wolfson, "Layers of Subcontracted Services Confuse and Frustrate Medi-Cal Patients," *Kaiser Health News*, December 22, 2021.

190. Chad Terhune, "Coverage Denied: Medicaid Patients Suffer as Layers of Private Companies Profit," *California Healthline,* December 19, 2018.

191. Ibid.

192. California Legislative Analyst's Office, "The 2022–23 Budget: Analysis of the Medi-Cal Budget," February 9, 2022, https://lao.ca.gov/Publications/Report/4522. According to budget documents prepared by the governor's office, total spending on Medi-Cal more than doubled in the past decade, from under $60 billion in 2013 to a projected $124 billion in 2022.

193. Department of Health Care Services, Auditor of the State of California, *Millions of Children in Medi-Cal Are Not Receiving Preventive Health Services* (Sacramento, CA: Department of Health Care Services, Auditor of the State of California, 2019).

194. Ibid., 6, 13.

195. Bernard J. Wolfson, "Record Fines Might Mean California Is Finally Serious About Improving Medi-Cal," *Kaiser Health News*, April 4, 2022.

196. Samantha Young, "'Somebody Is Gonna Die': Medi-Cal Patients Struggle to Fill Prescriptions," *Kaiser Health News*, February 9, 2022, https://khn.org/news/article/california-medicaid-patients-struggle-to-fill-prescriptions-medi-cal-rx/.

197. California Department of Health Care Services, "California Takes a Historic Step in Transforming the Medi-Cal Program," press release, August 25, 2022, https://www.dhcs.ca.gov/formsandpubs/publications/oc/Documents/2022/22-10-MCP-Selections-8-25-22.pdf.

198. California regulators have fined Molina at least three times since 2015. Ron Shinkman, "Molina Healthcare Slapped with Large Fine for Lapses in Handling Grievances," *California Health Report*, January 9, 2019, https://www.calhealthreport.org/2019/01/09/molina-healthcare-slapped-large-fine-lapses-handling-grievances/.

199. Bernard J. Wolfson, "Why Almost 2 Million Californians May Need to Switch Health Insurance Plans," *San Francisco Chronicle*, September 26, 2022.

200. Although this letter was taken down, a web archive version is available at https://web.archive.org/web/20221012235338/https://www.standupforhealthcare.com/open-letter.

201. Howard Fine, "Molina Wins Spur Lawsuits," *Los Angeles Business Journal*, November 21, 2022, https://labusinessjournal.com/featured/molina-wins-spur-lawsuits/.

202. Daniel Hatcher's book, *The Poverty Industry*, offers a thorough and devastating analysis of the schemes states have concocted, often with

private-sector help, to squeeze both the federal government and their own constituents for revenues. Daniel L. Hatcher, *The Poverty Industry: The Exploitation of America's Most Vulnerable Citizens* (New York: NYU Press, 2016).

203. "Maximum Harm: MAXIMUS' Medicaid Management Failures," Maximus Accountability Project, November 2019, https://maximusaccountability.org/news/maximum-harm-maximus-medicaid-management-failures.

204. Ibid., 8.

205. Ibid.

206. U.S. Congress, Committee on Oversight and Government Reform, Subcommittee on Health Care, District of Columbia, Census, and the National Archives and the Subcommittee on Regulatory Affairs, Stimulus Oversight and Government Spending, *Is Government Adequately Protecting Taxpayers from Medicaid Fraud?*, report prepared for the use of the Committee on Oversight and Government Reform, 112th Cong., 2nd Sess., 2012, Committee Print 112-151, 2 (statement of Senator Charles E. Grassley).

207. Committee on Oversight and Government Reform, *Is Government Adequately Protecting Taxpayers from Medicaid Fraud?*, 36, 38 (statement of David Feinwachs, Minnesota Hospital Association).

208. U.S. Department of Health and Human Services, Office of Inspector General, *California Medicaid Managed Care Organizations Received Capitation Payments After Beneficiaries' Deaths* (Washington, D.C.: U.S. Department of Health and Human Services, Office of Inspector General, 2019); U.S. Department of Health and Human Services, Office of Inspector General, *Ohio Medicaid Managed Care Organizations Received Capitation Payments After Beneficiaries' Deaths* (Washington, D.C.: U.S. Department of Health and Human Services, Office of Inspector General, 2018).

209. U.S. Department of Health and Human Services, Office of Inspector General, *Data on Medicaid Managed Care Payments to Providers Are Incomplete and Inaccurate* (Washington, D.C.: U.S. Department of Health and Human Services, Office of Inspector General, 2021).

210. "PERM Error Rate Findings and Reports," Centers for Medicare and Medicaid Services, last modified September 6, 2023, https://www.cms.gov/Research-Statistics-Data-and-Systems/Monitoring-Programs/Medicaid-and-CHIP-Compliance/PERM/PERMErrorRateFindingsandReport.

211. Donald F. Kettl, *Government by Proxy: (Mis)Managing Federal Programs* (Washington, D.C.: CQ Press, 1987).

212. U.S. Government Accountability Office, *Medicaid Managed Care: Compensation of Medicaid Directors and Managed Care Organization Executives in Selected States in 2015* (Washington, D.C.: U.S. Government Accountability Office, 2017).

213. Ibid., 5.

214. Ibid., 8.

215. Ibid.

216. Medicaid and CHIP Payment and Access Commission (MACPAC), *Report to the Congress on Medicaid and CHIP* (Washington, D.C.: Medicaid and CHIP Payment and Access Commission, 2014).

217. Ibid., 187.

218. "Chronic Kidney Disease (CKD)," National Kidney Foundation, https://www.kidney.org/atoz/content/about-chronic-kidney-disease.

219. National Institutes of Health, National Institute of Diabetes and Digestive and Kidney Diseases, "Incidence, Prevalence, Patient Characteristics, and Treatment Modalities," in *2022 Annual Data Report: End Stage Renal Disease* (Washington, D.C.: National Institutes of Health, National Institute of Diabetes and Digestive and Kidney Diseases, 2022), https://usrds-adr.niddk.nih.gov/2022/end-stage-renal-disease/1-incidence-prevalence-patient-characteristics-and-treatment-modalities. In 2020, 130,522 people were diagnosed with end stage renal disease.

220. "Dialysis Facility Compare, Davita GWU Southeast Dialysis," Medicare.gov, https://www.medicare.gov/care-compare/details/dialysis-facility/092517?city=Washington&state=DC&zipcode=#ProviderDetailsLocations.

221. "The Kidney Project," University of California San Francisco, https://pharm.ucsf.edu/kidney/need/statistics; Melissa W. Wachterman, Ann M. O'Hare, Omari-Khalid Rahman, et al., "One-Year Mortality After Dialysis Initiation Among Older Adults," *JAMA International Medicine* 179, no. 7 (July 2019): 987–90, doi: 10.1001/jamainternmed.2019.0125.

222. Ibid.

223. Email to author from Patrice Miles, coordinator of MOTTEP (Minority Organ Tissue and Transplant Education Program) at Howard University.

224. "Summary Health Statistics: National Health Institute Survey, 2018, Table A-4a. Age-adjusted percentages (with standard errors) of selected diseases and conditions among adults aged 18 and over, by selected characteristics: United States, 2018," U.S. Department of Health and Human Services, National Center for Health Statistics, https://ftp.cdc.gov/pub/Health_Statistics/NCHS/NHIS/SHS/2018_SHS_Table_A-4.pdf.

225. National Institutes of Health, National Institute of Diabetes and Digestive and Kidney Diseases, "Kidney Disease Statistics for the United States," September 2021, https://www.niddk.nih.gov/health-information/health-statistics/kidney-disease; Deidra C. Crews, Orlando M. Gutiérrez, Stacey A. Fedewa, et al., "Low Income, Community Poverty and Risk of End

Stage Renal Disease." *BMC Nephrology* 15, no. 192 (2014), https://doi.org/10.1186/1471-2369-15-192.

226. Medicare Payment Advisory Commission, "Outpatient Dialysis Services," in *2022 Report to Congress, Outpatient Dialysis Services* (Washington, D.C.: Medicare Payment Advisory Commission, 2022), 193–230, 199.

227. "Adults with Diabetes," DC Health Matters, https://www.dchealthmatters.org/indicators/index/view?indicatorId=81&localeId=130951&localeChartIdxs=1|4; "Dialysis Facility Compare," Medicare.gov, https://www.medicare.gov/care-compare/results?searchType=DialysisFacility&page=1&city=Washington&state=DC&zipcode=&radius=5&sort=closest.

228. Medicare.gov, "Dialysis Facility Compare."

229. Medicare Payment Advisory Commission, *2022 Report to Congress*, 205.

230. Ibid., 208.

231. DaVita Inc., *Annual Report on Form 10-K for the Fiscal Year Ended December 31, 2022* (Denver, CO: DaVita Inc., 2022), 6.

232. Ibid., 62.

233. Ibid., 64. This is down significantly from 2020, when the company administered more than 30.3 million dialysis treatments. Because dialysis patients are extremely medically vulnerable, the industry lost many patients due to the coronavirus pandemic.

234. Joel W. Greer, "End Stage Renal Disease and Medicare," *Health Care Financing Review*, 24, no. 4 (2003): 1–5, PMID: 14628396.

235. National Institutes of Health, National Institute of Diabetes and Digestive and Kidney Diseases, "Healthcare Expenditures for Persons with ESRD," in *2022 Annual Data Report*, https://usrds-adr.niddk.nih.gov/2022/end-stage-renal-disease/9-healthcare-expenditures-for-persons-with-esrd. According to the U.S. Renal Data Service, the government spent $38.8 billion in 2019 to care for ESRD patients, compared to $543.8 billion in total Medicare expenditures that year. Total federal spending in 2019 was $4.4 trillion. "The Federal Budget in 2019: An Infographic," Congressional Budget Office, April 15, 2020, https://www.cbo.gov/publication/56324.

236. Ibid., Figure 9.6(a).

237. Interview with author.

238. American Renal Associates Holdings, Inc., *Annual Report on Form 10-K for the Fiscal Year Ended December 31, 2019* (Beverly, MA: American Renal Associates Holdings, Inc., 2019). Archive version available at https://www.sec.gov/ix?doc=/Archives/edgar/data/0001498068/000149806820000037/ara1231201910-kxdocume.htm#s8E802A32FD615BFAAF871CA757BBC766, 9. In 2021, American Renal Associates was acquired by

Innovative Renal Care, a subsidiary of the private equity firm Nautic Partners. Innovative Renal Care, "American Renal Associates Completes Transaction with Innovative Renal Care, a Nautic Partners Portfolio Company," press release, January 26, 2021, https://innovativerenal.com/2021/01/american renal-associates-completes-transaction-with-innovative-renal-care-a-nautic -partners-portfolio-company/.

239. "Bugs & Infestations: Managing Patient Care," Quality Insights, Renal Network 5, accessed November 7, 2023, https://www.qirn5.org/Dialysis -Providers/Bugs-Infestations.aspx.

240. Interview with author.

241. Interview with author.

242. Interview with author.

243. Interview with author.

244. "Hemodialysis," National Institutes of Health, National Institute of Diabetes and Digestive and Kidney Diseases, last modified January 2018, https://www.niddk.nih.gov/health-information/kidney-disease/kidney-failure /hemodialysis/vascular-access.

245. National Institutes of Health, National Institute of Diabetes and Digestive and Kidney Diseases, "Mortality," in *2022 Annual Data Report*, https://usrds-adr.niddk.nih.gov/2022/end-stage-renal-disease/6-mortality.

246. Interview with author.

247. National Institutes of Health, National Institute of Diabetes and Digestive and Kidney Diseases, "Incidence, Prevalence, Patient Characteristics and Treatment Modalities," in *2022 Annual Data Report*; Ruyi Cai, Jinshi Zhang, Yin Zhu, et al., "Mortality in Chronic Kidney Disease Patients with COVID-19: A Systematic Review and Meta-analysis," *International Urology and Nephrology* 53 (2021): 1623–29; Stephen Salerno, Joseph Messana, Garrett W. Gremel, et al., "Covid-19 Risk Factors and Mortality Outcomes Among Medicare Patients Receiving Long-term Dialysis," *JAMA Network Open* 4, no. 11 (2021): e2135379.

248. National Institutes of Health, National Institute of Diabetes and Digestive and Kidney Diseases, "Incidence, Prevalence, Patient Characteristics and Treatment Modalities," in *2022 Annual Data* Report, Figure 1.10.

249. Ibid.

250. Shana Alexander, "They Decide Who Lives, Who Dies," *Life*, November 9, 1962.

251. Richard A. Rettig, "Origins of the Medicare Kidney Disease Entitlement: The Social Security Amendments of 1972," in *Biomedical Politics*, ed. Kathi E. Hanna (Washington, D.C.: National Academies Press, 1991).

252. Dialysis Clinic, Inc., https://www.dciinc.org.

253. Fresenius Medical Care, *2022 Annual Report* (Bad Homburg, Germany: Fresenius Medical Care, 2022).

254. Fresenius Medical Care, *2022 Annual Report*, 20.

255. DaVita Inc., *Annual Report on Form 10-K for the Fiscal Year Ended December 31, 2021* (Denver, CO: Davita Inc., 2021), 22.

256. Centers for Medicare and Medicaid Services, "Calendar Year 2023 End-Stage Renal Disease (ESRD) Prospective Payment System (PPS) Final Rules (CMS-1768-F)," October 31, 2022, https://www.cms.gov/newsroom/fact-sheets/calendar-year-2023-end-stage-renal-disease-esrd-prospective-payment-system-pps-final-rule-cms-1768-f.

257. "Dialysis: Last Week Tonight with John Oliver (HBO)," YouTube, https://www.youtube.com/watch?v=yw_nqzVfxFQ.

258. Ibid.

259. Interview with author.

260. Interview with author.

261. Jennifer M. Kaplan, Jingbo Niu, Vivian Ho, Wolfgang C. Winkelmayer, and Kevin F. Erickson, "A Comparison of US Medicare Expenditures for Hemodialysis and Peritoneal Dialysis," *Journal of the American Society of Nephrology* 33, no. 11 (2022): 2059–70.

262. Home Dialyzors United, https://www.homedialyzorsunited.org.

263. Interview with author, 2022.

264. Interview with author, 2022.

265. National Institutes of Health, National Institute of Diabetes and Digestive and Kidney Diseases, "Incidence, Prevalence, Patient Characteristics and Treatment Modalities," in *2022 Annual Data Report*. In 2020, 11.2 percent of white kidney failure patients used home-based modalities for dialysis, versus 8.2 percent of Black patients and 8.4 percent of Hispanic patients.

266. Centers for Medicare and Medicaid Services, "HHS to Transform Care Delivery for Patients with Chronic Kidney Disease," press release, July 10, 2019, https://www.cms.gov/newsroom/press-releases/hhs-transform-care-delivery-patients-chronic-kidney-disease.

267. "Kidney Care Choices (KCC) Model," Centers for Medicare and Medicaid Services, https://innovation.cms.gov/innovation-models/kidney-care-choices-kcc-model.

268. Ibid.

269. Charlotte Huff, "How Artificial Kidneys and Miniaturized Dialysis Could Save Millions of Lives," *Nature.com*, March 11, 2020.

270. Sandra Blakeslee, "Willem Wolff, Doctor Who Invented Kidney and Heart Machines, Dies at 97," *New York Times*, February 12, 2009.

271. Rettig, "Origins of the Medicare Kidney Disease Entitlement."

272. Joseph B. Lockridge and Sindhu Chandran, "The Scribner Shunt: 50 Years Later," *Kidney International* 81, no. 1 (January 2012): 120.

273. "Preparing for Dialysis (AV Fistula)," Yale School of Medicine, https://www.yalemedicine.org/conditions/preparing-dialysis-av-fistula.

274. "About KidneyX," Kidney Innovation Accelerator, https://www.kidneyx.org/about-kidneyx/.

275. Fresenius Medical Care, *2021 Annual Report* (Bad Homburg, Germany: Fresenius Medical Care, 2021), 52.

276. "Physician Self Referral," Centers for Medicare and Medicaid Services, https://www.cms.gov/Medicare/Fraud-and-Abuse/PhysicianSelfReferral/index?redirect=/physicianselfreferral/.

277. Interview with author.

278. Medicare Payment Advisory Commission, "Outpatient Dialysis Services," in *Report to the Congress: Medicare Payment Policy* (Washington, D.C.: Medicare Payment Advisory Commission, 2016), 147–72, 162.

279. American Renal Associates Holdings, Inc., *2019 Annual Report*.

280. DaVita Inc., *2021 Annual Report*, 8.

281. DaVita Inc., *2022 Annual Report*, 49.

282. U.S. Department of Justice, Office of Public Affairs, "DaVita to Pay $350 Million to Resolve Allegations of Illegal Kickbacks," press release, October 22, 2014, https://www.justice.gov/opa/pr/davita-pay-350-million-resolve-allegations-illegal-kickbacks.

283. Ibid.

284. National Institutes of Health, National Institute of Diabetes and Digestive and Kidney Diseases, *2022 Annual Data Report*, Figure 6.7.

285. Interview with author.

286. Interview with author.

287. Yi Zhang, Mae Thamer, Onkar Kshirsagar, Dennis J. Cotter, and Mark J. Schlesinger, "Dialysis Chains and Placement on the Waiting List for a Cadaveric Kidney Transplant," *Transplantation* 98, no. 5 (September 15, 2014): 543–51.

288. Federal Trade Commission, "FTC Accepts Settlement to Remedy DaVita's Acquisition of Rival Outpatient Dialysis Clinic Provider Gambro," press release, October 4, 2005, https://www.ftc.gov/news-events/news/press-releases/2005/10/ftc-accepts-settlement-remedy-davitas-acquisition-rival-outpatient-dialysis-clinic-provider-gambro.

289. Ibid.

290. "Fresenius Medical Care Acquires Renal Advantage," *Mergr*, December 20, 2010.

291. Defendants' Joint Motion to Dismiss, United States v. DaVita Inc and

Kent Thiry, No. 21-cr-0229-RBJ (D. Colo. September 14, 2021), https://fingfx.thomsonreuters.com/gfx/legaldocs/myvmnjoqjpr/davita%20motion%20dismiss.pdf; Mike Scarcella, "DaVita Loses Bid to Dismiss DOJ's Criminal Antitrust Charges," *Reuters*, January 28, 2022; Sam Tabachnik, "Jury Acquits DaVita, Ex-CEO Ken Thiry in Landmark Antitrust Prosecution of Non-poaching Agreements," *Denver Post*, April 15, 2022.

292. Tabachnik, "Jury Acquits DaVita."

293. Andrew Pollack, "Dialysis Equipment Maker Settles Lawsuit for $250 Million," *New York Times*, February 18, 2016.

294. Fresenius Medical Care, internal memo, November 4, 2011, http://graphics8.nytimes.com/packages/pdf/business/fresenius-memo.pdf.

295. Andrew Pollack, "Dialysis Company's Failure to Warn of Product Risk Draws Inquiry," *New York Times*, June 14, 2012.

296. Nate Raymond, "U.S. Jury Orders DaVita to Pay $383.5 Million in Wrongful Death Lawsuits," *Reuters*, June 28, 2018.

297. Lydia Wheeler, "DaVita, Fresenius Accused of Putting Minority Patients at Risk," *Bloomberg Law*, January 11, 2022.

298. SEIU-UHW, National Health Law Program, and Feinberg, Jackson, Worthman &Wasow LLP, "Administrative Complaint, Re: High-Speed Hemodialysis Has a Disparate Impact on Latino and Asian American Patients," January 11, 2022, https://aboutblaw.com/1cM, 2.

299. Ibid., 12.

300. U.S. Department of Justice, Office of Public Affairs, "DaVita to Pay $450 Million to Resolve Allegations That It Sought Reimbursement for Unnecessary Drug Wastage," press release, June 24, 2015, https://www.justice.gov/opa/pr/davita-pay-450-million-resolve-allegations-it-sought-reimbursement-unnecessary-drug-wastage.

301. Ibid.

302. United States Attorney's Office, Northern District of Texas, "DaVita Rx Agrees to Pay $63.7 Million to Resolve False Claims Act Allegations," press release, December 14, 2017, https://www.justice.gov/usao-ndtx/pr/davita-rx-agrees-pay-637-million-resolve-false-claims-act-allegations.

303. Shawn Shinneman, "Davita Rx to Close Coppell Facility, Lay Off 869 Employees After Sale to Walgreens," *Dallas Magazine*, August 1, 2018.

304. "DaVita Securities Litigation," https://www.davitasecuritieslitigation.com.

305. Amended Class Action Complaint for Violations of the Federal Securities Laws and Jury Trial Demand, Peace Officers' Annuity and Benefit Fund of Georgia v. DaVita Inc., Kent J. Thiry, James K. Holger and

Javier J. Rodriguez (D. Colo., January 12, 2018), https://www.saxenawhite.com/wp-content/uploads/2019/11/Davita-Amended.pdf, 18.

306. Ibid., 19.

307. Ibid., 20.

308. Ibid., 20.

309. "Medicare's Coverage of Dialysis and Kidney Transplant Benefits," Medicare.gov, https://www.medicare.gov/Pubs/pdf/11360-Medicare-Dialysis-Kidney-Transplant.pdf.

310. Reed Abelson and Katie Thomas, "Top Kidney Charity Directed Aid to Patients at DaVita and Fresenius Clinics, Lawsuit Claims," *New York Times*, August 2, 2019.

311. Samantha Young, "Dialysis Industry Spends Millions, Emerges as Power Player in California Politics," *Modern Healthcare*, December 10, 2020.

312. Victoria Collier, "Federal Court Considers Whether to Halt California Dialysis Law," *POLITICOPro*, October 26, 2022; "Assembly Passes Bill to Address Inflated Medical Claims by Dialysis Industry," United Healthcare Workers West, September 10, 2019, https://www.seiu-uhw.org/press/assembly-passes-bill-to-address-inflated-medical-claims-by-dialysis-industry/.

313. Liz Kreutz, "Proposition 29: Californians Reject Measure to Alter Dialysis Clinic Rules, AP Projects," KGO-TV, November 9, 2022, https://abc7news.com/california-proposition-29-2022-dialysis-clinic-prop-election/12295409/; "2022 Elections Money Tracker," *Los Angeles Times*, https://www.latimes.com/projects/2022-california-election-proposition-29-kidney-dialysis-money-tracker/.

314. "DaVita Inc., Summary," OpenSecrets.org, https://www.opensecrets.org/orgs/davita-inc/summary?id=D000021951; "Fresenius Medical Care, Summary," OpenSecrets.org, https://www.opensecrets.org/orgs/fresenius-medical-care/summary?id=D000025929.

315. OpenSecrets.org, "Fresenius Medical Care, Summary."

316. Young, "Dialysis Industry Spends Millions."

317. "Kidney Disease Surveillance System," U.S. Centers for Disease Control and Prevention, https://nccd.cdc.gov/CKD/default.aspx; "Chronic Kidney Disease Initiative," U.S. Centers for Disease Control and Prevention, http://www.cdc.gov/ckd.

318. "Prevalence of CKD Among U.S. Adults," U.S. Centers for Disease Control and Prevention, https://nccd.cdc.gov/CKD/detail.aspx?Qnum=Q9#refreshPosition.

5. Crime Pays: The Business of Criminal "Justice"

1. A&E, *Dog the Bounty Hunter,* https://www.aetv.com/shows/dog-the-bounty-hunter.

2. Emily Rome, "'Dog the Bounty Hunter' canceled," *Entertainment Weekly,* May 21, 2012; Jackie Willis, "Dog the Bounty Hunter Reacts to Daughter Bonnie Claiming He's Racist and Homophobic (Exclusive)," *ET Online,* September 1, 2021, https://web.archive.org/web/20210906220700/https://www.etonline.com/dog-the-bounty-hunter-reacts-to-daughter-bonnie-claiming-hes-racist-and-homophobic-exclusive-171378 (archive); Da Kine Bail Bonds, http://www.dakinebail.com/index.html.

3. "Dog's Most Wanted," DogtheBountyHunter.com; "Grounds for Arrest Bounty Brew," accessed November 9, 2023, https://coffee.dogthebountyhunter.com.

4. Federal Bureau of Investigation, "Crime in the United States 2019: Table 29, Estimated Number of Arrests," https://ucr.fbi.gov/crime-in-the-u.s/2019/crime-in-the-u.s.-2019/tables/table-29. Federal Bureau of Investigation, "Crime in the United States 2018: Table 29, Estimated Number of Arrests," https://ucr.fbi.gov/crime-in-the-u.s/2018/crime-in-the-u.s.-2018/tables/table-29. Police arrested approximately 10.3 million people in 2018 and nearly 10.1 million in 2019. (These are the latest data available as of this writing.)

5. Kristen M. Budd and Niki Monazzam, "Private Prisons in the United States," The Sentencing Project, updated June 15, 2023, https://www.sentencingproject.org/publications/private-prisons-united-states/.

6. "Dog the Bounty Hunter Joins Legal Fight Against Bail Reform," *CBS Philadelphia,* July 1, 2017, https://www.cbsnews.com/philadelphia/news/dog-the-bounty-hunter-nj-bail-reform/; Meghan Lopez, "Dog the Bounty Hunter Speaks Out Against Colorado's Jail Reform Bill," *ABC Denver,* May 7, 2021 (updated May 10, 2021), https://www.denver7.com/news/politics/dog-the-bounty-hunter-speaks-out-against-colorados-jail-reform-bill.

7. "Dog the Bounty Hunter Rips Bail Reform: 'People Are Dying,'" *Fox News,* November 23, 2021, https://www.foxnews.com/media/dog-bounty-hunter-bail-reform-people-dying.

8. "About Bail – What Is Bail," Professional Bail Agents of the United States, accessed November 8, 2023, https://www.pbus.com/page/1.

9. Matt Keyser, "'I Just Felt So Violated': Harvard Researcher's Study Shows 'Devastating' Effects of Jailing People Pretrial," National Partnership for Pretrial Justice, undated, http://www.pretrialpartnership.org/news/i-just-felt-so-violated-harvard-researchers-study-shows-devastating-effects-of-jailing-people-pretrial/.

10. This section stands on the shoulders of incredible work on pretrial

justice by a broad coalition of organizations, including Arnold Ventures, the Pretrial Justice Institute (now Go Bright), the Fines and Fees Justice Center, the Sentencing Project, the Marshall Project, the Brennan Center, the Justice Policy Institute, the ACLU, the Prison Policy Initiative, and countless others.

11. Full details of Rafiq's story were first published in the *Washington Monthly*, later syndicated to the *Baltimore City Paper* and *The Atlantic*. Anne Kim, "How Cash Bail Keeps the Poor in Jail," *The Atlantic*, January 15, 2017.

12. Maryland Office of the Public Defender, *The High Cost of Bail: How Maryland's Reliance on Money Bail Jails the Poor and Costs the Community Millions* (Baltimore, MD: Maryland Office of the Public Defender, 2016), 4.

13. "Frequently Asked Questions," Office of the State's Attorney for Baltimore City, accessed November 9, 2023, https://www.stattorney.org/resources/faqs/29-bail-bond.

14. And yes, *Aarow* is spelled with two "a's," presumably so that this business is listed first alphabetically. Dan Barto, "Do You Get Your Bail Money Back?," Aarrow Bail Bonds, updated February 3, 2020, https://www.aarrowbailbonds.com/bail-bond-blog/do-you-get-your-bail-money-back/.

15. Interview with author.

16. "About Bail—How to Become a Bail Agent," Professional Bail Agents of the United States, accessed November 8, 2023, http://www.pbus.com/?3.

17. American Civil Liberties Union and Color of Change, *Commitments to Anti-Racism Ring Hollow: Fairfax Financial Is the Last Big Insurance Holdout in the Dying Bail Industry* (Washington, D.C.: American Civil Liberties Union and Color of Change, 2021).

18. Zeke Jennings, "Bondsman Jeff Kirkpatrick Big Part of 'Dog and Beth: On the Hunt' Episode in Jackson," *Mlive*, May 13, 2013, https://www.mlive.com/entertainment/jackson/2013/05/bondsman_jeff_kirkpatrick_big.html; Danielle Salisbury, "Court of Appeals Affirms Convictions of Ricky Wheeldon, Racketeer Pursued by Bounty Hunter Duane 'Dog' Chapman," *Mlive*, May 24, 2014, https://www.mlive.com/news/jackson/2014/05/court_of_appeals_affirms_convi_3.html.

19. Alwyn Scott and Suzanne Barlyn, "U.S. Bail-Bond Insurers Spend Big to Keep Defendants Paying," *Reuters*, March 26, 2021.

20. "Bail Bonds Forms," Lexington National, accessed November 9, 2023, https://lexingtonnational.com/bail-bonds/bail-bonds-forms/.

21. "Bail Bond Application and Agreement," Lexington National, accessed November 9, https://www.lexingtonnational.com/wp-content/uploads/2015/10/Bail-Standard-Form-No.-1.pdf.

22. Ibid.

23. "Bail Bond Premium Receipt and Statement of Charges," Lexington National, accessed November 9, 2023, https://lexingtonnational.com/wp-content/uploads/Forms/Standard/Bail%20Standard%20Form%20No-3%20NCR.pdf.

24. Interview with author.

25. U.S. Commission on Civil Rights, *The Civil Rights Implications of Cash Bail* (Washington, D.C.: U.S. Commission on Civil Rights, 2022), 71.

26. Ibid.

27. "Recovery Agents," Professional Bail Agents of the United States, accessed November 8, 2023, https://www.pbus.com/page/A3.

28. "Bail Bond Services Industry in the U.S.—Market Research Report," IBISWorld, October 29, 2022, https://www.ibisworld.com/united-states/market-research-reports/bail-bond-services-industry/.

29. "The High Price of Bail," Justice Policy Institute, https://justicepolicy.org/wp-content/uploads/2022/02/high_price_of_bail_-_final.pdf.

30. Ibid.

31. Ibid.

32. These model policies have been taken down from the ALEC website but are available from the internet archive. "Crimes with Bail Restrictions Act," American Legislative Exchange Council, https://web.archive.org/web/20161008032906/https://www.alec.org/model-policy/crimes-with-bail-restrictions-act/ (archive).

33. "2022 Felony Bail Schedule," Superior Court of California, County of Los Angeles, https://www.lacourt.org/division/criminal/pdf/felony.pdf.

34. "California's Cannabis Laws," State of California Department of Cannabis Control, https://cannabis.ca.gov/cannabis-laws/laws-and-regulations/; Michel Martin, "5 Years After California Legalized Weed, the Illicit Market Dominates," *NPR*, November 7, 2021.

35. "Bail Forfeiture Relief and Remission Act," American Legislative Exchange Council, https://web.archive.org/web/20170413084531/https://www.alec.org/model-policy/bail-forfeiture-relief-and-remission-act/ (archive).

36. §903.28, Fla. Stat. (2005).

37. Ibid.

38. Va. Code Ann., §9.1-185.8 (2019). This law provides that "a licensed bail bondsman shall not charge a bail bond premium less than 10 percent or more than 15 percent of the amount of the bond."

39. Zhen Zeng, *Jail Inmates in 2021: Statistical Tables* (Washington, D.C.: U.S. Department of Justice, Bureau of Justice Statistics, 2022), 1.

40. Ibid.

41. "The Hidden Costs of Pretrial Detention Revisited," Arnold Ventures, March 21, 2022, https://craftmediabucket.s3.amazonaws.com/uploads/HiddenCosts.pdf.

42. Wendy Sawyer, "How Race Impacts Who Is Detained Pretrial," Prison Policy Initiative, October 9, 2019, https://www.prisonpolicy.org/blog/2019/10/09/pretrial_race/.

43. "Criminal Justice Reform," New Jersey Courts, https://www.njcourts.gov/public/concerns/criminal-justice-reform.

44. Oveta Wiggins and Ann E. Marimow, "Maryland's Highest Court Overhauls the State's Cash-Based Bail System," *Washington Post*, February 7, 2017.

45. Pretrial Release or Detention: Pretrial Services, SB-10, 2017-2018 Leg., Reg. Sess. (Cal. 2018); "The Facts on Bail Reform," NYCLU, ACLU of New York, https://www.nyclu.org/en/campaigns/facts-bail-reform; Ames Grawert and Noah Kim, "The Facts on Bail Reform and Crime Rates in New York State," Brennan Center for Justice, updated May 9, 2023, https://www.brennancenter.org/our-work/research-reports/facts-bail-reform-and-crime-rates-new-york-state.

46. Nicole Moeder, Devin Dwyer, and Isabella Meneses, "Illinois Set to Become 1st State to Eliminate Cash Bail," *ABC News*, December 19, 2022.

47. Taryn A. Merkl and Leily Arzy, "California's Referendum to Eliminate Cash Bail, Explained," Brennan Center for Justice, October 2, 2020, https://www.brennancenter.org/our-work/analysis-opinion/californias-referendum-eliminate-cash-bail-explained.

48. Nigel Duara, "What the Failure of Prop. 25 Means for Racial Justice in California," *CalMatters*, November 5, 2020 (updated February 24, 2021); Patrick McGreevy, "Prop. 25 Rejected in 2020 California Election," *Los Angeles Times*, November 4, 2020.

49. Don Thompson, "California Stalls Scaled Down Bail Reform After Year's Delay," *Associated Press*, September 1, 2022.

50. State of New York, Bail Reform Amendments, S.7506-B/A. 9506-B (Part UU), https://perma.cc/4CPC-YZ4E.

51. New York State Senate Assembly, S8006C (2021), https://perma.cc/4CRD-ADM8.

52. "Illinois High Court Halts Elimination of Cash Bail," *Associated Press*, January 1, 2023.

53. "Miami Mayor to President Biden: 'End Cash Bail' Policies a Failure," American Bail Coalition, January 24, 2023, https://ambailcoalition.org/miami-mayor-to-president-biden-end-cash-bail-policies-a-failure/;

"Effectiveness and Cost," American Bail Coalition, accessed November 9, 2023, https://ambailcoalition.org/effectiveness-and-cost/.

54. "Pretrial Roadmap: 2023," American Bail Coalition, January 4, 2023, https://ambailcoalition.org/pretrial-roadmap-2023/.

55. "About," American Bail Coalition, accessed November 9, 2023, https://ambailcoalition.org/our-team/; "Factbox—Major Insurers of US Bail Bonds," *Reuters*, March 26, 2021, https://www.reuters.com/article/usa-insurance-bail-jails-idCNL1N2LL176; Bankers Financial Corporation, https://bankersfinancialcorp.com; AIA Surety, https://www.aiasurety.com.

56. Scott and Barlyn, "U.S. Bail-Bond Insurers Spend Big."

57. Michael Janofsky, "Baltimore Opening High-Tech Central Booking Center," *New York Times*, November 23, 1995.

58. "Central Booking Headquarters Bail Bond Inc.," Cmac.ws, accessed November 9, 2023, https://bail-bond-providers.cmac.ws/central-booking-headquarters-bail-bond-inc/3728/.

59. Advantage Sentencing Alternative Programs, Inc. & Electronic Monitoring Services (EMS), accessed November 9, 2023, http://02ddb6b.netsolhost.com/index.htm.

60. "Electronic Monitoring in Maryland, PA & WV," Alert Home Detention, accessed November 9, 2023, http://alertinc.info/index.htm; A1 Trusted Monitoring LLC, accessed November 9, 2023, https://a1trusted.com.

61. Interview with author.

62. "About SCRAM Systems," SCRAM Systems, accessed November 9, 2023, https://www.scramsystems.com/our-company/about-us/.

63. Josh Wigler, "Lindsay Lohan's SCRAM Bracelet: How Does It Work?," MTV.com, May 24, 2010, https://www.mtv.com/news/qep3px/lindsay-lohans-scram-bracelet-how-does-it-work.

64. SCRAM Systems, "About."

65. "Electronic Monitoring Equipment & Service," Alert Home Detention, http://alertinc.info/electronic_monitoring_equipment.htm; "How We Can Help You," A1 Trusted Monitoring LLC, https://a1trusted.com/services/; "GPS Solutions," Securus Monitoring, https://securusmonitoring.com/our-solutions/hardware_solutions/gps-solutions/.

66. "Our Applications," A1 Trusted Monitoring LLC, accessed March 15, 2023, https://a1trusted.com/applications/; "Welcome to ASAP Home Detention," Advantage Sentencing Alternative Programs, Inc. & Electronic Monitoring Services (EMS), accessed March 15, 2023, http://02ddb6b.netsolhost.com/index.htm.

67. "Participant Rules and Agreement," Advantage Sentencing Alternative Programs, Inc., accessed March 15, 2023, http://02ddb6b.netsolhost

.com/forms/participantrulesandagreement.pdf. In particular, clients must agree that "while bathing I must have my leg over the side of the bath tub, out of the water. While showering, I understand that I must thoroughly cleanse the area around the transmitter with soap and water, and dry underneath."

68. "Maryland Division of Pretrial Detention and Services," Maryland.gov, https://www.dpscs.state.md.us/agencies/dpds.shtml.

69. Tim Prudente, "Delayed Trials, Home Detention and Hundreds of Dollars in Ankle-Monitoring Costs," *Washington Post*, September 9, 2020.

70. Baltimore County Government, "Baltimore County Eliminates Home Monitoring Fees," press release, January 4, 2021, https://www.baltimorecountymd.gov/county-news/2021/01/04/baltimore-county-eliminates-home-monitoring-fees; Md. Const., Art. II, §17(c).

71. Fines and Fees Justice Center, *Electronic Monitoring Fees: A 50-State Survey of the Costs Assessed to People on E-Supervision* (New York: Fines and Fees Justice Center, 2022).

72. "Use of Electronic Offender-Tracking Devices Expands Sharply," Pew Charitable Trusts, September 7, 2016, https://www.pewtrusts.org/en/research-and-analysis/issue-briefs/2016/09/use-of-electronic-offender-tracking-devices-expands-sharply.

73. "Electronic Monitoring-FAQs," Challenging E-Carceration, December 5, 2021, https://www.challengingecarceration.org/my-blog.

74. Ibid.

75. The COVID Prison Project, https://covidprisonproject.com.

76. Ibid.

77. Izabela Zaluska, "Iowa Sheriff's Office Implementing Pretrial Electronic Monitoring Pilot Program," *The Gazette*, January 24, 2022, https://www.corrections1.com/gps-monitoring/articles/iowa-sheriffs-office-implementing-pretrial-electronic-monitoring-pilot-program-rIkdc2ZqKJXJoXgV; Helen Outland, "Electronic Monitoring to Save Money," *Carteret County News-Times*, January 11, 2009, https://www.carolinacoastonline.com/news_times/news/article_aa0f948b-68b3-54f4-86bf-920832347c13.html.

78. Ibid.

79. "Home Detention in West Virginia," Alert Home Detention, accessed November 9, 2023, https://www.alertinc.info/house-arrest-west-virgina.html; "Electronic Monitoring in Maryland, PA & WV," Alert Home Detention, https://www.alertinc.info/house-arrest-maryland.html.

80. Kate Weisburd, *Electronic Prisons: The Operation of Ankle Monitoring in the Criminal Legal System* (Washington, D.C.: George Washington University Law School, 2021), 15.

81. Ibid., 15.

82. Fines and Fees Justice Center, *Electronic Monitoring Fees*, 8.

83. Md. Code §5-201.

84. Fines and Fees Justice Center, *Electronic Monitoring Fees*, 5.

85. Ibid., 9.

86. Weisburd, *Electronic Prisons*, 1.

87. Ibid.

88. Patrice James, James Kilgore, Gabriela Kirk, et al., *Cages Without Bars: Pretrial Electronic Monitoring Across the United States* (Chicago, IL: Shriver Center on Poverty Law, MediaJustice and Chicago Appleseed Center for Fair Courts, 2022), 35.

89. Fines and Fees Justice Center, *Electronic Monitoring Fees*, 8.

90. Ibid.

91. Interview with author.

92. James et al., *Cages Without Bars*.

93. Ibid., 6.

94. Ibid., 28.

95. Ibid., 13.

96. Ibid., 36.

97. 3M, "3M Attenti Renames Its Offender Monitoring Business to 3M Electronic Monitoring," press release, undated, https://news.3m.com/2011-09-27-3M-Attenti-Renames-its-Offender-Monitoring-Business-to-3M-Electronic-Monitoring. In 2010, 3M acquired Attenti for $230 million. Alexia Tsotsis, "3M Captures Attenti for $230 Million," *TechCrunch*, August 31, 2010. In 2022, Attenti became a subsidiary of global firm Allied Universal. Allied Universal, "Allied Universal Completes Acquisition of Attenti to Create the Global Leader in Electronic Monitoring," press release, August 2022, https://www.aus.com/press-releases/allied-universal-completes-acquisition-attenti-create-global-leader-electronic.

98. James et al., *Cages Without Bars*, 18.

99. Ibid.

100. "Private Equity–Owned Firms Dominate Prison and Detention Services," Private Equity Stakeholder Project, December 2018, https://pestakeholder.org/wp-content/uploads/2018/09/PE-Incarceration-Detention-PESP-122018.pdf.

101. "Sentinel Offender Services," Bison Capital, accessed March 14, 2023, https://bisoncapital.com/portfolio-items/sentinel-offender-services/.

102. "Sierra Wireless Completes Divestiture of Offender Monitoring Business for US $37.6 Million," *Business Wire*, April 18, 2022. Sierra Wireless was itself purchased by Semtech in 2023 for $1.2 billion. Alan Burkitt-Gray,

"Semtech Completes $1.2bn Acquisition of Sierra Wireless," *Capacity*, January 13, 2023.

103. "About Us," Securus Monitoring, accessed November 9, 2023, https://securusmonitoring.com/about-us/; "GPS Solutions," Securus Monitoring, accessed November 9, 2023, https://securusmonitoring.com/our-solutions/hardware_solutions/gps-solutions/; Aventiv, https://www.aventiv.com.

104. "JPay," Aventiv, https://www.aventiv.com/jpay/.

105. Weisburd, *Electronic Prisons*, 22.

106. Ibid.

107. Lynh Bui, "Reforms Intended to End Excessive Cash Bail in Md. Are Keeping More in Jail Longer, Report Says," *Washington Post*, July 2, 2018.

108. Interview with author.

109. Prison Policy Initiative, "Economics of Incarceration," updated March 12, 2023, https://www.prisonpolicy.org/research/economics_of_incarceration; Bureau of Economic Analysis, "Gross Domestic Product by State and Personal Income by State, 3rd Quarter 2022," press release, https://www.bea.gov/sites/default/files/2022-12/stgdppi3q22.pdf. Delaware's 2021 GDP was about $81.1 billion.

110. "Local Spending on Jails Tops $25 Billion in Latest Nationwide Data," Pew Charitable Trusts, January 29, 2021, https://www.pewtrusts.org/en/research-and-analysis/issue-briefs/2021/01/local-spending-on-jails-tops-$25-billion-in-latest-nationwide-data.

111. "State Profile: Delaware," State Higher Education Finance, https://shef.sheeo.org/state-profile/delaware/; "2021 Budget: Correction," State of Delaware, https://budget.delaware.gov/budget/fy2021/documents/operating/correction.pdf.

112. State of Oregon Legislative Fiscal Office, "Budget Information Brief/2021-1," https://www.oregonlegislature.gov/lfo/Documents/2021-1%20LAB%20Summary%202021-23.pdf.

113. "GEO Group History Timeline," The GEO Group, Inc., accessed November 9, 2023, https://www.geogroup.com/history_timeline.

114. Eunice Cho, "More of the Same: Private Prison Corporations and Immigration Detention Under the Biden Administration," American Civil Liberties Union, October 5, 2021, https://www.aclu.org/news/immigrants-rights/more-of-the-same-private-prison-corporations-and-immigration-detention-under-the-biden-administration.

115. Byron Eugene Price, *Merchandizing Prisoners: Who Really Pays for Prison Privatization?* (Westport, CT: Praeger Publishers, 2006), 2.

116. Ibid.

117. Matthew T. King, "A History of Private Prisons," in *Prison Privatization:*

The Many Facets of a Controversial Industry, ed. Byron E. Price and John Morris (Santa Barbara, CA: Praeger, 2012), 24.

118. Ibid., 8.

119. Bill Carey, "Fried Chicken, the Colonel and the Nashville Businessman," *Winchester Sun*, December 6, 2021, https://www.winchestersun.com/2021/12/06/fried-chicken-the-colonel-and-the-nashville-businessman/. "Colonel" Sanders was never actually a colonel in the military—he was awarded an honorary title by the Kentucky legislature in 1935 because of the fame of his chicken. "Colonel Harland Sanders," Biography.com, https://www.biography.com/business-leaders/colonel-harland-sanders. Sanders also reportedly turned down stock in exchange for his interest in his company, telling John Massey's partner, John Brown, that KFC stock was "not going to be worth toilet paper." Carey, "Fried Chicken, the Colonel and the Nashville Businessman"; "Top Ten Largest Health Systems in the U.S. by Number of Hospitals Affiliated," *Hospital Management*, May 26, 2022, https://www.hospitalmanagement.net/features/top-ten-largest-health-systems-in-the-us-by-number-of-hospitals-affiliated/.

120. David A. Vise, "Private Company Asks for Control of Tenn. Prisons," *Washington Post*, September 22, 1985.

121. Kristen M. Budd and Niki Monazzam, "Private Prisons in the United States," The Sentencing Project, June 15, 2023, https://www.sentencingproject.org/publications/private-prisons-united-states/.

122. Price, *Merchandizing Prisoners*, xvi–xvii.

123. Ibid., 36.

124. Gerald G. Gaes, Scott D. Camp, Julianne B. Nelson, and William G. Saylor, *Measuring Prison Performance: Government Privatization and Accountability* (Walnut Creek, CA: AltaMira Press, 2004), 47, citing Elaine Cummins, *Private Prisons in Texas, 1987–2000*. Unpublished doctoral dissertation, American University, Washington, D.C., 2001.

125. Gaes et al., *Measuring Prison Performance*, 47.

126. Texas had 9,748 privately housed inmates in 2021. Budd and Monazzam, "Private Prisons in the United States."

127. A.W. Geiger, "U.S. Private Prison Population Has Declined in Recent Years," Pew Research Center, April 11, 2017, https://www.pewresearch.org/short-reads/2017/04/11/u-s-private-prison-population-has-declined-in-recent-years/.

128. Budd and Monazzam, "Private Prisons in the United States."

129. Ibid.

130. Several analyses have dissected ALEC's role in helping the prison industry take flight in the 1990s. See, e.g., Price, *Merchandizing Prisoners*, 133;

Mike Elk and Bob Sloan, "The Hidden History of ALEC and Prison Labor," *The Nation*, August 1, 2011. American Civil Liberties Union, *Banking on Bondage: Private Prisons and Mass Incarceration* (New York: American Civil Liberties Union, 2011), 15.

131. American Civil Liberties Union, *Banking on Bondage*, 15.

132. In the Public Interest, *Criminal: How Lockup Quotas and "Low-Crime Taxes" Guarantee Profits for Private Prison Corporations* (Oakland, CA: In the Public Interest, 2013), 2.

133. Ibid., 5.

134. CoreCivic, Inc., *2021 Annual Report* (Brentwood, TN: CoreCivic, Inc., 2021), 7.

135. Anne Lee, "Private Prisons and Community Corrections," in *Pri$on Privatization: The Many Facets of a Controversial Industry. Volume 1: The Environment of Private Prisons*, eds. Byron Eugene Price and John Charles Morris (Santa Barbara, CA: Praeger, 2012), 258.

136. Ibid.

137. Jamiles Lartey, "Think Private Prison Companies Are Going Away Under Biden? They Have Other Plans," *The Marshall Project*, November 17, 2020, https://www.themarshallproject.org/2020/11/17/think-private-prison-companies-are-going-away-under-biden-they-have-other-plans.

138. White House, "Executive Order on Reforming Our Incarceration System to Eliminate the Use of Privately Operated Criminal Detention Facilities," January 26, 2021, https://www.whitehouse.gov/briefing-room/presidential-actions/2021/01/26/executive-order-reforming-our-incarceration-system-to-eliminate-the-use-of-privately-operated-criminal-detention-facilities/.

139. Jaanvi Kaur, "ACLU Condemns Biden Administration for Enormous Enlargement of ICE Personal Immigration Detention [Center] in Georgia," *Georgia Law News.com*, March 26, 2022.

140. As of September 24, 2023, ICE held more than 35,289 detainees in custody. "Immigration Detention Quick Facts," TRAC Immigration, Syracuse University, https://trac.syr.edu/immigration/quickfacts/. In 1994, in comparison, the average number of immigrant detainees was just 6,785. American Civil Liberties Union, *Banking on Bondage*.

141. Cho, "More of the Same: Private Prison Corporations and Immigration Detention Under the Biden Administration."

142. CoreCivic, *2021 Annual Report*, 8, 39.

143. Cho, "More of the Same: Private Prison Corporations and Immigration Detention Under the Biden Administration."

144. Jeremy Redmon and Lautaro Grinspan, "Exclusive: Ga. Immigration

Facility to Become One of Nation's Largest," *Atlanta Journal-Constitution*, February 4, 2022.

145. Ibid.

146. Ted Hesson and Mica Rosenberg, "Private Prisons Company to Test U.S. House Arrest Program for Immigrants," *Reuters*, February 16, 2022.

147. Casey Tolan, "Biden Vowed to Close Federal Private Prisons, but Prison Companies Are Finding Loopholes to Keep Them Open," *CNN*, November 12, 2021.

148. Ibid.

149. Liz Kiesche, "GEO Group, CoreCivic Stocks Climb as They Replace Federal Prison Contracts," *Seeking Alpha*, October 8, 2021, https://seekingalpha.com/news/3751019-geo-group-corecivic-stocks-climb-as-they-replace-federal-prison-contracts.

150. CoreCivic, Inc., *Annual Report on Form 10-K for the Fiscal Year Ended December 31, 2022* (Brentwood, TN: CoreCivic, Inc., 2022), 73; The GEO Group, Inc., *Annual Report on Form 10-K for the Fiscal Year Ended December 31, 2022* (Boca Raton, FL: The GEO Group, Inc.), 53.

151. "Building a Path for Second Chances," Aramark Correctional Services, https://www.aramark.com/industries/business-and-government/corrections. Worth Rises maintains an excellent map of the various sectors profiting from prison operations. Worth Rises, "The Prison Industrial Complex: Mapping Private Sector Players," April 2019, https://static1.squarespace.com/static/58e127cb1b10e31ed45b20f4/t/5cc7c27b9e3a8d00018649c5/1556595324791/The+Prison+Industrial+Complex+-+Mapping+Private+Sector+Players+-+2019.pdf.

152. David Dayen, "The True Cost: Why the Private Prison Industry Is About So Much More Than Prisons," *Talking Points Memo*, 2016.

153. "Inmate Care Package Services," Maryland Department of Public Safety and Correctional Services, accessed November 9, 2023, https://news.maryland.gov/dpscs/inmate-care-packages/.

154. Access Securepak, https://www.accesscatalog.com/index.html?PageID=22; "About Keefe Group," Keefe Group, https://www.keefegroup.com.

155. "Access Corrections," Keefe Group, https://www.keefegroup.com/companies/access-corrections-114.

156. "Inmate Banking Services," Maryland Department of Public Safety and Correctional Services, accessed November 9, 2023, https://news.maryland.gov/dpscs/inmate-trust-fund-services/.

157. Pete Wagner and Alexi Jones, "State of Phone Justice: Local Jails, State Prisons and Private Phone Providers," Prison Policy Initiative, February 2019, https://www.prisonpolicy.org/phones/state_of_phone_justice.html.

158. Ibid.

159. Peter Wagner and Wanda Bertram, "State of Phone Justice 2022: The Problem, the Progress, and What's Next," Prison Policy Initiative, December 2022, https://www.prisonpolicy.org/phones/state_of_phone_justice_2022.html.

160. Ibid.; Wanda Bertram, "Since You Asked: What's Next For Prison and Jail Phone Justice Now That the Martha Wright-Reed Just and Reasonable Communications Act Is Law?," Prison Policy Initiative, January 19, 2023, https://www.prisonpolicy.org/blog/2023/01/19/martha-wright-reed-act/.

161. Bernadette Rabuy and Peter Wagner, "Screening Out Family Time: The For-Profit Video Visitation Industry in Prisons and Jails," Prison Policy Initiative, January 2015, https://www.prisonpolicy.org/visitation/report.html.

162. Ibid., 11.

163. Wagner and Bertram, "State of Phone Justice 2022."

164. Rabuy and Wagner, "Screening Out Family Time"; "HomeWAV Celebrates Milestones in Company Growth," HomeWAV, press release, January 31, 2023, https://www.homewav.com/homewav-celebrates-milestones-in-company-growth/.

165. Private Equity Stakeholder Project, "Private Equity–Owned Firms Dominate Prison and Detention Services."

166. Stephen Raher, "The Company Store: A Deeper Look at Prison Commissaries," Prison Policy Initiative, May 2018, https://www.prisonpolicy.org/reports/commissary.html.

167. Ibid.

168. Ibid.

169. "Order Form, Maryland DOC," Access Securepak, accessed November 9, 2023, https://www.accesscatalog.com/downloads/OrderForms/MD_DOC_2021_OrderForm_P2.pdf.

170. "Inmate Devices & Content," ConnectNetwork, https://web.connectnetwork.com/inmate-devices-content/streaming-music/.

171. "Prison Music Kiosk PDF Guide," Prison Kiosk, accessed November 9, 2023, https://prisonkiosk.net/product/prison-music-kiosk-pdf-guide/.

172. Consumer Financial Protection Bureau, *Justice-Involved Individuals and the Consumer Financial Marketplace* (Washington, D.C.: Consumer Financial Protection Bureau, 2022), 18.

173. Ibid.

174. New York City Comptroller, Bureau of Budget and Bureau of Policy and Research, *Fees, Fines and Fairness: How Monetary Charges Drive Inequity in New York City's Criminal Justice System* (New York: New York City Comptroller, Bureau of Budget and Bureau of Policy Research, 2019), 51.

175. Consumer Financial Protection Bureau, *Justice-Involved Individuals and the Consumer Financial Marketplace*, 19.

176. Some states also mark up the cost of commissary items far above what Securepak charges. In 2021, the state of Nevada reportedly made more than $2.8 million in profits from prison commissary sales. Nick Shepack, "Why Is the Nevada Department of Corrections Profiting Off Struggling Families?," *Nevada Independent*, August 5, 2022.

177. Pat Eaton-Robb, "At $249 Per Day Prison Stays Leave Ex-inmates Deep in Debt," *Associated Press*, August 27, 2022.

178. Tanzina Vega, "Costly Prison Fees Are Putting Inmates Deep in Debt," *CNN*, September 18, 2015.

179. Tiana Herring, "Prisons Shouldn't Be Charging Medical Co-pays—Especially During a Pandemic," Prison Policy Initiative, December 21, 2020, https://www.prisonpolicy.org/blog/2020/12/21/copay-survey/.

180. Tiana Herring, "COVID Looks Like It May Stay. That Means Prison Medical Copays Must Go," Prison Policy Initiative, February 1, 2022, https://www.prisonpolicy.org/blog/2022/02/01/pandemic_copays/.

181. "State Audit: Nevada Inmates Overpay for Medical, Store Items," *Associated Press*, March 7, 2022.

182. Shepack, "Why Is the Nevada Department of Corrections Profiting."

183. New York City Comptroller, *Fees, Fines and Fairness*, 6.

184. Ibid.

185. Consumer Financial Protection Bureau, *Justice-Involved Individuals and the Consumer Financial Marketplace*, 15.

186. Ibid.

187. "UNICOR, Program Details," Federal Bureau of Prisons, https://www.bop.gov/inmates/custody_and_care/unicor_about.jsp; "Alphabetical Schedule of Products and Services," UNICOR, https://www.unicor.gov/SopAlphaList.aspx.

188. Federal Bureau of Prisons, "UNICOR."

189. U.S. Department of Justice, Bureau of Justice Assistance, "Prison Industry Enhancement Certification Program," November 1995, https://www.ojp.gov/pdffiles/pie.pdf.

190. "About PRIDE," PRIDE Enterprises, accessed November 9, 2023, https://www.pride-enterprises.org/#AvailableProducts.

191. "Prison Rehabilitative Industries and Diversified Enterprises, Inc.," State of Florida, Office of Program Policy Analysis and Government Accountability, https://oppaga.fl.gov/ProgramSummary/ProgramDetailPrint?programNumber=1037.

192. Tiffany Barfield-Cottledge, "An Overview and Profile of Private

Prisons," in *Pri$on Privatization: The Many Facets of a Controversial Industry. Volume 1: The Environment of Private Prisons*, eds. Byron Eugene Price and John Charles Morris (Santa Barbara, CA: Praeger, 2012).

193. "Researchers Find Prison Privatization Can Impede Job Growth," *Washington State University Insider*, January 28, 2013.

194. Ibid.

195. U.S. Department of Justice, Office of the Inspector General, *Review of the Federal Bureau of Prisons' Monitoring of Contract Prisons* (Washington, D.C.: U.S. Department of Justice, Office of the Inspector General, 2016), ii.

196. Ibid., 19.

197. In the Public Interest, *How Private Prison Companies Increase Recidivism* (Oakland, CA: In the Public Interest, 2016), 4.

198. Brian Highsmith, *Commercialized (In)justice: Consumer Abuses in the Bail and Corrections Industry* (Washington, D.C.: National Consumer Law Center, 2019).

199. Shepack, "Why Is the Nevada Department of Corrections Profiting."

200. Civic Works Center for Sustainable Careers, http://sustainablecareers.civicworks.com.

201. "Our Impact," Civic Works Center for Sustainable Careers, http://sustainablecareers.civicworks.com/our-impact/.

202. Interview with author.

203. "Baltimore City Department of Transportation: Towing Division," City of Baltimore, accessed November 9, 2023, https://transportation.baltimorecity.gov/towing.

204. Ibid.

205. "Baltimore City to Waive Towing Fees for Stolen Vehicles," *CBS News-Baltimore*, January 13, 2022, https://www.cbsnews.com/baltimore/news/baltimore-city-to-waive-towing-fees-for-stolen-vehicles/.

206. "Frequently Asked Questions," Baltimore City Department of Finance, https://web.archive.org/web/20221004041939/https://finance.baltimorecity.gov/public-info/faq (archive).

207. "Frequently Asked Questions," Baltimore City Department of Finance, accessed November 9, 2023, https://finance.baltimorecity.gov/public-info/faq.

208. "Statewide Debt Collection Services, Contract Award Information," State of Maryland Department of Budget and Management, https://dbm.maryland.gov/contracts/Pages/contract-library/Services/DebtCollection2015.aspx.

209. "Request for Proposals (RFP), Statewide Debt Collection Services," State of Maryland Department of Budget and Management, October 8, 2014,

https://dbm.maryland.gov/contracts/Documents/ContractLibrary/Services/DebtCollection2015/DebtCollection2015.pdf. According to the RFP, "typical debts include college tuition and fees, a small number of student loans, public assistance and food stamp overpayments, Parole and Probation restitution/Supervisory Fees/Court Cost accounts, Motor Vehicle Administration insurance lapse default fines, reimbursement for damage to State property, returned checks, reimbursement for care at a State hospital, unpaid workers' compensation insurance premiums, Home Improvement Commission awards, and environmental fines."

210. The Fines and Fees Justice Center's Free to Drive campaign has been extraordinarily successful in this regard. Over five years, the campaign won legislative action in twenty-two states to end or limit driver's license suspensions for failure to pay. Free to Drive, https://www.freetodrive.org.

211. I am using initials only to protect the privacy of the trainees who spoke with me.

212. "Uninsured Vehicle Owners," Maryland Department of Transportation, Motor Vehicle Administration, accessed November 9, 2023, https://mva.maryland.gov/vehicles/Pages/insurance-uninsured.aspx.

213. I shared some of these trainees' stories in this piece: Anne Kim, "You're Out of Prison. Now You Have to Get Your Driver's License Back," *Washington Post*, April 4, 2019; "Maryland Senate Bill 234: Vehicle Laws—Suspension of Driver's License or Registration—Unpaid Citations or Judgements," Fines and Fees Justice Center, March 17, 2020, https://finesandfeesjusticecenter.org/articles/maryland-senate-bill-234-vehicle-laws-suspension-of-drivers-license-or-registration-unpaid-citations-or-judgements/.

214. The state of Maryland is particularly zealous about collecting child support, and lists numerous "enforcement tools" for collecting these obligations, including drivers license suspensions. "Child Support Administration," Maryland Department of Human Services, accessed November 9, 2023, https://dhs.maryland.gov/child-support-services/child-support-resources/enforcement-tools/. A description of every state's laws on suspensions for unpaid fines and fees is available from the Free to Drive campaign, run by the Fines and Fees Justice Center, Free to Drive, https://www.freetodrive.org/maps/#page-content.

215. Interview with author.

6. Sheltering Profits, Feeding Industry

1. "Housing and Community Development Expenditures," Urban Institute, accessed March 15, 2023, https://www.urban.org/policy-centers/cross-center-initiatives/state-and-local-finance-initiative/state-and-local-backgrounders/housing-and-community-development-expenditures.

2. "The Federal Government's Support for Low-Income Housing Expanded During the Pandemic," Peter G. Peterson Foundation, June 24, 2022, https://www.pgpf.org/blog/2022/06/how-does-the-federal-government-support-housing-for-low-income-households.

3. Corianne Payton Scally, Amanda Gold, Carl Hedman, Matthew Gerken, and Nicole DuBois, *The Low-Income Housing Credit: Past Achievements, Future Challenges* (Washington, D.C.: Urban Institute, 2018); Congressional Research Service, *An Introduction to the Low-Income Housing Tax Credit* (Washington, D.C.: Congressional Research Service, 2023).

4. "Lyon Homes Apartments," Apartments.com, accessed March 15, 2023, https://www.apartments.com/lyon-homes-apartments-townhomes-dundalk-md/rlxltj2/.

5. "Annual Expenditures for Affordable Rental Housing in Baltimore City," Baltimore City Department of Housing & Community Development, accessed March 15, 2023, https://dhcd.baltimorecity.gov/nd/affordable-housing-inventory.

6. Ibid.

7. "Supportive Housing Programs," Baltimore County Government, https://www.baltimorecountymd.gov/departments/housing/housing-programs.

8. Eva Rosen, *The Voucher Promise: "Section 8" and the Fate of an American Neighborhood* (Princeton and Oxford: Princeton University Press, 2020), 103.

9. Frederick J. Eggers, *Characteristics of HUD-Assisted Renters and Their Units in 2019* (Washington, D.C.: U.S. Department of Housing and Urban Development, Office of Policy Development and Research, 2021), ES-1, ES-2.

10. U.S. Department of Housing and Urban Development, *Worst Case Housing Needs: 2021 Report to Congress* (Washington, D.C.: U.S. Department of Housing and Urban Development, 2021), iii.

11. Eggers, *Characteristics of HUD-Assisted Renters*, ES-2.

12. Sonya Acosta and Erik Gartland, *Families Wait Years for Housing Vouchers Due to Inadequate Funding* (Washington, D.C.: Center on Budget and Policy Priorities, 2021).

13. Andrew Aurand, Dan Emmanuel, Diane Yentel, Ellen Errico, Zoe Chapin, Gar Meng Leong, and Kate Rodrigues, *Housing Spotlight: The Long Wait for a Home* (Washington, D.C.: The National Low Income Housing Coalition, 2016), 3.

14. "Waiting List Status," Prince George's County, Maryland, accessed November 8, 2023, https://www.princegeorgescountymd.gov/community/housing/housing-authority/tenant-resources/application-process/check-wait-list-status.

15. Hiren Nisar, Jim Murdoch, Elgin Dallas, Mallory Vachon, and charles

horseman, *Landlord Participation Study* (Washington, D.C.: U.S. Department of Housing and Urban Development, Office of Policy Development and Research, 2018), 1.

16. Congressional Research Service, *An Overview of the Section 8 Housing Program* (Washington, D.C.: Congressional Research Service, 2014), 1.

17. Barbara Sard and Jennifer Daskal, "Housing and Welfare Reform: Some Background Information," Center on Budget and Policy Priorities, November 5, 1998, https://www.cbpp.org/sites/default/files/archive/hous212.htm; The Housing Choice Voucher program is primarily tenant-based—meaning that the voucher travels with the tenant. A small number of public housing authorities, however, have "project based" vouchers attached to units in a project (but these work exactly like tenant-based vouchers). For the sake of simplicity, research on vouchers treats both tenant-based and project-based vouchers as "vouchers"; Eggers, *Characteristics of HUD-Assisted Renters*.

18. Center on Budget and Policy Priorities, *Policy Basics: The Housing Choice Voucher Program* (Washington, D.C.: Center on Budget and Policy Priorities, 2021).

19. Eggers, *Characteristics of HUD-Assisted Renters*, ES-4.

20. "Endicott Peabody, the Man with the Thickest Skin in New England," New England Historical Society, 2022, https://newenglandhistoricalsociety.com/endicott-peabody-man-thickest-skin-new-england/.

21. Anne Kim, "The Monthly Interview: The Man Who Reinvented Public Housing," *Washington Monthly*, June 30, 2016.

22. Alison Stateman, "Breaking Down LA's Jordan Downs," *Commercial Observer*, March 26, 2018, https://commercialobserver.com/2018/03/breaking-down-las-jordan-downs; Karen Hawkins, "Chicago Shutters Infamous Public Housing Complex," *NBC News*, December 1, 2010, https://www.nbcnews.com/id/wbna40450463.

23. Sara Rimer, "Minoru Yamasaki, Architect of World Trade Center, Dies," *New York Times*, February 9, 1986.

24. Colin Marshall, "Pruitt-Igoe: The Troubled High-Rise That Came to Define Urban America," *The Guardian*, April 22, 2015.

25. Kim, "The Man Who Reinvented Public Housing."

26. For a useful primer on "neighborhood effects" on socioeconomic outcomes, see Steven N. Durlauf, "Neighborhood Effects," *Handbook of Regional and Urban Economics, Volume 4* (New York: Elsevier, 2004), 2173–2242, https://doi.org/10.1016/S1574-0080(04)80007-5.

27. Raj Chetty, Nathaniel Hendren, and Lawrence F. Katz, "The Effects of Exposure to Better Neighborhoods on Children: New Evidence from the Moving to Opportunity Experiment," National Bureau of Economic

Research Working Paper 21156, May 2015, revised September 2015, JEL No. H53,I32,I38,R38, https://www.nber.org/papers/w21156; Jens Ludwig, Greg J. Duncan, Lisa A. Gennetian, Lawrence F. Katz, Ronald C. Kessler, Jeffrey R. Kling, and Lisa Sanbonmatsu, "Long-Term Neighborhood Effects on Low-Income Families: Evidence from Moving to Opportunity," NBER Working Paper No. 18772, February 2013, Revised April 2013, JEL No. H43,I18,I38,J38, http://www.nber.org/papers/w18772. In potential contradiction of the 2015 study by Chetty et al., however, this study showed "no detectable effect on economic outcomes, youth schooling and youth physical health; and mixed results by gender on other youth outcomes, with girls doing better on some measures and boys doing worse."

28. Lance Freeman, *The Impact of Source of Income Laws on Voucher Utilization and Locational Outcomes* (Washington, D.C.: U.S. Department of Housing and Urban Development, Office of Policy Development and Research, 2011), vii.

29. U.S. Department of Housing and Urban Development, Office of Inspector General, *HUD's Oversight of Voucher Utilization and Reallocation in the Housing Choice Voucher Program* (Washington, D.C.: U.S. Department of Housing and Urban Development, Office of Inspector General, 2021), 7.

30. Ibid., 10.

31. Rosen, *The Voucher Promise*, 20.

32. Alison Bell, Barbara Sard, and Becky Koepnick, *Prohibiting Discrimination Against Renters Using Housing Vouchers Improves Results* (Washington, D.C.: Center on Budget and Policy Priorities, 2018).

33. Mary K. Cunningham and Audrey Droesch, *Neighborhood Quality and Racial Segregation* (Washington, D.C.: Urban Institute, 2005).

34. Ingrid Gould Ellen and Keren Mertens Horn, *Do Federally Assisted Households Have Access to High Performing Public Schools?* (Washington, D.C.: Poverty and Race Research Action Council, 2012), 5.

35. "Dundalk Elementary, 2021–2022 School Report Card," Maryland State Department of Education, Baltimore County, https://reportcard.msde.maryland.gov/Graphs/#/ReportCards/ReportCardSchool/1/E/1/03/1202/0. "Dundalk High, 2021–2022 School Report Card," Maryland State Department of Education, Baltimore County, https://reportcard.msde.maryland.gov/Graphs/#/ReportCards/ReportCardSchool/1/H/1/03/1273/.

36. Philip Garboden, Eva Rosen, Meredith Greif, Stefanie DeLuca, and Kathryn Edin, *Urban Landlords and the Housing Choice Voucher Program: A Research Report* (Washington, D.C.: U.S. Department of Housing and Urban Development, 2018), 26.

37. Ibid., 18.

38. Mary Cunningham, Martha Galvez, Claudia L. Aranda, et al., *A Pilot Study of Landlord Acceptance of Housing Choice Vouchers* (Washington, D.C.: U.S. Department of Housing and Urban Development, 2018), iii.

39. Daniel Teles and Yipeng Su, *Source of Income Protections and Access to Low-Poverty Neighborhoods* (Washington, D.C.: Urban Institute, 2022).

40. Ibid.

41. Kristian Hernandez, "States Consider Source-of-Income Laws to Fight Housing Voucher Discrimination," *Planning Magazine*, June 1, 2021, https://www.planning.org/planning/2021/spring/states-tackle-housing-voucher-discrimination-with-source-of-income-laws/.

42. Edgar Walters and Neena Satija, "Section 8 Vouchers Are Supposed to Help the Poor Reach Better Neighborhoods. Texas Law Gets in the Way," *Texas Tribune*, November 19, 2018. Fair housing advocates have challenged the Texas law and similar laws in other jurisdictions. As of early 2023, this litigation was still pending. Sarah Holder and Kristin Capps, "A Legal Showdown Over Section 8 Discrimination Is Brewing in Dallas Suburb," *Bloomberg*, July 29, 2022.

43. Rosen, *The Voucher Promise*, 24. A once-thriving neighborhood, Park Heights is now beset by poverty and crime. Half the children in Park Heights live below the poverty line. Luke Broadwater, "In Park Heights, a Struggle to Save a Neighborhood—and a Horse Race," *Baltimore Sun*, May 13, 2017.

44. Steve Thompson and Dalton Bennett, "DC Overpays Landlords Millions to House the City's Poorest," *Washington Post*, February 16, 2023.

45. "Official Site of Commercial Real Estate Coach, Author and Investor Peter Harris," Peter Harris Real Estate, accessed October 15, 2023, http://www.peterharrisrealestate.com.

46. Donald Trump, Curtis Oakes, and Peter Harris, *Three Master Secrets of Real Estate Success (Audio CD)*, Trump University Press, 2006.

47. Peter Conti and Peter Harris, *Commercial Real Estate Investing for Dummies* (Hoboken, NJ: For Dummies, 2008).

48. "Commercial Real Estate Investor Seeks Protegé," Commercial Property Advisors, accessed November 9, 2023, https://www.commercialpropertyadvisors.com/protege-program/.

49. Peter Harris, "Investing in Section 8 Apartments," Peter Harris Real Estate, May 4, 2017, http://www.peterharrisrealestate.com/investing-in-section-8-apartments.

50. Ibid.

51. Ibid. Harris declined an emailed interview request, instead responding only with a link to an autobiographical video. "Peter Harris Real Estate,"

Commercial Property Advisors, https://www.commercialpropertyadvisors.com/peter-harris-real-estate/.

52. Congressional Research Service, *An Introduction to the Low-Income Housing Tax Credit.*

53. Andrew Aurand, Dan Emmanuel, Keely Stater, and Kelly McElwain, *Balancing Priorities: Preservation and Neighborhood Opportunity in the Low-Income Housing Tax Credit Program Beyond Year 30* (Washington, D.C.: National Low Income Housing Coalition and Public and Affordable Housing Research Corporation, 2018), 4. For units in less desirable neighborhoods, says the NLIHC, the expiration of LIHTC requirements (and subsidies) could mean a deterioration in housing quality, especially if landlords won't invest in improvements without further government aid.

54. Ibid., 13.

55. "2022 Federal LIHTC Information by State," Novogradac, Affordable Housing Resource Center, https://www.novoco.com/resource-centers/affordable-housing-tax-credits/2022-federal-lihtc-information-state. In 2023, states got an allocation equal to $2.75 per person (with a minimum allocation of $3.1 million).

56. At least 20 percent of units must go to tenants with incomes 50 percent or less of the area's gross median income. Alternatively, 40 percent must go to households making less than 60 percent of the median. Congressional Research Service, *An Introduction to the Low-Income Housing Tax Credit*, 4.

57. Congressional Research Service, *The Effectiveness of the Community Reinvestment Act* (Washington, D.C.: Congressional Research Service, 2019). The Community Reinvestment Act requires federally chartered banks to "meet the credit needs" of their customers (including low- and moderate-income populations) in order to maintain their charters. The CRA allows a broad variety of activities to satisfy this mandate, including community economic development activities such as investing in LIHTC projects.

58. Ibid.

59. "Low-Income Housing Tax Credit (LIHTC): Property Level Data," U.S. Department of Housing and Urban Development, updated May 4, 2023, https://www.huduser.gov/portal/datasets/lihtc/property.html.

60. Laura Sullivan and Meg Anderson, "Affordable Housing Program Costs More, Shelters Fewer," *NPR*, May 9, 2017. A 2018 report by the GAO likewise found wide variation in per-unit costs across twelve agencies it studied, from $104,000 for a project in Georgia to $606,000 per unit for a development in California, but little understanding of why costs varied so greatly. U.S. Government Accountability Office, *Improved Data and Oversight Would*

Strengthen Cost Assessment and Fraud Risk Management (Washington, D.C.: U.S. Government Accountability Office, 2018).

61. U.S. Congress, Joint Committee on Taxation, *Estimates of Federal Tax Expenditures for Fiscal Years 2022–2026*, (Washington, D.C.: U.S. Congress, Joint Committee on Taxation, 2022), 37. The Committee projects that the LIHTC will cost $15 billion in 2026. Provisions in the Inflation Reduction Act of 2022 and the Taxpayer Certainty and the Disaster Tax Relief Act of 2020 expanded the credit by, for instance, increasing allocation authority within disaster zones. Congressional Research Service, *An Introduction to the Low-Income Housing Tax Credit.*

62. U.S. Government Accountability Office, *Improved Data and Oversight.*

63. Ibid.

64. Sullivan and Anderson, "Affordable Housing Program Costs More, Shelters Fewer."

65. Government Accountability Office, *Improved Data and Oversight*, 1.

66. Ibid., 55, 59.

67. Ibid.

68. Donna Kimura, "2021 NMHC Top 10 Syndicators," *Multifamily Executive*, May 6, 2021, https://www.multifamilyexecutive.com/business-finance/top-50/2021-nmhc-top-10-syndicators_o.

69. Government Accountability Office, *Improved Data and Oversight*, 57.

70. National Council of State Housing Agencies, "Recommended Practices in Housing Credit Administration," December 2017, https://www.ncsha.org/wp-content/uploads/2018/05/NCSHA-Recommended-Practices-in-Housing-Credit-Administration-Updated-Dec-2017.pdf.

71. Missouri State Auditor, *Low Income Housing Tax Credit Program, Report No. 2014-014* (Jefferson City, MO: Missouri State Auditor, 2014).

72. Ibid. Missouri created a state LIHTC program to supplement the federal credit. "In 1990, Missouri began supplementing the federal program by allocating state income tax credits equal to 20 percent of the federal total. In 1994, the state credit increased to up to 40 percent of the federal credit for areas that lost housing in the 1993 flood. In 1997, the state credit increased to up to 100 percent of the federal credit for all areas and remains at that level." Ibid., 4.

73. Ibid.

74. Congressional Research Service, *An Introduction to the Low-Income Housing Tax Credit.*

75. Chris Edwards and Vanessa Brown Calder, "Low-Income Housing Tax Credit: Costly, Complex, and Corruption-Prone," CATO Institute *Tax &*

Budget Bulletin no. 79 (November 13, 2017), https://www.cato.org/sites/cato.org/files/pubs/pdf/tbb79.pdf.

76. Brandon M. Weiss, "Residual Value Capture in Subsidized Housing (July 6, 2016)," *Harvard Law & Policy Review* 10, no. 2 (2016): 522–63, 548, https://ssrn.com/abstract=2812718.

77. Abt Associates, *Development and Analysis of the National Low-Income Housing Tax Credit Database* (Washington, D.C.: U.S. Department of Housing and Urban Development, Office of Policy Development and Research, 1996).

78. U.S. Department of Housing and Urban Development, Office of Policy Development and Research, *Understanding Whom the LIHTC Serves: Data on Tenants in LIHTC Units as of December 31, 2017* (Washington, D.C.: U.S. Department of Housing and Urban Development, Office of Policy Development and Research, 2019), 9.

79. Ibid.

80. Ibid., 13.

81. Ibid., 20.

82. Jongho Won, "Exploring Spatial Clustering Over Time and Spillover Effects of the Low-Income Housing Tax Credit on Neighborhood-Level Income Segregation," *Urban Affairs Review* 58, no. 3 (2020): 799–831, https://doi.org/10.1177/1078087420973436.

83. Casey J. Dawkins, *Exploring the Spatial Distribution of Low Income Housing Tax Credit Properties* (Washington, D.C.: U.S. Department of Housing and Urban Development, Office of Policy Development and Research, 2011).

84. U.S. Senate, Committee on Finance, *America's Affordable Housing Crisis: Challenges and Solutions*, report prepared for the use of the Committee on Finance, 115th Cong., 1st Sess., 2017, Committee Print 115–288, 61 (statement of Kirk McClure, University of Kansas).

85. "LIHTC Admissions, Rents and Grievance Procedures," National Housing Law Project, April 27, 2018, https://www.nhlp.org/resources/lihtc-admissions-rents-grievance-procedures/.

86. Aurand et al., *Balancing Priorities*, 7.

87. Weiss, "Residual Value Capture," 525.

88. "Food Security and Nutrition Assistance," U.S. Department of Agriculture, Economic Research Service, last modified October 31, 2023, https://www.ers.usda.gov/data-products/ag-and-food-statistics-charting-the-essentials/food-security-and-nutrition-assistance/?topicId=d7627f77-6cee-4ab9-bbb9-8c74d4778941.

89. "National School Lunch Program," U.S. Department of Agriculture,

Economic Research Service, updated September 27, 2023, https://www.ers.usda.gov/topics/food-nutrition-assistance/child-nutrition-programs/national-school-lunch-program/.

90. Vance Cariaga, "Food Stamps: How Ending Enhanced SNAP Benefits Could Hurt Walmart, Dollar Stores," *Yahoo.com*, February 28, 2023; Krissy Clark, "The Secret Life of a Food Stamp Might Become a Little Less Secret," *Slate*, August 5, 2014.

91. "The Rise of Dollar Stores: How the Proliferation of Discount Stores May Limit Healthy Food Access," Center for Science in the Public Interest, February 2020, https://www.cspinet.org/sites/default/files/2022-03/Dollar%20Store%20Fact%20Sheet.pdf.

92. Center on Budget and Policy Priorities, *Policy Basics: The Supplemental Nutrition Assistance Program (SNAP)* (Washington, D.C.: Center on Budget and Policy Priorities, 2022).

93. Dottie Rosenbaum, Katie Bergh, and Lauren Hall, *Temporary Pandemic SNAP Benefits Will End in Remaining 35 States in March 2023* (Washington, D.C.: Center on Budget and Policy Priorities, 2023).

94. Center on Budget and Policy Priorities, *Policy Basics: SNAP*; "SNAP Participation Fell between 2013 and 2019 across United States," U.S. Department of Agriculture, Economic Research Service, January 21, 2021, https://www.ers.usda.gov/data-products/chart-gallery/gallery/chart-detail/?chartId=100254. According to the USDA, SNAP spending in fiscal 2019 was $60.4 billion.

95. Tim Craig, "A Mile-Long Line for Free Food Offers a Warning as Covid Benefits End," *Washington Post*, March 4, 2023.

96. Jinjoo Lee, "Food Stamps Are About to Spoil Grocery Stores' Outlook," *Wall Street Journal*, February 20, 2023.

97. Grocery Outlet is an "extreme value" discounter with 430 stores in eight states as of early 2023. Diane Adam, "Grocery Outlet Opens New Store in New Jersey," *Insight Grocery Business*, February 2, 2023. The chain specializes in closeouts and overstocks—it's essentially the TJ Maxx of grocery stores. Mackenzie Chung Fegan, "The Inflation-Proof Joys of Grocery Outlet Bargain Market," *Bon Appétit*, August 9, 2022.

98. Lee, "Food Stamps Are About to Spoil Grocery Stores' Outlook."

99. Michele Simon, *Food Stamps: Follow the Money* (n.p.: EatDrinkPolitics, 2012), 3.

100. As of 2018, just one-third of U.S. counties had one or more farmers markets that accepted SNAP benefits, according to USDA. "One-third of U.S. Counties in 2018 Had One or More Farmers Markets That Accepted SNAP Benefits," U.S. Department of Agriculture, Economic Research Service,

last modified November 18, 2020, https://www.ers.usda.gov/data-products/chart-gallery/gallery/chart-detail/?chartId=99829. The SNAP Farmers Market Coalition reports $22 million in SNAP redemptions at farmers markets in 2017, a minuscule fraction of the $70 billion spent on SNAP that year. "Supplemental Nutrition Assistance Program (SNAP)," Farmers Market Coalition, https://farmersmarketcoalition.org/advocacy/snap/.

101. "Top 50 Food and Grocery Retailers by Sales," *Supermarket News*, July 6, 2021, https://www.supermarketnews.com/retail-financial/top-50-food-and-grocery-retailers-sales. Groceries accounted for nearly half of Walmart's total 2021 sales of $433 billion. Kroger, in contrast, reported $132.5 billion in 2021 sales, while Albertson's (which includes Safeway, Vons, and other brands) reported $69.7 billion. The number-two grocery in 2021 was Amazon.

102. "Profile of Craigsville, Virginia," U.S. Census Bureau, accessed November 7, 2023, https://data.census.gov/profile?g=1600000US5119904.

103. Ibid.

104. Dollar General Corporation, *2022 Annual Report and 2023 Proxy Statement* (Goodlettsville, TN: Dollar General Corporation, 2023), 6. (Page references here and below refer to the company's Form 10-K, included in the 2022 Annual Report.)

105. "About Us," Dollar General, accessed November 9, 2023, https://www.dollargeneral.com/about-us.html; Dollar General, *2022 Annual Report*, 5.

106. "Location Facts," Walmart, accessed November 9, 2023, https://corporate.walmart.com/about/location-facts.

107. Liam Gravvat, "Number of McDonald's Locations in the United States, North America and World in 2022," *USA Today*, July 30, 2022.

108. *Supermarket News*, "Top 50 Grocery Retailers."

109. Dollar General, *2022 Annual Report*, 7.

110. "Healthy People 2030: Access to Foods That Support Healthy Dietary Patterns," U.S. Department of Health and Human Services, Office of Disease Prevention and Health Promotion, https://health.gov/healthypeople/priority-areas/social-determinants-health/literature-summaries/access-foods-support-healthy-dietary-patterns.

111. Community Development Financial Institutions Fund, *Searching for Markets: The Geography of Inequitable Access to Health and Affordable Food in the United States* (Washington, D.C.: Community Development Financial Institutions Fund, 2012), 2.

112. Ibid.

113. Community Development Financial Institutions Fund, *Searching for Markets*, 52.

114. U.S. Department of Health and Human Services, Office of Disease

Prevention and Health Promotion, "Healthy People 2030, Access to Foods That Support Healthy Dietary Patterns."

115. Mike Troy, "Dollar General Adding Produce to 10,000 Stores," *Progressive Grocer.com*, June 30, 2021, https://progressivegrocer.com/dollar-general-adding-produce-10000-stores. In July 2023, the company announced that it had expanded its produce offerings to 3,900 stores nationwide and was planning to reach 5,000 stores by early 2024. Dollar General, "Dollar General Extends Feeding America Partnership," July 11, 2023, https://www.businesswire.com/news/home/20230711804000/en/Dollar-General-Extends-Feeding-America®-Partnership

116. Dollar General, *2022 Annual Report*, 7. The company reports that the "typical store is operated by a store manager, one or more assistant store managers, and three or more sales associates."

117. Heather Lalley, "Dollar General Replaces an Illinois Store with a Produce-Focused DG Market," *Winsight Grocery Business*, October 17, 2022, https://www.winsightgrocerybusiness.com/fresh-food/dollar-general-replaces-illinois-store-produce-focused-dg-market.

118. "Dollar General Opens First DG Market and Popshelf Stores in TENNESSEE," *Retail Insight Network*, July 29, 2021, https://www.retail-insight-network.com/news/dollar-general-popshelf/.

119. Stacy Mitchell and Marie Donahue, "Dollar Stores Are Targeting Struggling Urban Neighborhoods and Small Towns. One Community Is Showing How to Fight Back," Institute for Local Self-Reliance, December 5, 2018, https://ilsr.org/dollar-stores-target-cities-towns-one-fights-back/.

120. "The Rise of Dollar Stores: How the Proliferation of Discount Stores May Limit Healthy Food Access," Center for Science in the Public Interest, February 2020, https://www.cspinet.org/sites/default/files/2022-03/Dollar%20Store%20Fact%20Sheet.pdf.

121. Ibid.

122. Tony Romm, "Republicans Take Aim at Food Stamps in Growing Fight over Federal Debt," *Washington Post*, February 16, 2023; Under new rules announced by the Trump administration in 2019, "ABAWDs" must work for at least eighty hours a month in order to receive benefits. "Supplemental Nutrition Assistance Program (SNAP): SNAP Work Requirements," U.S. Department of Agriculture, Food and Nutrition Service, September 1, 2023, https://www.fns.usda.gov/snap/work-requirements. These requirements were suspended during the pandemic but are now again being enforced. Prepandemic analyses by the USDA estimated that the Trump rules would push nearly 700,000 people out of SNAP. Laura Reiley, "Trump Administration

Tightens Work Requirements for SNAP, Which Could Cut Hundreds of Thousands from Food Stamps," *Washington Post*, December 4, 2019.

123. "Burke County Free/Reduced Statistics," Burke County Public Schools, accessed November 8, 2023, https://www.burke.k12.ga.us/apps/pages/index.jsp?uREC_ID=323896&type=d&pREC_ID=732401.

124. Jennie Montgomery, "First Lady Visits Rural Farm-to-School Program in Burke County, Georgia," *WJBF-TV*, April 7, 2016, https://www.wjbf.com/news/first-lady-visits-rural-farm-to-school-program-in-burke-county-georgia/.

125. "About Us," Fairfax County Public Schools, accessed November 9, 2023, https://www.fcps.edu/about-fcps; "Free and Reduced-Price Meals (FRM)," Fairfax County Public Schools, accessed November 9, 2023, https://www.fcps.edu/frm.

126. "Contract Details," Fairfax County, Virginia, accessed November 7, 2023, https://www.fairfaxcounty.gov/cregister/ContractDetails.aspx?contractNumber=4400009132. Premier, Inc. and U.S. Foods have a partnership to offer "cooperative purchasing" to "members" that buy food service items in bulk. "Partnership Information," US Foods/Premier, accessed November 7, 2023, https://legacy.premierinc.com/costs/tools-services/targeted-communities/foodservice/uscommunities/.

127. "Lunch Menu, Justice High School, March 2023," Fairfax County Public Schools, accessed March 10, 2023, https://fcps.nutrislice.com/menu/justice-high-school/hs-lunch-2/2023-03-09. (To its credit, Fairfax County did add a "salad bar" in the fall of 2023, which offers a wider variety of fresh fruit and vegetables, including celery sticks, grape tomatoes, cucumber slices, and grapes. The entrees, however, are the same.)

128. Ibid.

129. "McDonald's USA Nutrition Facts for Popular Menu Items," McDonald's, http://nutrition.mcdonalds.com/nutrition1/nutritionfacts.pdf.

130. Heather Hamner, et al., "Fruit, Vegetable and Sugar-Sweetened Beverage Intake Among Young Children, by State—United States, 2021," U.S. Centers for Disease Control and Prevention, *Morbidity and Mortality Weekly Report* 72, no. 7 (February 2023): 165–70, http://dx.doi.org/10.15585/mmwr.mm7207a1.

131. Lisa M. Powell, Binh T. Nguyen, and William H. Dietz, "Energy and Nutrient Intake from Pizza in the United States," *Pediatrics* 135, no. 2 (2015): 322–30, https://doi.org/10.1542/peds.2014-1844.

132. "Childhood Obesity Facts, Prevalence of Childhood Obesity in the United States," U.S. Centers for Disease Control and Prevention, last reviewed May 17, 2022, https://www.cdc.gov/obesity/data/childhood.html;

U.S. Centers for Disease Control and Prevention, "Future Surge in Diabetes Could Dramatically Impact People Under 20 in U.S.," press release, December 29, 2022.

133. "School Meal Statistics," School Nutrition Association, accessed March 15, 2023, https://schoolnutrition.org/about-school-meals/school-meal-statistics/.

134. National Center for Education Statistics, "Digest of Education Statistics, Table 204.10, Number and Percentage of Public School Students Eligible for Free or Reduced-Price Lunch, by state: Selected Years, 2000–2001 through 2021–22," https://nces.ed.gov/programs/digest/d22/tables/dt22_204.10.asp.

135. Katherine Ralston, Katie Treen, Alisha Coleman-Jensen, and Joanne Guthrie, *Children's Food Security and USDA Child Nutrition Programs* (Washington, D.C.: U.S. Department of Agriculture, Economic Research Service, 2017).

136. "The School Breakfast Program: A Smart Investment for Student Success," School Nutrition Association, https://schoolnutrition.org/wp-content/uploads/2022/06/Breakfast-Benefits-final.pdf.

137. School Nutrition Association, "School Meal Statistics."

138. Department of Agriculture, Food and Nutrition Service, "National School Lunch, Special Milk, and School Breakfast Programs, National Average Payments/Maximum Reimbursement Rates," *Federal Register* 87, no. 142 (July 28, 2022): 44328.

139. School Nutrition Association, *2023 School Nutrition Trends Report* (Arlington, VA: School Nutrition Association, 2023). Federal reimbursements were already falling short pre-pandemic. According to a 2019 report by Mathematica for the USDA, the average reported cost of a lunch was $3.81 in 2014, while the average federal reimbursement was $3.32. Mary Kay Fox and Elizabeth Gearan, *School Nutrition and Meal Cost Study: Summary of Findings* (Washington, D.C.: U.S. Department of Agriculture, Food and Nutrition Service, 2019), 32.

140. Interview with author.

141. School Nutrition Association, *2023 School Nutrition Trends Report*.

142. Pew Charitable Trusts, "States Need Updated School Kitchen Equipment," March 26, 2014, https://www.pewtrusts.org/en/research-and-analysis/reports/2014/03/26/states-need-updated-school-kitchen-equipment-b. Pew Charitable Trusts, "U.S. Department of Agriculture Equipment Grants Improve School Kitchens," June 14, 2016, https://www.pewtrusts.org/en/research-and-analysis/data-visualizations/2016/usda-school-kitchen-equipment-grants.

143. U.S. Department of Agriculture, Food and Nutrition Service, "Child Nutrition Programs: Transitional Standards for Milk, Whole Grains and Sodium," 7 CFR Parts 210, 215, 220, and 226; "Smoothies Offered in Child Nutrition Programs," U.S. Department of Agriculture, memo dated September 23, 2019, https://fns-prod.azureedge.us/sites/default/files/resource-files/SP40-CACFP17-SFSP17-2019os.pdf.

144. "Aramark," Investigate, A Project of the American Friends Service Committee, March 18, 2021, https://investigate.afsc.org/company/aramark.

145. "Are These 3 Outsourcing Misconceptions Limiting Your District Meal Program?," Aramark, accessed March 9, 2023, https://k12insights.aramark.com/blog/misconceptions-limiting-your-district-meal-program.

146. "Outsourcing Is Not a Dirty Word," Aramark, accessed March 9, 2023, https://k12insights.aramark.com/outsourcing-not-a-dirty-word?hsCtaTracking=53b2549e-dd3c-47e5-adcb-a4c7c2a903fd%7C00feb737-d141-47a8-b1b7-0c7aa25192bc.

147. Ellen Flax, "Food-Service Companies Eye $5-Billion School-Lunch Market," *EducationWeek*, April 11, 1990.

148. By 2014, 17 percent of districts relied on private food services, according to the Kids' Safe and Healthful Food Project by the Pew Charitable Trusts. Pew Charitable Trusts, "States Need Updated School Kitchen Equipment."

149. Mike Buzalka, "The Top 50's Nine Largest K–12 Market Operators," *Food Management*, March 29, 2022, https://www.food-management.com/top-50-contract-companies/top-50-s-nine-largest-k-12-market-operators, slides 1–3.

150. Physicians Committee for Responsible Medicine, "Who's Making Money from Overweight Kids?," *Good Medicine* XXIV, no. 3 (summer 2015): 6.

151. Emily Heil, "Lunchables in School Cafeterias Have Child-Nutrition Experts Concerned," *Washington Post*, March 16, 2023.

152. Domino's SmartSlice, accessed November 9, 2023, https://biz.dominos.com/school-lunch/. Domino's "NSLP compliant" pizza, the site says, can be made with "ingredients like 100% real lite mozzarella cheese, reduced fat pepperoni, and dough that's rich in whole grain." It is, however, still pizza.

153. "A+ Pizza School Lunch Program," Pizza Hut, accessed November 9, 2023, https://www.pizzahut.com/assets/w/marketingpages/schoollunch/School_Lunch_Program_8MB_r2.pdf.

154. "USDA Foods in Schools/Child Nutrition USDA Foods Program," U.S. Department of Agriculture, Food and Nutrition Service Nutrition Program, fact sheet, January 2020, https://www.fns.usda.gov/usda-fis/factsheet-2022.

155. "USDA Foods Further Processing," U.S. Department of Agriculture,

Food and Nutrition Service Food Distribution, fact sheet, March 2018, https://fns-prod.azureedge.us/sites/default/files/resource-files/Processing FactSheet.pdf.

156. Ibid. The USDA, by the way, spends millions of dollars purchasing surplus bulk foods from meat and dairy producers. In 2013, according to the Physicians Committee for Responsible Medicine, the USDA "paid more than $500 million to 62 meat and dairy producers for beef, chicken, turkey, pork, fish, dairy, eggs and lamb that ended up in school meals." The biggest beneficiaries were Tyson Foods, which received $89 million for sales of chicken, beef, and pork to the USDA, and Pilgrim's Pride Corporation, which received $70.1 million for sales of chicken. Physicians Committee, "Who's Making Money," 6.

157. Lucy Komisar, "How the Food Industry Eats Your Kid's Lunch," *New York Times*, December 3, 2011.

158. Interview with author.

159. Masooma Hussain and Joshua Stearns, *Contracting Out School Food Services Failed to Control Costs as Promised* (Washington, D.C.: Office of the District of Columbia Auditor, 2016).

160. Michael Alison Chandler, "DC Schools Food Vendor Pays $19 Million to Settle Whistleblower Lawsuit," *Washington Post*, June 5, 2015.

161. Ibid.

162. Hussain and Stearns, *Contracting Out School Food Services Failed to Control Costs*, 23.

Conclusion: Who's Really Fighting the War on Poverty?

1. Background on the double-bottom-line movement is available here: Catherine Clark, David Long, Sara Olsen, and William Rosenzweig, *Double Bottom Line Project Report: Assessing Social Impact in Double Bottom Line Ventures: Methods Catalog* (New York: Rockefeller Foundation, 2004).

2. "Coffee Impact Report: 2020," Fair Trade America, September 16, 2021, https://www.fairtradeamerica.org/why-fairtrade/global-impact/reports-trends /coffee-impact-report-2020/.

3. Jens Hainmueller, Michael J. Hiscox, and Sandra Sequeira, "Consumer Demand for Fair Trade: Evidence from a Multistore Field Experiment," *Review of Economics and Statistics* 97, no. 2 (May 2015): 242–56.

4. U.S. Department of Health and Human Services, Administration for Children and Families Office of Child Care, "Profiles: Successful Public-Private Partnerships," https://childcareta.acf.hhs.gov/sites/default/files/public /utah_profile.pdf.

5. Ibid.

6. Anne Kim, "Mayor Ben McAdams of Salt Lake County: Financing Preschool with 'Social Impact Bonds,'" Republic 3-0.com, March 2014, https://web.archive.org/web/20160320232709/http://republic3-0.com/qa-paying-for-success-in-salt-lake-county/.

7. Nathaniel Popper, "Success Metrics Questioned in School Program Funded by Goldman," *New York Times*, November 3, 2015.

8. Ibid.

9. Allison E. Tse and Mildred E. Warner, "The Razor's Edge: Social Impact Bonds and the Financialization of Early Childhood Services," *Journal of Urban Affairs* 42, no. 6 (2020): 816–32, https://doi.org/10.1080/07352166.2018.1465347.

10. Nadine Pequeneza, "The Downside of Social Impact Bonds," *Stanford Social Innovation Review*, May 13, 2019, https://ssir.org/articles/entry/the_downside_of_social_impact_bonds.

11. Ibid.

12. "What Does a High-Quality Preschool Program Look Like?," National Association for the Education of Young Children, https://www.naeyc.org/our-work/families/what-does-high-quality-program-for-preschool-look-like.

13. In the case of contractors, they *are* the government, which raises a host of issues too complex to address here. There is a wealth of literature, for instance, on the constitutionality of private prisons acting on behalf of the state to detain individuals and to make decisions about their freedom. Some of that literature is alluded to in chapter 5.

14. "Nursing Home Care," U.S. Centers for Disease Control and Prevention, National Center for Health Statistics, December 15, 2022, https://www.cdc.gov/nchs/fastats/nursing-home-care.htm; Susan Jaffe, "Medicaid Weighs Attaching Strings to Nursing Home Payments to Improve Patient Care," *Kaiser Health News*, June 10, 2022.

15. Mimi Kirk, "Does Privatized Foster Care Put Kids at Risk?," *Bloomberg*, June 15, 2018.

16. Aram Roston and Jeremy Singer-Vine, "Fostering Profits: Abuse and Neglect at America's Biggest For-Profit Foster Care Company," *BuzzFeed News*, February 20, 2015.

17. This conviction that under-investment is a root cause of persistent poverty is why the Biden administration's original "Build Back Better" plan was set to cost $3.5 trillion. The pared-down, $2.2 trillion package later passed by the House included a $203 billion expansion of the EITC, $166 billion for affordable housing, plus more money for child nutrition, among a host of other priorities. It also included $33 billion for job training programs, including $500 million for Job Corps and $6.9 billion to create the "Civilian

Climate Corps," a new "green jobs" program for young adults. After protracted negotiations with a closely divided Senate, what ultimately became law (as the Inflation Reduction Act) included virtually none of these priorities. Tami Luhby and Katie Lobosco, "Here's What's in Biden's Build Back Better Plan," *CNN*, November 19, 2021. LaDonna Pavetti and Gina Azito Thompson, "Important Investments in Build Back Better Would Expand Pathways to Quality Jobs, Promote Equity," Center on Budget and Policy Priorities, February 9, 2022, https://www.cbpp.org/research/poverty-and-inequality/important-investments-in-build-back-better-would-expand-pathways-to. "FACT SHEET: The Inflation Reduction Act Supports Workers and Families," The White House, press release, August 16, 2022, https://www.whitehouse.gov/briefing-room/statements-releases/2022/08/19/fact-sheet-the-inflation-reduction-act-supports-workers-and-families/.

Index

About the Author

Anne Kim is a writer, lawyer, and public policy expert with a long career in Washington, DC–based think tanks working in and around Capitol Hill. She is also a contributing editor at *Washington Monthly*, where she was a senior writer. Her work has appeared in the *Washington Post*, *Governing*, TheAtlantic.com, the *Wall Street Journal*, *Democracy*, and numerous other publications. She is the author of *Abandoned: America's Lost Youth and the Crisis of Disconnection*.

Publishing in the Public Interest

Thank you for reading this book published by The New Press; we hope you enjoyed it. New Press books and authors play a crucial role in sparking conversations about the key political and social issues of our day.

We hope that you will stay in touch with us. Here are a few ways to keep up to date with our books, events, and the issues we cover:

- Sign up at www.thenewpress.com/subscribe to receive updates on New Press authors and issues and to be notified about local events
- www.facebook.com/newpressbooks
- www.twitter.com/thenewpress
- www.instagram.com/thenewpress

Please consider buying New Press books not only for yourself, but also for friends and family and to donate to schools, libraries, community centers, prison libraries, and other organizations involved with the issues our authors write about.

The New Press is a 501(c)(3) nonprofit organization; if you wish to support our work with a tax-deductible gift please visit www.thenewpress.com/donate or use the QR code below.